Jan Saudek

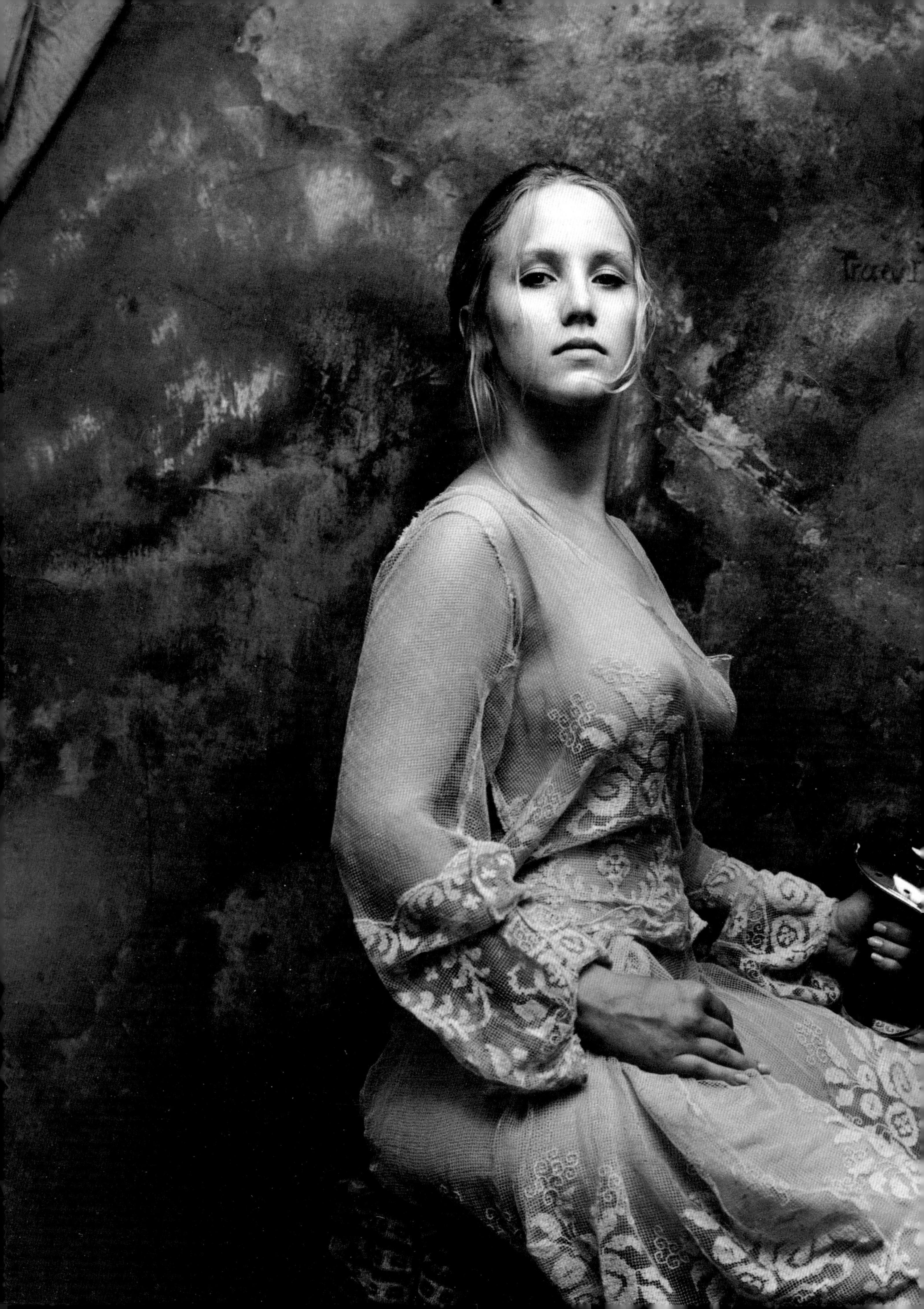

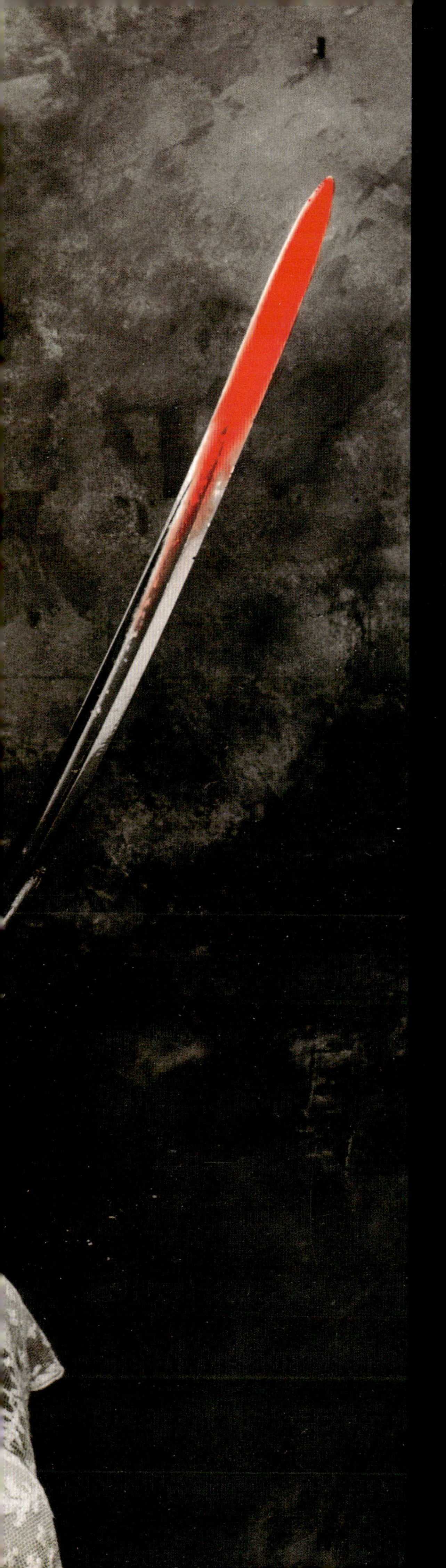

Jan Saudek

Essay by · Essay von · Essaie de
Christiane Fricke

TASCHEN
KÖLN LISBOA LONDON NEW YORK PARIS TOKYO

Front cover · Umschlagvorderseite · Couverture:
Marie no. 142, 1972

Back cover · Umschlagrückseite · Dos de Couverture:
Czech Girl Singing, 1990
Singendes tschechisches Mädchen
Jeune fille tchèque chantant

Page 2/3 · Seite 2/3
The Sabre, 1994
Der Säbel
Le Sabre

© 1998 Benedikt Taschen Verlag GmbH
Hohenzollernring 53, D–50672 Köln
© for the illustrations: Jan Saudek, Prague
Edited by Michael Konze, Cologne
Design: Claudia Frey, Cologne
English translation: Fiona Elliott, Edinburgh
French translation: Thérèse Chatelain-Südkamp, Lohmar

Printed in Spain
ISBN 3-8228-7429-9

Contents
Inhalt
Sommaire

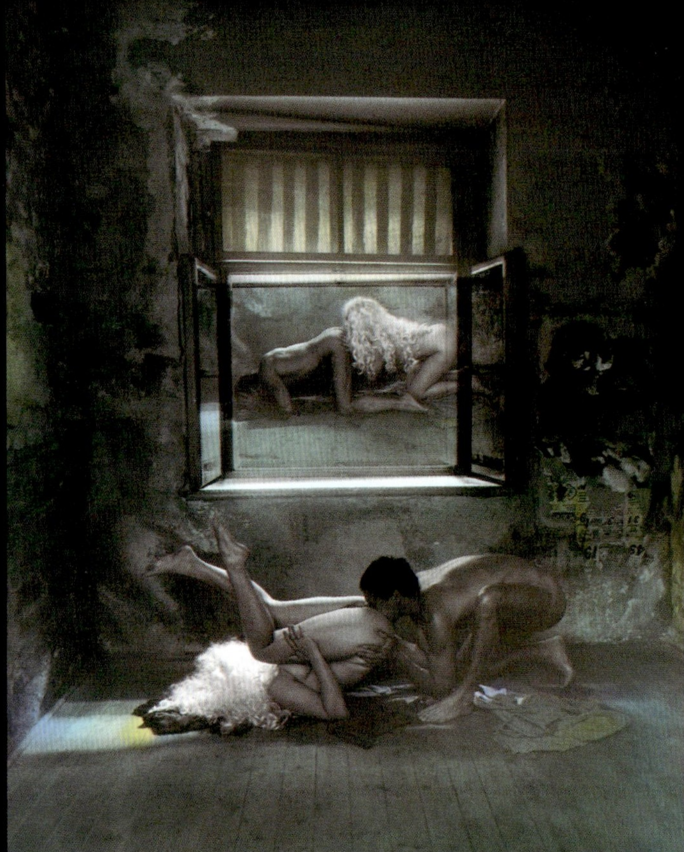

Karolina, Marie and the Faces of Love

Once there was a man who worked in a factory from six in the morning until three in the afternoon. He lived in a basement with the plaster crumbling off the mouldy walls, and all he could see through the window was a gloomy enclosed area. That man was Jan Saudek, and he owned little more than the bicycle he rode to the factory and an old Pentacon six. His most valuable assets were certainly his immense energy and relentless ambition. In the early 1970s, when he found himself in this basement converted into a makeshift home, his life took a significant new turn. By no stretch of the imagination could he have continued to photograph here as he had done before. In the 60s his pictorial world had been peopled with family members, children and friends. Their lives determined the geographical reach of his own activities. He often took photographs in the street, by courtyard walls or in gardens – frequently snapping his subjects quite spontaneously. The highpoint of this relatively extrovert period of his career as a photographer was his journey to the United States in 1969. After 1970 his photographs concentrated increasingly on "the room" with the decaying walls that became a synonym for his photographic output.

It is hard to imagine which direction Saudek's work might have taken had he not moved into the basement. The fact is that photographing landscapes and isolated objects has never interested him. There is documentary evidence of his ambitions regarding live-photography, and as late as 1974, when he was already mainly taking photographs of nudes, he told a friend that he was occasionally trying his hand at reportage. Perhaps circumstances prevented further experiments in this direction. While his paid work in the factory did at least allow him to survive, it left him little chance of pursuing his photographic work in daylight.

Censorship and Success

In certain respects Saudek's work has a solitary character. In contrast to many other photographers of his day the trauma of 1968 did not prevent him from developing new ideas. Social reality had no place in his visual world – neither before nor after 1968. He paid little attention to political events until that terrible day when the student Jan Palach burnt himself alive. For Saudek the late 60s were above all a time of personal upheaval.

According to a diplomatic comment by Zdenek Primus, nowadays Saudek is viewed in his native land as one of the artists who pursued their own path in the 70s, independent of social change around them – and without the protection of any artists' union or other state authority. Put rather more bluntly, this means that he was simply cut dead by the latter. Saudek himself tells of periods when people thought he was living in another country or was working as an FBI agent or had recently died. Apparently the Czech Ministry of Culture even denied his existence altogether in response to one enquiry from abroad.

As an observer from the West, one tends to view Saudek purely as a victim of the political situation. The fact is, however, that his increasing international recognition from 1975 onwards meant that he was able to pursue a successful career untroubled by financial concerns. Naturally this aroused a certain amount of jealousy which might have contributed to Saudek's lack of contact with other photographers in his own country. However, the root cause of his isolated position is most probably the fact that in his work with nude subjects he was concentrating on a theme that was not of particular interest to many other serious Czech photographers at the time. In the 70s, when Saudek was starting to focus on human sexuality, Czech photography was predominantly documentary. Vladimír Birgus, professor at the Academy of Fine Arts in Prague and himself a photographer, even maintained that the nude photography of the 70s was qualitatively and quantitatively well below the standards achieved in the 60s both in its understanding of classical nude photography and in its 'staged' images. In his view, part of the responsibility for this must be attributed to the various, often absurd, decrees and bans that had made it impossible to exhibit or to publish photographs of nudes.

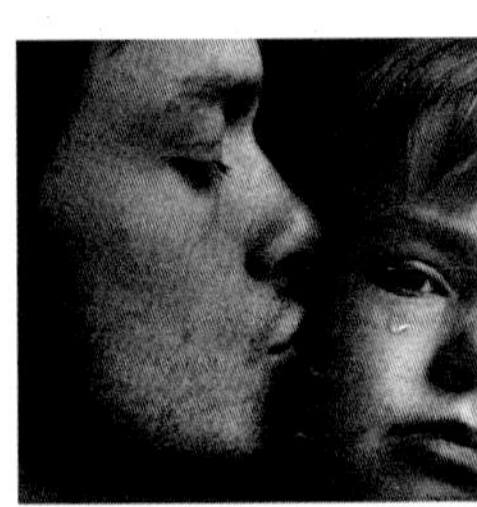

Thus Saudek was on a collision course – and this was not without consequences. His flat was repeatedly searched. Prints and negatives were confiscated, when they could not be hidden away in time, and the State Security pursued individuals who appeared in his photographs and interviewed his friends and relations. At times Saudek was obliged to report at regular intervals to the police.

Doubtless this sometimes extremely burdensome situation arose from the obvious interest his work generated abroad in the form of exhibitions and publications. Since his first presentation at the University of Indiana in Bloomington in 1969, scarcely a year has passed without a solo exhibition of his work in the USA. He has also achieved notable success in Australia and France where he soon made inroads into leading exhibitions and collections.

However, he owes his wider breakthrough to a Dutch publishing house that specialises in publishing and distributing postcards, posters and books. In the mid-80s, when he was able to give up his factory job, 'Art Unlimited' closed a contract with him. For nearly ten years he produced work for them – even to the point of exhaustion.

In Germany, to date, Saudek has been treated with extreme caution. Though he has enjoyed commercial success there since 1978, so far no museum or gallery has felt they could honour Saudek with a solo exhibition. With the exception of the Gruber Collection in the Museum Ludwig in Cologne one may seek him in vain in any of the leading collections. Even in Czechoslovakia there was a distinct reluctance to recognise his work. Anna Fárová, former director of the photographic collection set up in 1970 by the Prague Museum of Arts and Crafts, made no secret of the difficulties she had with Saudek's work: "I hated his leaning towards bad taste and kitsch," she wrote in 1983. "I equally disliked the unnatural air and the brittle sentimentality of his early pictures." At the same time she did admit that "in his own way, this man from Prague was extraordinary." There is, of course, no denying that in exhibitions and photo-journals his pictures always caught the reader's eye – they were so unusual compared to the reportage style and the realism of his contemporaries.

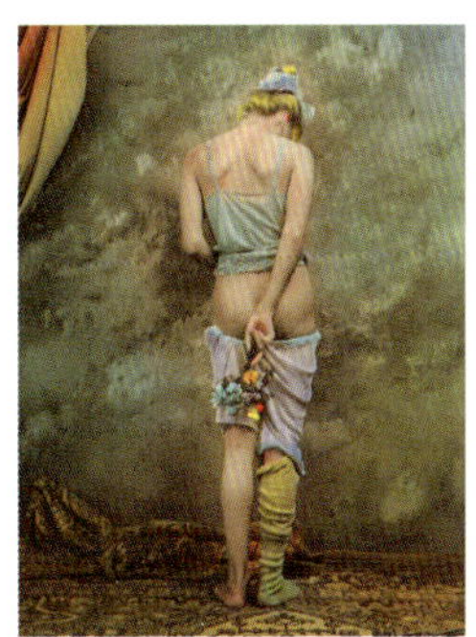

Fifteen years later Fárová's assessment has by no means lost its relevance. Opinions are still sharply divided when it comes to Saudek's work. Experts in the field either reject his work over the last decades altogether or are at least very restrained in their response. And as to his paintings – silence seems to be the preferred option. Yet while some are still hesitating, others have long cast their vote and in no uncertain terms either – for it is not only in Czech bookshops and souvenir shops that sales of Saudek's postcards, calendars and books easily outstrip all other artworks except those bearing the name of Picasso or Matisse.

Icons of Longing

"In 1935 my mother gave birth to a son, Kaja, and not long afterwards as something of an afterthought, to yours truly." – Saudek's first sentence in his life-story. He goes on to tell how this meant that all his life he played number two. Kaja (Karl) Saudek, a successful graphic- and comic-strip artist by the 60s, was both a dearly beloved friend and challenging rival. The younger Saudek took rather more time to discover that his strongest talent lay in photography rather than in drama, dance or painting. His parents were unable to help him. They were fighting for their own existence. His father, a Jew and up until 1939 a respected employee in a bank, was the only brother in his family to have survived the concentration camp Theresienstadt. After the war, as a native German speaker, he was refused permission to take up his previous employment. His youngest son, Jan, had to leave school at fifteen because his marks were so poor. When Jan started to work for a reprographics business at the age of sixteen, he was a restless spirit, with nothing but women in his head and corresponding problems with completing his quota of work. His brother tells us that with his photographic skills Jan could at most have assisted Nadar or Mathew B. Brady. People mocked his first photographs, taken with a Baby Brownie, so for the time being he abandoned photography again.

Today it is hard to fully understand the upset that Saudek caused in Prague in 1963 when he first exhibited his work. His earliest work, from 1951, shows a young, semi-naked man lying on his back on the ground with his arms outstretched as though he wanted to embrace the universe. The broad-shouldered man in *Hey, Joe!* (1959, ill. p. 37) who has stopped his motor-scooter on the banks of the Moldau conveys a feeling of tense expectation. *Chains of Love* (1960) shows a young couple from above wearing only blue jeans, lying face downwards on the ground with their wrists chained together. Pictures like these express something of the impetuous energy of a young man who still does not know where he should invest his strength, and whose relish for life and love has already, far too soon, swept him into the harbour of marriage.

The success which later came to Saudek must be ascribed to his ability to express deep-seated longings in universally comprehensible images. He rarely tells the viewer anything about his own everyday life – instead his work reveals all the more clearly something of the feelings of a person living under a rigid Communist regime, longing for freedom and only able to imagine this as some kind of a dream. This power of imagination in the face of all kinds of difficulties also made him extremely receptive to Edward Steichen's beautiful dream of the 'Family of Man'. That exhibition in the Museum of Modern Art in New

York showed photographs of people of every colour at existential moments in their lives, from birth to death. The exhibition travelled to 44 capital cities with its optimistic message that there is more uniting the nations of the world than separating them. "We begin and end," Steichen wrote in a press release – "there is none amongst us who could do any differently. We are all human beings, one like the other."

In 1963, deeply moved by the catalogue of 'The Family of Man' which had by now been on tour all over the world for eight years, Saudek decided to portray human life from birth to death. He blithely set about this self-imposed task, entirely unbothered by the fact that Steichen's exhibition in fact brought together hundreds of photographs from all four corners of the earth. He was similarly unworried by the fact that these photographs largely addressed their subject matter using the techniques of live-photography. Aside from a few photographs that were clearly inspired by 'The Family of Man' Saudek did quite the opposite. Instead of observing the behaviour of a particular person and releasing the shutter at the decisive moment, he imagined a scene and then proceeded to stage it for the camera. In his own way, Saudek was continuing in the tradition of the "tableau vivant" and the "pose plastique" which had their roots in the leisure pursuits of the aristocracy in the 18th century and lingered on into the 19th century in official photographs of Queen Victoria's children.

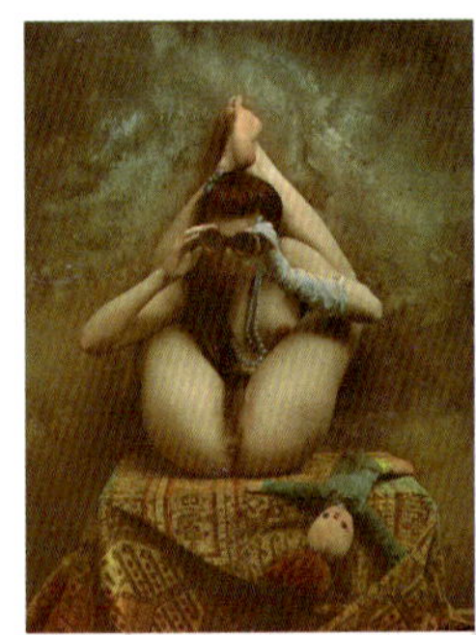

Saudek's method is well illustrated by the genesis of his famous picture, *Life*, which he took in 1966 (ill. p. 44). The photographer had hit upon the idea of a big, strong father holding his tiny, new-born child close to his chest in a protective, loving gesture. It struck him that a weightlifter in his circle of friends might be the ideal model. However, during the photo sessions it became abundantly clear that this man did not have the slightest idea of how a father holds his own baby in his arms. Saudek therefore substituted himself as the father and, in doing so, came to a surprising conclusion: it is not the sight of swelling muscles but rather the relationship between father and child which is crucial to the impact of the pictorial message.

The Lover Arrives

Jan Saudek's work after 1970 creates the impression that the artist has turned his back on the world outside. It may well be – leaving aside his personal circumstances – that his move into the basement was a subconscious strategy to withdraw from the field of battle and to remove himself from the controlling hand of the authorities. Life in the open could become extremely precarious for a controversial figure like Saudek. It hardly even counted when he had to run home once in his underwear – in the early 60s – because the police had confiscated his blue jeans. Even today, nine years after the lifting of the Iron Curtain, visitors from abroad are still perplexed to find his curtains drawn in the middle of the day – lending any visit to the artist's flat the air of an intimate rendezvous, hidden from prying eyes.

When one looks more closely at the few photographs taken in the open air it soon becomes clear that these were as carefully set up as his studio photographs. Reality never enters his pictures. In *120 km/hr* (1975, ill. p. 41) the message is concentrated into a few details which are all the more telling in view of the passport and travel restrictions that were in force at the time: a steam locomotive rushes by at a closed railway crossing; a young man sits on the barrier, overgrown gravel in the foreground showing that this crossing has not been used for a long time now. This is one of many pictures that Saudek tinted by hand after 1977, heightening the surreal atmosphere. In *Destiny Walks Down to the River* (1971) the town with its filthy chimneys is the perfect backdrop to a mother striding towards the valley with her two unruly daughters. The girls – clinging to the proud young woman in her best clothes – are naked; the street is empty; no cars, no people in sight who might have added a touch of the everyday to the image. Saudek knows how to turn a location into a set.

Unlike photographs by his American colleague Joel-Peter Witkin, who consciously sought out pain and distress, Saudek's images are rarely disturbing. He works in a room cut off from the outside world. Whoever steps into the twilight of his studio enters a territory controlled by Saudek with its own laws. He himself once referred to the way that he creates a dream world for his models, which then automatically takes on a life of its own. The American portrait photographer Irving Penn worked in a similar manner, although in his case it meant taking a portable tent-studio round the world with him: "When I took people out of their natural surroundings and put them in front of the camera in my studio, this didn't just isolate them, it completely transformed them." Saudek, unlike Penn, is not satisfied with this transformation alone. He takes action; he divests his models of their usual clothes, brings props into play. In her 1991 monograph Daniela Mrázková has talked about women "willingly joining in the game," saying that "they simply allow themselves to be undressed and dressed, to be moulded according to his vision."

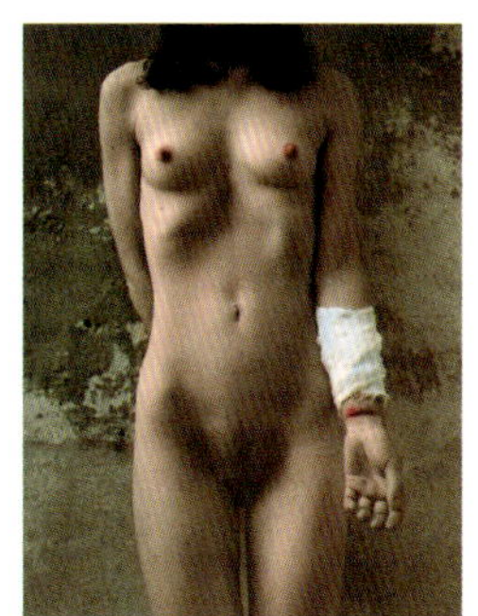

One would have to be unusually naive to see Saudek's images as no more than an apotheosis of woman offering herself to man. Indeed the poet August von Platen once wrote that "creatures reflect the joy of their Creator." Even aside from questions regarding the level of intimacy and personality that comes across despite the poses, it is clear that no other photographer has worked with women as closely and over as long a time as Jan Saudek. In his photography he has explored all possible aspects of the miracle of womanhood – and not just as an observer, but as one who is himself utterly bound up in the whole process. He himself has been very clear about what this means: "I don't have the capacity to portray other people's lives. I am portraying my own."

Doubtless the most interesting pictures for the viewer are those where Saudek captures something of the 'chemistry' of the relationship between himself and the model: like the provocatively inviting gesture of the young woman in *Marie no. 142* (1972, ill. p. 54) pulling up her sweater with her teeth; the self-confident, relaxed ease of the androgynous *Susanna* (1978, ill. p. 78) with her wreath; or *Oh, That Virgin Els!* (1985, ill. p. 77) defiantly exposing her meagre chest. Looking at these photographs one has the sense of witnessing an intimate dialogue. The photographer's gaze is concentrated on his opposite number, showing her from the knees upwards and rarely – at least in the early 70s – at full length. But Saudek also brings in the decaying surroundings. The wall shows the ravages of life that have, as yet, left no trace on the softly lit bodies of his young models. By contrast, other bodies reveal the effect that age has had on their form and appearance. In some images he focuses on specifically female behaviour: young women staring at their own reflection from behind, how they handle their own breasts or how they display submission. Saudek often brings to mind thoughts of Milan Kundera's character Tomas who was obsessed with the desire to find in each new woman he conquered even a "millionth of something different" that would distinguish her from all the others.

Grief only ever enters Saudek's works with a lyrical overlay: for example, the profile of a friend he lost after his divorce, shown in a small medallion held in someone's hand (1970, ill. p. 34); or the sadness at a 'love story' that has come to an end – a rose in flower that gradually loses its petals one by one (1974, ill. p. 35). Real disaster is generally kept at bay or only shown – as in the hanged woman – in a theatrical guise (1977, ill. p. 118/119). The utter confusion that he felt during his stay in the USA in 1969 is reflected in the picture of a man hanging from an oversized billboard (1969, ill. p. 39). Only once, in 1976, did he abandon the stage of the Saudek 'theatre of life' in order to photograph his father, worn out and old, in amongst the gravestones in an overgrown Jewish cemetery. It is a simple, completely unpretentious picture, an exception in Saudek's increasingly lavish, theatrical world – an image filled with sadness (1975, ill. p. 33).

Throughout the ages the Czech people have had to accept circumstances that were forced upon them. One aspect of their adaptability is the capacity to create their own imaginary, magical reality. Saudek, who could never bring himself to emigrate, has become a true master of the imagination. In 1976/77 he began to photograph dreamlike scenes set in the window looking out onto that dismal inner area. Significantly, these were soon followed by his first attempts at colouring black and white prints by hand. Anna Fárová has talked in this connection of colours that go against nature; Daniela Mrázková saw it as his final break with reality.

Saudek's window pictures quite rightly remind one of Josef Sudek's cycle "The Window of My Studio". During the Second World War, under the Nazi threat, Sudek retreated into his studio in the backyard. There he discovered the window – the glass clouded, spattered with raindrops, freezing over – and used it as a projection surface for his own ideas like a mysterious veil between himself and the outside world. However, where Sudek's thoughtful gaze lingered contentedly on the phantasmagoria that revealed itself before his eyes, Saudek radically alters what he finds. Using light-montage, he copies in fleeting images of pedestrians hurrying by, or the vapour trails of aeroplanes in the cloudy sky, or the moon and stars. Yet there ist something strange about all of this: while the window offer many wondrons sights – we even see a lover arriving – we never see anyone leaving.

On the reverse side of Saudek's vitality are the existential fears that Daniel Mrázková vividly describes. These are not simply the fears a person would feel who was exposed to permanent danger as a child, growing up amidst the Nazi persecution of the Jews, and whose family again had to fight for their survival in 1954, merely because of their German ancestry. Saudek's fears are also those of an outsider who for long periods was subjected to scrutiny by the state. In addition, Daniela Mrázková describes the artist's fear of losing his creative powers, his constant self-doubts and consequent fear of decline and death. Every five years Saudek photographed his lover Veronica (ill. p. 82/83) – clearly an attempt by the artist to combat his own share of uncertainty: the endeavour to save individual moments of this life as 'pars pro toto' while it moves inexorably onwards.

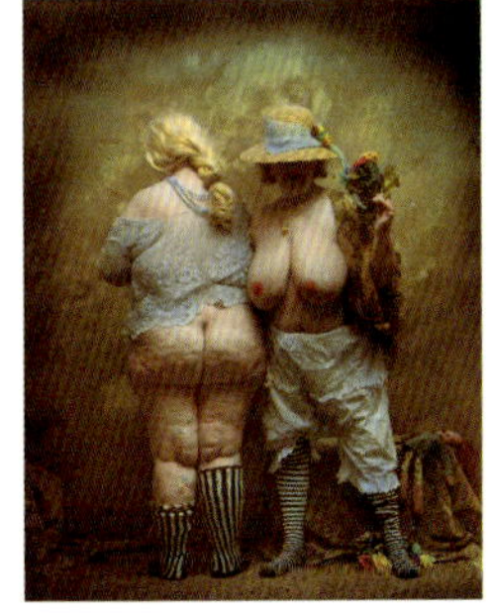

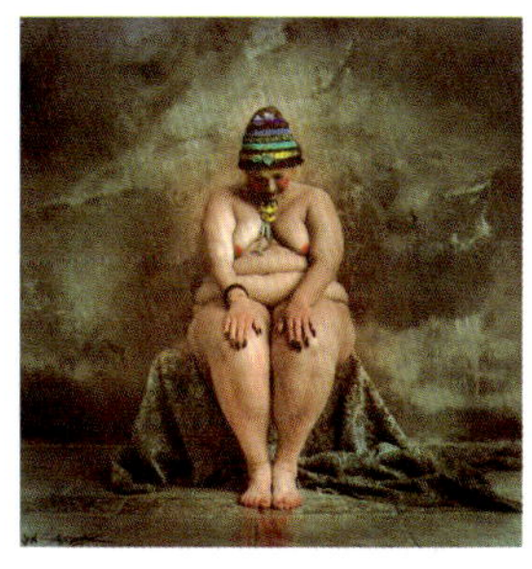

The show must go on

Saudek's work after 1984 provokes mixed feelings above all in those who previously gladly succumbed to the magic of his poetic, once powerfully nostalgic visual world. Now they gaze in consternation at pictures, which seem at times to be indulging in extremes of Mannerism and outrageous imagery. Yet all the time it is perfectly obvious that Saudek could not spend his whole artistic career as the worshipful lover or as the besotted father. The most innocuous of these works are the decorative scenes, composed using light-montage to create mirror images, like the playing cards (1984–1987) or *Purgatory no. 2* (1987, ill. p. 155).

Many of his works from the 80s already bear witness to the toll that his breakneck love life and disputes with wives and lovers have taken. The adoration of womanhood in the early works later becomes quite the opposite and at times disintegrates into sheer spite. *Deep Desire* (1985, ill. p. 110) for example, shows a husband kneeling before his nagging wife, pleading with her as though she were Jesus Christ in person. In the mid-80s he made the *Portrait of Woman and Man* (ill. p. 114/115) with himself as a macho-figure, complacently lighting up a cigarette while his partner is on the point of shooting herself with an old-fashioned pistol. The irony is unmistakable and often goes hand in hand with open cynicism. The lively, erotic tension between photographer and model of the earlier works becomes increasingly rare. In extreme cases the artist no longer seeks the mysterium in the interaction of the participants but tries to capture it visually by aiming specifically at the taboo areas of the female form.

Saudek balks at nothing. In *Photographer as Jesus* (1991, ill. p. 163) he hangs between two scantily dressed women like Jesus on the Cross between the thieves. In a self-portrait he strikes a Hamlet-style pose, clad, it seems, in the meagre clothing of a concentration camp prisoner. It is only on closer examination that one discovers that this is in fact a designer jacket by the firm of "Matsuda", for whom he took fashion shots in 1989 and 1991. Instead of a skull he is holding a camera in his hand.

Saudek reaches as casually into the treasury of historical pictorial motifs as he might do into the box of props that he once bought from a theatre in Prague. Again and again one comes across tableaus in his work with clearly Christian origins or ideas borrowed from contemporary colleagues. Most of all, however, one finds scenes based on erotic photographs and postcards from the turn of the century. In his early works Saudek used wreaths of flowers, diadems, animal skins and scraps of tulle to lend his images the sensual, rather sultry atmosphere of a "fin de siècle boudoir". After the mid-70s his models wear whimsical, old-fashioned clothes, are swathed in pearls and loll naked on luxurious fabrics as they might have done a hundred years ago. In the 80s Saudek did many more photoseries based on picture postcards. He staged small wanton scenes of maids going to bed, but also more salacious, pornographic sequences with threesomes indulging each other.

As a young man, Saudek believed he had "what it takes to stand in front of the camera". However, later he admitted that life had taught him that his place was behind and not in front of the camera. The fact is, that Saudek is just as impassioned an actor as he is a director. If he does not see himself as such, then perhaps this is only because he has long since become an integral part of his own stage – whether in art or in life, whether behind or in front of the camera. "The show must go on."

Christiane Fricke

Karolina, Marie und die Gesichter der Liebe

Der Mann, der von sechs Uhr in der Früh bis drei Uhr nachmittags in einer Fabrik arbeitete, bewohnte einen Kellerraum, dessen Fenster sich in einen trüben Lichtschacht öffnete; von den feuchten Wänden bröckelte der Putz ab. Jan Saudek besaß nicht viel mehr als ein Fahrrad, mit dem er zur Arbeit fuhr, und eine alte Pentacon six. Sein größtes Kapital waren zweifellos eine ungeheure Energie und ein rastloser Ehrgeiz.

Als er sich zu Beginn der siebziger Jahre, nach einer seiner Scheidungen, in diesem notdürftig zum Wohnen umfunktionierten Kellerraum wiederfand, nahm sein Leben eine äußerst folgenreiche Wende. Unmöglich hätte er in dieser Situation so weiter photographieren können wie bisher. In den sechziger Jahren bevölkerten Familienangehörige, Kinder und Freunde seine Bildwelt. Ihr Bewegungsspielraum bestimmte die geographische Ausdehnung seiner Aktivitäten. Oft photographierte er auf der Straße, an Hofmauern oder im Garten, und nicht selten bediente er sich dabei der Techniken der Momentaufnahme. Den Höhepunkt dieser vergleichsweise extrovertierten Schaffensphase bildete eine Amerikareise im Jahre 1969. Nach 1970 konzentrierte sich der Schauplatz mehr und mehr auf den »Raum«, dessen morbide Wand, vom Künstler im Jahre 1972 entdeckt, zum Synomym seines bildnerischen Schaffens wurde.

Schwer vorstellbar ist, in welche Richtung sich Saudeks Arbeit ohne seinen Umzug in den Keller entwickelt hätte. Tatsache ist, daß ihn Landschafts- und Sachphotographie nicht interessiert haben. Verbrieft sind seine Ambitionen für die Live-Photographie. Noch im Jahre 1974, als er bereits überwiegend Akte aufnahm, schrieb er einem Freund, er versuche manchmal, Reportagen zu gestalten. Vielleicht scheiterte die weitere Erprobung derartiger Neigungen auch an den Umständen. Die lohnabhängige Arbeit sicherte zwar das Überleben, ließ jedoch wenig Spielraum für eine photographische Betätigung bei Tageslicht.

Zensur und Erfolg

Das Werk Saudeks besitzt in verschiedener Hinsicht solitären Charakter. Anders als viele seiner photographierenden Zeitgenossen hinderte ihn das Trauma von 1968 nicht daran, Neues zu schaffen. In seiner Bildwelt hatte weder vor noch nach '68 die gesellschaftliche Realität einen Platz. Dem politischen Geschehen zollte er wenig Aufmerksamkeit, bis zu jenem schrecklichen Tag, an dem sich der Student Jan Palach selbst verbrannte. Alles in allem erlebte Saudek das Ende des Jahrzehnts wohl hauptsächlich als eine Zeit des persönlichen Umbruchs.

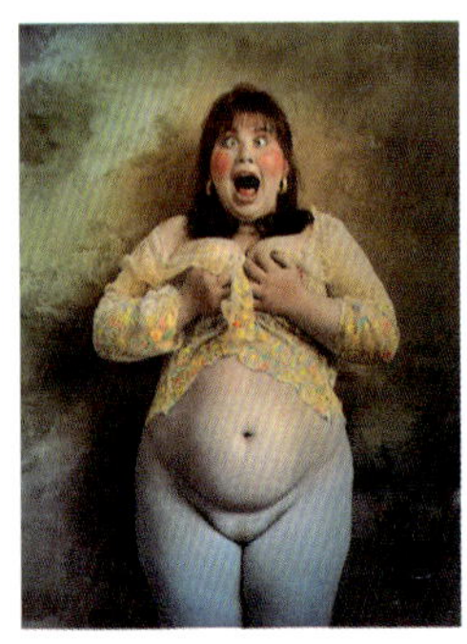

Einer diplomatisch formulierten Einschätzung von Zdenek Primus zufolge gilt Saudek in seinem Land inzwischen als eine der wenigen Persönlichkeiten, die in den siebziger Jahren unabhängig von den gesellschaftlichen Veränderungen ihren eigenen Weg als Künstler gingen – ohne Rückendeckung durch einen Künstlerverband oder andere staatliche Einrichtungen. Im Klartext bedeutete dies, totgeschwiegen zu werden. Saudek weiß von Zeiten zu berichten, in denen die einen annahmen, er lebe bereits in einem anderen Land, während die anderen der Meinung waren, er sei ein Agent des FBI oder unlängst verstorben. Das tschechoslowakische Kulturministerium soll eine Anfrage aus dem Ausland mit der Antwort beschieden haben, er sei überhaupt nicht existent.

Als westlicher Beobachter neigt man dazu, in der Person Saudek allein ein Opfer politischer Umstände zu sehen. Tatsächlich jedoch gelang es ihm, mit zunehmendem, nach 1975 einsetzendem internationalen Bekanntheitsgrad, fern von materieller Not erfolgreich zu arbeiten. Sicherlich gab es genügend Neider, was vielleicht auch einer der Gründe gewesen sein mochte, warum Saudek keinen freundschaftlichen Austausch mit Kollegen im eigenen Land pflegte. Entscheidend für seine isolierte Position dürfte jedoch der Umstand gewesen sein, daß er mit seiner Konzentration auf die Nacktheit des Menschen ein Themengebiet behandelte, auf dem zu seiner Zeit nicht viele ernst zu nehmende tschechoslowakische Photographen tätig waren. In den siebziger Jahren, in denen er die Geschlechtlichkeit des Menschen in den Fokus seiner Kamera zu rücken begann, dominierten dokumentarische Tendenzen die gesamte Photographie des Landes. Vladimír Birgus, Professor an der Akademie der Schönen Künste in Prag und selbst Photograph, vertritt sogar die Ansicht, die Aktphotographie der siebziger Jahre habe sowohl in ihrer klassischen gestalterischen Auffassung als auch in den inszenierten Darstellungen qualitativ und quantitativ weit unter dem Niveau der sechziger Jahre gelegen. Verantwortlich für diese Situation seien auch die verschiedenen, oft absurden Verbote gewesen, die es nahezu unmöglich gemacht hätten, photographische Akte auszustellen und zu veröffentlichen. Saudek befand sich mit seinem Tun also auf Konfrontationskurs – und das hatte Folgen. Wiederholt kam es zu Wohnungsdurchsuchungen. Positiv- und Negativmaterial wurde beschlagnahmt, soweit es nicht vorher in Sicherheit gebracht werden konnte; die Staatssicherheit heftete sich auf die Spur abgebildeter Personen und verhörte Freunde und Bekannte. Saudek unterlag zeitweise sogar polizeilicher Meldepflicht.

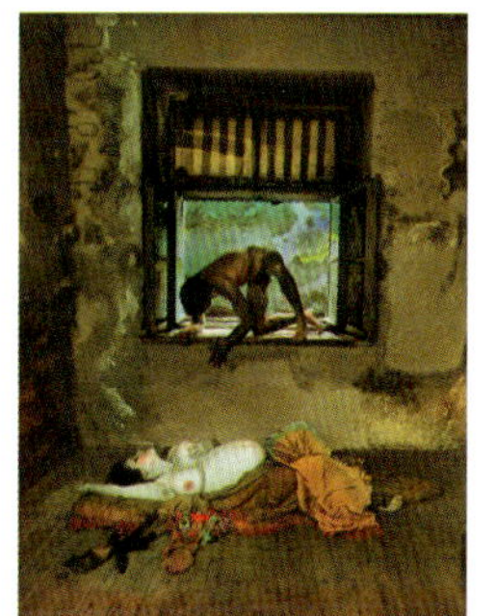

Entscheidenden Anteil an dieser bisweilen extrem belastenden Situation hatte zweifellos das Interesse, das ihm in Form von Publikationen und Ausstellungen im Ausland entgegengebracht wurde. Seit seiner ersten Präsentation an der Universität von Indiana in Bloomington 1969 verging kaum ein Jahr, in dem er nicht mit einer Einzelausstellung in den USA vertreten war. Bemerkenswerte Erfolge erzielte Saudek auch in Australien und Frankreich, wo es ihm schon früh gelang, an repräsentativer Stelle ausgestellt und gesammelt zu werden.

Den Durchbruch auf breiter Ebene verdankt er jedoch einem niederländischen Verlag, der sich auf die Herstellung und den Vertrieb von Postkarten, Plakaten und Büchern spezialisiert hat. »Art Unlimited« nahm ihn 1990 unter Vertrag. Annähernd fünf Jahre produzierte er für dieses Unternehmen – bis zur Erschöpfung.

In Deutschland wurde Saudek bislang nur mit spitzen Fingern angefaßt. Zwar wird er seit 1978 mit relativ gutem wirtschaftlichen Erfolg präsentiert, doch hat sich noch kein Museum dazu entschließen können, den Künstler mit einer Einzelausstellung zu würdigen. In den einschlägigen photographischen Sammlungen sucht man ihn – von der Sammlung Gruber im Museum Ludwig in Köln einmal abgesehen – vergebens. Auch in der CSSR nahm man ihn nur unwillig zur Kenntnis. Anna Fárová, ehemals Leiterin der 1970 neu gegründeten Photosammlung des Prager Kunstgewerbemuseums, machte aus ihren Schwierigkeiten mit Saudek keinen Hehl. »Ich haßte seine Vorliebe für Geschmacklosigkeiten und Kitsch«, schrieb sie 1983. »Ebensowenig gefiel mir die Unnatürlichkeit, die spröde Sentimentalität, die klar aus einigen seiner frühen Bilder sprach.« Zugleich gestand sie ein, »daß dieser Mann aus Prag außergewöhnlich war«. Es sei nicht zu leugnen, daß seine Bilder in Ausstellungen und Photozeitschriften die Aufmerksamkeit auf sich zögen – so ungewöhnlich seien sie, verglichen mit dem Reportagestil und Realismus seiner Zeitgenossen.

Fárovás Einschätzung hat auch nach 15 Jahren nichts von ihrer Aktualität verloren. An Saudek scheiden sich noch immer die Geister. Die Fachleute stehen namentlich seinem Schaffen des letzten Jahrzehnts ablehnend oder zumindest sehr verhalten gegenüber. Über seine Malerei schweigt man lieber. Und während die einen noch hadern, haben andere ihr Votum schon längst und in aller Eindeutigkeit gefällt. Nicht nur in den Buchhandlungen und Souvenirläden Tschechiens laufen Postkarten, Wandkalender und Bücher von Saudek allem den Rang ab, was nicht Picasso oder Matisse heißt.

Ikonen der Sehnsucht

»1935 bringt meine Mutter einen Sohn Kaja zur Welt und gleich darauf mich, quasi als Dreingabe«, lautet Saudeks erster Satz in seinem Lebenslauf. Dies habe ihn dazu bestimmt, sein Leben lang die Nummer zwei zu spielen. Kaja (dt. Karl) Saudek, der es schon in den sechziger Jahren zum erfolgreichen Graphiker und Comiczeichner gebracht hatte, war für Jan ebenso geliebte Bezugsperson wie herausfordernde Konkurrenz. Der jüngere Saudek brauchte mehr Zeit, um herauszufinden, daß die Photographie und nicht die Schauspielerei, der Tanz oder die Malerei seine tragfähigste Begabung werden sollte. Seine Eltern konnten ihm dabei nicht helfen. Sie kämpften um ihre Existenz. Der Vater, Jude und vor 1939 angesehener Angestellter einer Bank, hatte als einziger von sieben Brüdern das Konzentrationslager Theresienstadt überlebt. Nach dem Krieg wurde ihm aufgrund seiner deutschen Muttersprache die Rückkehr in seinen Beruf verwehrt. Sein jüngster Sohn mußte aufgrund seiner schlechten Noten die Schule schon im Alter von 15 Jahren verlassen. Als er mit 16 anfing zu photographieren, arbeitete er in einer Repro-Anstalt, deren technische Anlagen noch aus der Zeit der Jahrhundertwende stammten. Saudek war damals ein unruhiger Geist, hatte nichts als Frauen im Kopf und dementsprechend große Schwierigkeiten, sein Plansoll zu erfüllen. Von seinem Bruder erfahren wir, daß er mit seinen photographischen Kenntnissen allenfalls Nadar oder Mathew B. Brady hätte assistieren können. Mit Spott habe man auf seine ersten, mit einer Baby Brownie aufgenommenen Photographien reagiert, und so habe Jan das Photographieren zunächst einmal wieder fallengelassen.

Heute kann man den Aufruhr nur noch schwer nachvollziehen, der entstand, als Saudek 1963 zum ersten Mal in Prag ausstellte. Auf seinem ältesten, 1951 entstandenen Bild sieht man einen jungen, halbnackten Mann, der rücklings auf dem Boden liegt und die Arme ausbreitet, als wolle er das Universum umarmen. Der breitschultrige Mann, der in *Hey, Joe!* (1959, Abb. S. 37) auf seinem Motorroller am Ufer der Moldau haltgemacht hat, verrät hochgespannte Erwartung. *Fesseln der Liebe* (1960) zeigt aus der Vogelperspektive ein junges, nur mit Bluejeans bekleidetes Paar, das bäuchlings mit aneinandergeketteten Handgelenken auf dem Boden liegt. Solche Bilder verraten etwas von der ungestümen Energie eines jungen Mannes, der noch nicht weiß, in was er seine Kräfte investieren soll und den die Lust auf das Leben und die Liebe schon viel zu früh in den Hafen der Ehe geführt hat.

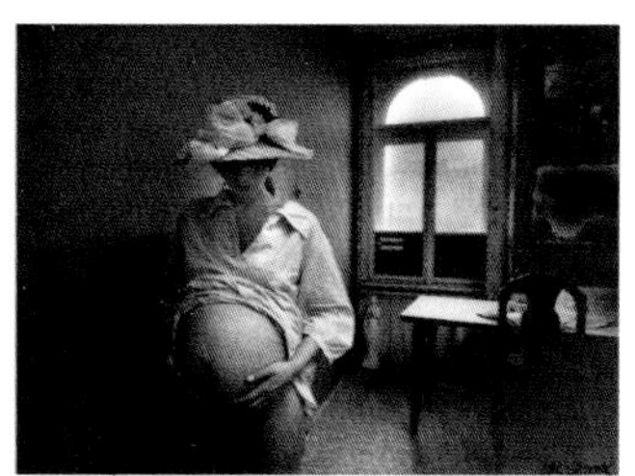

Wenn Saudek erfolgreich werden konnte, dann lag dies ganz sicher an seiner Fähigkeit, Sehnsüchte in allgemeinverständliche Bilder zu fassen. Nur selten teilt er dem Betrachter etwas über seinen Alltag mit. Um so entschiedener offenbart sich die Befindlichkeit eines Menschen, der sich in einem unbeweglichen, kommunistisch regierten Land nach einer Freiheit sehnt, die er sich nur in der Gestalt eines Traums vorstellen kann. Diese, sich über jedwede Unbilden hinwegsetzende Bereitschaft zur Imagination machte ihn auch empfänglich für Edward Steichens schönen Traum von der »Family of Man«. Die am New Yorker Museum of Modern Art organisierte Ausstellung zeigte Photographien von Menschen aller Hautfarben in existentiellen Lebenssituationen, von der Geburt bis zum Tod. In 44 Großstädte der Welt brachte die Ausstellung ihre optimistische Botschaft, derzufolge es unter den Völkern mehr Verbindendes als Trennendes gebe. »Wir beginnen und enden«, hieß es in einer Pressenotiz von Steichen. »Keiner ist unter uns, der da aus der Reihe tanzen könnte. Wir sind alle Menschen, einer wie der andere.«

1963, unter dem Eindruck des Katalogs dieser bereits seit acht Jahren durch die halbe Welt tourenden Ausstellung, beschloß Saudek, das Leben des Menschen von der Geburt bis zum Tod darzustellen. Er machte sich unbekümmert an die Arbeit. Dabei spielte es für ihn keine Rolle, daß am Zustandekommen dieser Ausstellung Hunderte von Photographen aus allen Teilen der Welt beteiligt waren. Ebensowenig ließ er sich von der Tatsache irritieren, daß sich diese Photographen dem Gegenstand ihres Interesses mit den Aufnahmetechniken der Live-Photographie genähert hatten. Saudek tat, bis auf wenige, offenkundig von »The Family of Man« inspirierte Ausnahmen, das Gegenteil. Anstatt das Verhalten des Menschen zu beobachten und im entscheidenden Moment den Auslöser zu betätigen, imaginierte er ein Bild und ging anschließend daran, es für die Kamera in Szene zu setzen. Auf seine Art setzt Saudek damit die Tradition des »tableau vivant« oder der »pose plastique« fort, die ihren Ursprung als aristokratische Freizeitbeschäftigung im 18. Jahrhundert hatte und nach deren Vorbild sich im 19. Jahrhundert noch Queen Victorias Kinder vom Hofphotographen ablichten ließen.

Ein gutes Beispiel für Saudeks Vorgehensweise liefern die Entstehungsumstände seines berühmten Bildes *Life* aus dem Jahre 1966 (Abb. S. 44). Der Photograph hatte die Vorstellung von einem starken, großen Vater, der sein winziges Neugeborenes mit schützender, liebender Geste an seine Brust preßt. Er glaubte, ein befreundeter Gewichtheber könnte das ideale Modell abgeben. Während der Aufnahme stellte sich jedoch heraus, daß dieser Mann nicht die geringste Ahnung davon hatte, wie ein Vater sein Baby in den Armen hält. Saudek realisierte die Aufnahme schließlich mit sich selbst als Modell und machte eine überraschende Erfahrung: Nicht die Muskelpakete, sondern die Beziehung zwischen Vater und Kind erwiesen sich als entscheidend für die Überzeugungskraft der Bildaussage.

Der Eintritt des Liebhabers

Das nach 1970 entstandene photographische Œuvre Saudeks vermittelt den Eindruck, der Künstler habe der Welt draußen den Rücken gekehrt. Möglicherweise war auch sein Umzug in den Keller – wenn man einmal die privaten Umstände beiseite läßt – zugleich eine unbewußte Strategie, sich selbst aus dem Gefechtsfeld zu bringen und sich der Kontrolle durch die Obrigkeit zu entziehen. Für eine aufrei-

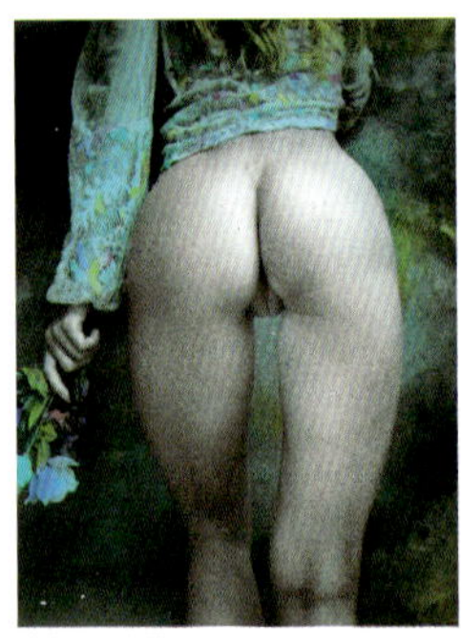

zende Persönlichkeit wie Saudek konnte der Aufenthalt in der Öffentlichkeit durchaus prekär werden. Da war es noch harmlos, wenn er in Unterwäsche nach Hause laufen mußte, weil ihm – so geschehen in den frühen sechziger Jahren – die Polizei die Bluejeans wegnahm. Noch heute, neun Jahre nach dem Fall des Eisernen Vorhangs, wundert sich der ausländische Gast über zugezogene Gardinen am hellichten Tag, die jedem Verweilen in der Wohnung des Künstlers den Charakter einer intimen, vor fremden Blicken abgeschirmten Zusammenkunft geben.

Unterzieht man die wenigen, unter freiem Himmel aufgenommenen Arbeiten einer näheren Betrachtung, fällt auf, daß sie ebenso sorgfältig inszeniert wurden wie seine Atelierphotographien. Die Wirklichkeit dringt nicht in seine Bilder ein. Auf dem Photo *120 km/h* (1975, Abb. S. 41) verdichtet sich die Bildaussage auf wenige Details, die vor dem Hintergrund der eingeschränkten Bewegungs- bzw. Reisefreiheit höchste Brisanz erhalten: die an der geschlossenen Schranke vorbeirauschende Dampflokomotive, ein junger Mann, der auf der Schranke sitzt, der grasüberwachsene Schotter im Vordergrund, der anzeigt, daß dieser Bahnübergang schon länger nicht mehr benutzt wurde. Wie viele andere Bilder hat Saudek auch diese Aufnahme nach 1977 von Hand koloriert und damit der Atmosphäre einen zusätzlichen Anstrich von Irrealität gegeben. In *Das Schicksal geht hinunter zum Fluß* (1971) gelingt es ihm, die Stadt mit ihren schmutzigen Schloten zur perfekten Kulisse für den Auftritt einer ins Tal schreitenden Mutter mit ihren beiden widerspenstigen Töchtern zu machen. Die Kinder, die sich an die stolze, festlich gekleidete junge Frau mit den blonden Haaren drängen, sind nackt; die Straße ist leer – kein Auto, keine Menschen sind sichtbar, die den Alltag in das Bild tragen könnten. Saudek weiß – und das hat er bereits 1959 mit *Hey, Joe!* unter Beweis gestellt –, wie man einen Ort in einen Schauplatz verwandelt.

Nur selten wirken Saudeks Arbeiten – anders als die seines amerikanischen Kollegen Joel-Peter Witkin, der das ihn Verstörende und den Schmerz bewußt gesucht hat – beunruhigend. Vielleicht ist für ihn auch deshalb die Arbeit in einem von der Außenwelt abgeschotteten, überschaubaren Raum obligatorisch. Wer auch immer den Fuß in das Dämmerlicht seines Ateliers setzt, betritt von Saudek kontrolliertes Terrain, und dort herrschen eigene Gesetze. Er schaffe für seine Modelle eine Traumwelt, so formulierte er einmal, und automatisch beginne darin, irgendein besonderer Faktor zu wirken. Ähnliche Erfahrungen machte der amerikanische Porträtphotograph Irving Penn, der allerdings mit einem transportablen Studio-Zelt in der Welt herumreiste: »Wenn ich die Menschen aus ihren natürlichen Lebensumständen herausnahm und sie in mein Studio vor die Kamera stellte, so wurden sie nicht einfach isoliert, sie wurden umgewandelt.« Saudek beläßt es im Gegensatz zu Penn nicht bei dieser Umwandlung. Er greift ein, nimmt den Modellen ihre Alltagsgarderobe, bringt Requisiten ins Spiel. Manchmal hilft er auch mit einem Gläschen Likör nach. Von Frauen, die »von sich aus willig zu Spielgefährtinnen« werden, berichtet Daniela Mrázková in ihrer 1991 erschienenen Monographie. »Sie lassen sich be- und entkleiden, sich in die Gestalt seiner Visionen kneten.«

Man müßte schon sehr naiv sein, um in Saudeks Werk nur eine Apotheose der sich dem Mann darbietenden Weiblichkeit zu sehen. »Geschöpfe«, so schrieb bereits der Dichter August von Platen, »spiegeln ihres Schöpfers Wonne.« Aber unabhängig von der Frage, wieviel an Intimität bzw. Persönlichkeit sich im Wettstreit mit der Pose noch behaupten mag: kein zweiter Photograph hat sich mit einer solchen Gründlichkeit und über einen so langen Zeitraum mit der Frau als seinem Gegenüber befaßt, wie Jan Saudek. In allen denkbaren Aspekten erforscht der Photograph dieses Mirakel – und zwar nicht allein als Beobachter, sondern als einer, der in diesen Prozeß zutiefst verstrickt ist. Er selbst hat unmißverständlich deutlich gemacht, was damit gemeint ist: »Ich habe nicht die Möglichkeit, das Leben anderer Menschen zu porträtieren. Ich porträtiere mein eigenes.«

Zweifellos sind für den Betrachter jene Bilder am interessantesten, in denen Saudek etwas von der »Chemie« der Beziehung zwischen sich und seinem Modell einfängt: die provokativ auffordernde Geste der jungen Frau etwa, die sich in *Marie Nr. 142* (1972, Abb. S. 54) mit den Zähnen ihren Pullover hochzieht, die selbstbewußte, souveräne Gelassenheit der bekränzten, androgynen *Susanna* (1978, Abb. S. 78) oder die dem Betrachter trotzig ihre magere Brust entgegenstreckende *Els!* (1985, Abb. S. 77). Man hat bei diesen Photographien das Gefühl, einem intimen Dialog beizuwohnen. Der

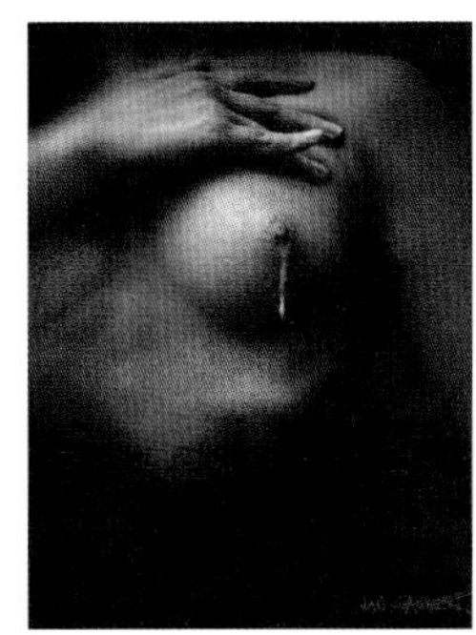

Blick des Photographen konzentriert sich auf sein Gegenüber, das von den Knien aufwärts, seltener, zumindest in den frühen siebziger Jahren, ganzfigurig erfaßt ist. Saudek hat den Bildausschnitt jedoch so gewählt, daß auch die Hinfälligkeit des Ambientes sichtbar ist. Die Wand trägt die Spuren des Lebens, die sich in die jungen, vom weichen Licht modellierten Körper noch nicht eingegraben haben. Andere Körper dagegen offenbaren im Akt der Entblößung ihre vom Alter gezeichnete Fleischlichkeit und Formung. In einigen Bildern spürt er weiblichen Verhaltensweisen nach: junge Frauen, die sich gebannt mit dem Spiegelbild ihrer Kehrseite befassen, die Art und Weise, wie sie sich ihren Brüsten widmen oder ihre Hingabe demonstrieren. Nicht selten erinnert Saudek an Milan Kunderas literarische Gestalt des Tomas, der besessen ist von dem Wunsch, in jeder neu eroberten Frau das »Millionstel an Unähnlichem« zu entdecken, das sie von allen anderen unterscheidet.

Trauer findet in Saudeks Werk allenfalls in lyrischer Verbrämung Eingang: zum Beispiel der Verlust eines Freundes, dessen Profil er in ein kleines, in der Hand geborgenes Medaillon hinein belichtete (1970, Abb. S. 34) oder der Kummer über eine zu Ende gegangene »Liebesgeschichte«, dargestellt an einer aufblühenden Rose, die nach und nach ihre Blätter verliert (1974, Abb. S. 35). Das Desaströse bleibt gewöhnlich außen vor oder erscheint, wie das Beispiel der erhängten Frau zeigt, in theatralischem Gewand (1977, Abb. S. 118/119). Von der heillosen Verwirrung, die seinen Amerikaaufenthalt im Jahre 1969 begleitete, erzählt das Bild eines an einer überdimensionalen Plakatwand aufgeknüpften Mannes (1969, Abb. S. 39). Nur einmal, 1976, verließ er die Bühne des Saudekschen »Theater des Lebens«, um seinen müden, alten Vater zwischen den Gräbern des verwilderten jüdischen Friedhofs zu photographieren. Es ist ein schlichtes, völlig unprätentiöses Bild, eine Ausnahme in der mit der Zeit immer üppiger und aufwendiger inszenierten Welt des Photographen, ein Bild voller Trauer (1975, Abb. S. 33).

Von jeher waren die Tschechen angehalten, sich mit Verhältnissen zu arrangieren, die ihnen aufgezwungen wurden. Ein Aspekt ihrer Anpassungsfähigkeit ist die Gabe, sich imaginierenderweise eine eigene, magische Realität zu erschaffen. Saudek, der sich nie dazu entschließen konnte, zu emigrieren, hat es auf diesem Gebiet zu einer wahren Meisterschaft gebracht. Um 1976/77 begann er, in das sich in einen unfreundlichen Lichtschacht öffnende Fenster traumhafte Szenerien hineinzubelichten. Nicht viel später datieren bezeichnenderweise auch seine ersten Versuche, Schwarzweißabzüge von Hand zu kolorieren. Anna Fárová sprach in diesem Zusammenhang von Farben, die sich gegen die Natur wenden, Daniela Mrázková von seinem letzten gewichtigen Bruch seiner Bindungen an die Realität.

Mit Recht erinnert man sich angesichts von Saudeks Fensterbildern an Josef Sudeks Zyklus »Fenster meines Ateliers«. Sudek, der während des 2. Weltkriegs angesichts des Naziterrors den Rückzug in sein Hinterhofatelier antrat, entdeckte die beschlagene, mit Regentropfen übersäte und zufrierende Fensterscheibe als eine Projektionsfläche, die sich gleich einem Schleier voller Rätsel vor die Außenwelt legte. Doch wo sein versonnener Blick selbstgenügsam auf den sich ihm darbietenden Phantasmagorien verweilte, verwandelt Saudek das Vorhandene radikal. Im Lichtmontageverfahren werden die flüchtigen Schemen vorübereilender Fußgänger, heitere, von den Kondensstreifen der Flugzeuge durchkreuzte Wolkenhimmel oder Mond und Sterne einkopiert. Etwas erscheint jedoch eigentümlich: das Fenster erlaubt zwar diverse wundersame Ausblicke und es erlaubt sogar den Eintritt des Liebhabers. Aber nie sieht man jemanden hinaussteigen.

Auf der Kehrseite der Saudekschen Vitalität stehen Existenzängste, die Daniela Mrázková eindringlich beschrieben hat. Es sind nicht allein die Ängste eines Menschen, der unter der nationalsozialistischen Judenverfolgung schon als Kind permanenter Gefährdung ausgesetzt war und dessen Familie nach 1945 wieder, und zwar nun aufgrund ihrer deutschen Wurzeln, um die blanke Existenz kämpfen mußte. Es sind auch die Ängste einer unangepaßten Persönlichkeit, die über lange Zeiträume immer wieder im Visier staatlicher Aufsichtsbehörden stand. Daniela Mrázková beschreibt außerdem die Furcht des Künstlers vor dem Verlust seiner kreativen Potenz, die steten Selbstzweifel und die damit zusammenhängende Angst vor Verfall und Tod. Wenn Saudek seine Geliebte Veronika in Abständen von fünf Jahren wieder vor seine Kamera treten läßt (Abb. S. 82/83), dann verbirgt sich dahinter gewiß auch ein gehöriges Maß an Erschütterung, dem der Künstler etwas entgegensetzen möchte: Es ist der Versuch, einzelne Momente dieses Lebens als pars pro toto einer unerbittlich fortschreitenden Biographie zu retten.

The show must go on

Dem nach 1984 entstandenen Werk Saudeks stehen vor allem jene mit gemischten Gefühlen gegenüber, die sich willig von der Magie seiner poetischen und einstmals stark nostalgisch gefärbten Bildwelt gefangennehmen ließen. Nun blicken sie konsterniert auf seine jüngsten Arbeiten, die sich in mancherlei auf die Spitze getriebenen Manierismen und Despektierlichkeiten gefallen. Dabei liegt es eigentlich auf der Hand, daß Saudek nicht lebenslang aus der Perspektive des andachtsvollen Freiers oder des liebevollen, in seine Kinder vernarrten Vaters ans Werk gehen konnte. Zu den unverfänglichsten Arbeiten zählen noch die dekorativen, mit Hilfe der Lichtmontage spiegelbildlich komponierten Szenen, darunter die zwischen 1984 und 1987 entstandenen Spielkarten oder das Bild *Fegefeuer Nr. 2* (1987, Abb. S. 155), auf dem sich Saudek und seine wohlgestaltete Partnerin in perfekter, artistischer Pose annähern.

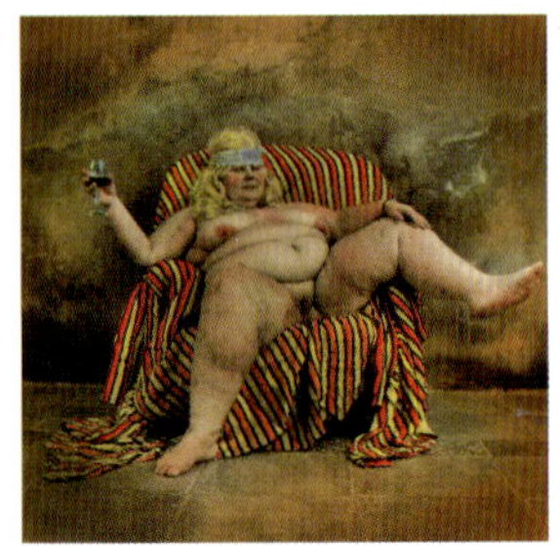

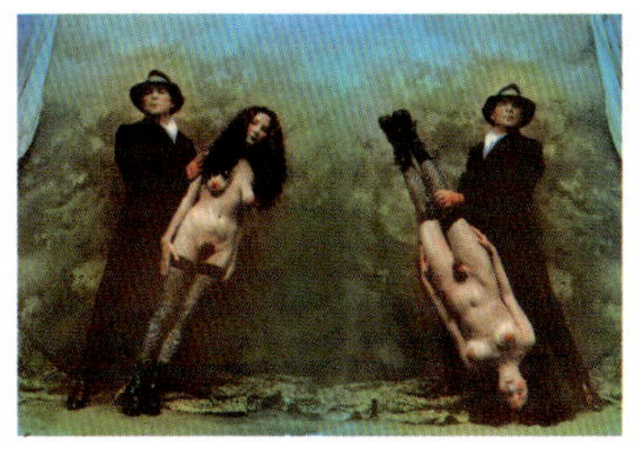

Daß Saudek aus seinem rastlosen Liebesleben, den Auseinandersetzungen mit Ehefrauen und Liebhaberinnen nicht ohne Federn zu lassen hervorgehen konnte, davon erzählen bereits viele Arbeiten der achtziger Jahre. Die in früheren Jahren immer wieder beschworene Vergötterung der Frau verkehrt sich in ihr Gegenteil und gerinnt nicht selten zu Gehässigkeit. So sieht man ihn in *Tiefes Verlangen* (1985, Abb. S. 110) in der Rolle des bittenden, vor seiner keifenden Frau wie vor Jesus Christus in die Knie gesunkenen Ehemanns. In dem Mitte der achtziger Jahre entstandenen *Porträt einer Frau und eines Mannes* (Abb. S. 114/115) gefällt er sich als Macho, der sich seelenruhig eine Zigarette anzündet, während seine Partnerin dabei ist, sich mit einer altertümlichen Pistole umzubringen. Die Ironie ist unübersehbar und paart sich nicht selten mit Zynismus. Immer häufiger bleibt dabei die einstmals lebendige erotische Spannung zwischen Modell und Photograph auf der Strecke. Im Extremfall sucht der Künstler das Mysterium nicht mehr in der Interaktion der Beteiligten, sondern versucht, es optisch dingfest zu machen, indem er mit seiner Kamera den Tabuzonen des Körpers im wörtlichen Sinne zu Leibe rückt.

Saudek schreckt vor nichts zurück. In *Der Photograph als Jesus* (1991, Abb. S. 163) hängt er zwischen zwei leicht geschürzten Frauen wie der Gekreuzigte zwischen den Schächern. Ein Selbstporträt zeigt ihn in der Pose des Hamlet, der, so scheint es, im Kostüm eines KZ-Häftling auftritt. Erst bei genauerem Hinsehen entdeckt man, daß es sich um ein Designerjacket der Firma »Matsuda« handelt, für die er 1989 und 1991 Modeaufnahmen machte. Anstelle des Totenkopfes hält er seine Kamera in der Hand.

Saudek greift so lässig in den Fundus historischer Bildmotive wie in die Requisitenkiste, die er einstmals einem Prager Theater abkaufen konnte. Immer wieder stößt man bei ihm auf christlich inspirierte Konfigurationen oder entdeckt Anleihen, die er bei zeitgenössischen Kollegen tätigt. Am häufigsten finden sich allerdings Szenerien, für die erotische Photographien und Postkarten der Jahrhundertwende die Vorlagen liefern. Zunächst sind es nur einzelne Accessoires wie der Blumenkranz, das Diadem, ein Fell oder ein Fetzen Tüll, die dem Geschehen vor seiner Kamera das sinnliche, etwas schwüle Flair der »Boudoirs« des Fin de siècle verleihen. Seit der zweiten Hälfte der siebziger Jahre tragen seine Modelle verspielte, altertümliche Kleider, sind mit Perlenketten behängt oder räkeln sich nackt auf üppigen Stoffen wie ihresgleichen vor hundert Jahren. In den achtziger Jahren beginnt Saudek verstärkt, nach dem Vorbild der Bildpostkarten in Serie zu arbeiten. Er inszeniert kleine lüsterne Anekdoten von Dienstmädchen, die schlafen gehen, aber auch pikantere, pornographische Sequenzen, in denen man sich zu Dritt miteinander vergnügt.

Als junger Mann glaubte Saudek, »das Zeug zu haben, vor der Kamera stehen zu können«. Das Leben selbst habe ihn davon überzeugt, gestand er später, daß er hinter und nicht vor der Kamera seinen Platz habe. Tatsache ist, daß Saudek mindestens so leidenschaftlich Schauspieler wie Regisseur ist. Wenn er sich in dieser Rolle nicht wiederzuerkennen vermag, dann vielleicht deshalb, weil er längst integraler Bestandteil der von ihm geschaffenen Bühne geworden ist – ob in der Kunst oder im Leben, ob vor oder hinter der Kamera. »The show must go on.«

Christiane Fricke

Karolina, Marie et les Visages de l'Amour

L'homme qui travaillait à l'usine de six heures du matin à trois heures de l'après-midi habitait dans une cave dont la fenêtre donnait sur une cour triste. Les murs étaient recouverts de moisissure, le plâtre s'effritait. Jan Saudek ne possédait guère plus qu'une bicyclette qu'il empruntait pour aller travailler et un vieux Pentacon six. Sa plus grande richesse était sans nul doute son immense énergie doublée d'une ambition sans limites. Lorsqu'il se retrouva au début des années soixante-dix, à l'issue de l'un de ses divorces, dans cette cave transformée en abri de fortune, sa vie prit un tournant décisif. Dans ces circonstances en effet, il aurait été incapable de continuer à photographier comme il l'avait fait jusque-là. Dans les années soixante, c'étaient les membres de sa famille, les enfants et les amis qui peuplaient ses photographies. Leur liberté de mouvements déterminait l'étendue géographique de ses activités. Il les photographiait bien souvent dans la rue, contre les murs de la cour ou dans le jardin et il se servait volontiers des techniques de l'instantané. Le point d'orgue de cette phase créatrice plutôt extravertie si on la compare à la suite fut un voyage en Amérique en 1969. Après 1970, le théâtre de ses activités se focalisa de plus en plus sur « la cave » dont le mur morbide découvert par l'artiste en 1972 devint le synonyme de son œuvre.

On peut difficilement concevoir dans quelle direction le travail de Saudek aurait évolué s'il n'avait pas emménagé dans cette cave. Une chose est sûre, il ne s'intéressait pas à la photographie technique ou de paysages. Ses ambitions le portaient à la photographie en direct. En 1974, alors qu'il photographiait déjà surtout des nus, il écrivit à un ami qu'il essayait parfois de faire des reportages. Peut-être ne put-il suivre ses goûts en raison des circonstances. Si son travail à l'usine lui permettait de gagner son pain, il ne lui laissait que peu d'occasions de prendre ses photos à la lumière du jour.

Censure et succès

Dans son œuvre, Saudek fait figure à plusieurs égards de cavalier seul. Contrairement à beaucoup de photographes contemporains, le traumatisme causé par les événements de 1968 ne l'empêcha pas de créer quelque chose de nouveau. Pas plus avant qu'après 1968, la réalité sociale n'eut de place dans l'univers pictural de Saudek. Quant aux événements politiques, il y prêta peu d'attention jusqu'à ce jour atroce où l'étudiant Jan Palach se laissa brûler vif. D'une façon générale, on peut dire que Saudek vécut la fin de cette décennie surtout comme une période de bouleversements personnels.

Selon un jugement de Zdenek Primus que celui-ci formule avec diplomatie, Saudek est désormais considéré dans son pays comme l'un des rares artistes à avoir suivi sa propre voie dans les années soixante-dix, indépendamment des changements sociaux et sans le soutien d'une association d'artistes ou d'autres institutions de l'Etat. En clair, cela signifie qu'on faisait le silence sur lui. Saudek se souvient de certaines époques où les uns supposaient qu'il vivait déjà dans un autre pays tandis que les autres croyaient qu'il était un agent du FBI ou qu'il venait de mourir. Le ministère de la Culture tchécoslovaque aurait coupé court à une demande de renseignements provenant de l'étranger en répondant qu'il n'existait pas de Jan Saudek.

Un observateur occidental aurait tendance à voir en Saudek une victime de la situation politique. Mais le fait est qu'à partir de 1975, il devint de plus en plus populaire sur le plan international et parvint

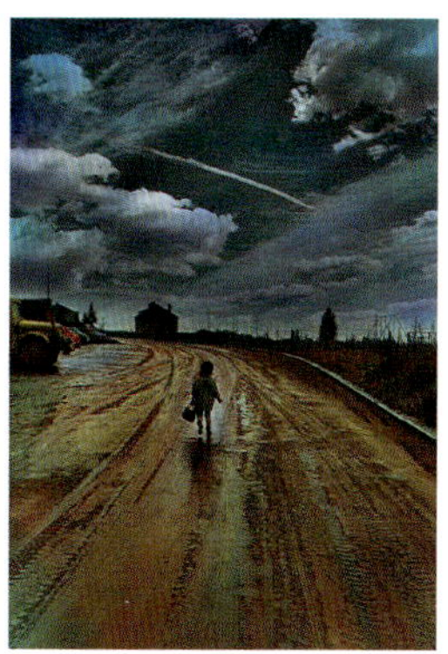

à travailler avec succès et sans soucis matériels. Bien sûr, les envieux ne manquaient pas, et c'est peut-être aussi l'une des raisons pour laquelle Saudek n'entretenait pas d'échanges amicaux avec les collègues de son pays. Pourtant, son isolement s'expliquerait plutôt par le fait qu'en se concentrant sur la nudité de l'homme il traitait un sujet sur lequel peu de photographes tchèques sérieux travaillaient à cette époque. Dans les années soixante-dix, quand il commença à montrer la sexualité de l'homme avec ses photos, les tendances documentaires dominaient toute la photographie de son pays. Vladimir Birgus, directeur de l'Institut de la Photographie appliquée de Prague et lui-même photographe, prétendit même que la photographie de nus des années soixante-dix était en qualité et en quantité bien inférieure à celle des années soixante, et ce aussi bien au niveau de la conception artistique classique qu'à celui de la mise en scène. Selon lui, les différentes interdictions, souvent absurdes, étaient responsables de cette situation puisqu'elles rendaient pratiquement impossible l'exposition et la publication de photos de nus.

Du fait de ses agissements, Saudek bravait les autorités, et cela ne resta pas sans conséquences. Son appartement fut fouillé à plusieurs reprises. Les épreuves positives et négatives qu'il n'avait pu mettre en sécurité furent confisquées. Les services de la Sûreté retrouvèrent la trace des personnes photographiées et interrogèrent amis et connaissances. Il y eut même des époques où on l'obligea à se présenter régulièrement au poste de police.

Cette situation parfois extrêmement éprouvante était due sans nul doute à l'intérêt qu'on lui portait à l'étranger sous forme de publications et d'expositions. Depuis sa première présentation à l'université d'Indiana à Bloomington en 1969, il ne se passait pas une année sans qu'il soit représenté aux Etats-Unis dans une exposition particulière. Saudek connut également beaucoup de succès en Australie et en France où ses œuvres furent très tôt collectionnées et exposées dans des lieux représentatifs.

Mais c'est une maison d'édition néerlandaise spécialisée dans la production et la vente de cartes postales, d'affiches et de livres qui lui permit de devenir vraiment populaire. « Art Unlimited » le prit sous contrat en 1990. Il travailla près de cinq ans pour cette maison, jusqu'à épuisement.

Jusqu'ici en Allemagne, on a montré peu de considération pour les œuvres de Saudek. Même s'il y est représenté depuis 1978 avec un certain succès économique, aucun musée n'a pu encore se décider à honorer l'artiste avec une exposition particulière. Mis à part la collection Gruber au Museum Ludwig de Cologne, on le cherchera en vain dans les collections photographiques. En Tchécoslovaquie aussi, c'est bien à contrecœur qu'on s'aperçut de son existence. Anna Fárová, ancienne directrice de la collection de photographies créée en 1970 au musée des Arts appliqués de Prague, ne fait pas mystère des difficultés qu'elle avait avec Saudek. « Je détestais son amour du mauvais goût et du kitsch », écrit-elle en 1983. Et elle poursuit : « Le manque de naturel, cette sentimentalité farouche, qui émanait clairement de ses premières photographies, me déplaisait tout autant. » Pourtant, elle concède aussi « que cet homme de Prague était exceptionnel ». Selon elle, on ne pouvait contester que ses photos présentées dans les expositions et les magazines attiraient l'attention, tant elles se démarquaient sur le plan du style et du réalisme des reportages de ses contemporains.

Même si elle date de 15 ans, l'opinion de Anna Fárová n'a rien perdu de son actualité. Quand il s'agit de Saudek, les avis aussi sont toujours autant partagés. Les experts rejettent surtout son œuvre des dix dernières années ou sont très réservés. On préfère se taire sur sa peinture. Et tandis que les uns se querellent encore, les autres ont prononcé leur jugement depuis bien longtemps et sans ambiguïté. Il n'y a pas que dans les librairies et les magasins de souvenirs de Tchéquie que les cartes postales, les calendriers muraux et les livres de Saudek supplantent tout ce qui n'est pas signé Picasso ou Matisse.

Les icones du désir

« En 1935, ma mère mit au monde un fils dénommé Kaja et moi tout de suite après, quasiment en prime », ainsi commence le récit de Saudek de sa propre vie. Cette situation l'aurait incité à être toute sa vie le numéro deux. Devenu dès les années soixante un dessinateur de bandes dessinées célèbre, Kaja Saudek, Charles en français, était à la fois un frère tendrement aimé et un rival qui le défiait. Le plus jeune des Saudek mit plus longtemps à découvrir que son avenir résidait dans la photographie et non dans la comédie, la danse ou la peinture. Ses parents ne purent l'aider, parvenant à peine à joindre les deux bouts. Le père, un juif, était un employé de banque estimé de tous avant 1939. Il fut le seul des frères Saudek, à survivre au camp de concentration de Theresienstadt. Après la guerre, on lui interdit de reprendre son ancien métier parce que l'allemand était sa langue maternelle. Son plus jeune fils dut quitter l'école à quinze ans en raison de ses mauvaises notes. Lorsqu'il commença à photographier à l'âge de seize ans, il travaillait dans un établissement de reproductions dont l'équipement technique datait du début du siècle. A l'époque Saudek était dissipé, n'ayant que les femmes en tête, et par conséquent il avait de grandes difficultés à satisfaire les normes de production imposées par le plan. On sait de son frère qu'avec ses connaissances en photographie, il aurait pu tout au plus être l'assistant de Nadar ou de Mathew B. Brady. Ses premières photos prises avec un Baby Brownie furent accueillies avec des moqueries de sorte que Jan laissa tomber la photographie pour un temps.

Aujourd'hui, il est difficile de comprendre l'agitation que provoqua à Prague la première exposition de Saudek en 1963. Sur sa plus ancienne photo, réalisée en 1951, on voit un jeune homme à moitié nu, allongé sur le dos et les bras écartés comme s'il voulait embrasser l'univers. L'homme aux larges épaules qui, dans *Hey, Joe!* (1959, ill. p. 37) a arrêté son scooter sur la rive de la Moldau, laisse transparaître ses attentes. Dans *Les liens de l'amour* (1960), on voit pris d'en haut deux jeunes gens vêtus uniquement de jeans, allongés sur le ventre et enchaînés l'un à l'autre aux poignets. De telles images trahissent la fougue d'un jeune homme qui ne sait pas encore dans quoi il doit investir ses pouvoirs et dont le désir de vivre et d'aimer l'a fait échouer bien trop tôt sur les rivages de la vie conjugale.

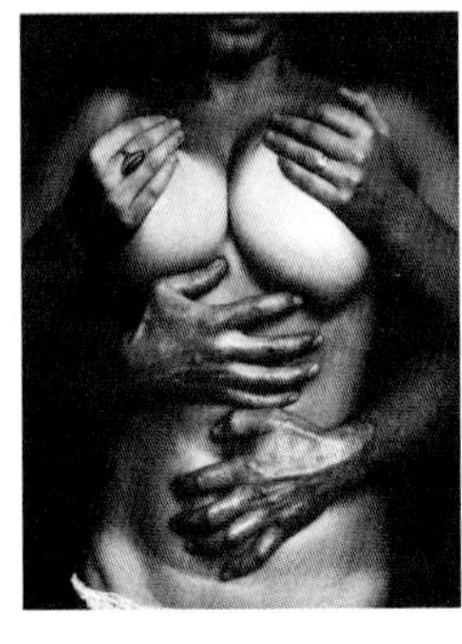

Si Saudek a pu devenir célèbre, c'est certainement parce qu'il a su exprimer des aspirations dans des photos à la portée de tous. Il est très rare qu'il révèle au spectateur quelque chose de sa vie quotidienne. Et c'est avec d'autant plus de résolution que se manifeste la sensibilité de cet homme qui, dans un pays en stagnation gouverné par les communistes, aspire à une liberté qu'il ne peut concevoir que sous la forme d'un rêve. Cette disposition naturelle à passer outre toutes les rigueurs pour se réfugier dans l'imaginaire l'a rendu sensible au beau rêve de la « Family of Man » d'Edward Steichen. L'exposition organisée au Museum of Modern Art montrait des photos d'hommes de

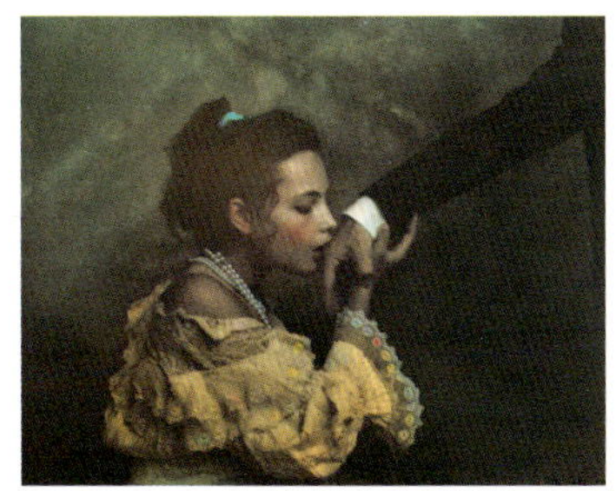

toutes couleurs de peau dans des situations existentielles, de la naissance à la mort. Cette exposition apporta dans 44 métropoles son message optimiste selon lequel les peuples ont plus de choses qui les réunissent que de choses qui les séparent. « Nous commençons et finissons », pouvait-on lire dans un entrefilet écrit par Steichen. « Il n'y a personne parmi nous qui pourrait se singulariser. Nous sommes tous des hommes, l'un pareil à l'autre. » En 1963, sous l'impression du catalogue de cette exposition qui depuis huit ans avait parcouru la moitié de la planète, Saudek décida de représenter la vie de l'homme de la naissance à la mort et se mit allègrement au travail. Il lui importait peu que cette exposition ait nécessité le concours de centaines de photographes du monde entier. Il ne se laissa pas non plus troubler par le fait que ces photographes avaient approché l'objet de leur intérêt en utilisant les techniques de la photographie en direct. A quelques rares exceptions près où il s'inspira manifestement de la « Family of Man », Saudek fit exactement le contraire. Au lieu d'observer le comportement de l'homme et d'appuyer au bon moment sur le déclencheur, il s'imagina d'abord la photo comme elle devrait être, puis s'occupa de la mise en scène. A sa façon, Saudek perpétuait ainsi la tradition du « tableau vivant » ou de la « pose plastique », une tradition née au XVIIIe siècle pour divertir la noblesse et que la reine Victoria poursuivit au siècle suivant en faisant photographier ses enfants par le photographe de la cour.

Les circonstances dans lesquelles fut réalisée *Life*, sa célèbre photo de 1966 (ill. p. 44), illustrent bien les techniques de Saudek. Le photographe avait en tête l'image d'un père grand et fort qui d'un geste tendre et protecteur presse contre sa poitrine son minuscule nouveau-né. Il crut qu'un haltérophile de ses amis pourrait faire parfaitement l'affaire. Pendant les prises de vue, il s'avéra toutefois que l'homme n'avait pas la moindre idée de la façon dont un père tient son bébé dans ses bras. Finalement, Saudek se prit lui-même comme modèle et découvrit avec surprise que ce n'était pas le physique athlétique mais la relation entre père et enfant qui était décisive pour que le message de la photo soit convaincant.

L'arrivée de l'amant

L'œuvre photographique de Saudek, réalisée après 1970, donne l'impression que l'artiste a tourné le dos au monde extérieur. Si on laisse de côté sa situation privée, il est possible que son installation dans la cave ait été une stratégie inconsciente pour se retirer du champ de bataille et se soustraire au contrôle des autorités. Pour une personnalité aussi provocante que Saudek, la vie en public pouvait s'avérer difficile. La fois où il dut rentrer chez lui en sous-vêtements – cela se passait au début des années soixante – parce que la police lui avait confisqué son jean fut l'un des épisodes les plus innocents. Aujourd'hui encore, neuf ans après la chute du « rideau de fer », l'invité venant de l'étranger s'étonne de voir ses rideaux fermés en plein jour, ce qui donne aux visites dans l'appartement de l'artiste le caractère d'une réunion intime protégée des regards extérieurs.

Si l'on étudie de plus près les quelques travaux réalisés en plein air, on constate qu'ils ont fait l'objet d'une mise en scène aussi scrupuleuse que ceux effectués en atelier. La réalité ne pénètre pas dans ses photos. Celle intitulée *120 km/h* (1975, ill. p. 41) se concentre sur un petit nombre de détails qui, vu les entraves faites à cette époque à la liberté de mouvements et de voyager, sont d'une actualité brûlante :

la locomotive à vapeur qui passe en chuintant devant la barrière fermée, un jeune homme assis sur cette barrière, les cailloux recouverts d'herbe au premier plan qui montrent que ce passage à niveau n'est plus en service depuis longtemps. Comme pour beaucoup d'autres photographies, Saudek a également colorié celle-ci à la main après 1977, renforçant ainsi son atmosphère irréelle. Dans *Le Destin descendant vers le fleuve* (1971), il réussit à transformer la ville avec ses cheminées noircies en décor parfait pour l'entrée en scène d'une mère marchant en direction de la vallée avec ses deux fillettes récalcitrantes. Les enfants qui se pressent contre la jeune femme fière en habits de fête sont nues; les rues sont désertes, on ne voit ni voitures ni être humains qui pourraient apporter dans cette photo quelque chose de la vie quotidienne. Saudek sait, et il l'a déjà prouvé en 1959 avec *Hey Joe!*, comment transformer un endroit en scène de théâtre.

Contrairement aux travaux de son confrère américain Joel-Peter Witkin, lequel a recherché consciemment la douleur et ce qui le bouleverse, il est bien rare que ceux de Saudek aient un caractère inquiétant. Peut-être est-ce pour cela qu'il considère comme impératif de travailler dans un endroit bien délimité et protégé du monde extérieur. Quiconque entre dans la pénombre de son atelier, pénètre dans un territoire contrôlé par Saudek et où règnent ses propres lois. Il a dit une fois qu'il créait pour ses modèles un monde imaginaire dans lequel un facteur particulier quelconque commençait automatiquement à opérer. Ce genre d'expériences a été fait également par le photographe de portrait américain Irving Penn lequel, toutefois, parcourait le monde avec sa tente-studio. « Si je retirais les hommes de leur cadre naturel pour les placer dans mon studio devant mon appareil photo, ils ne seraient pas simplement isolés, ils seraient transformés. » Saudek ne s'en tient pas à cette transformation, il intervient en privant ses modèles de leur garde-robe habituelle et en ajoutant des accessoires. Parfois, il leur vient en aide en leur offrant un petit verre de liqueur. Daniela Mrázková, dans sa monographie parue en 1991, fait état de femmes qui « se prêtent de bonne grâce à ses jeux. Elles se laissent habiller et déshabiller, acceptant d'être modelées pour devenir le personnage de ses visions ».

Il faudrait être bien naïf pour ne voir dans l'œuvre de Saudek qu'une apothéose de la féminité qui s'offre à l'homme. « Les créatures », écrivait déjà le poète August von Platen, « reflètent la joie de leur créateur. » Mais indépendamment de la question combien d'intimité ou de personnalité peut être encore conservée dans l'émulation de la pose, aucun autre photographe ne s'est penché avec autant de soin et aussi longtemps sur la femme qui lui faisait face. Saudek explore ce miracle sous tous ses aspects, et pas seulement en tant que spectateur, mais en étant profondément impliqué dans ce processus. Il a lui-même expliqué clairement et sans aucune ambiguïté ce qu'il entendait par là : « Je n'ai pas la possibilité de portraiturer la vie des autres. Je montre la mienne. »

Pour le spectateur, les photos les plus intéressantes sont sans nul doute celles où Saudek capte un peu de ce « fluide » qui passe entre lui et son modèle : comme le geste provocateur de la jeune femme qui, dans *Marie n°142* (1972, ill. p. 54), relève son pull-over avec les dents, ou le calme serein de l'androgyne *Susanna* (1978, ill. p. 78) à la tête couronnée, ou encore *Els!* (1985, ill. p. 77) qui tend avec défi sa poitrine maigre. Dans ses photos, on a l'impression d'assister à un dialogue intime. Le regard du photographe se concentre sur son vis-à-vis qui est représenté à partir des genoux et rarement, du moins au début des années soixante-dix, en entier. Toutefois, Saudek a choisi de telle sorte le détail photographique qu'il rend également visible la décrépitude du décor. Le mur porte les traces de la vie qui ne sont pas encore gravées sur le jeune corps modelé par la douce lumière. D'autres corps en revanche affichent en se dénudant une matérialité et des formes marquées par l'âge. Sur certaines photos, il cherche à pénétrer le comportement féminin : des jeunes femmes perdues dans la contemplation de leur dos dont l'image leur est renvoyée par le miroir, comment elles se préoccupent de leurs seins ou comment elles démontrent leur abandon. Saudek rappelle parfois le personnage de Milan Kundera, Toma, obsédé par le désir de découvrir dans chacune de ses nouvelles conquêtes féminines l'once de dissemblance qui la distinguait de toutes les autres.

Quand la tristesse entre dans l'œuvre de Saudek, elle le fait tout au plus sous forme d'enjolivement lyrique. Ainsi, la perte d'un ami dont il insère le profil dans un petit médaillon niché dans le creux de la main (1970, ill. p. 34) ou le chagrin d'une « histoire d'amour » parvenue à sa fin, représentée par une rose éclose qui perd ses pétales petit à petit (1974, ill. p. 35). Le tragique demeure généralement absent ou paraît sous une forme théâtrale, comme le montre l'exemple de la femme pendue (1977, ill. p. 118/119). La confusion inextricable qui entoura son séjour en Amérique en 1969, il la raconte par cette photo d'un homme pendu à un mur d'affichage démesuré (1969, ill. p. 39). Une seule et unique fois, en 1976, il quitta la scène du « Théâtre de la Vie » saudekien pour photographier son vieux père fatigué entre les tombes d'un cimetière juif laissé à l'abandon. Il s'agit d'une image sobre, sans prétentions, prise alors que l'univers du photographe devenait toujours plus exubérant et théâtral, une image pleine de tristesse (1975, ill. p. 33)

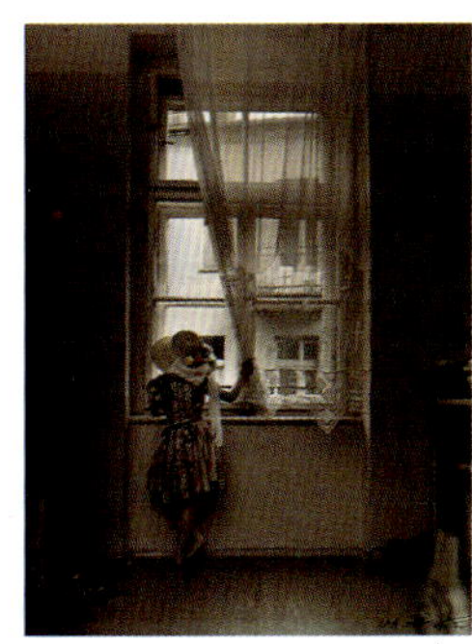

De tout temps, on a exigé des Tchèques qu'il s'arrangent d'une situation qu'on leur avait imposée. Leur capacité d'adaptation se traduit entre autres par ce don qu'ils ont de se créer une réalité magique bien à eux. Saudek, qui n'a jamais pu se résoudre à émigrer, est passé maître dans cet art. Aux alentours des années 1976/77, il commença à surexposer des scènes de rêve dans une fenêtre ouvrant sur une cour peu accueillante. Il est révélateur que ces premiers essais pour colorier à la main les épreuves en noir et blanc ne datent pas de beaucoup plus tard. A ce sujet Anna Fárová a parlé de couleurs qui s'opposent à la nature et Daniela Mrázková d'une dernière rupture importante avec ce qui le rattachait à la réalité.

Ses photographies de fenêtre rappellent à juste titre le cycle de Josef Sudek « Fenêtre de mon atelier ». Sudek, qui durant la Seconde Guerre mondiale s'était réfugié dans son atelier donnant sur une arrière-cour, avait découvert qu'une vitre recouverte de buée, de gouttes de pluie ou de givre est une surface de projection qui, tel un voile mystérieux, se place devant le monde extérieur. Mais, alors que Sudek portait avec contentement son regard songeur sur les fantasmagories qui s'offraient à lui, Saudek, lui, transforme ce qui existe de manière radicale. Par le biais de jeux d'éclairage, il reproduit les ombres fugitives de passants qui se hâtent, les nuages clairs traversés par les traînées de condensation des avions ou encore la lune et les étoiles. Une chose paraît toutefois étrange : la fenêtre offre certes des vues merveilleuses et permet même à l'amant d'entrer, mais on ne voit jamais personne en sortir.

Le revers de la vitalité saudekienne est marqué par des peurs existentielles sur lesquelles Daniela Mrázková a bien insisté. Ce ne sont pas seulement les angoisses d'un homme qui, dès l'enfance, s'est vu en permanence exposé aux dangers de la persécution nazie et dont la famille a dû, après 1945, se battre de nouveau pour survivre, cette fois-ci à cause de ses origines allemandes. Ce sont aussi les angoisses d'une personnalité qui, n'étant pas rentrée dans les rangs, s'est retrouvée longtemps sur la ligne de mire des services de contrôle de l'Etat. Daniela Mrázková par ailleurs a décrit en outre la crainte de l'artiste de perdre sa puissance créatrice, ses doutes permanents et, dans le même ordre d'idées, sa peur du déclin et de la mort. Quand Saudek fait poser tous les cinq ans sa chère Veronica (ill. p. 82/83), cela dissimule aussi certainement une bonne dose d'émotion à laquelle l'artiste voudrait opposer quelque chose. C'est une tentative de sauvegarder des moments isolés comme fragment d'une vie qui passe inexorablement.

The show must go on

Ceux qui s'étaient abandonnés à la magie de son monde poétique et très nostalgique de jadis considèrent avec des sentiments mitigés l'œuvre de Saudek réalisée après 1984. Déconcertés, ils regardent maintenant ses derniers travaux qui, à certains égards, se complaisent dans un maniérisme et un irrespect poussés à l'extrême. Pourtant, il fallait bien s'attendre à ce que Saudek ne puisse travailler toute sa vie en se plaçant dans la perspective du prétendant recueilli ou du père adorant ses enfants. Parmi les travaux les plus anodins, on peut compter encore les scènes décoratives reflétées par un miroir et réalisées à l'aide d'éclairages sophistiqués, dont entre autres les jeux de cartes effectués entre 1984 et 1987 et la photo *Purgatoire nº 2* (1987, ill. p. 155), sur laquelle Saudek et sa partenaire se rapprochent l'un de l'autre dans une pose artistique parfaite.

Beaucoup de travaux des années quatre-vingts nous racontent déjà que Saudek n'a pu sortir de ses liaisons amoureuses mouvementées, de ses conflits avec épouses et maîtresses sans y laisser des plumes. L'adulation de la femme se transforme en son contraire et se fige bien souvent en sentiment de haine. C'est ainsi qu'on le voit dans *Désir profond* (1985, ill. p. 110) dans le rôle de l'époux implorant, à genoux devant sa femme qui glapit, comme s'il avait devant lui Jésus-Christ. Dans le *Portrait d'une Femme et d'un Homme* (ill. p. 114/115), réalisé au milieu des années quatre-vingts, il se plaît en macho qui allume imperturbable une cigarette tandis que sa partenaire est en train de se tuer avec un vieux pistolet. L'ironie est flagrante et se double bien souvent de cynisme. De plus en plus souvent, elle prend le pas sur la tension érotique et vivante de jadis entre modèle et photographe. Dans les cas extrêmes, l'artiste ne cherche plus le mystère dans l'interaction des participants, mais essaie de le saisir visuellement en approchant son appareil photo des zones taboues du corps.

Saudek n'a peur de rien. Dans *Le Photographe en Jésus* (1991, ill. p. 163) il est pendu entre deux femmes légèrement vêtues comme le crucifié entre les deux larrons. Un autoportrait le montre dans la pose d'Hamlet qui, semble-t-il, se présente dans la tenue d'un détenu de camp de concentration. Ce n'est qu'en y regardant à deux fois que l'on découvre qu'il s'agit d'une veste du grand couturier « Matsuda » pour lequel il a fait des photos de mode en 1989 et 1991. A la place du crâne, il tient dans la main son appareil photo. Saudek puise dans le répertoire historique avec autant d'insouciance que dans sa caisse d'accessoires qu'il a pu acheter un jour à un théâtre de Prague. Chez lui, on tombe constamment sur des

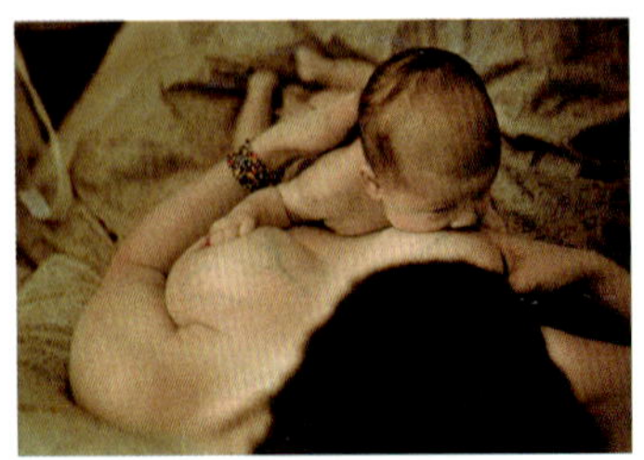

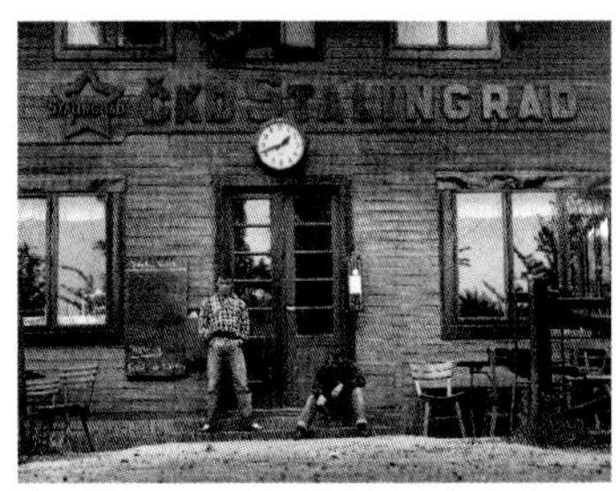

configurations d'inspiration chrétienne ou bien on découvre des emprunts qu'il a faits auprès de confrères contemporains. Le plus souvent toutefois, ce sont les photographies et les cartes postales érotiques du début du siècle qui servent de modèle. Au début, ce ne sont que des accessoires isolés comme la couronne de fleurs, le diadème, une fourrure ou un morceau de tulle qui confèrent à l'action ce côté sensuel, un peu capiteux, cette ambiance de « boudoir » fin de siècle. Depuis la seconde moitié des années soixante-dix, ses modèles portent des robes frivoles à l'ancienne, sont couvertes de colliers de perles ou s'étirent nues sur des étoffes luxueuses comme le faisaient leurs consœurs il y a un siècle. Aux débuts des années quatre-vingts, Saudek passe aux séries selon le modèle des cartes postales. Il met en scène de petites anecdotes libertines de femmes de chambre qui vont se coucher, mais aussi des séquences pornographiques plus salées où l'on s'amuse à trois.

Jeune homme, Saudek croyait qu'il « avait l'étoffe d'un modèle ». C'est la vie elle-même, avoua-t-il plus tard, qui le convainquit que sa place était derrière et non pas devant l'objectif. Une chose est sûre, Saudek est comédien avec au moins autant de passion que metteur en scène. S'il ne peut se reconnaître dans ce rôle, c'est peut-être parce qu'il est devenu depuis longtemps partie intégrante de ce théâtre qu'il a créé – que ce soit dans l'art ou dans la vie, devant ou derrière l'objectif. « The show must go on. »

Christiane Fricke

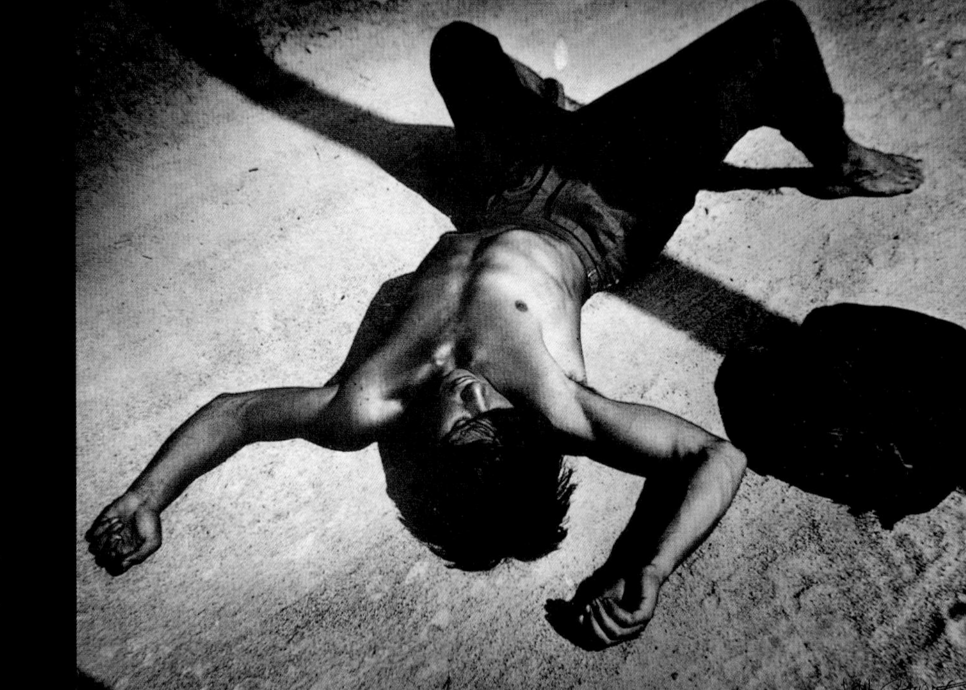

Into the Cellar
In den Keller
A la Cave

Seven of the very best and worst years of my life – for I lived in those 14 square metres, as if I were buried in a tomb – but then I was thirty years younger ...

Der Keller steht für sieben der besten und schlimmsten Jahre meines Lebens – denn ich lebte auf diesen 14 Quadratmetern und fühlte mich wie in einer Gruft begraben –, aber damals war ich dreißig Jahre jünger ...

C'est là que j'ai passé sept années de ma vie, les meilleures et les pires – puisque je vivais dans 14 mètres carrés et avais l'impression d'être dans une tombe –, mais j'avais aussi trente ans de moins ...

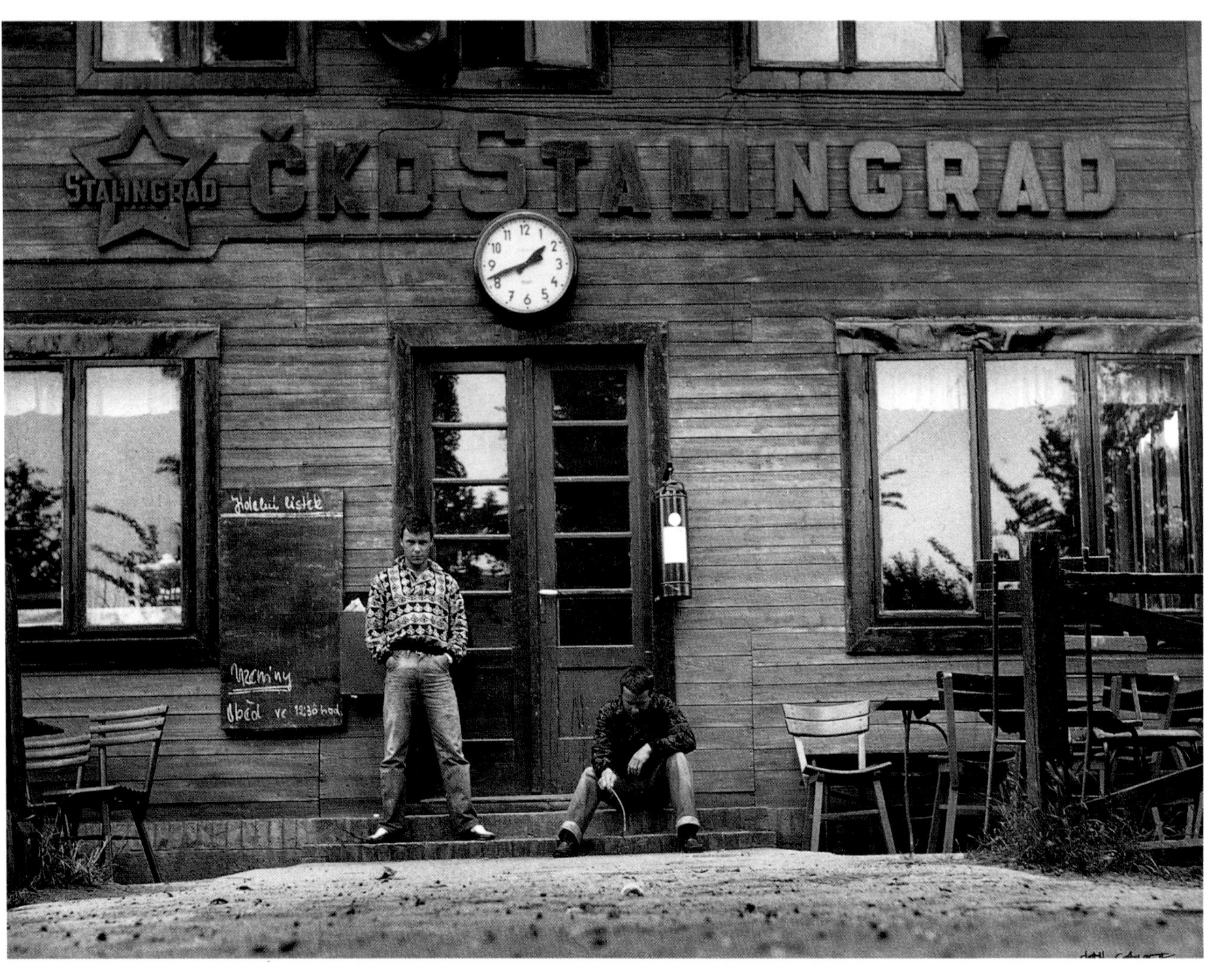
STALINGRAD
ČKD STALINGRAD
Jídelní lístek
Oběd ve 12:30 hod.

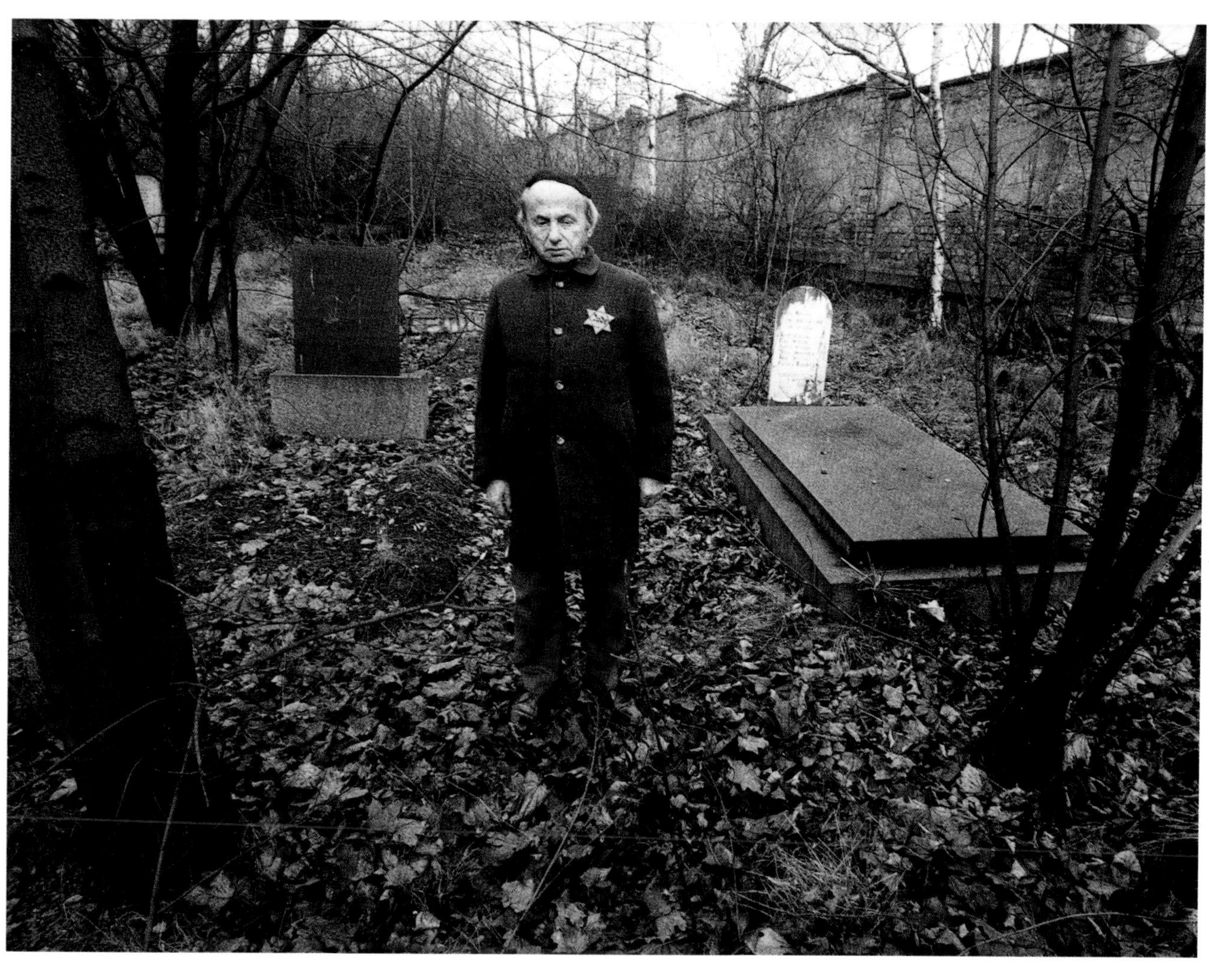

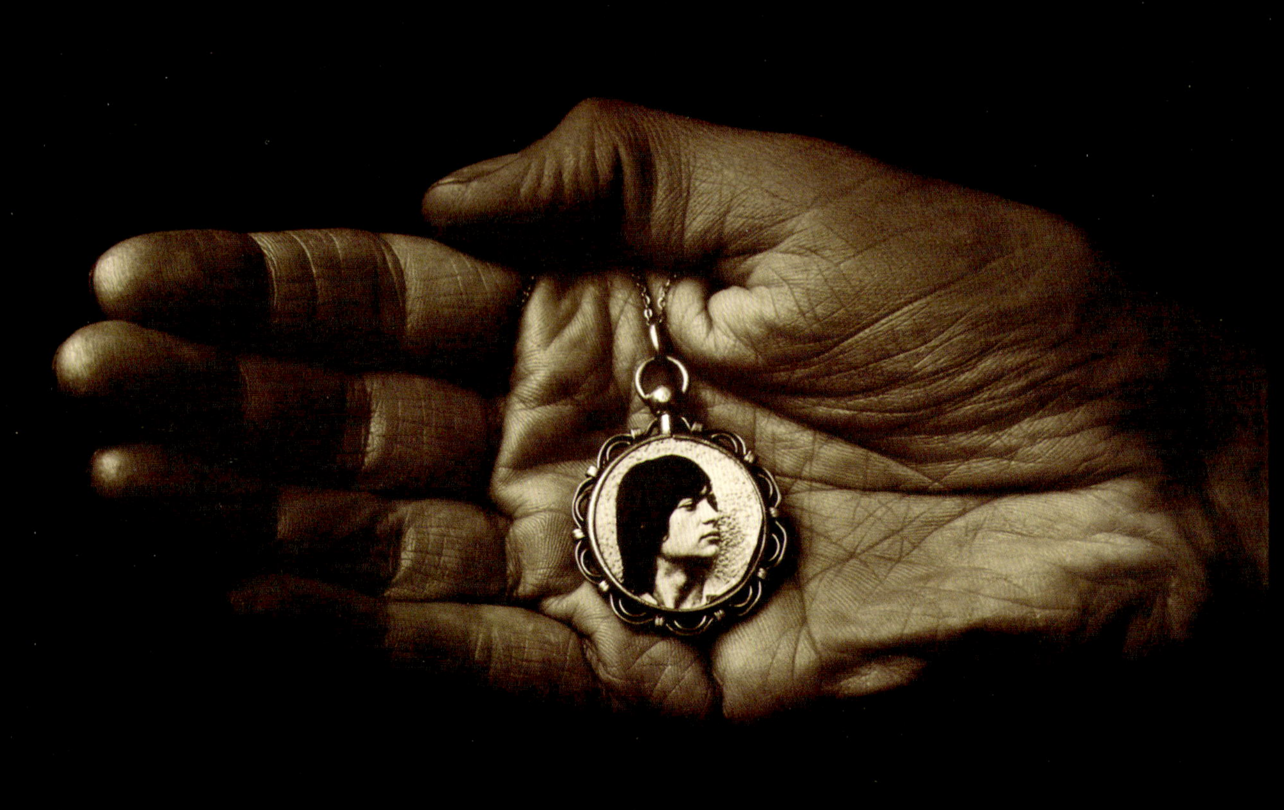

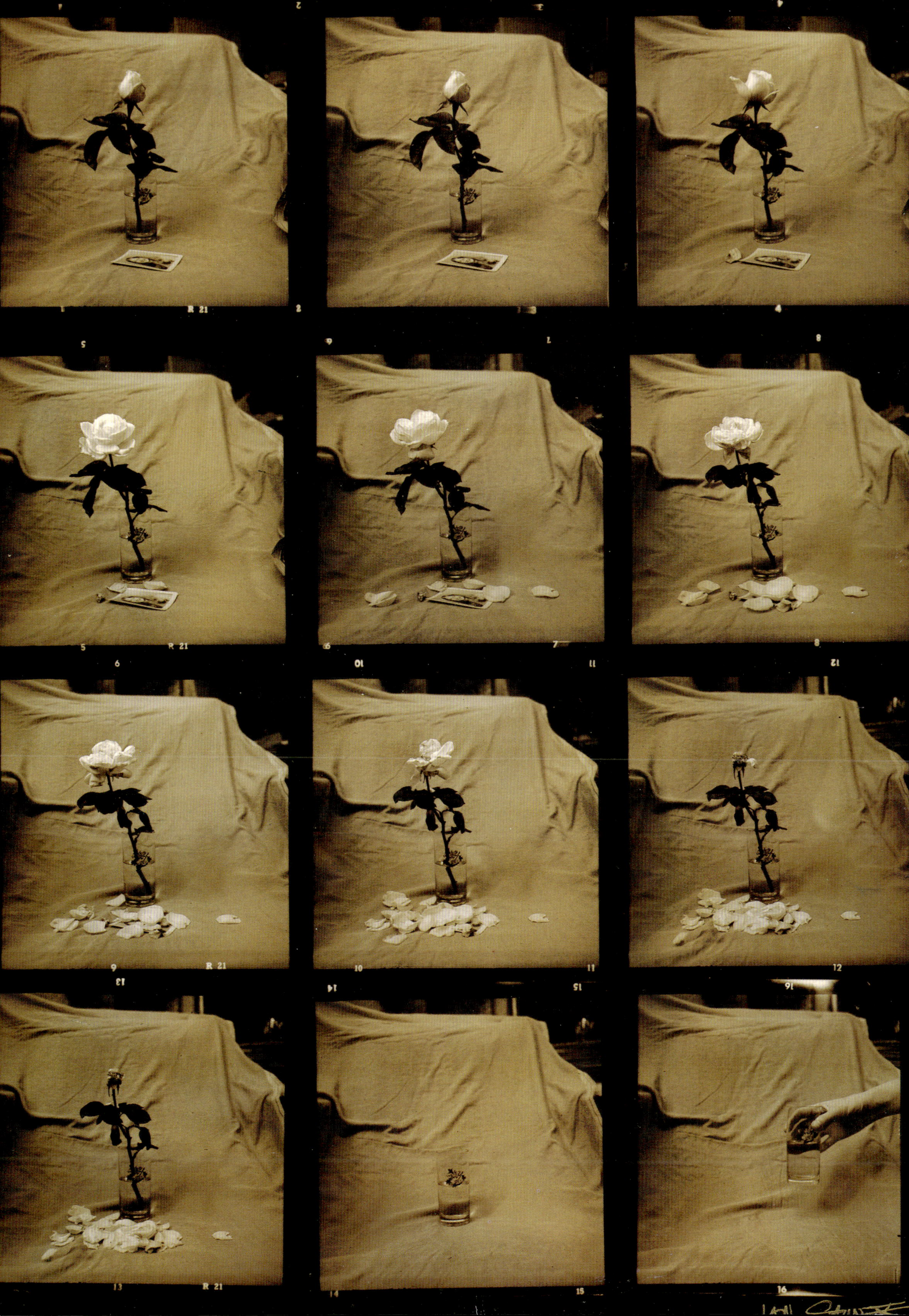

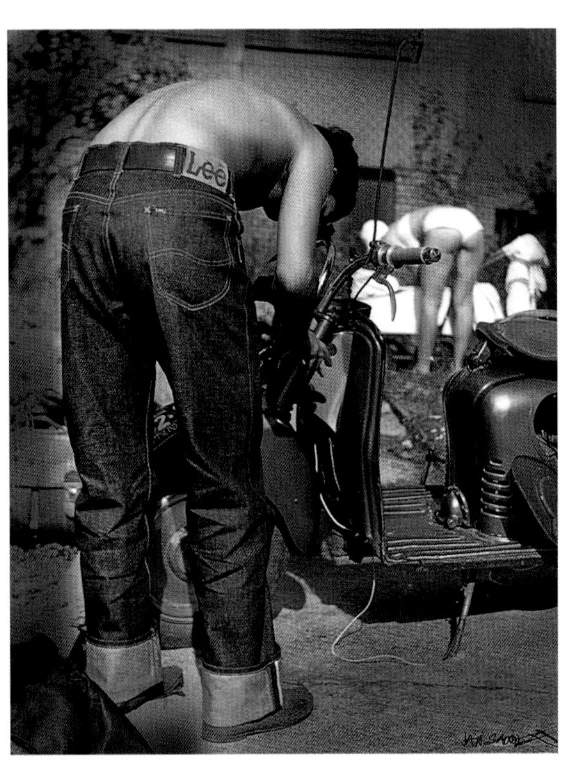
Lee

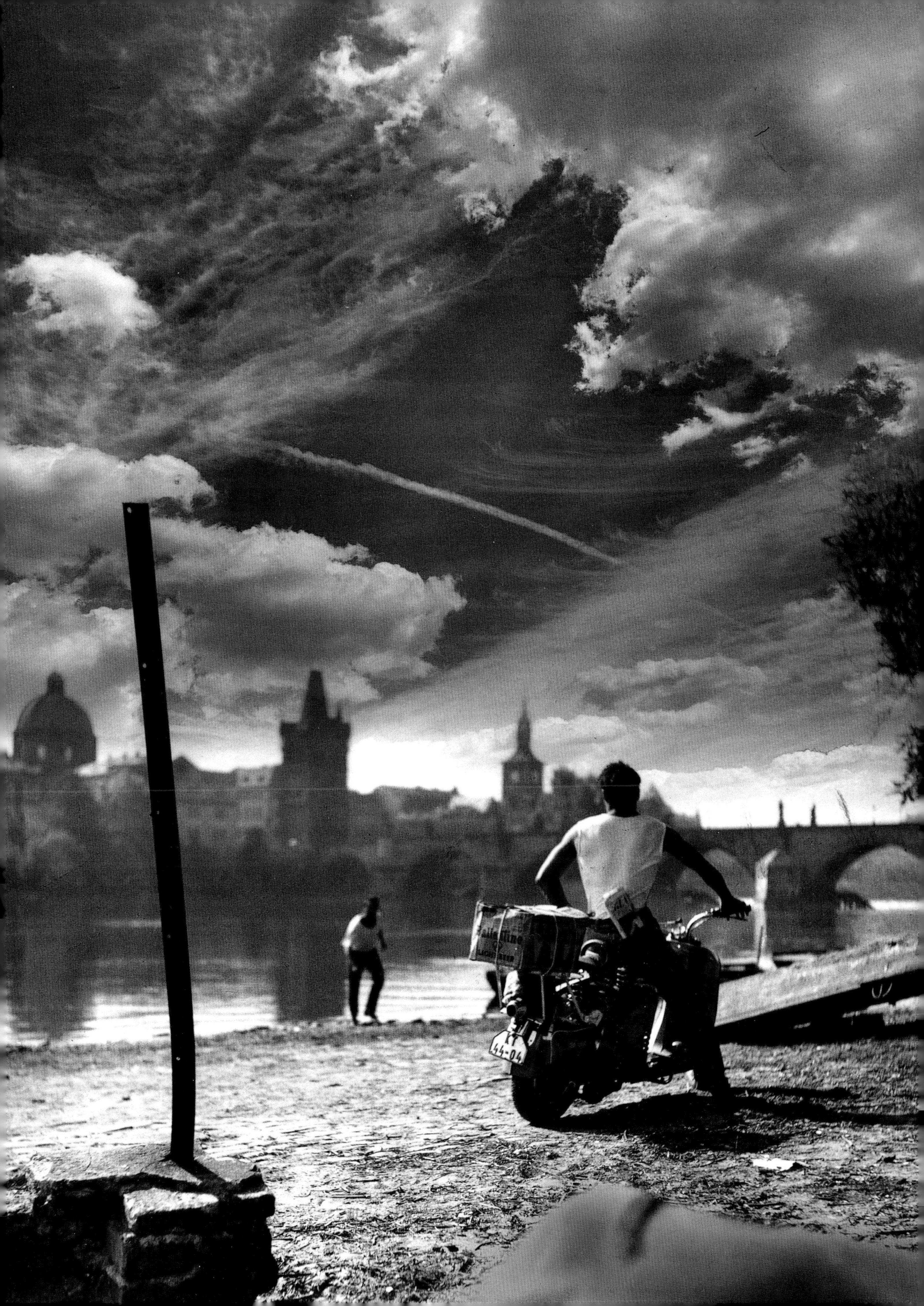
KY
44-04

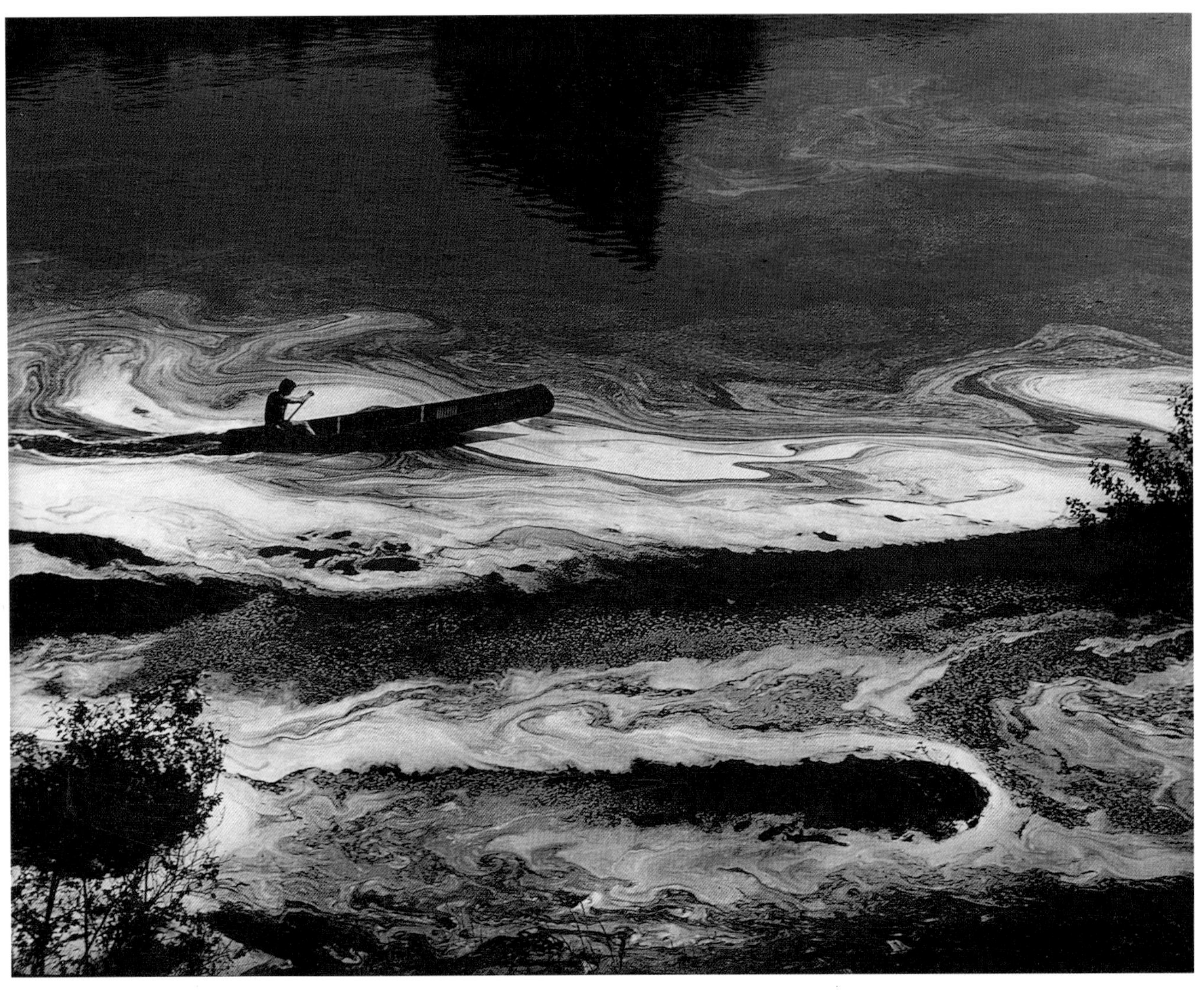

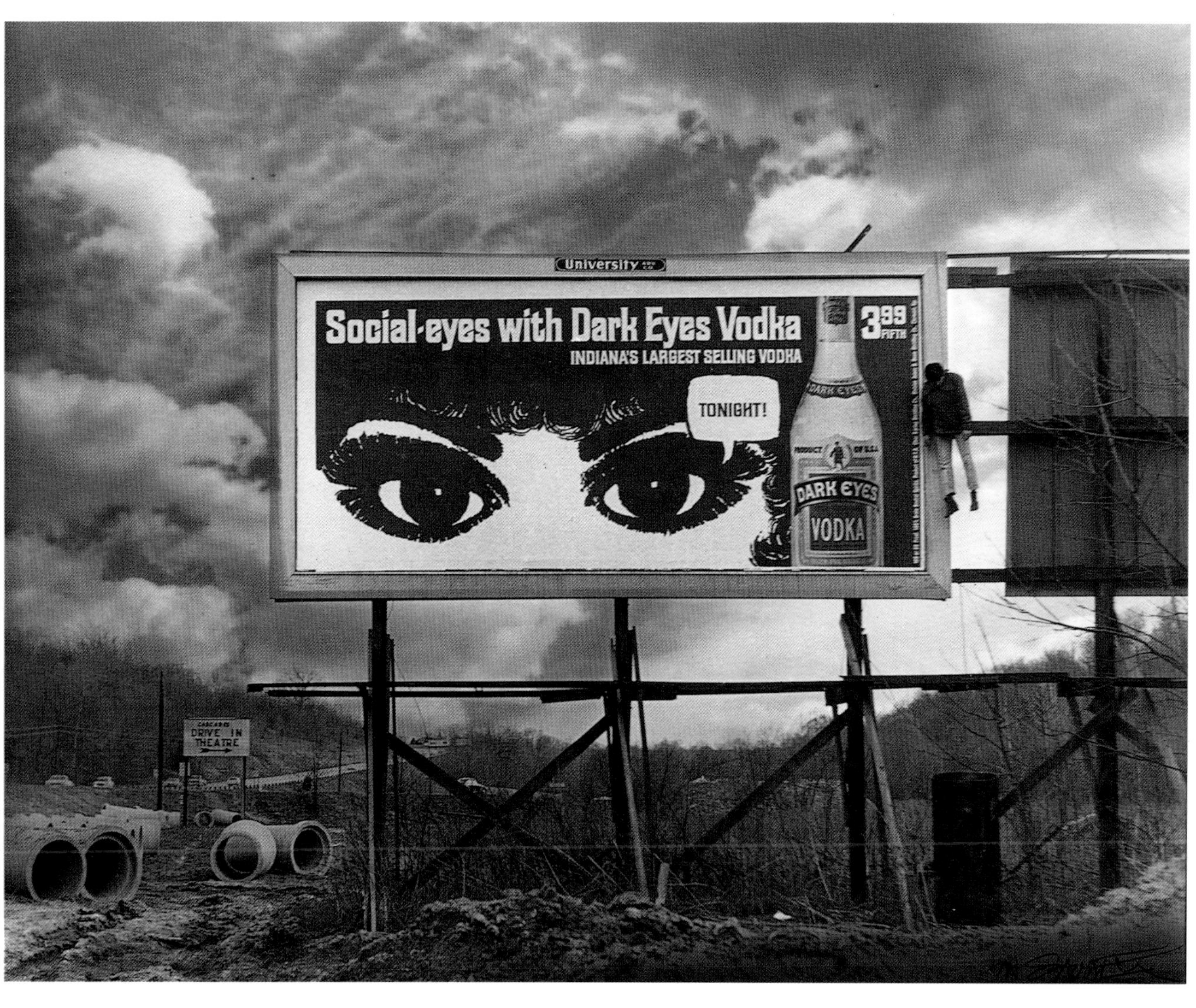
University
Social-eyes with Dark Eyes Vodka
INDIANA'S LARGEST SELLING VODKA
TONIGHT!
3.99 FIFTH
DARK EYES
VODKA
DRIVE IN THEATRE

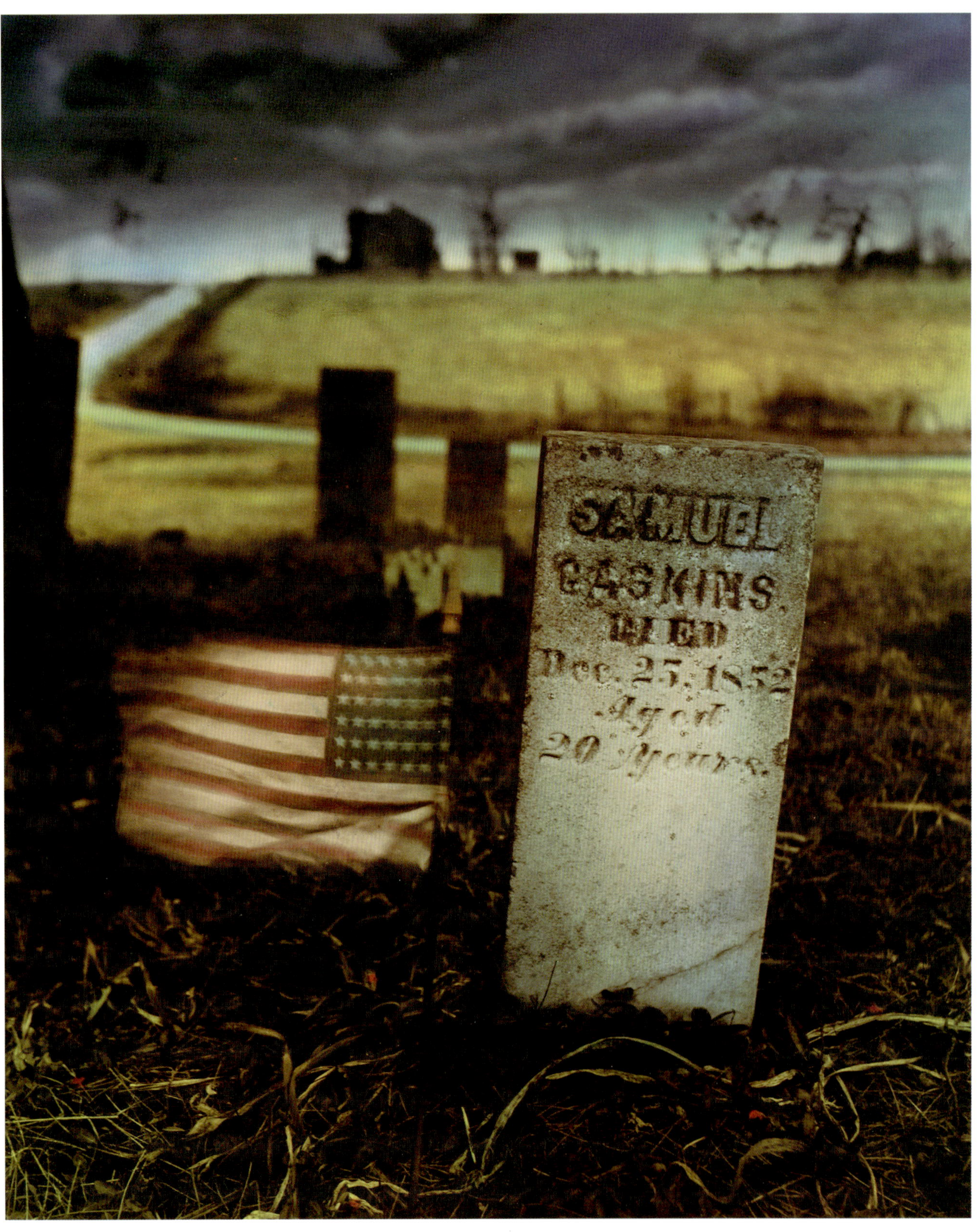
SAMUEL
GASKINS
DIED
Dec. 25, 1852
Aged
20 Years.

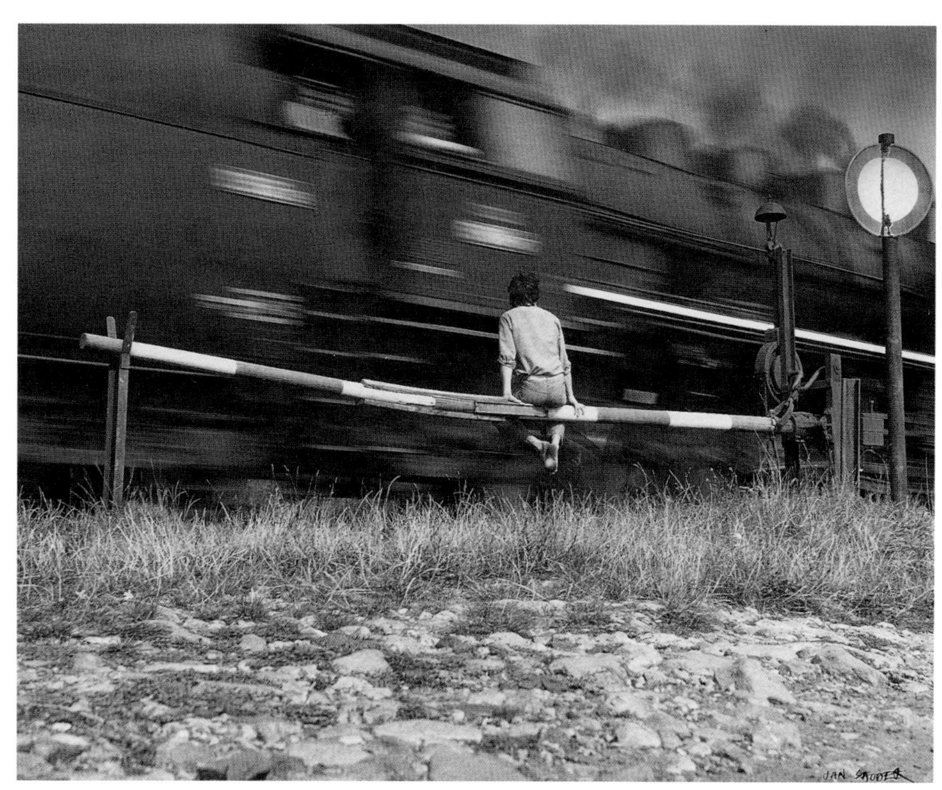
JAN SAUDEK

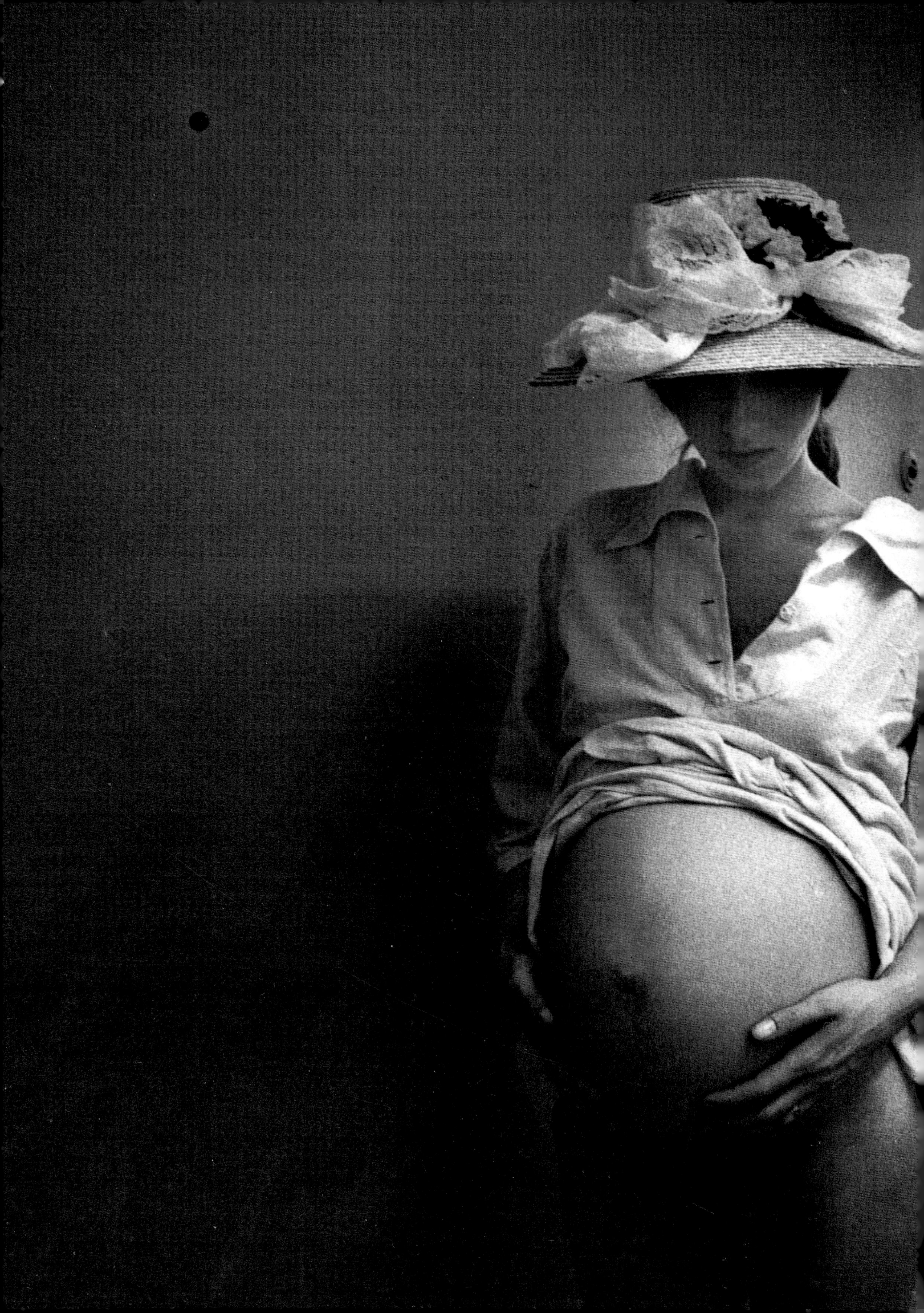

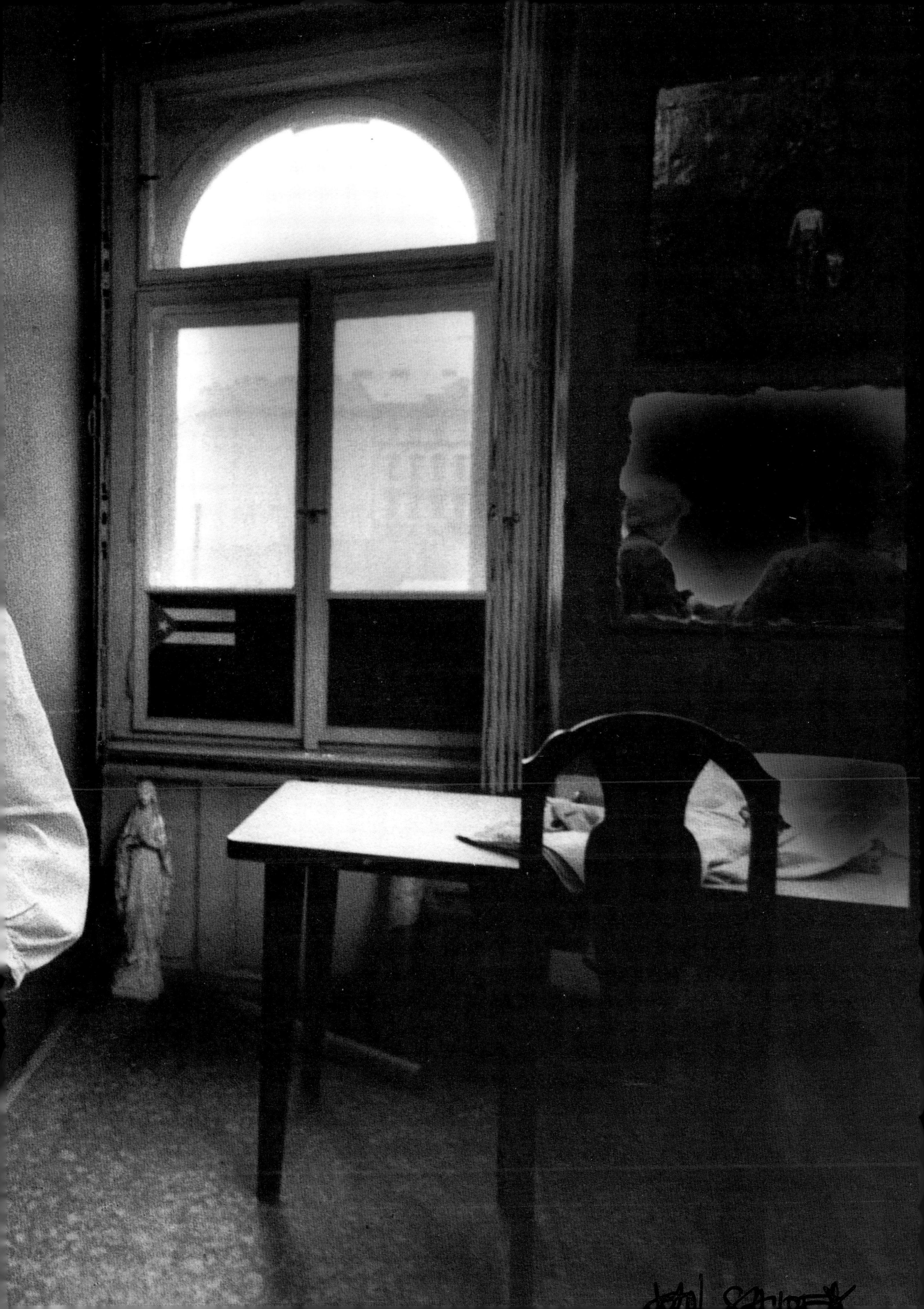

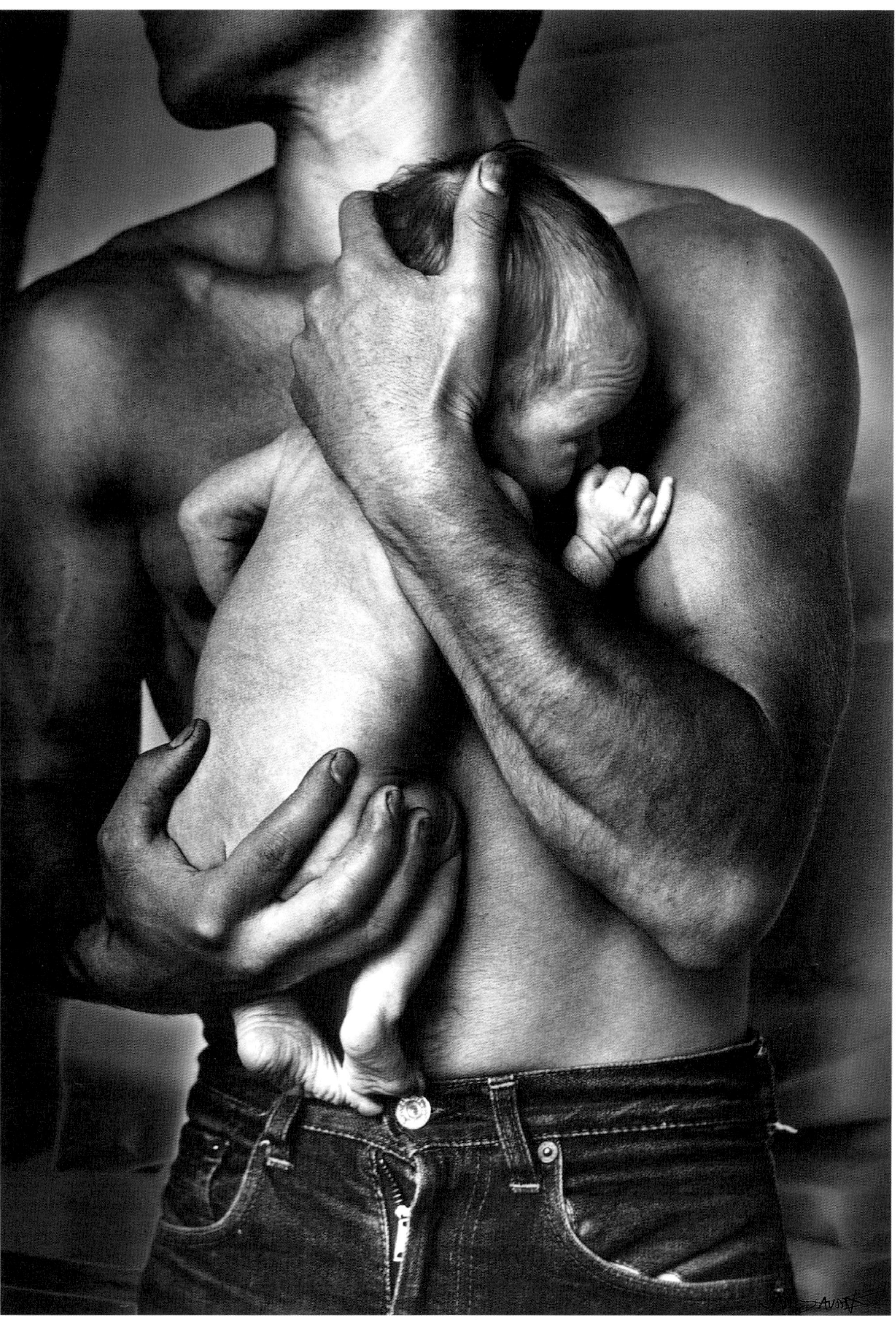

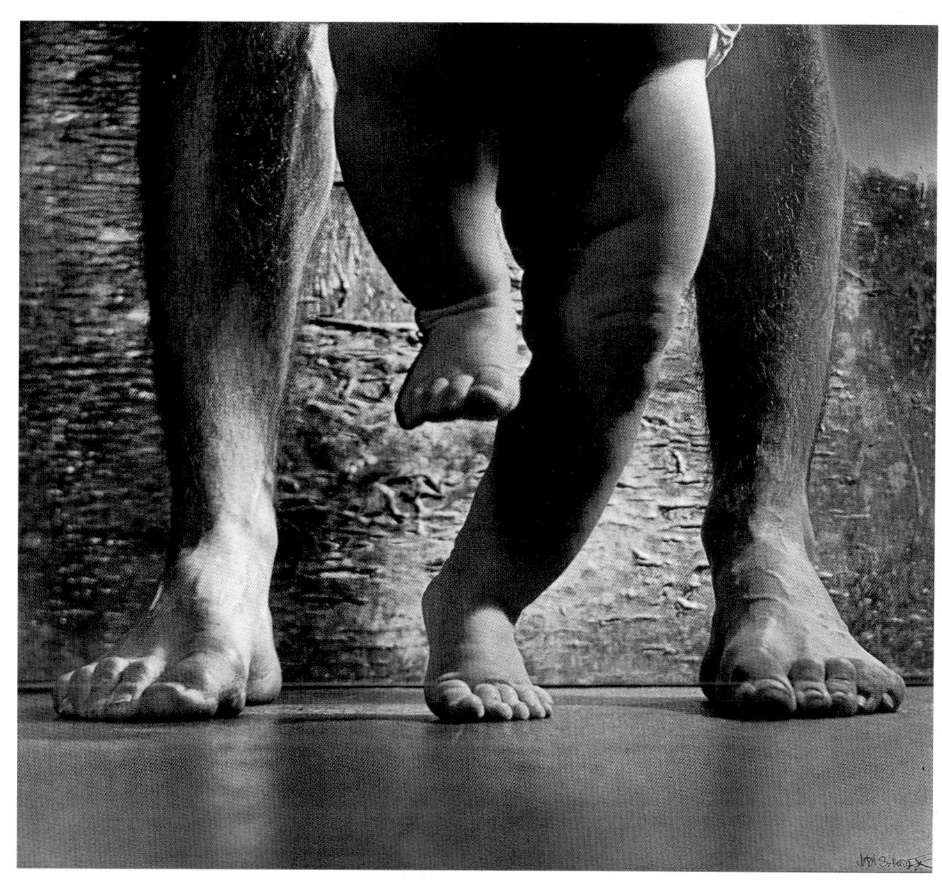

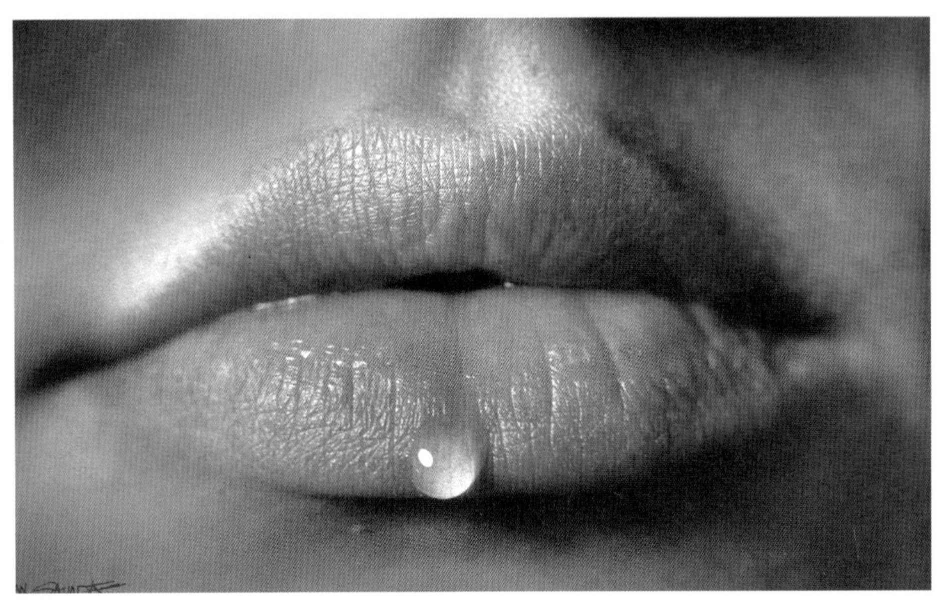

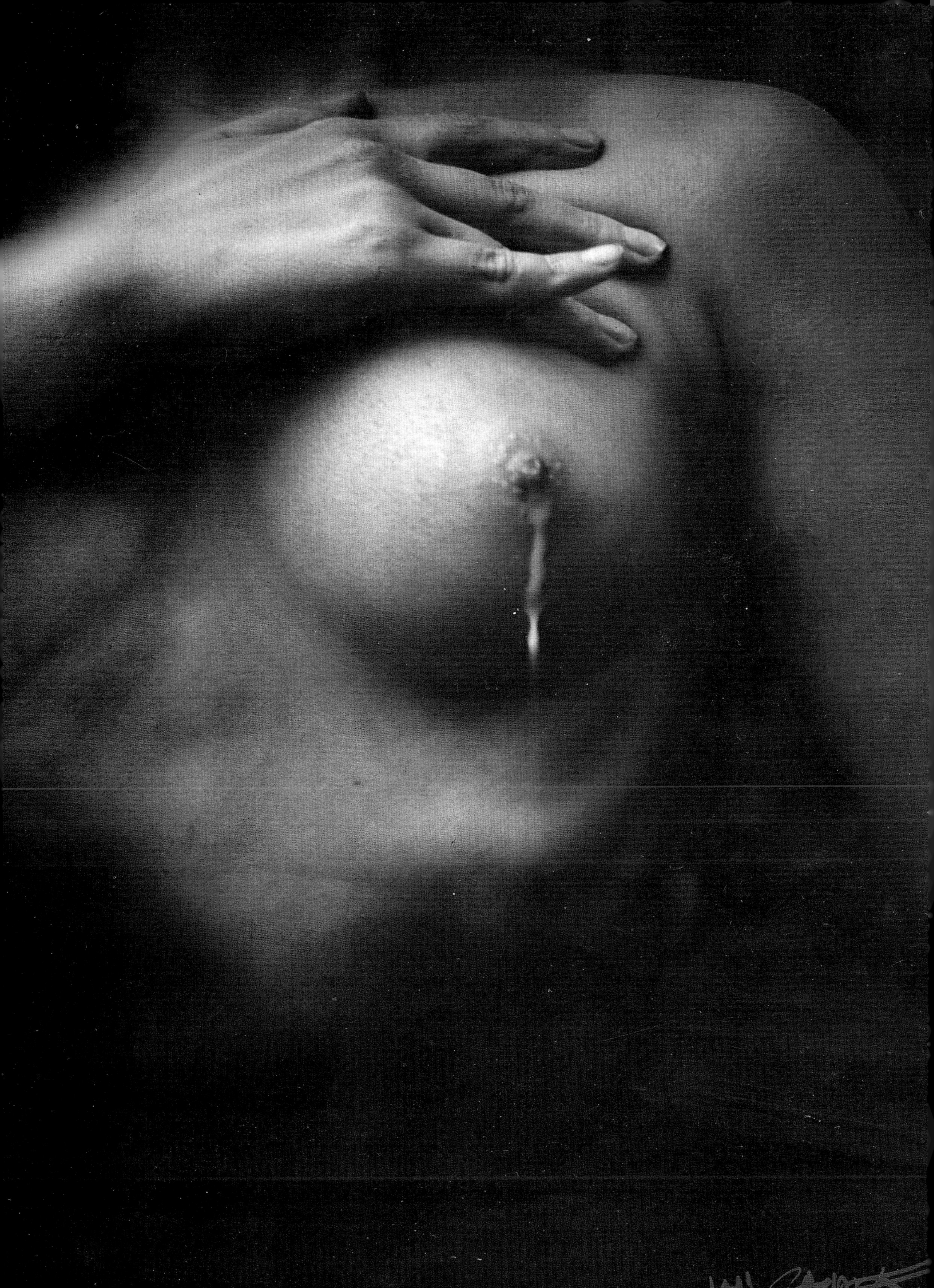
JAN SAUDEK

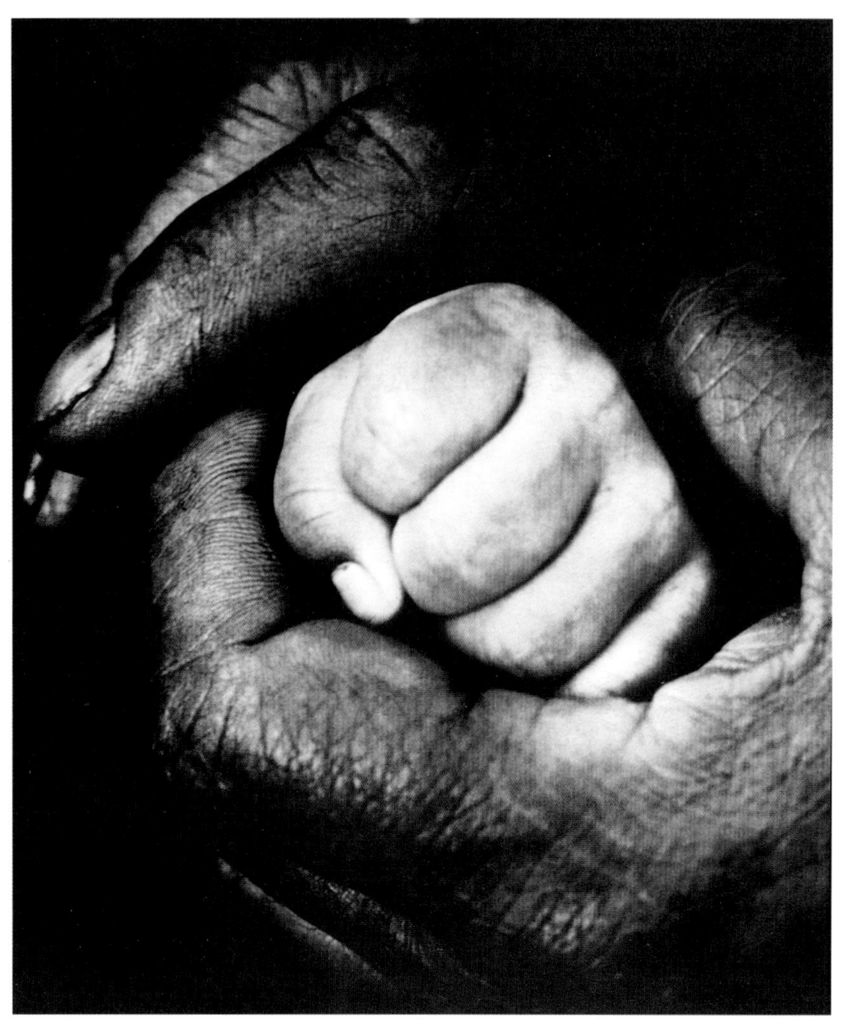

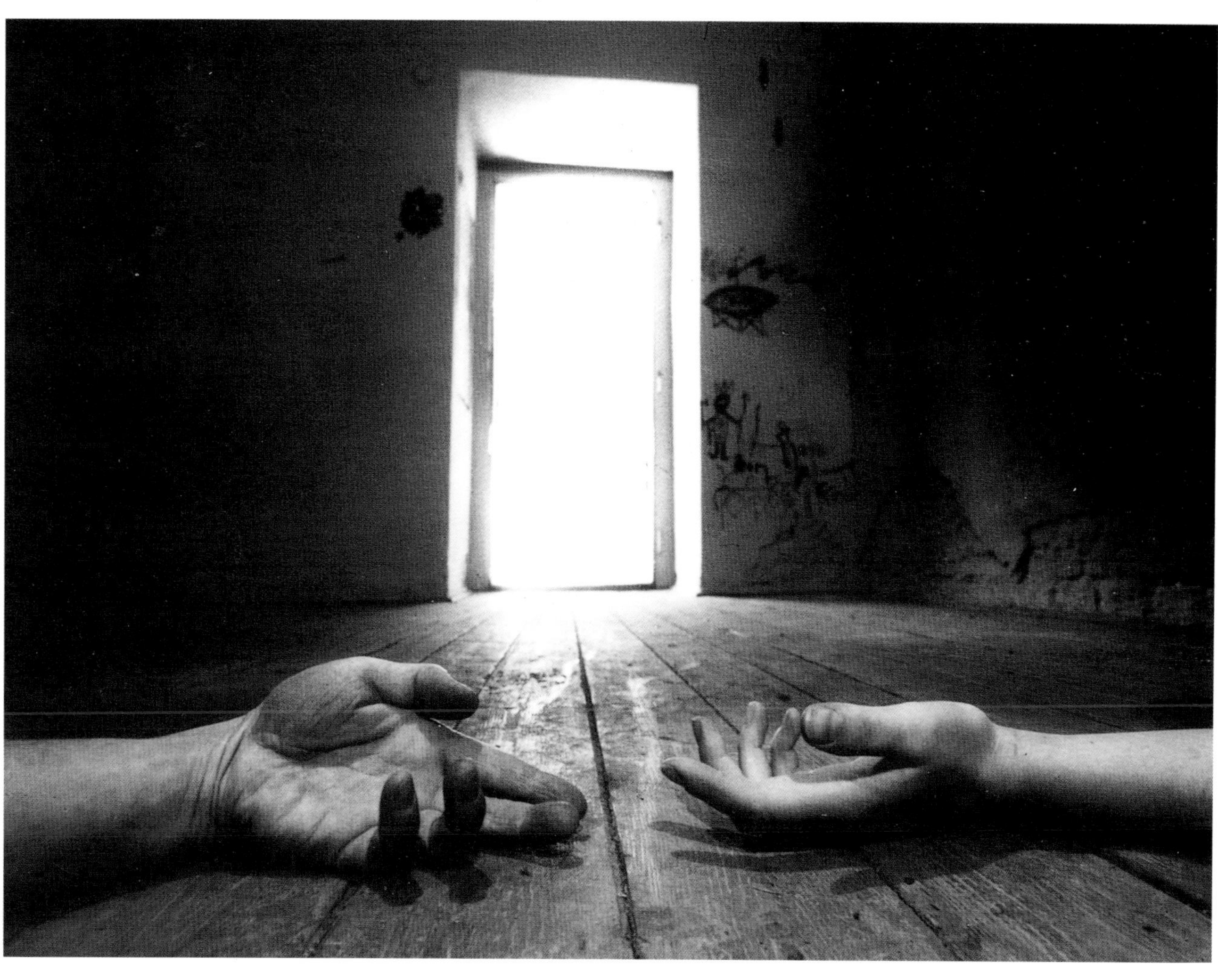

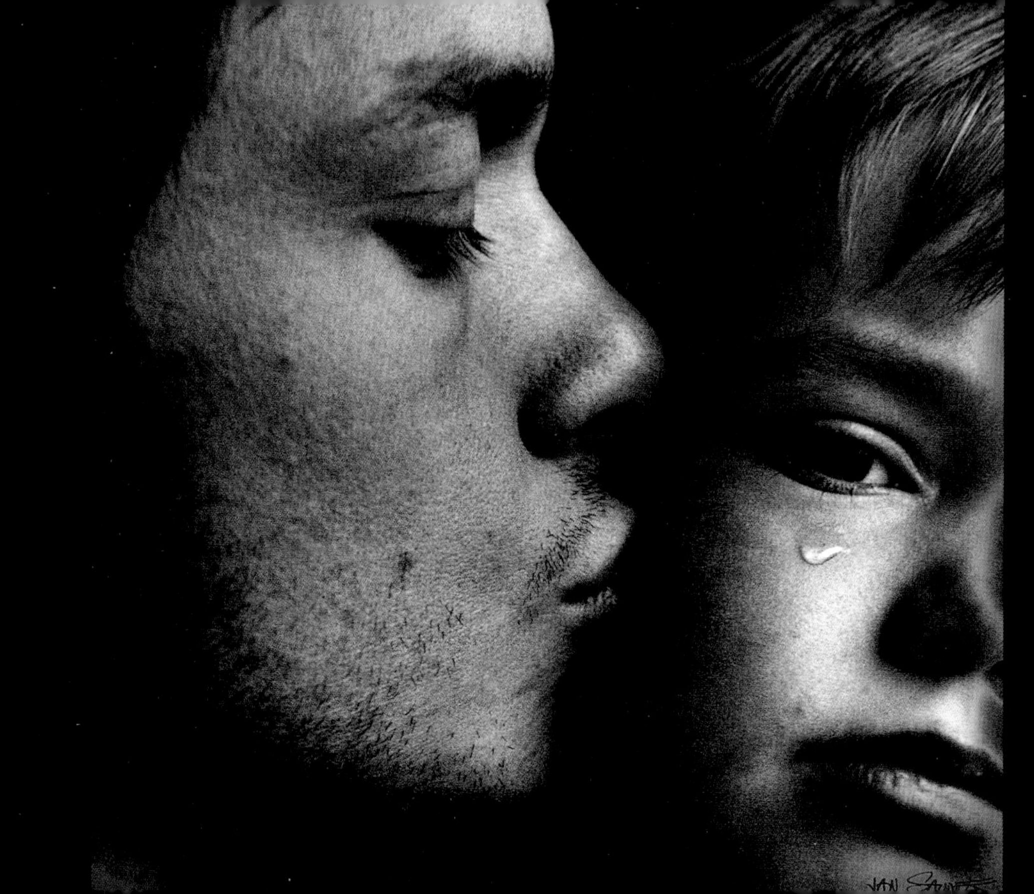

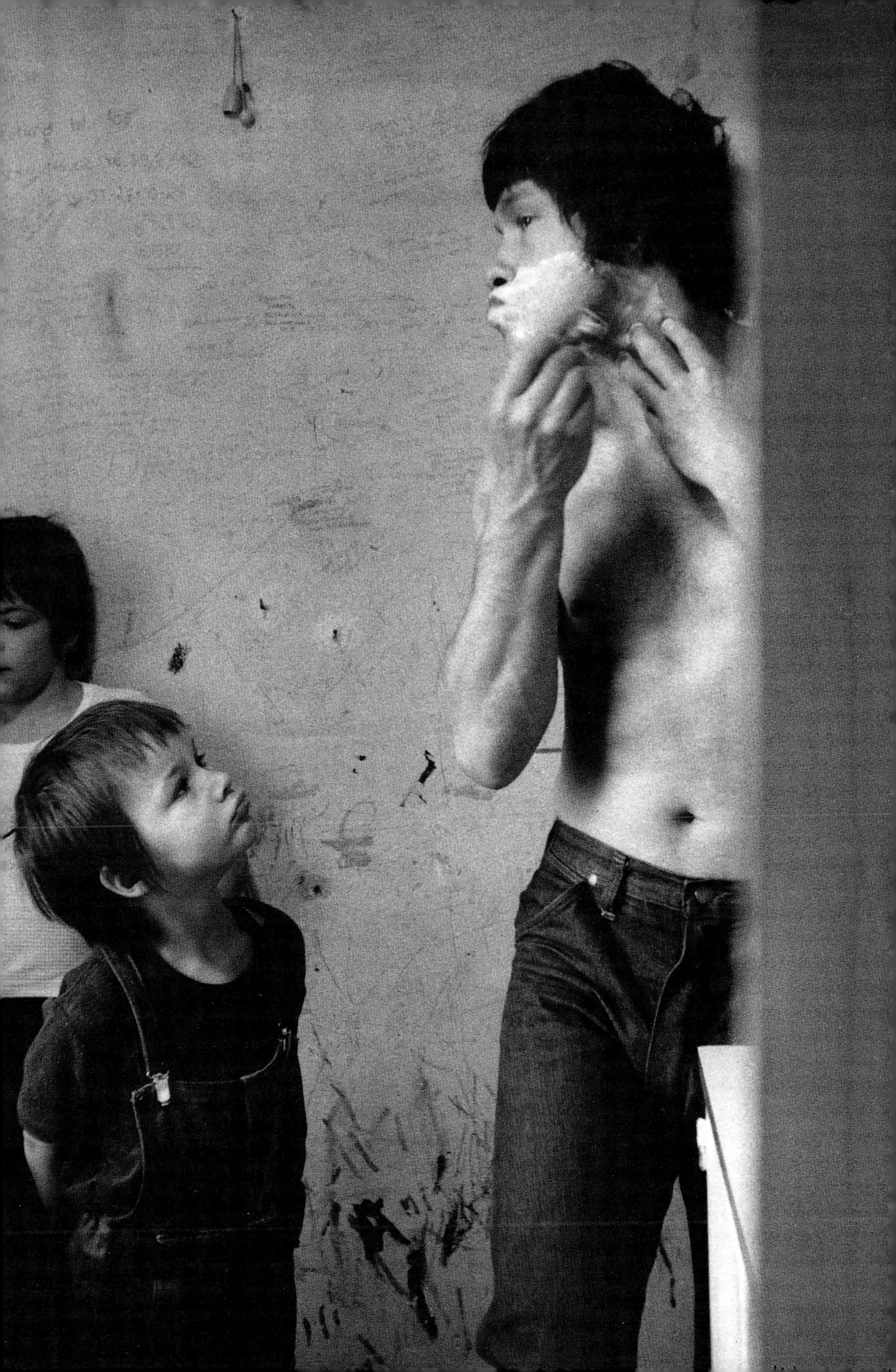

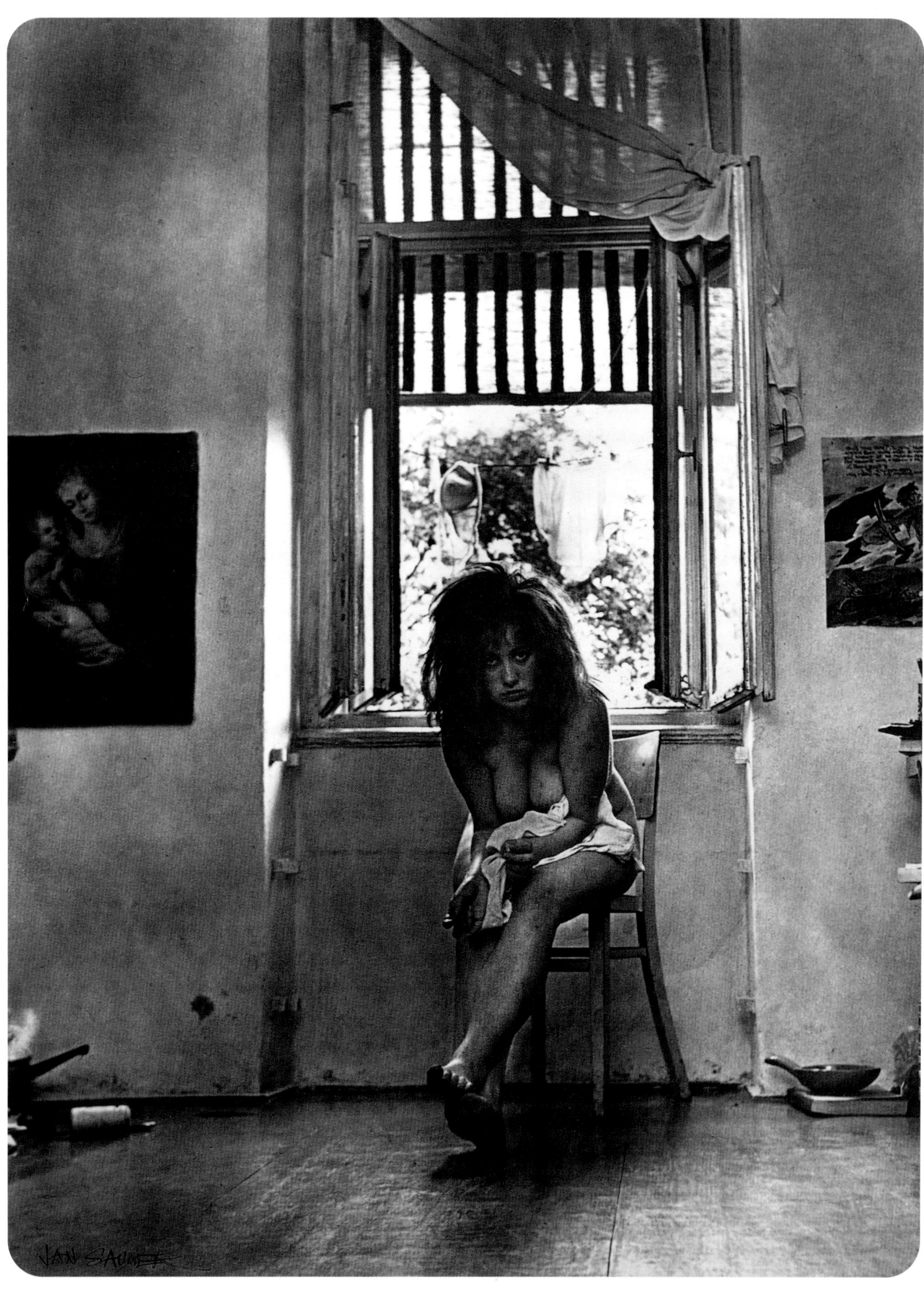

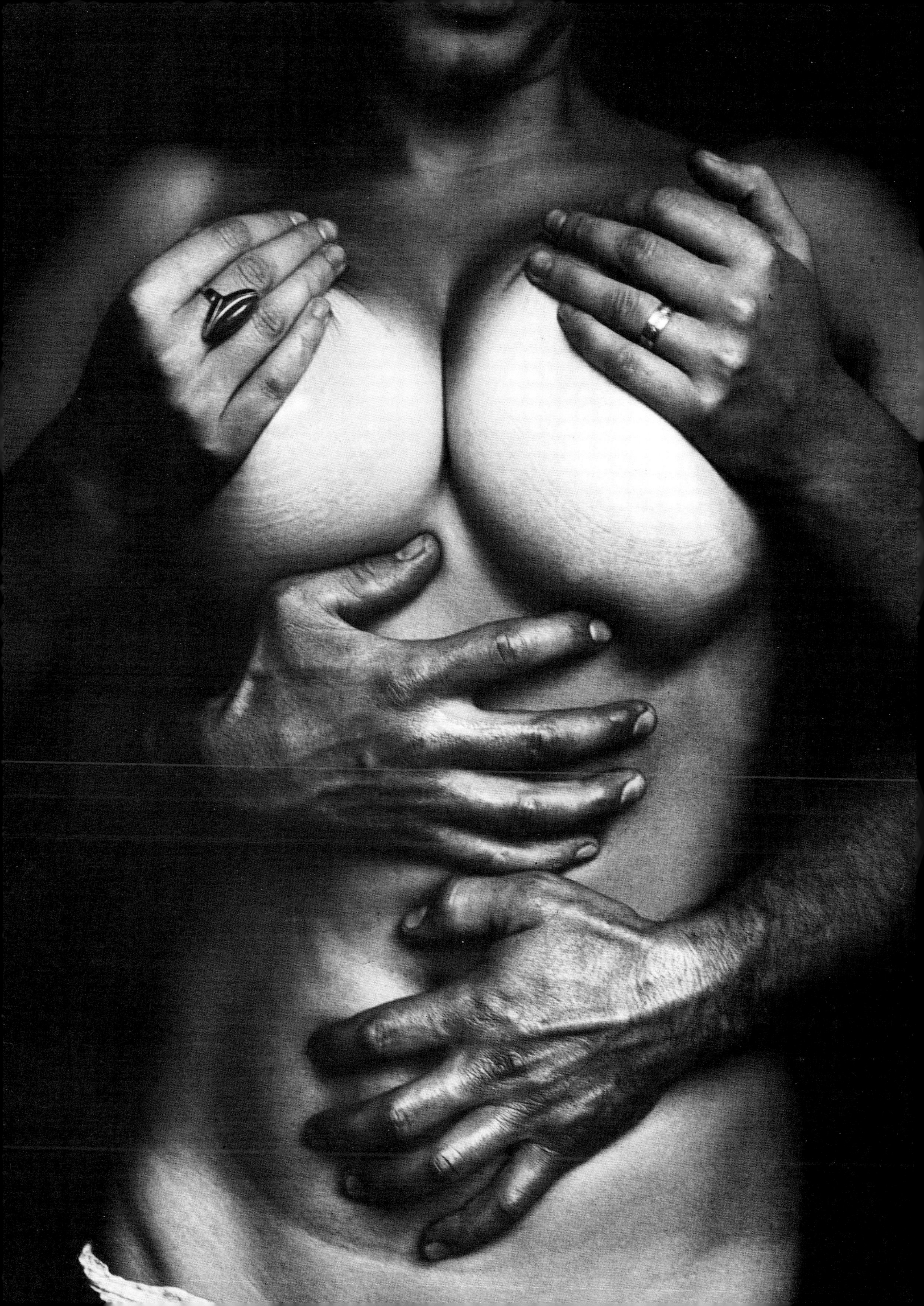

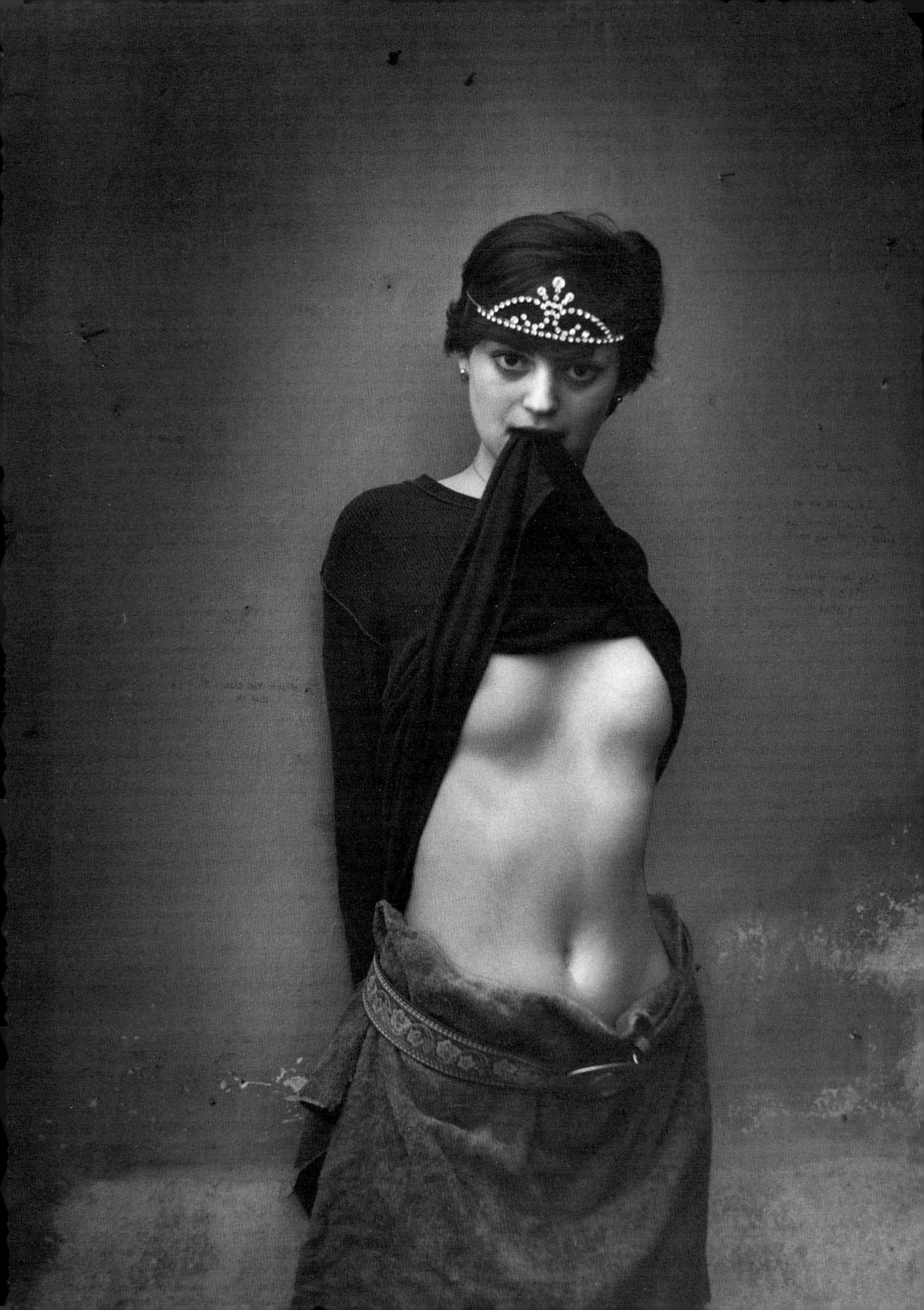

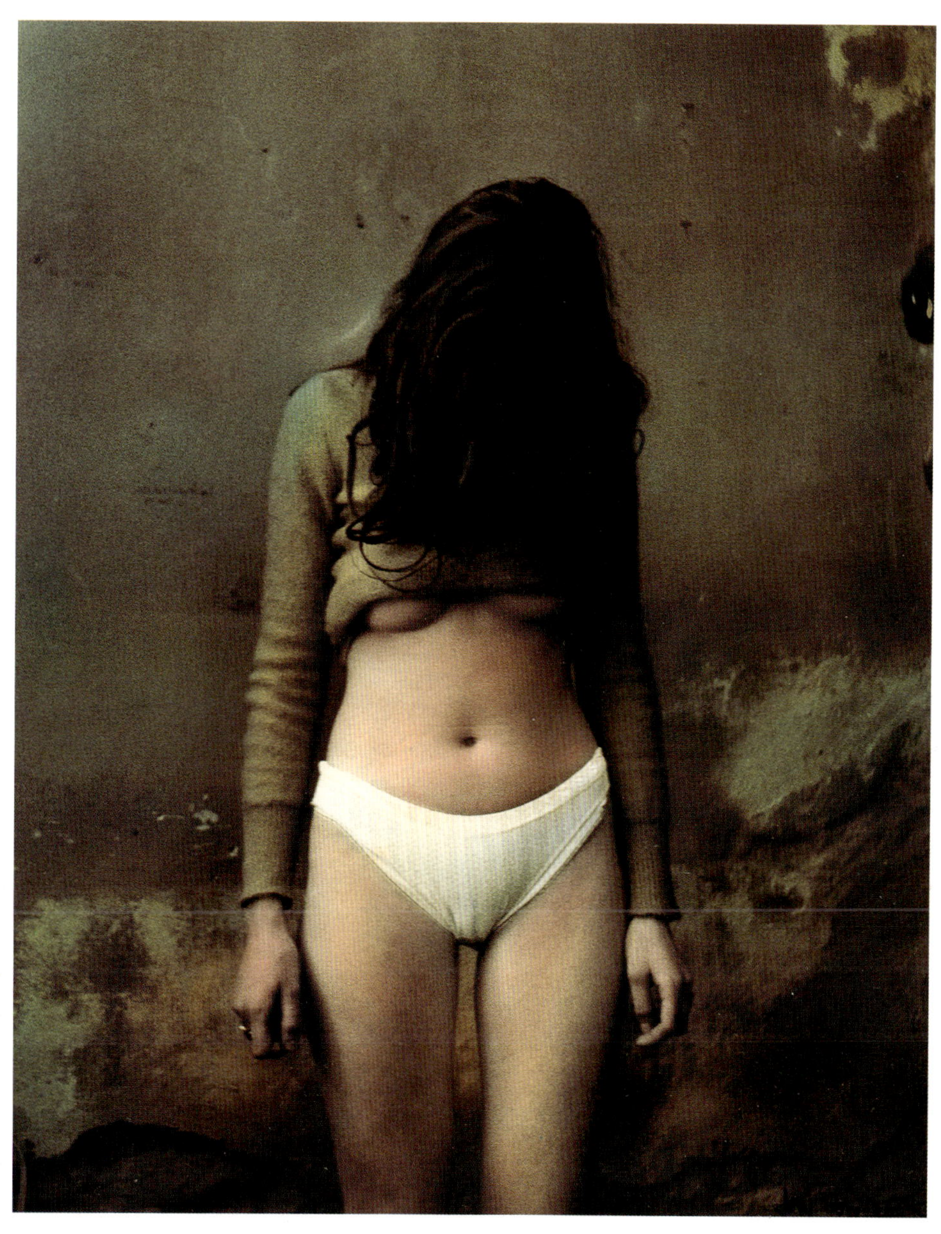

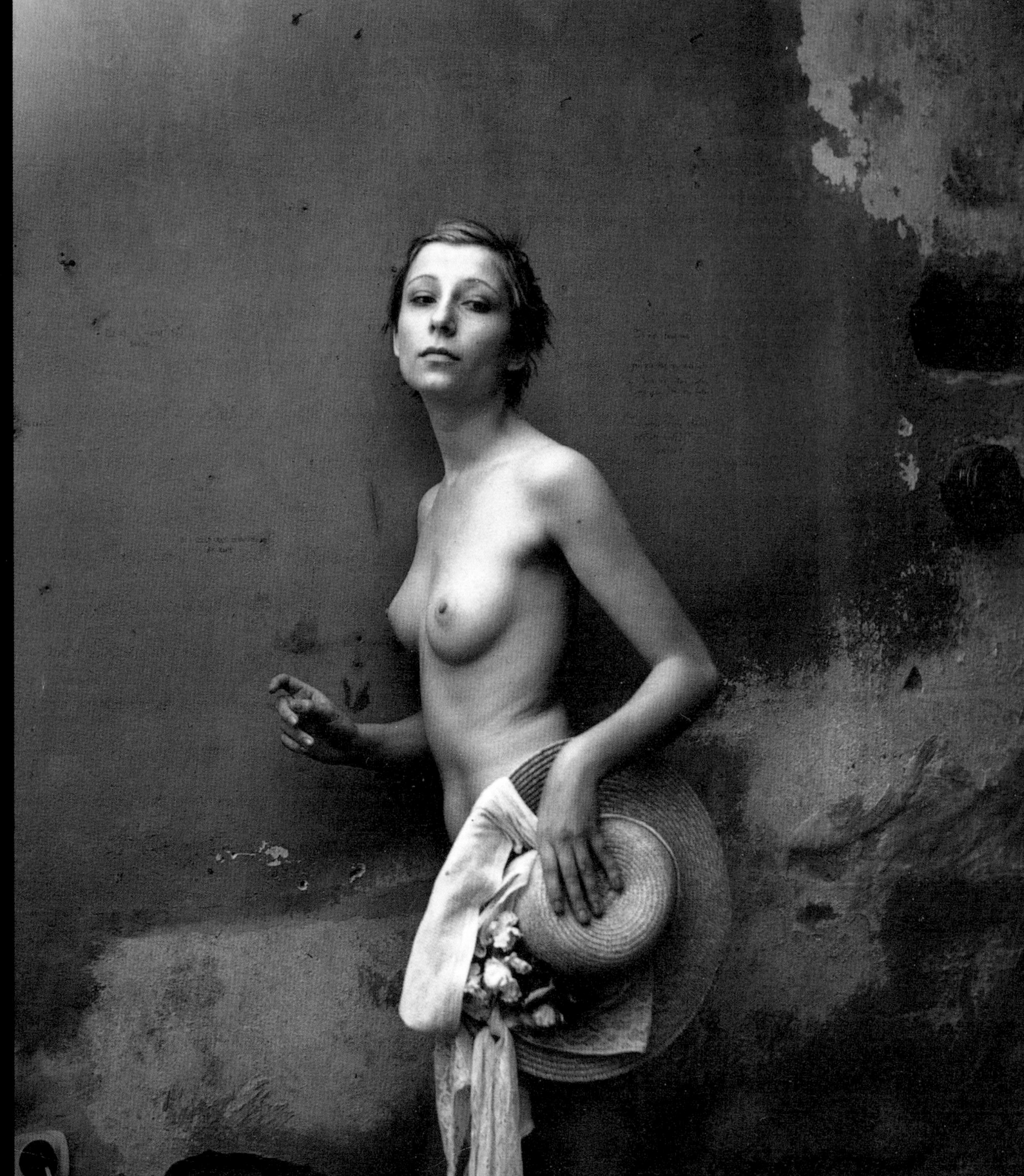

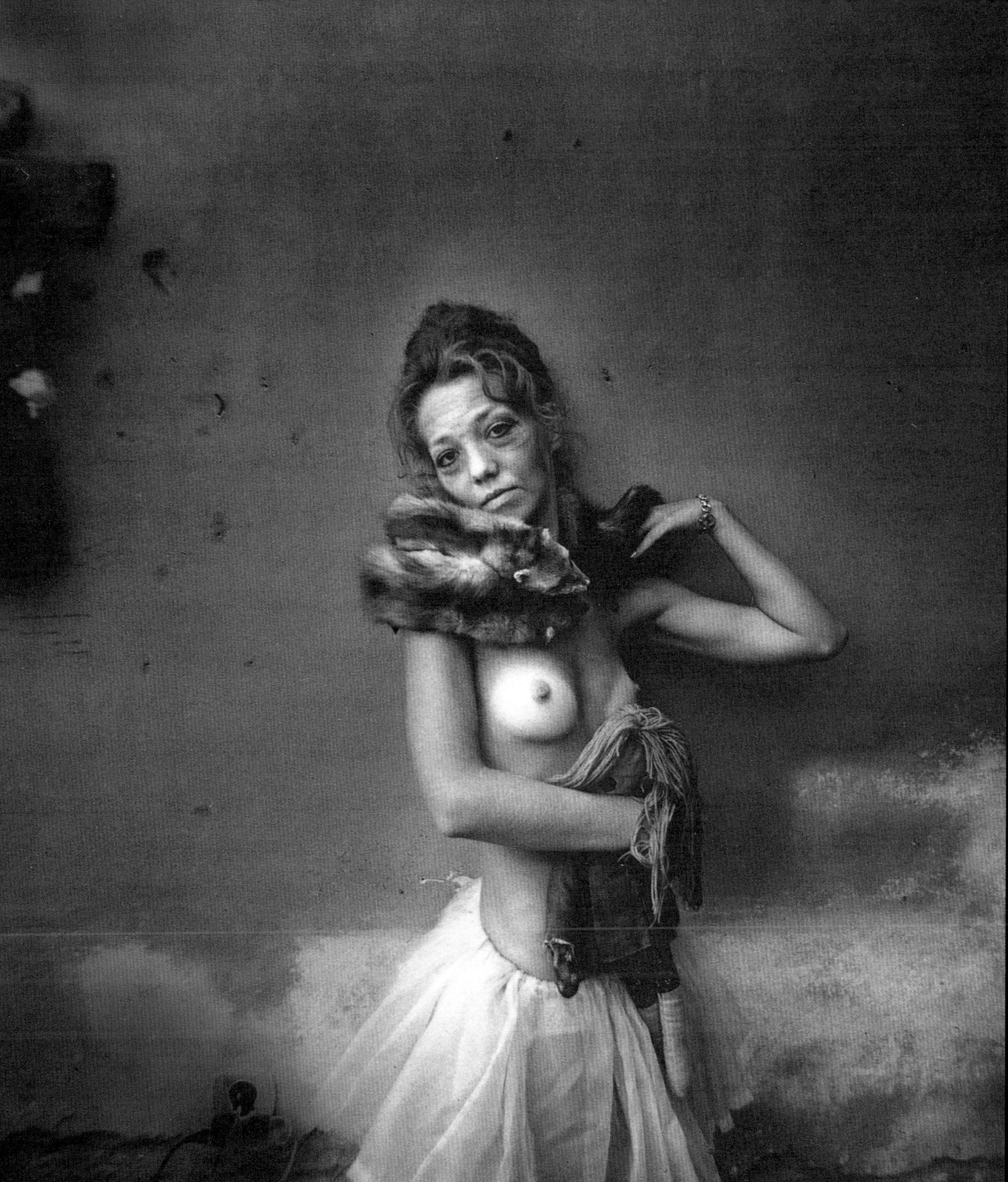

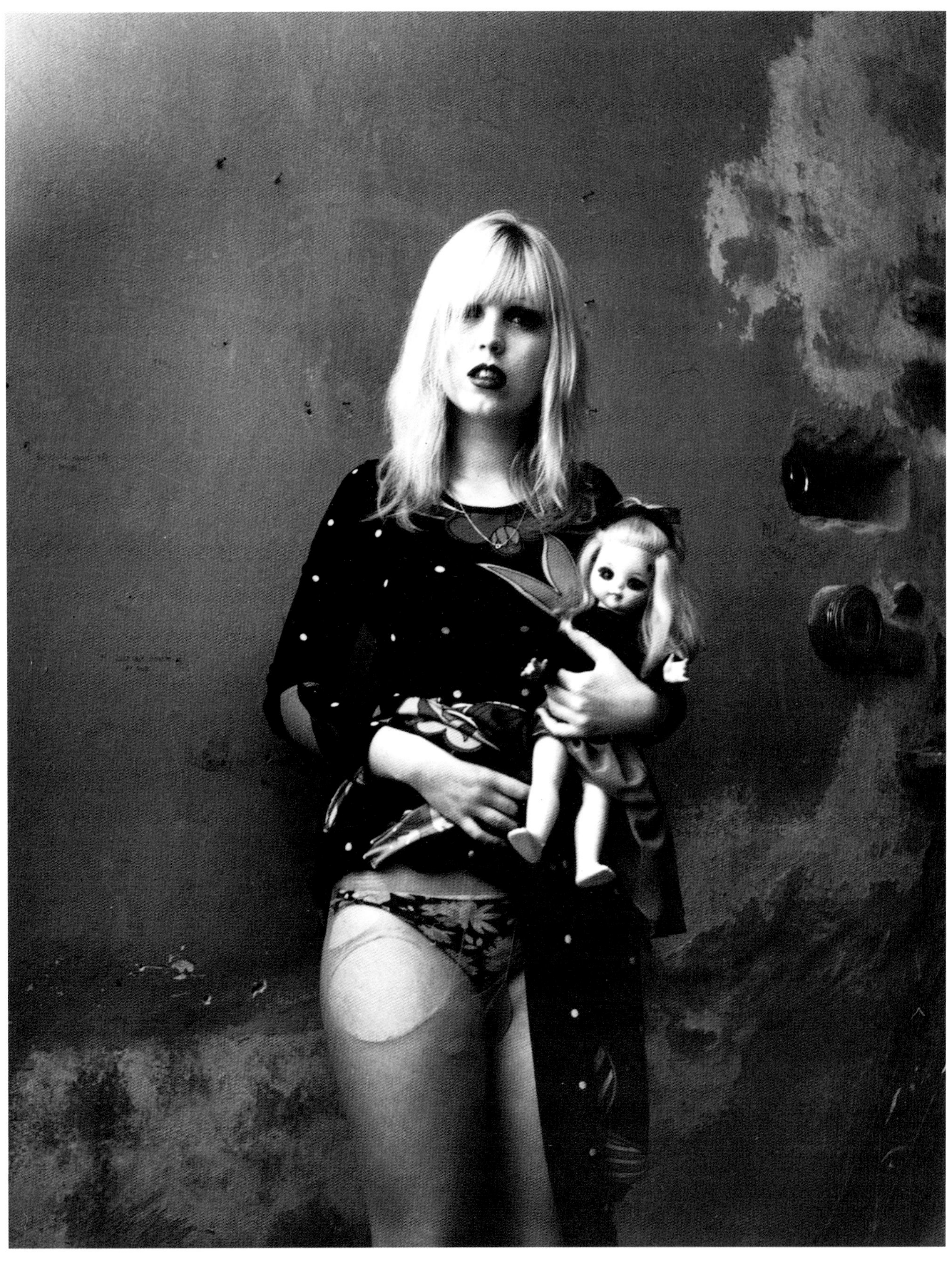

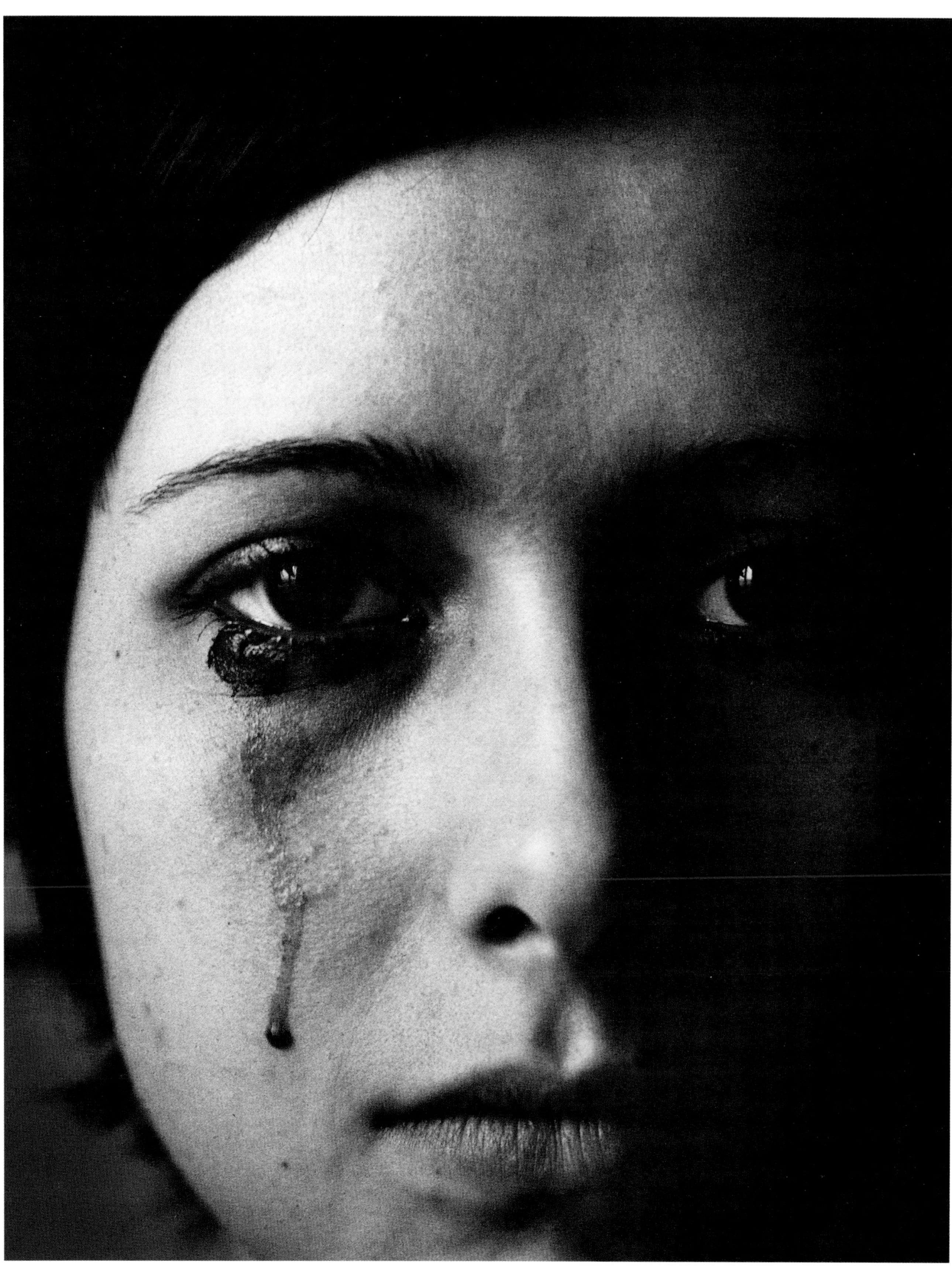

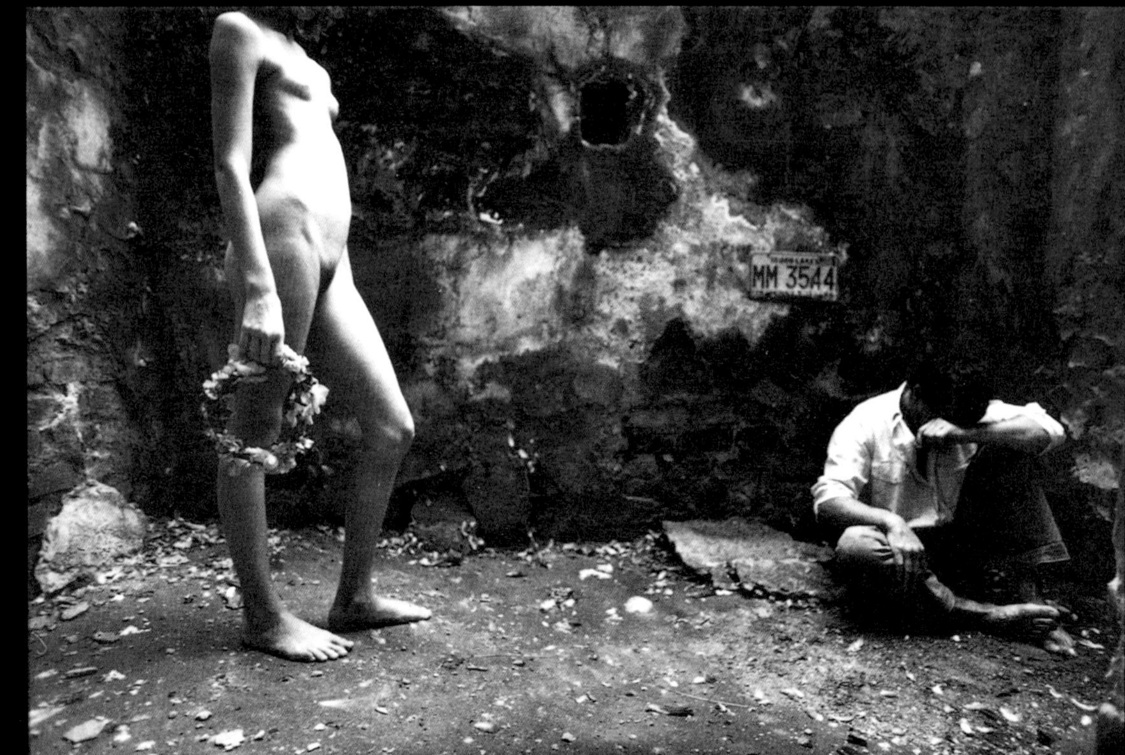
MM 3544

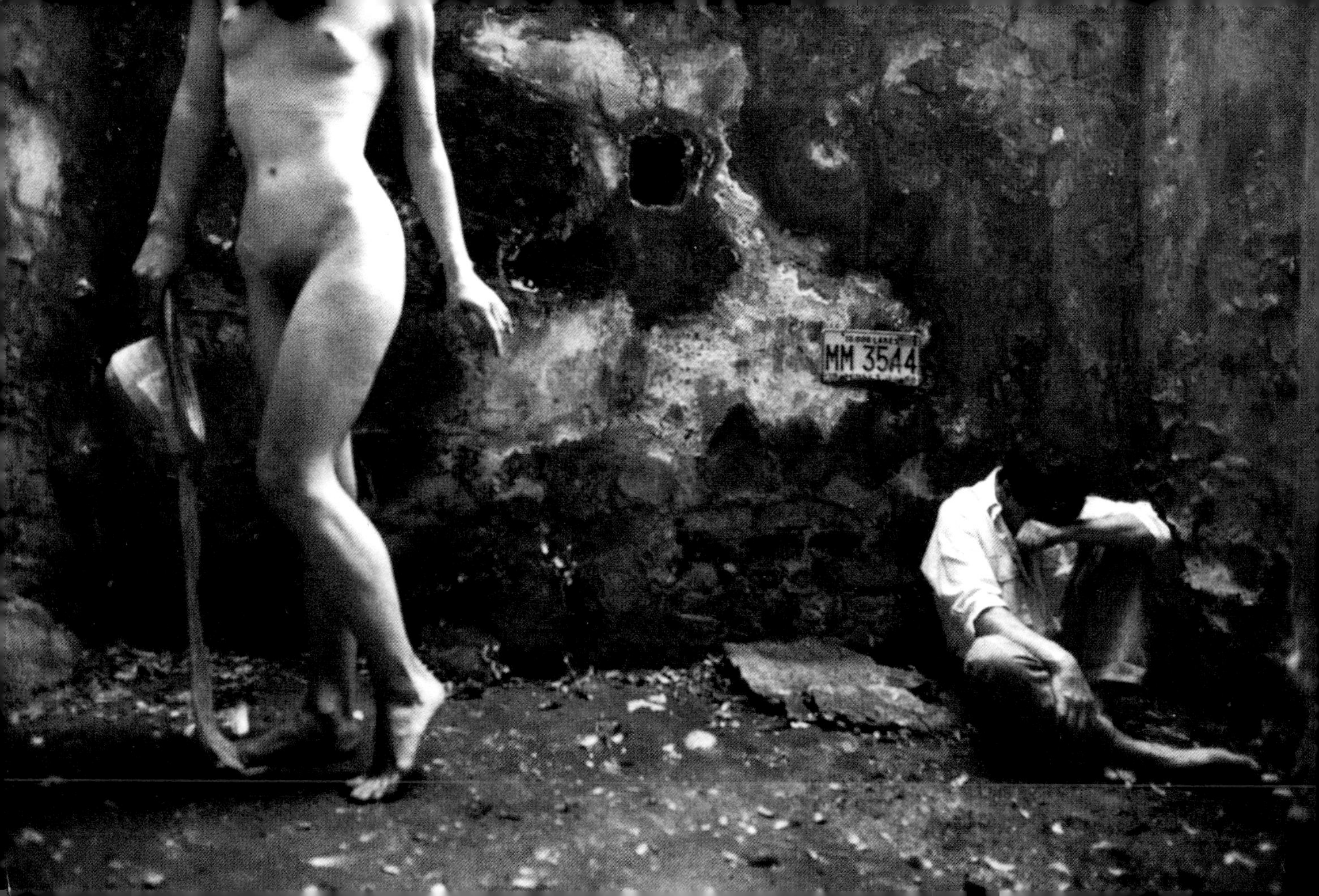
MM 3544

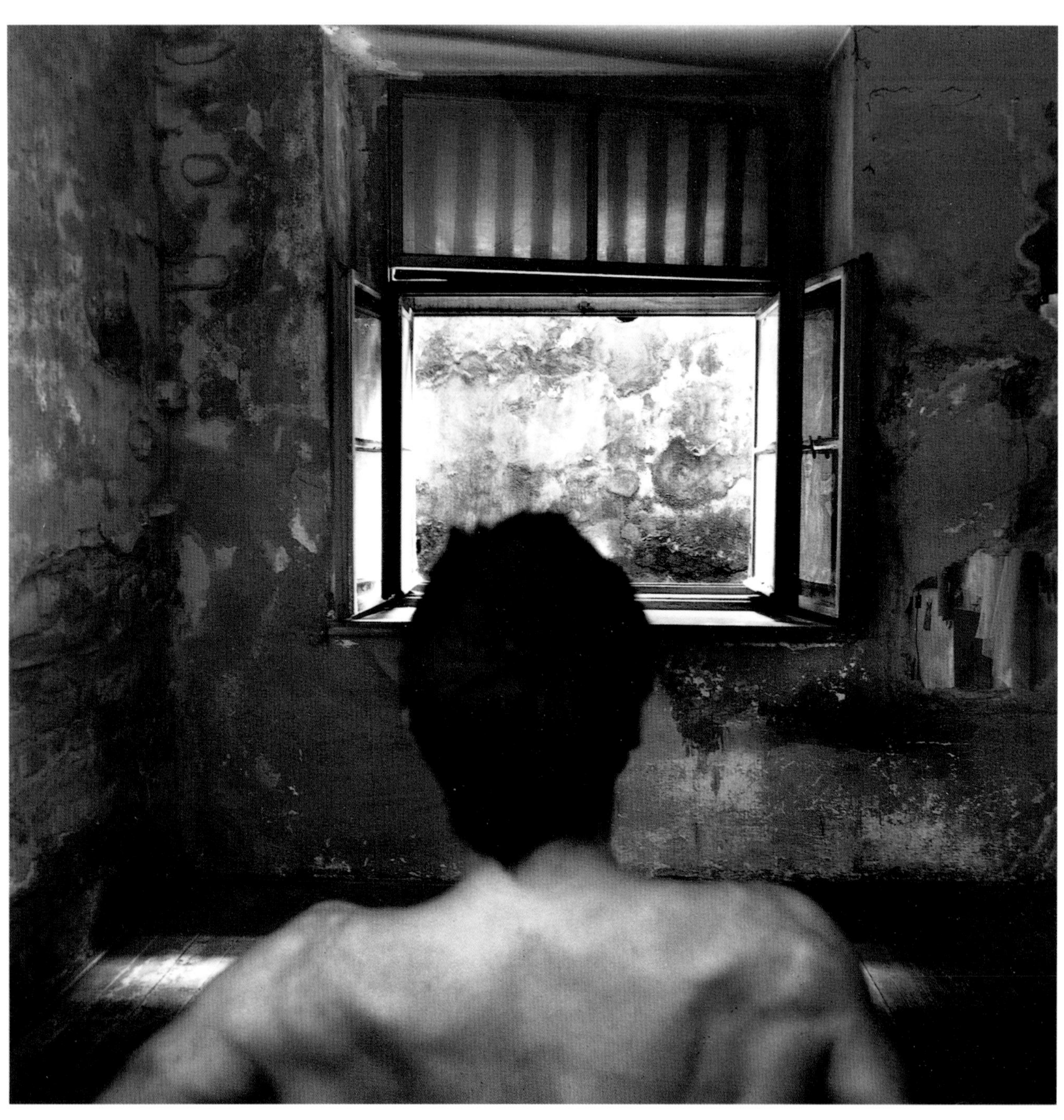

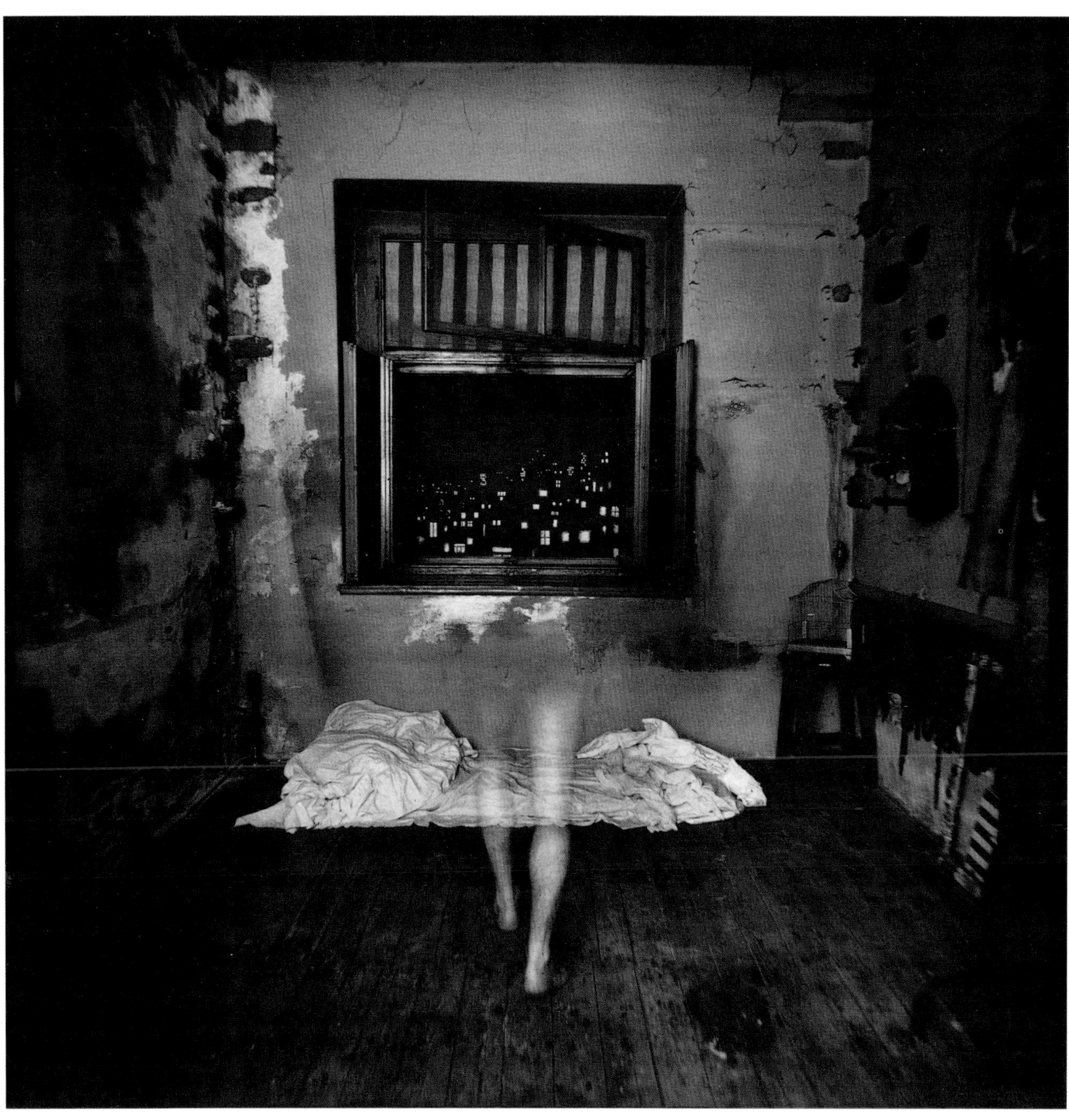

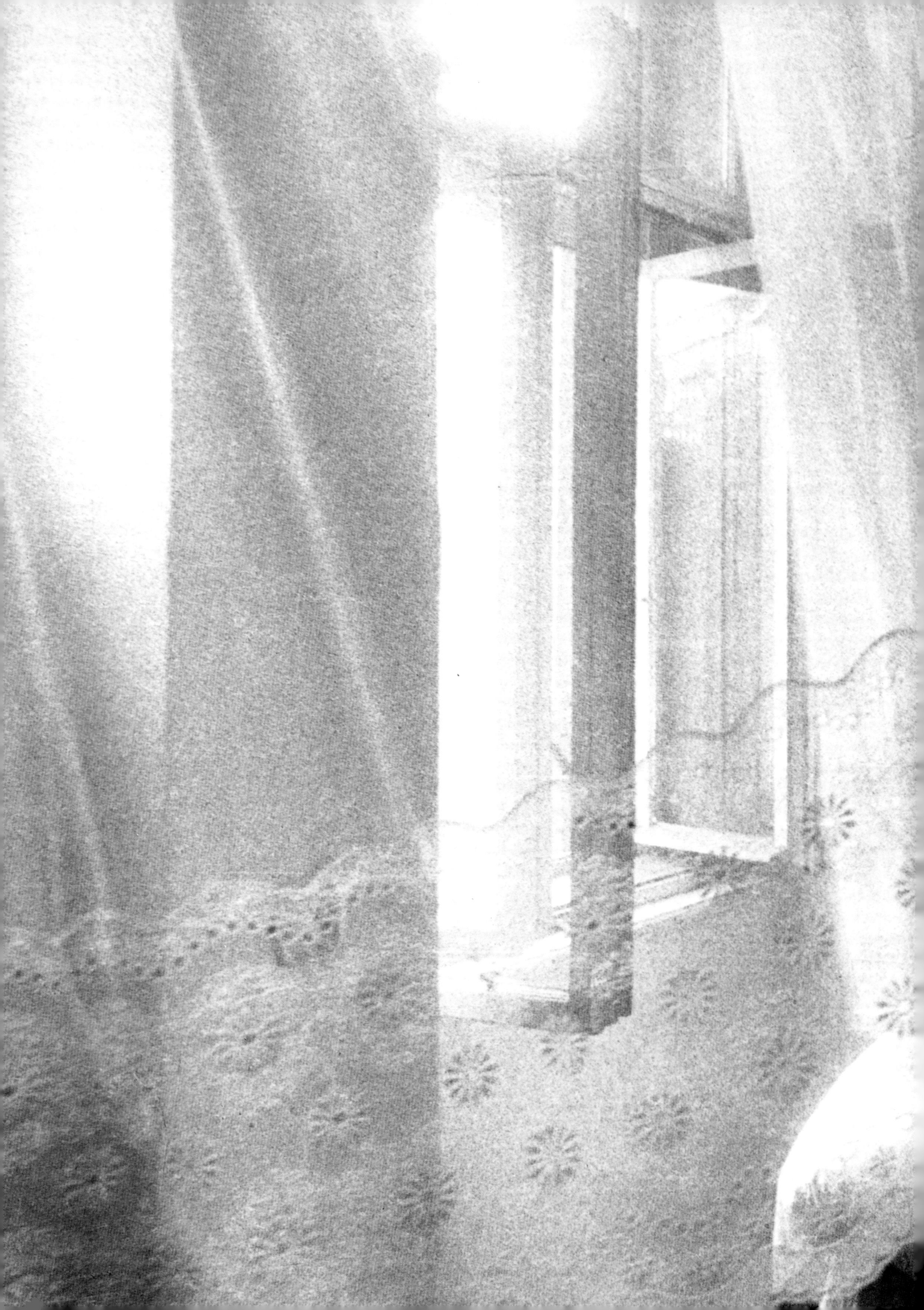

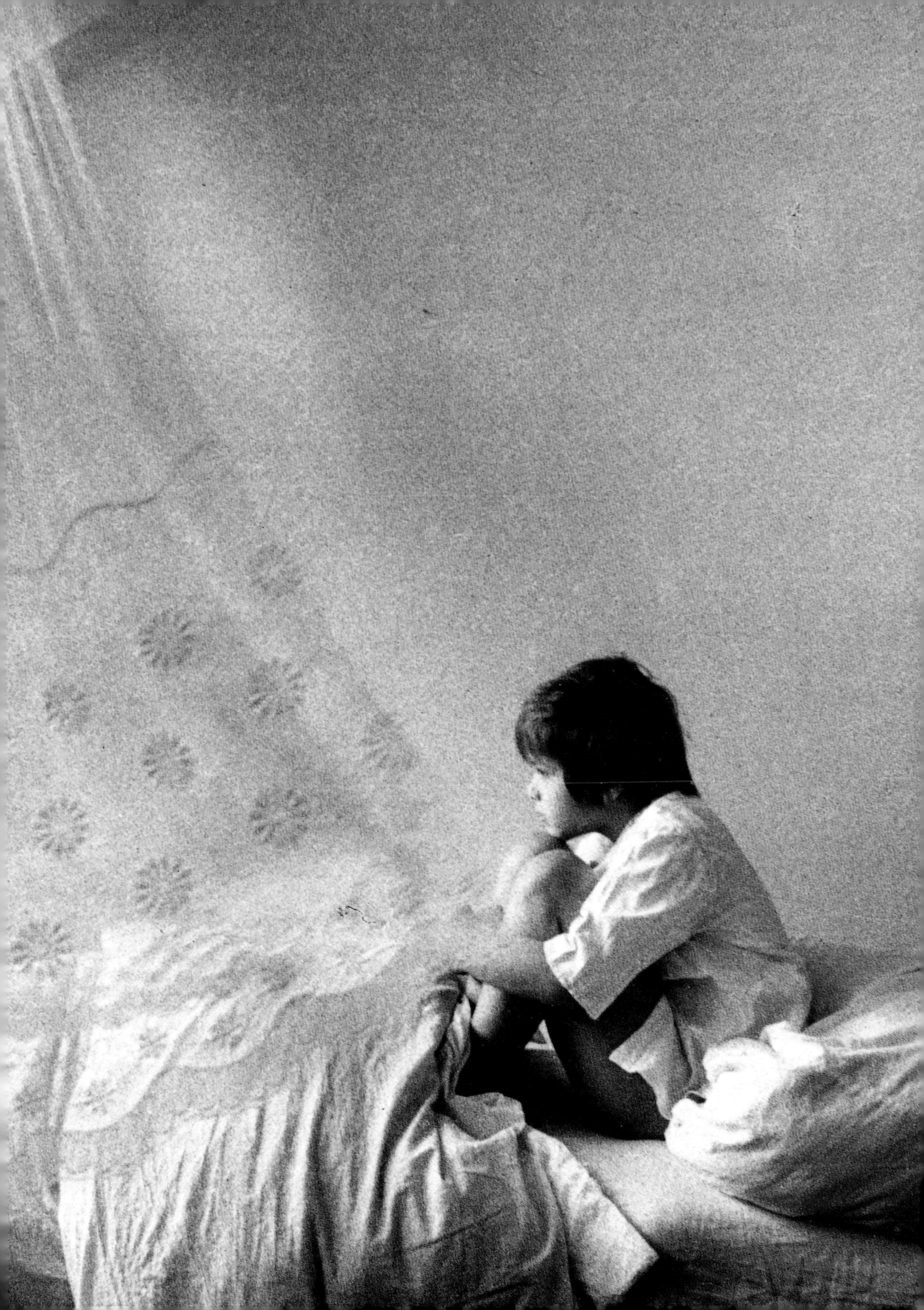

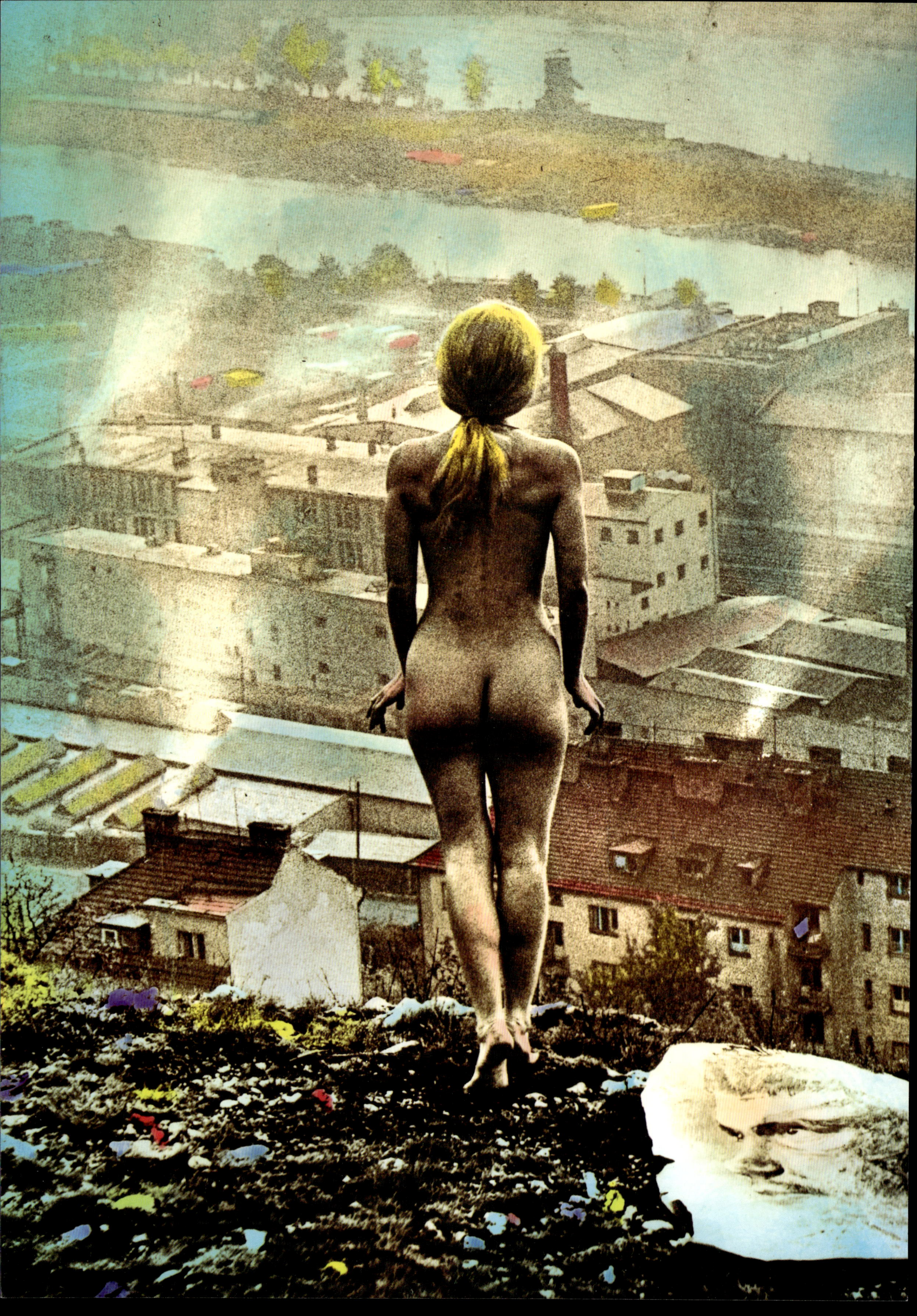

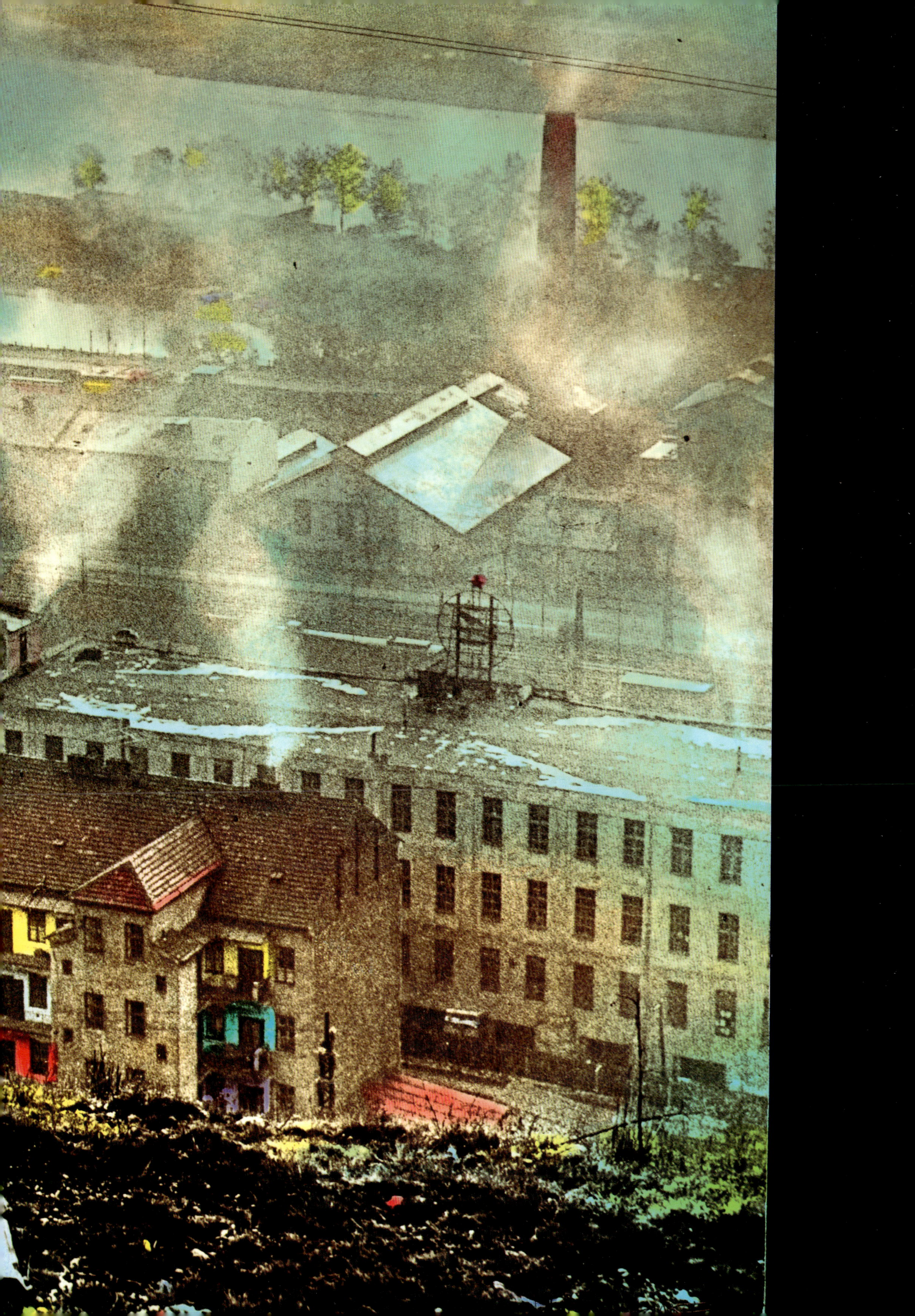

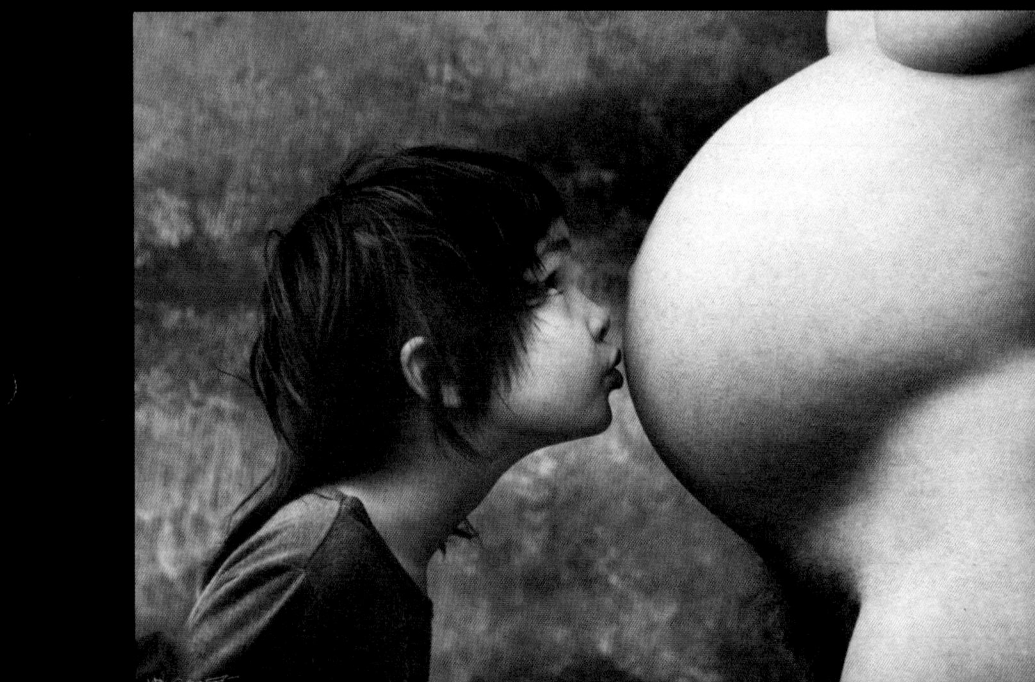

Stories
Geschichten
Histoires

If a photograph doesn't tell a story it's not a photograph, I say ...

Eine Photographie, die keine Geschichte erzählt, ist für mich keine Photographie ...

Pour moi, une photographie qui ne raconte pas d'histoire n'est pas une photographie ...

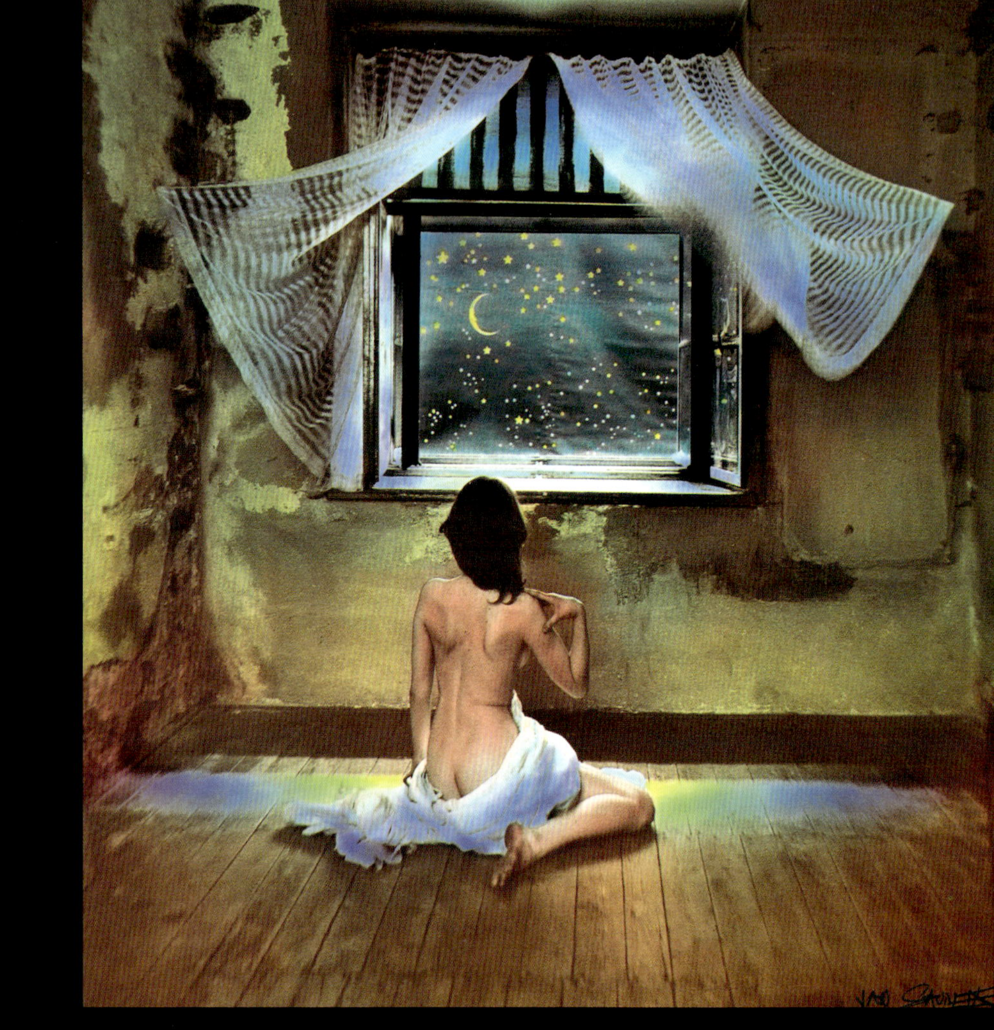

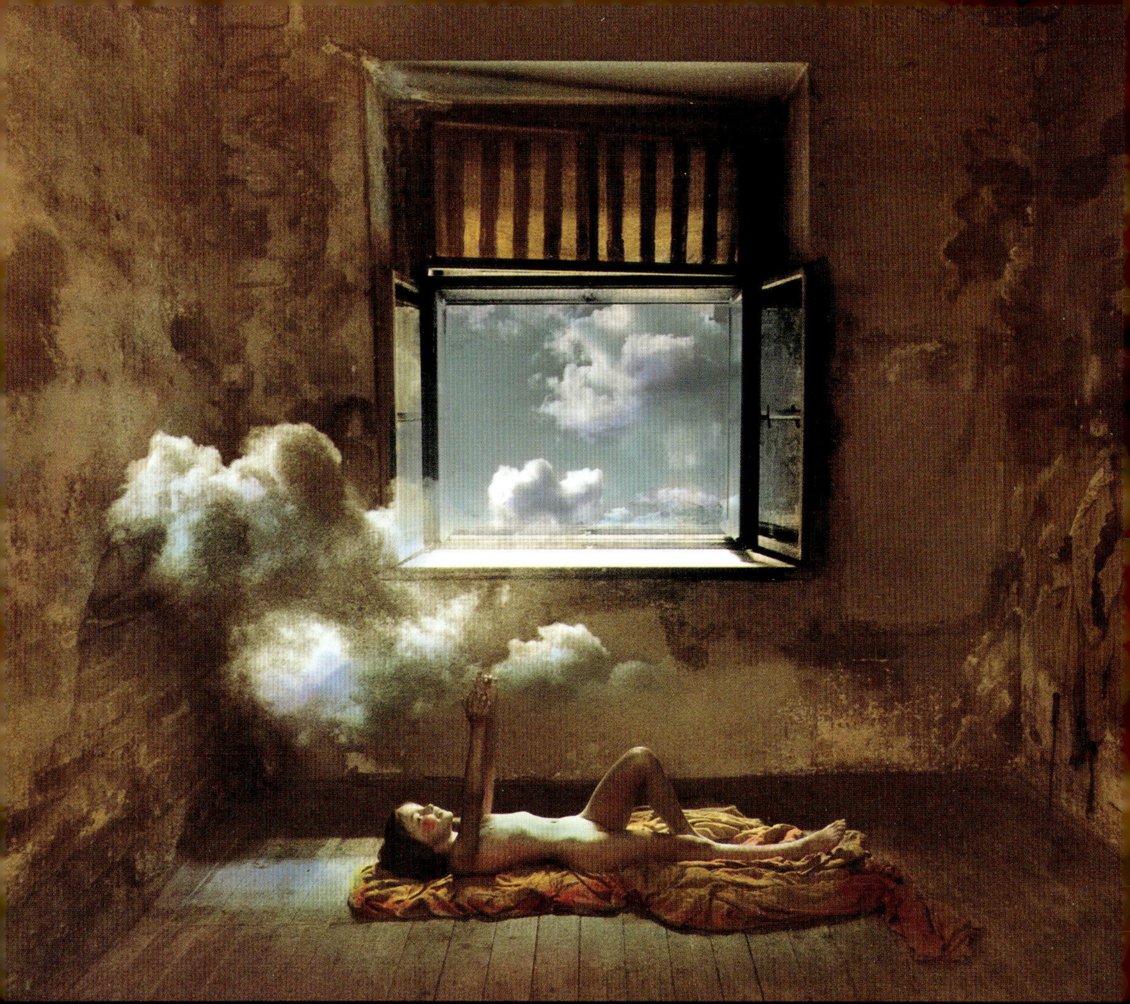

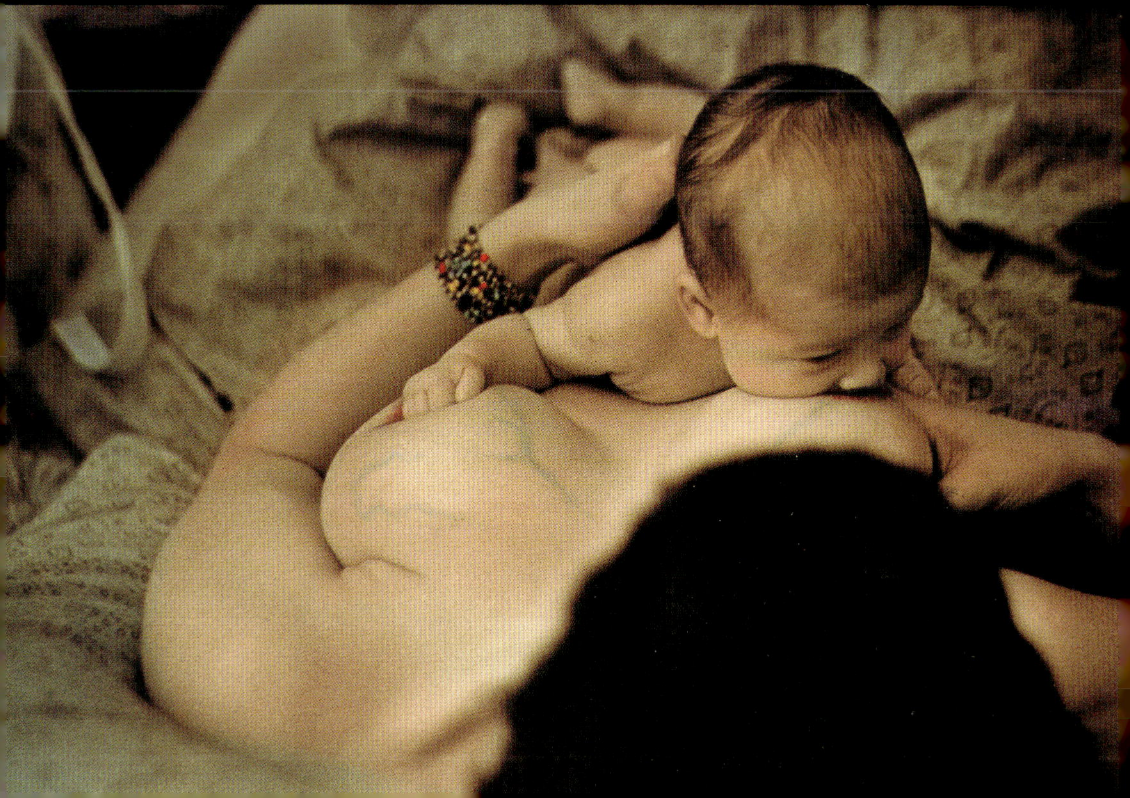

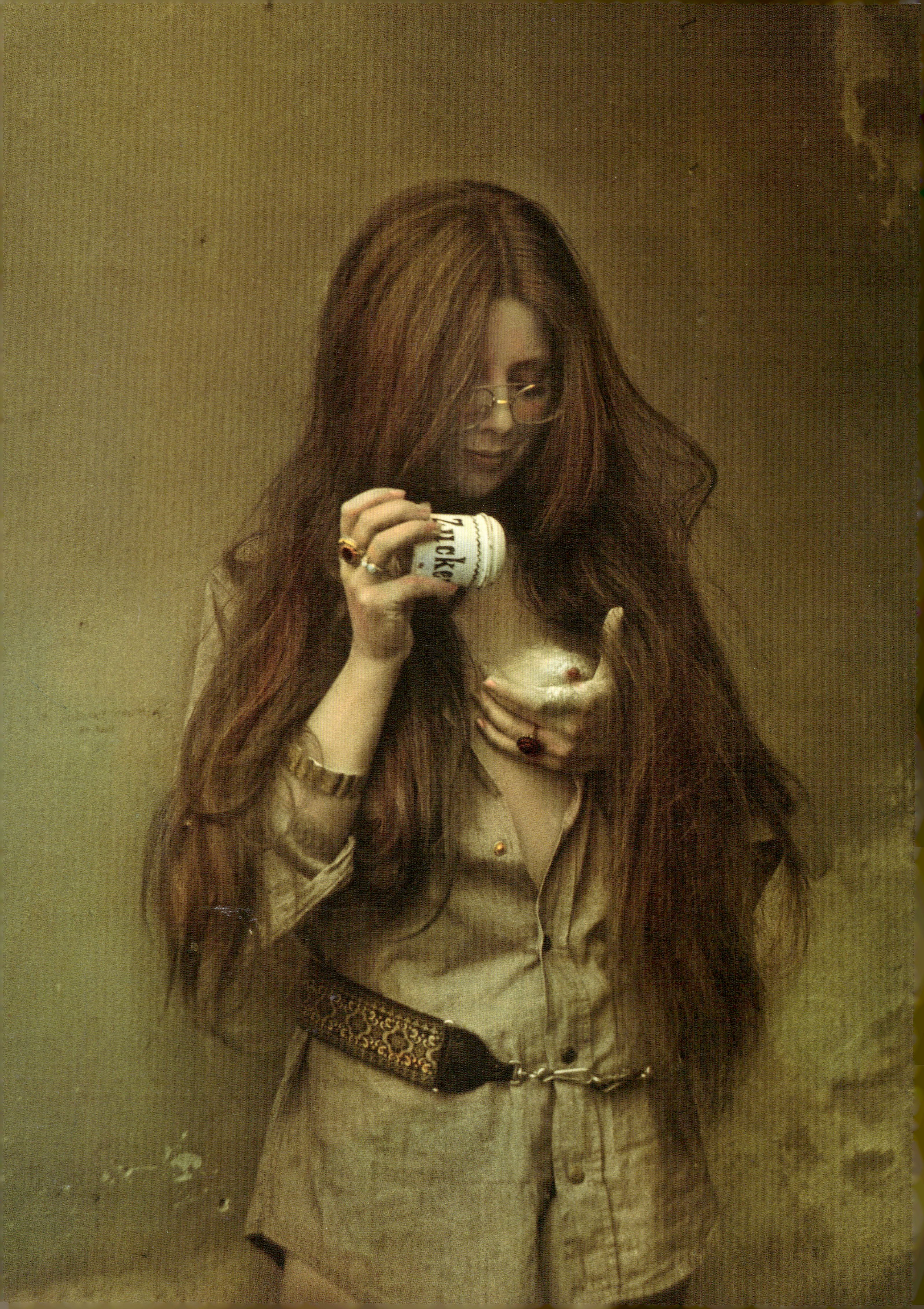

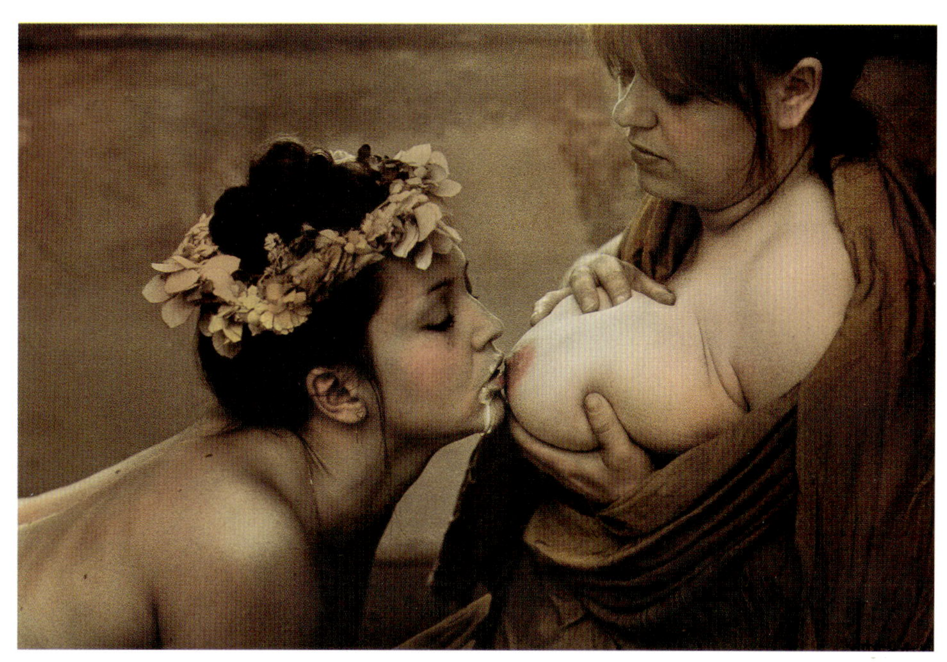

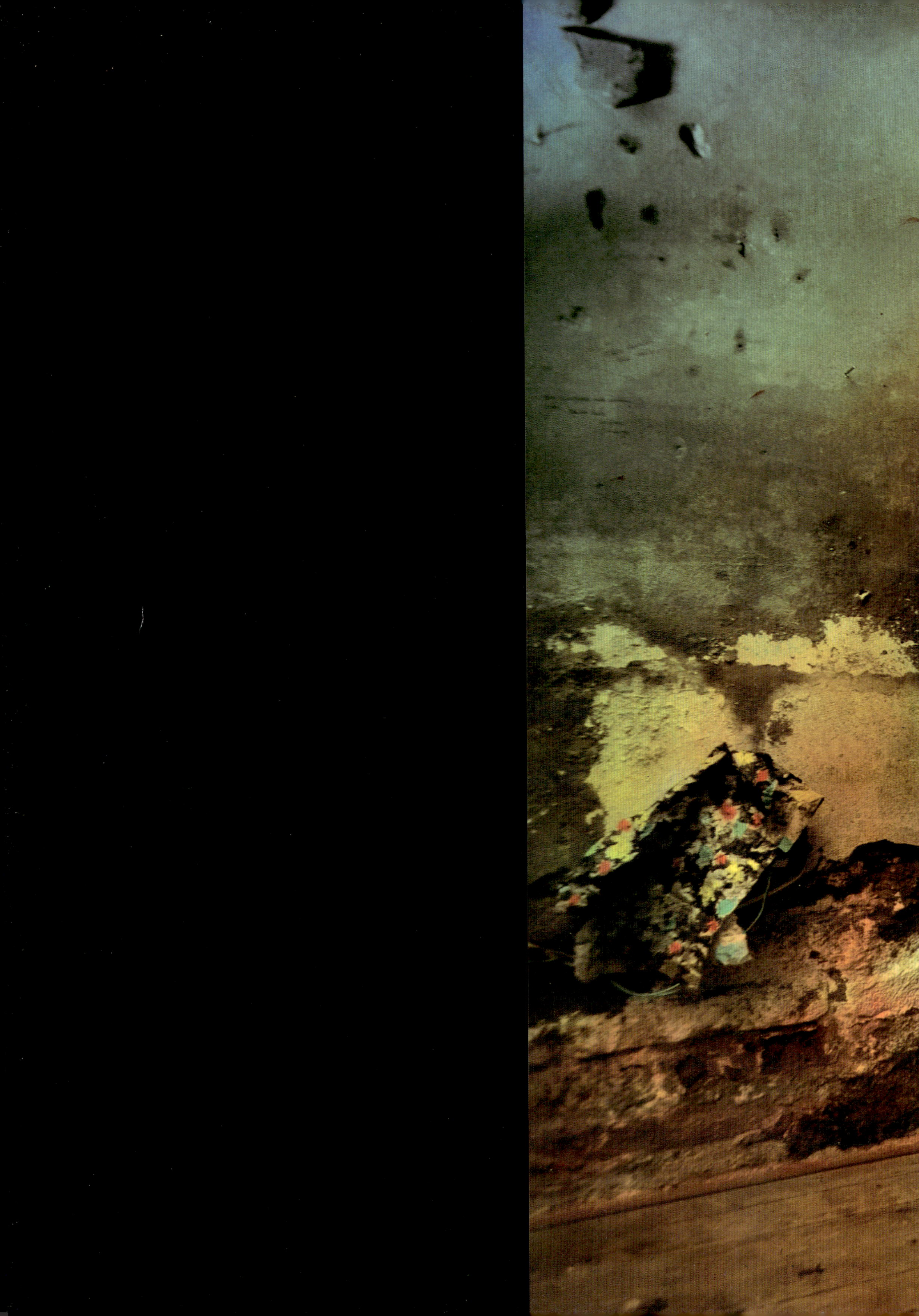

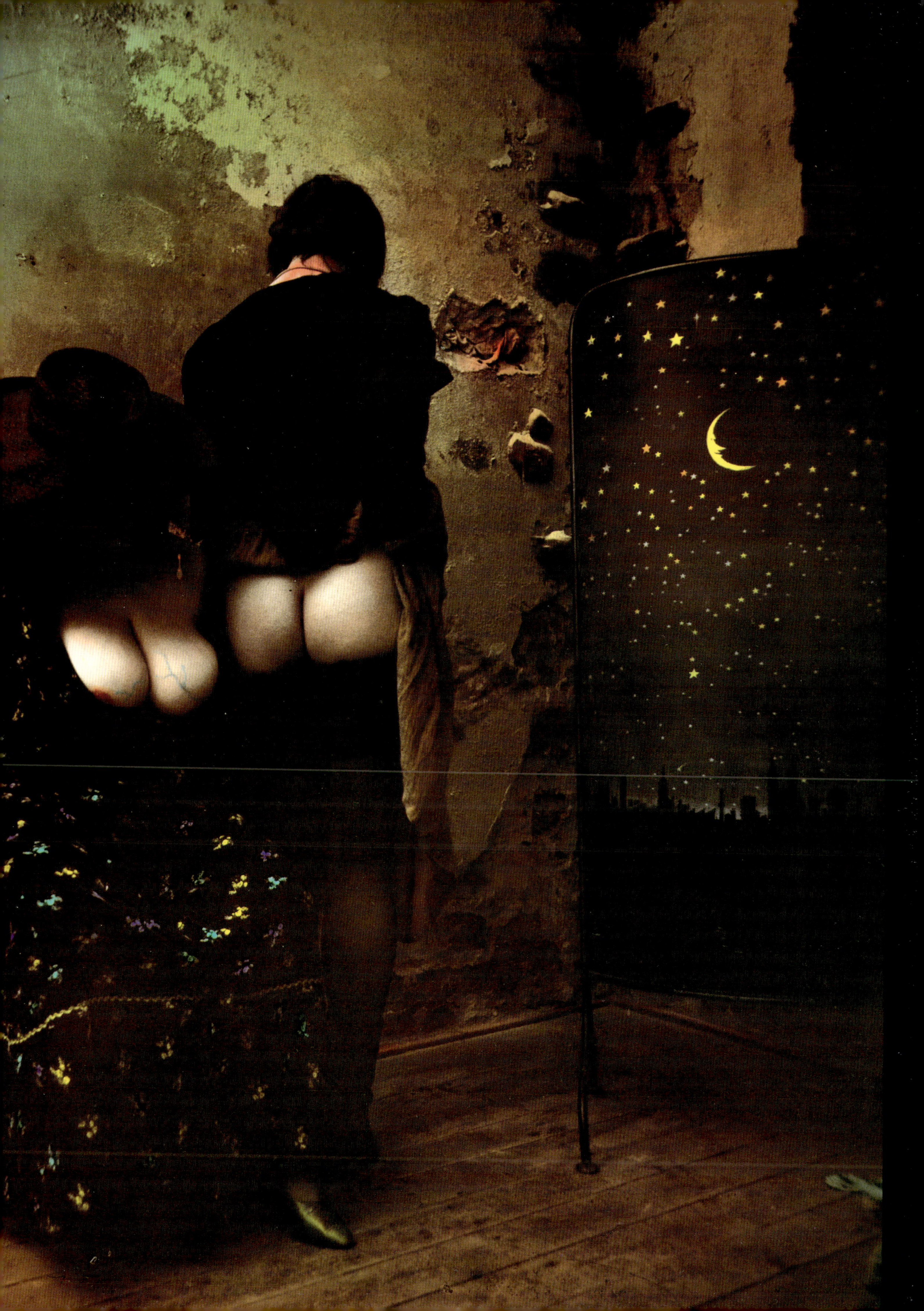

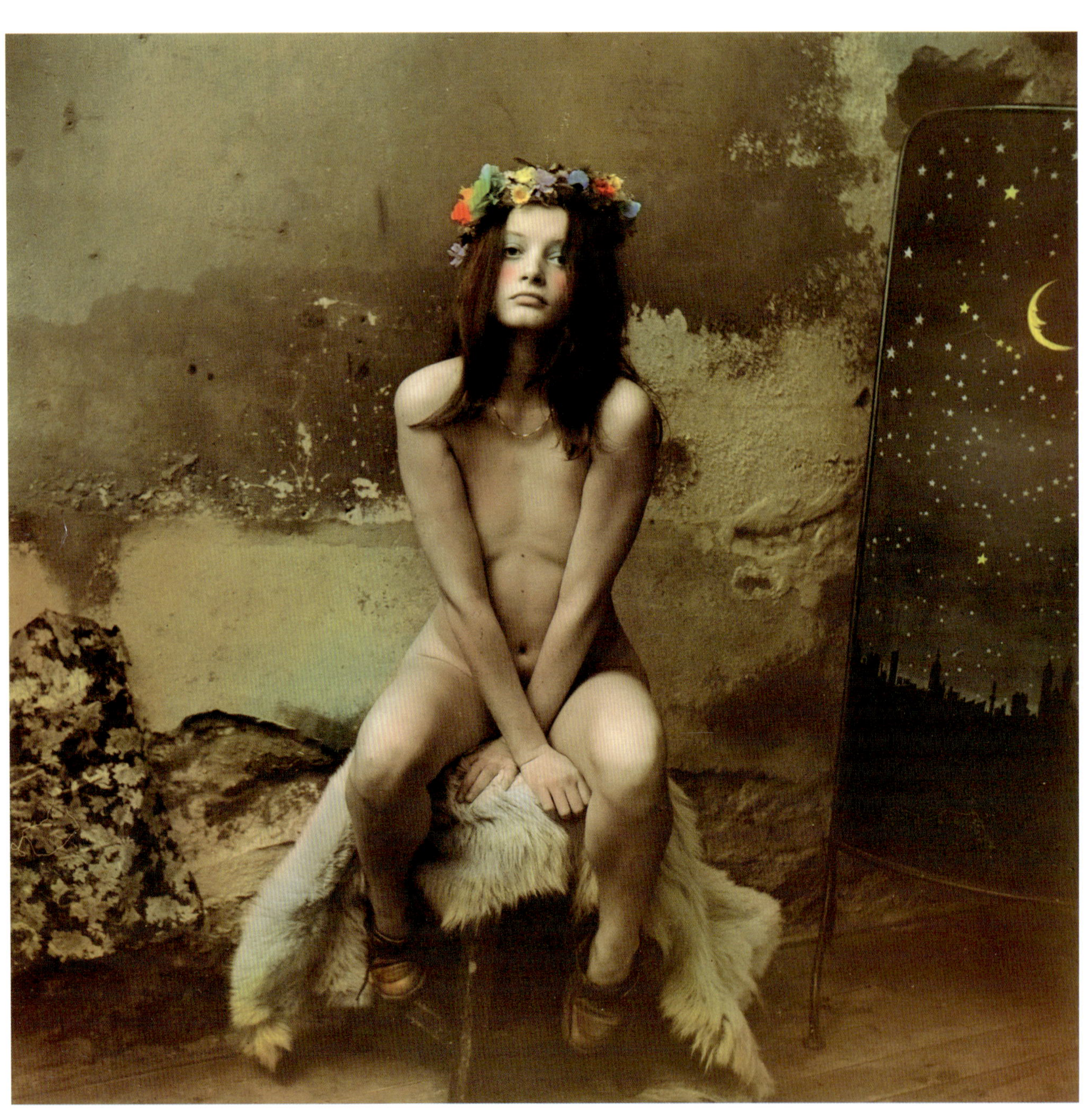

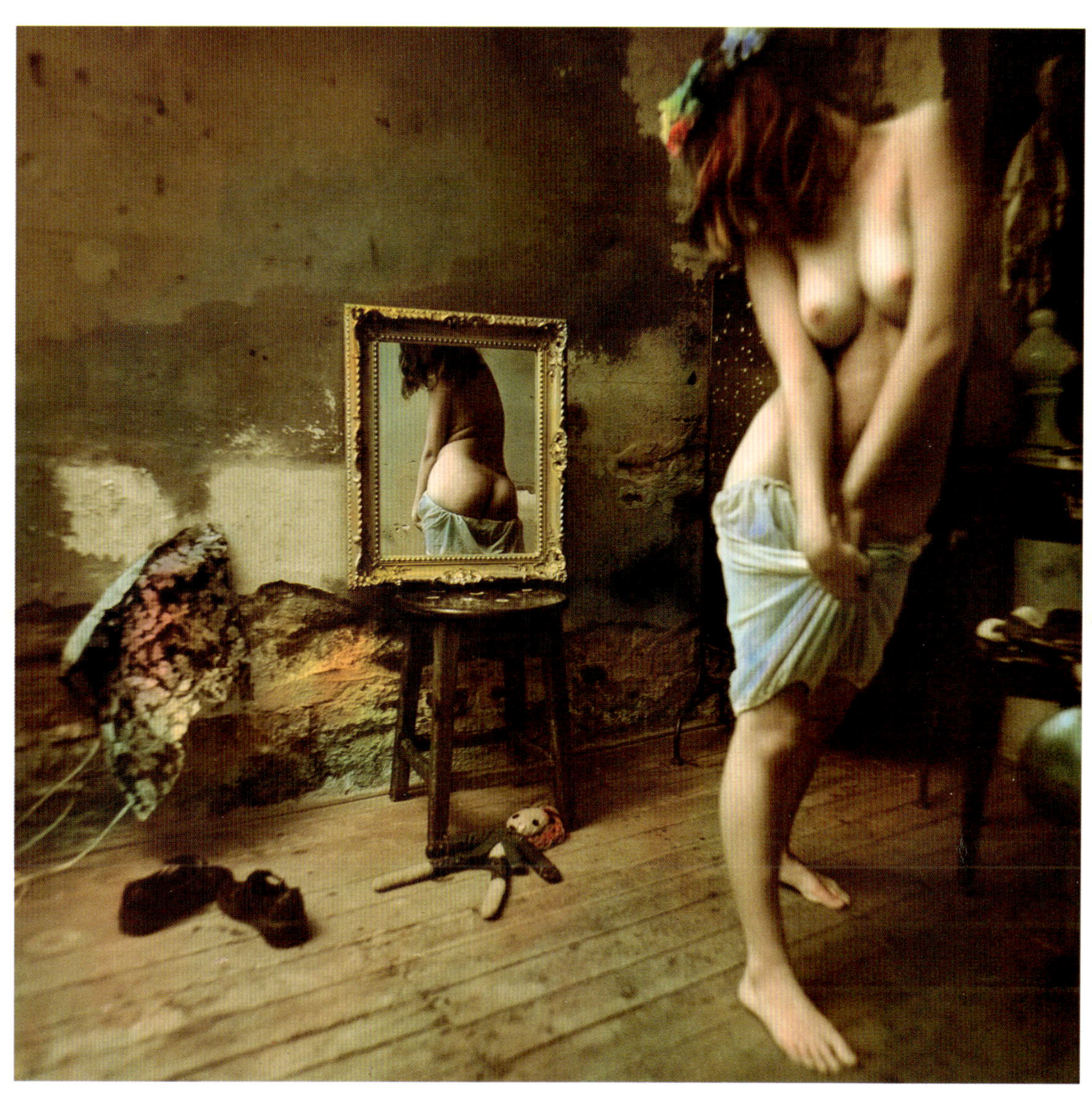

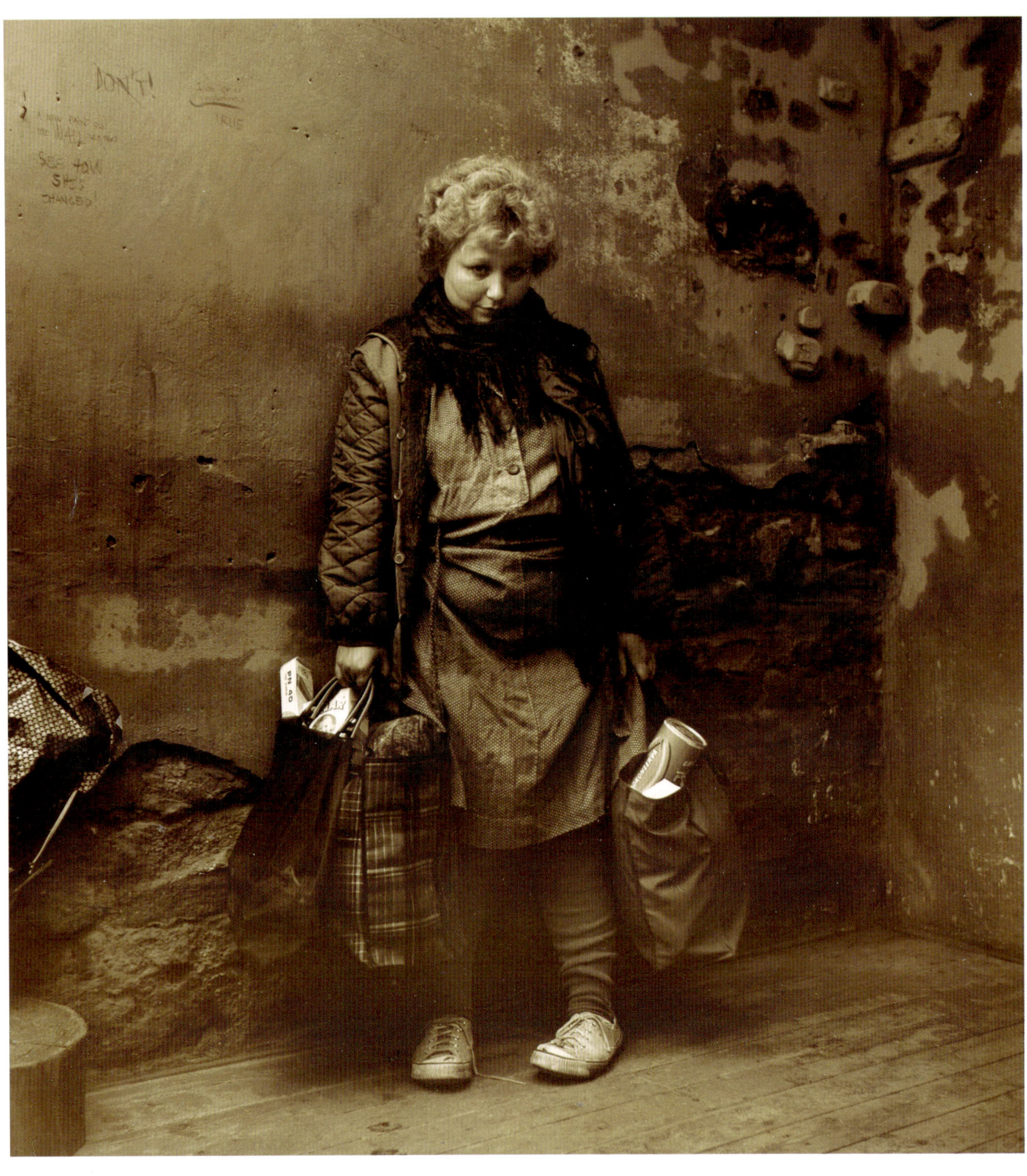
DON'T!
TRUE
SEE HOW
SHE'S
CHANGED!

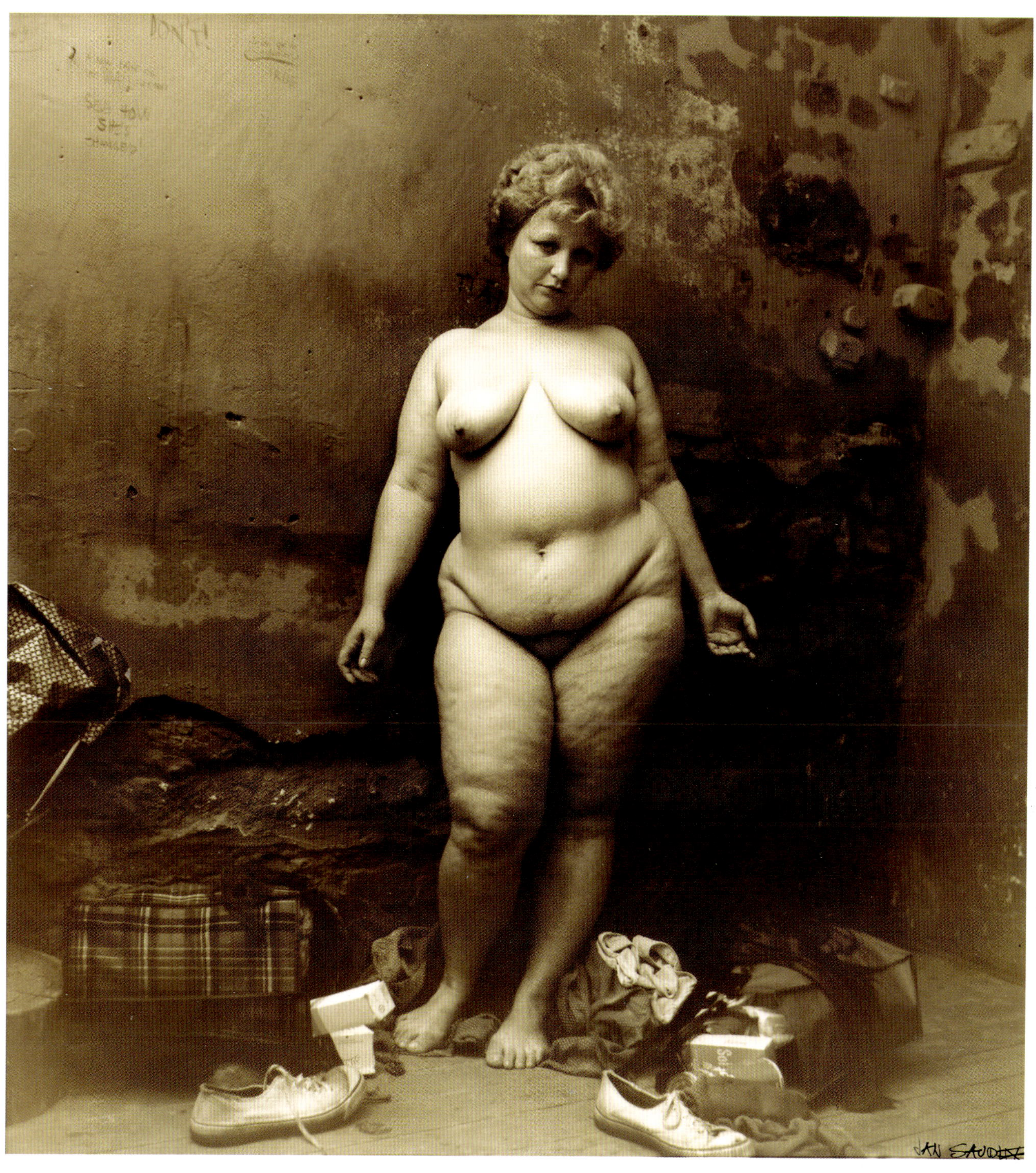
JAN SAUDEK

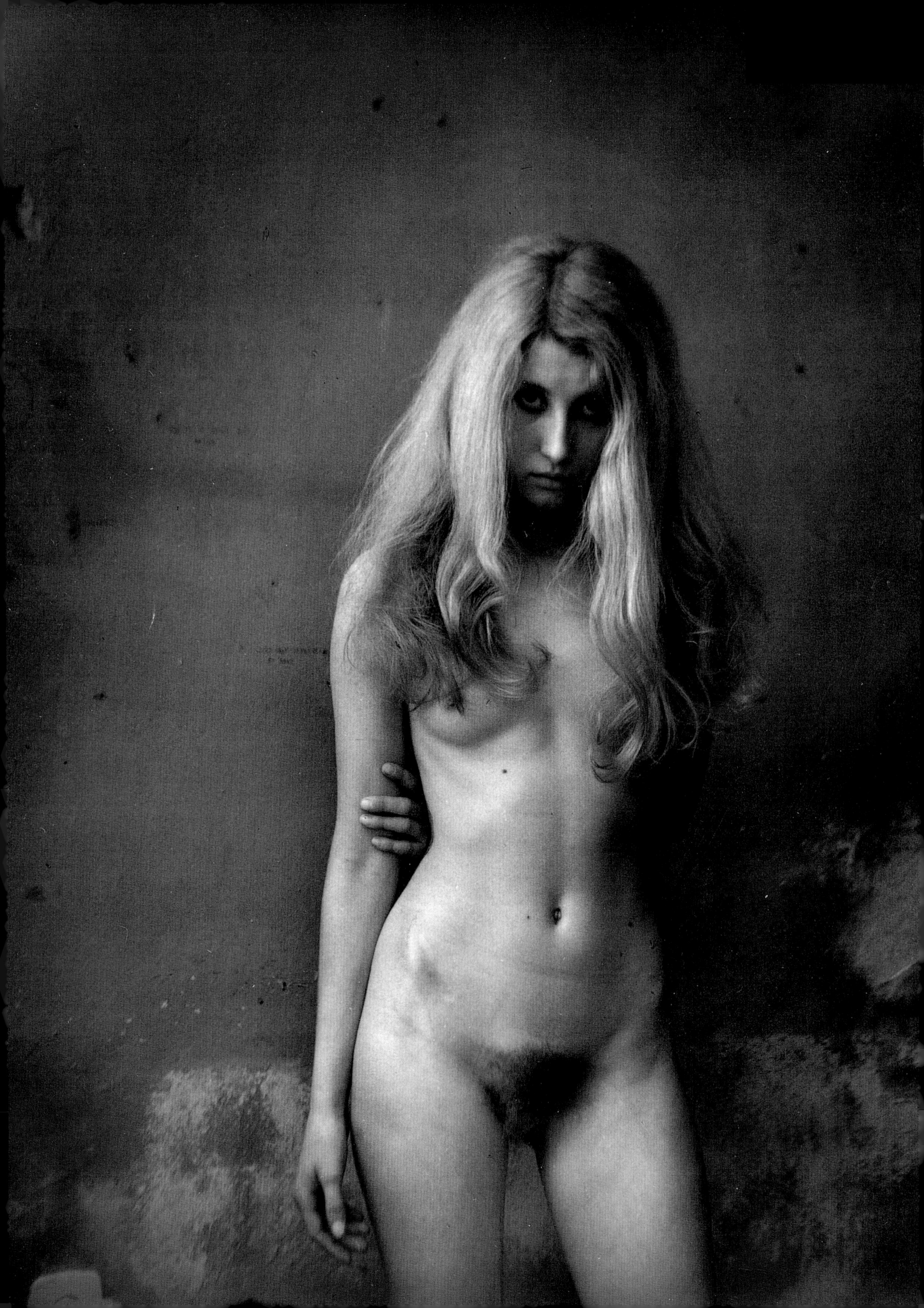

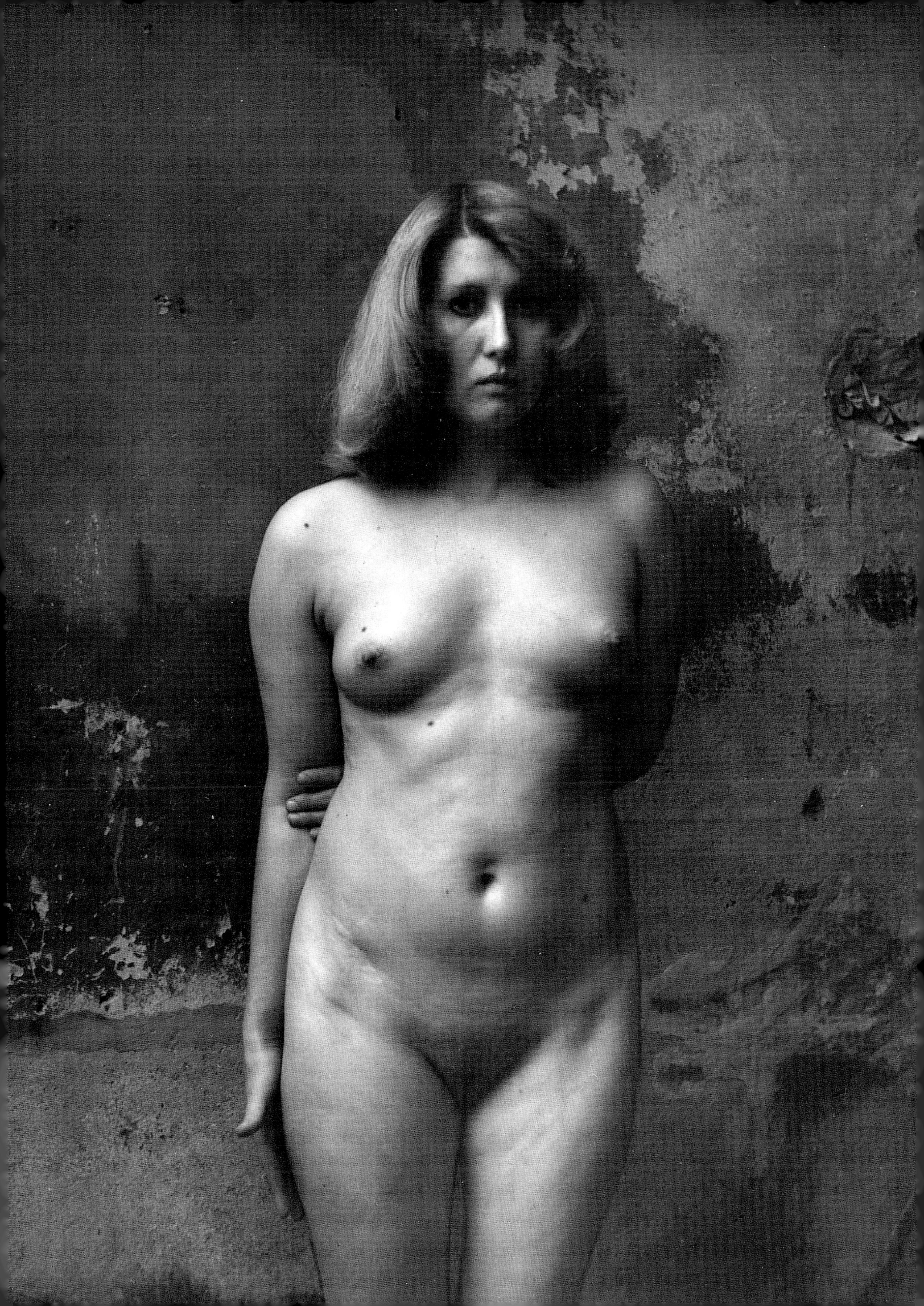

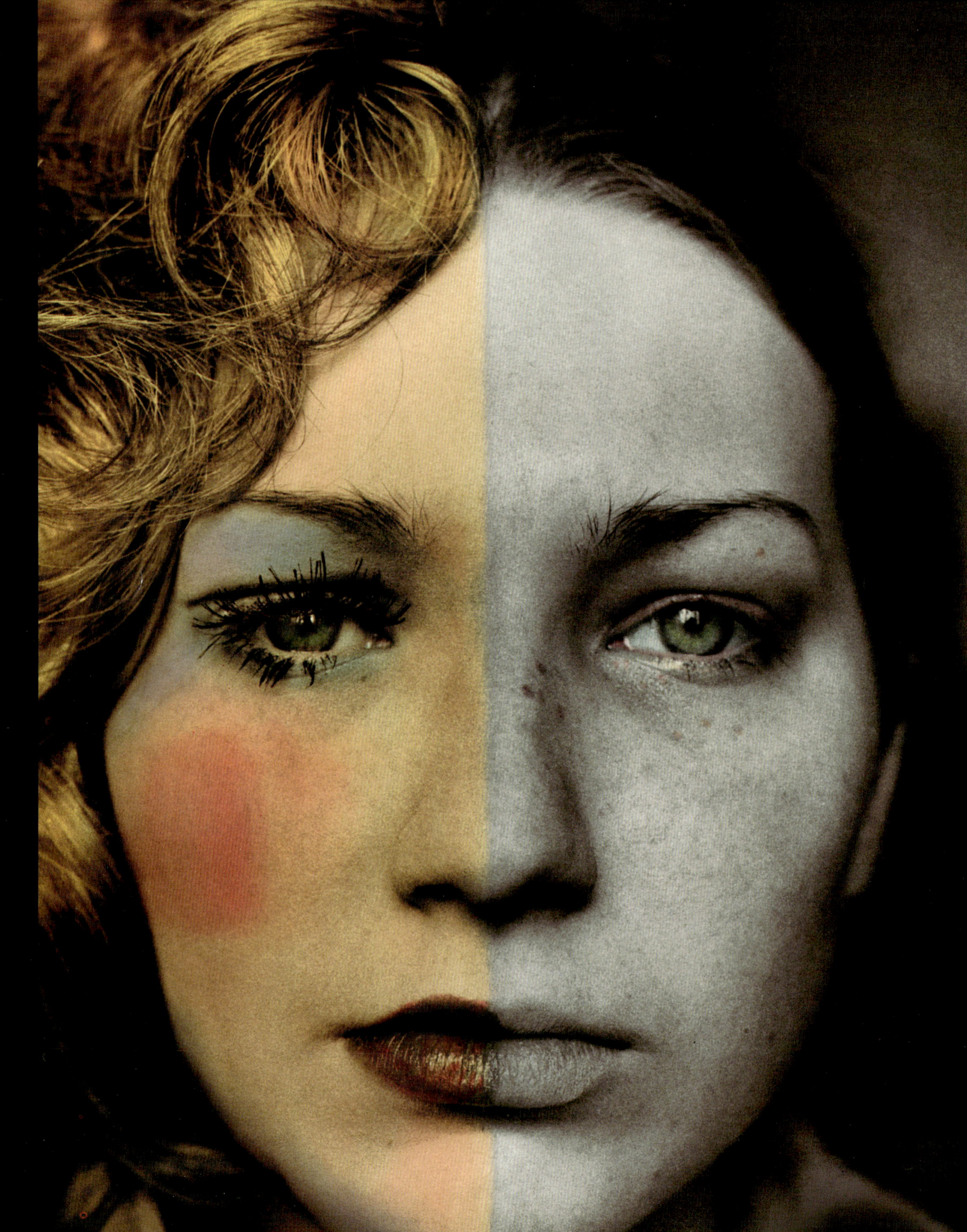

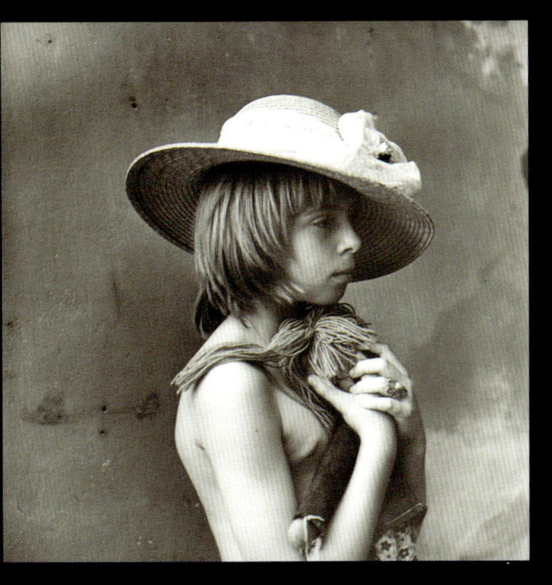

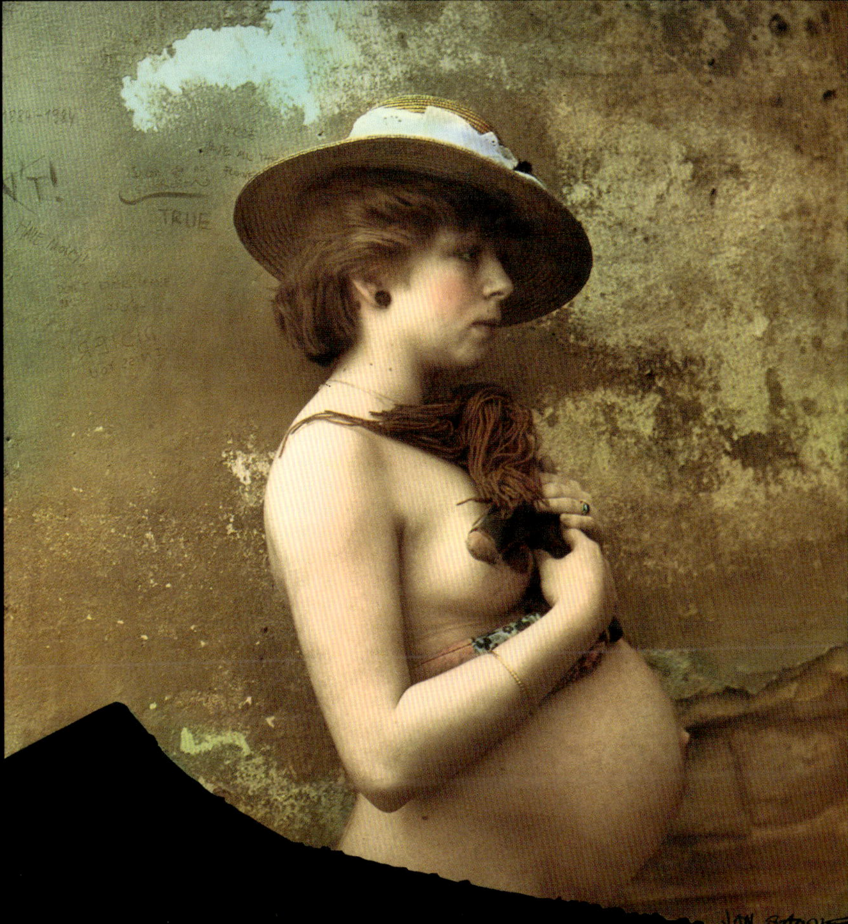

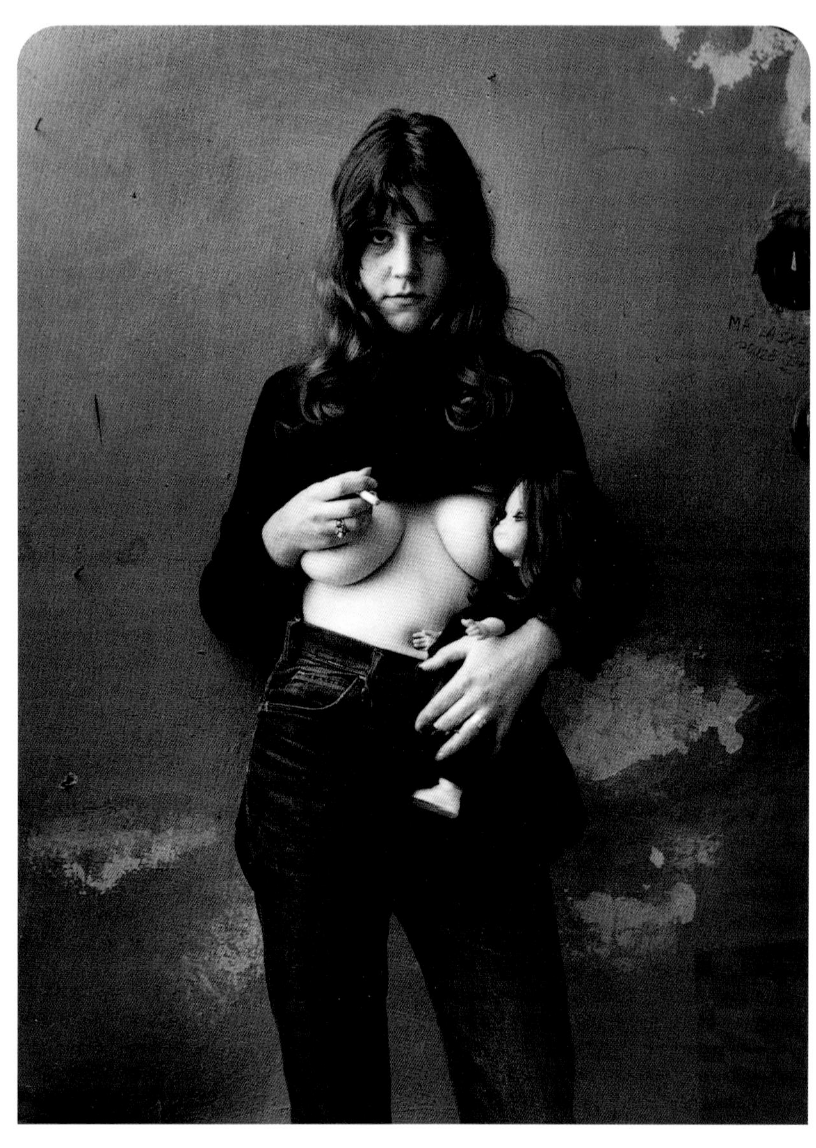

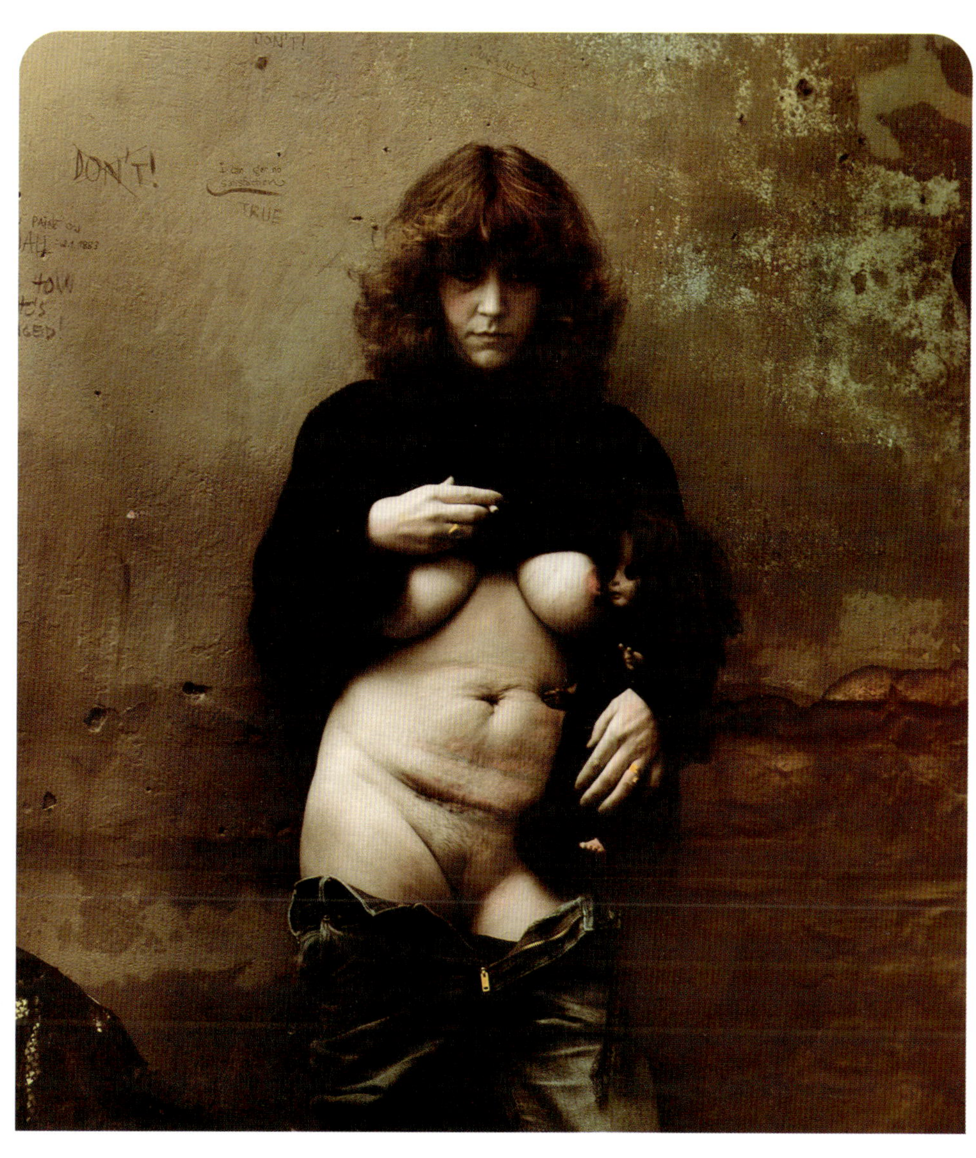
DON'T!
TRUE

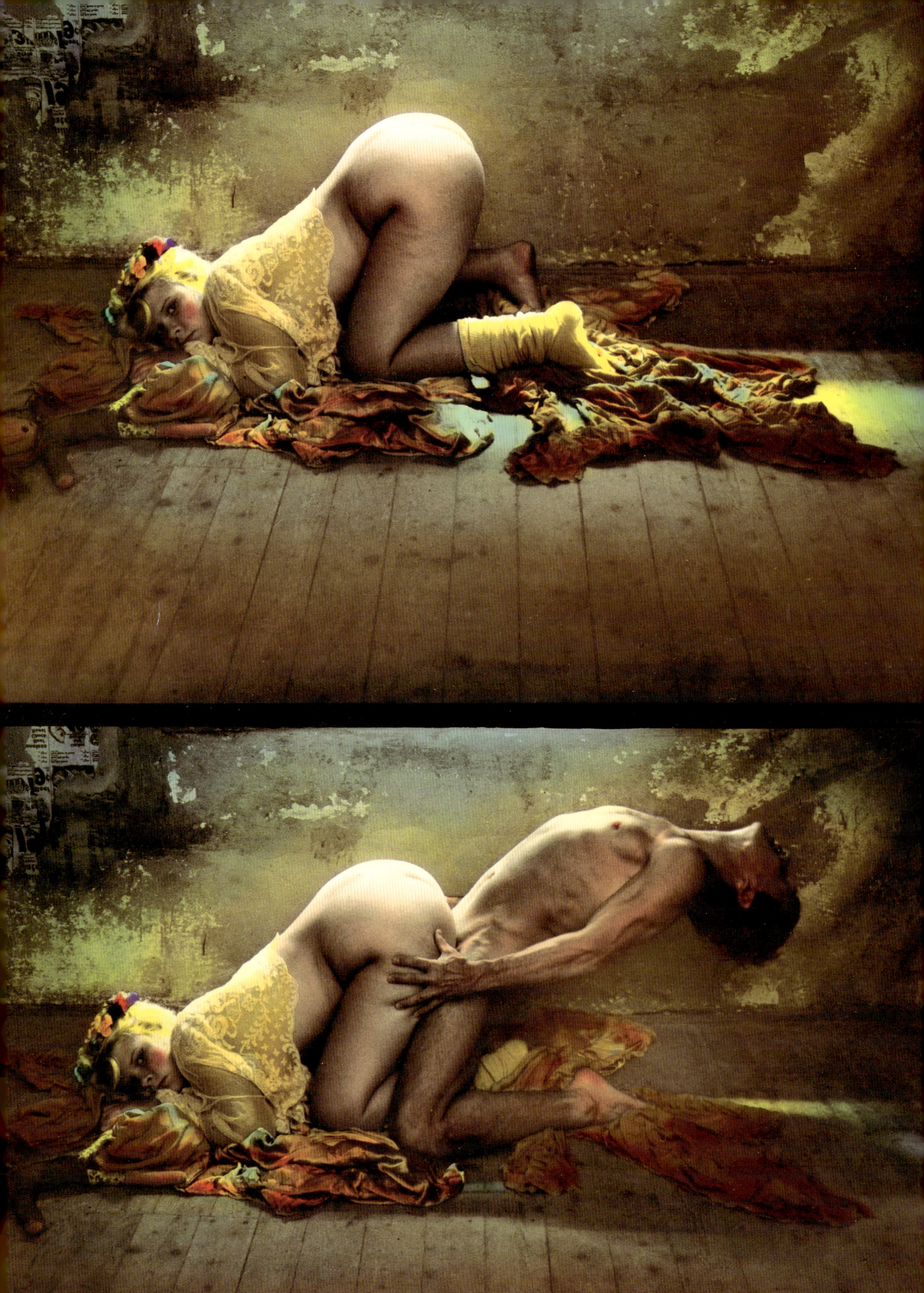

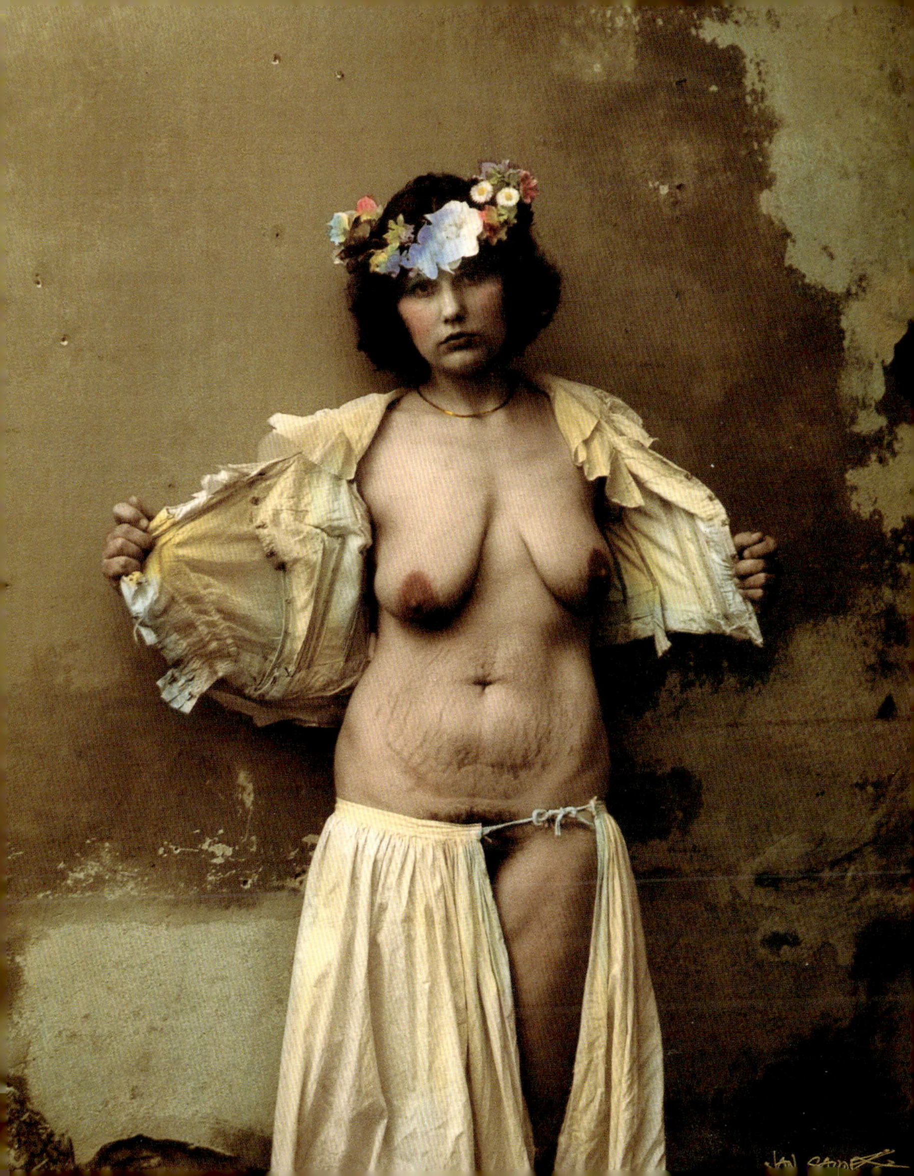

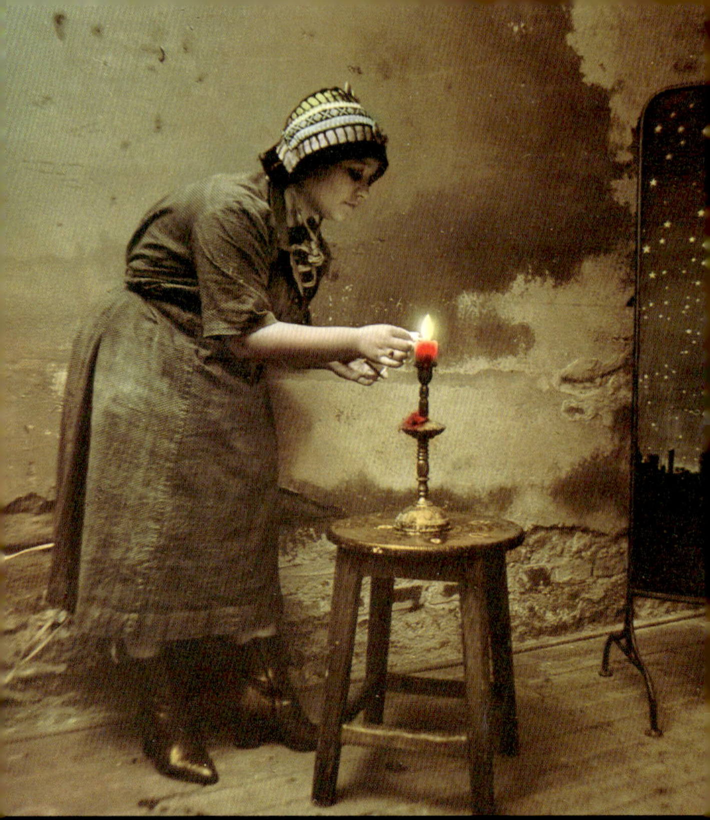

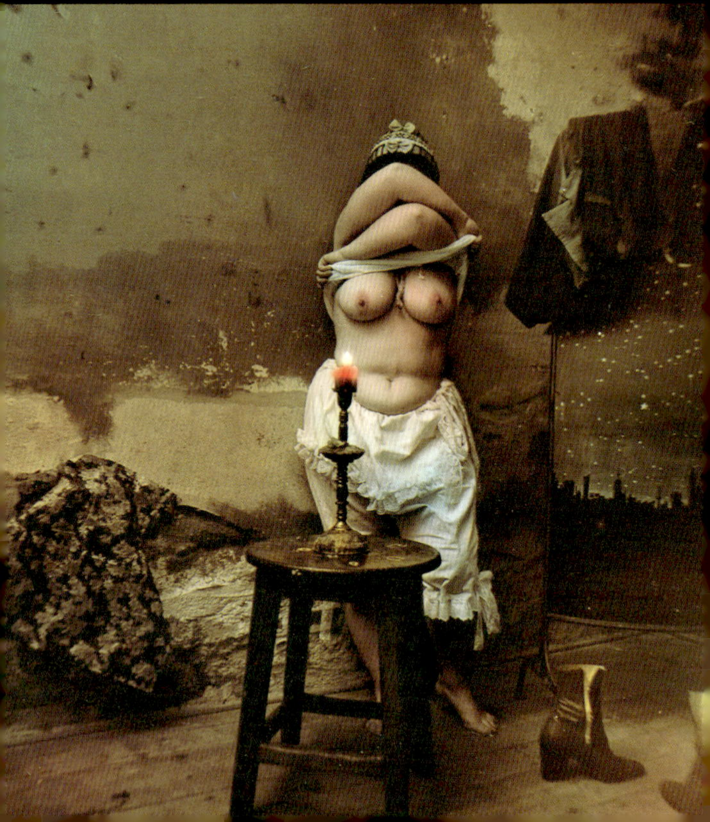

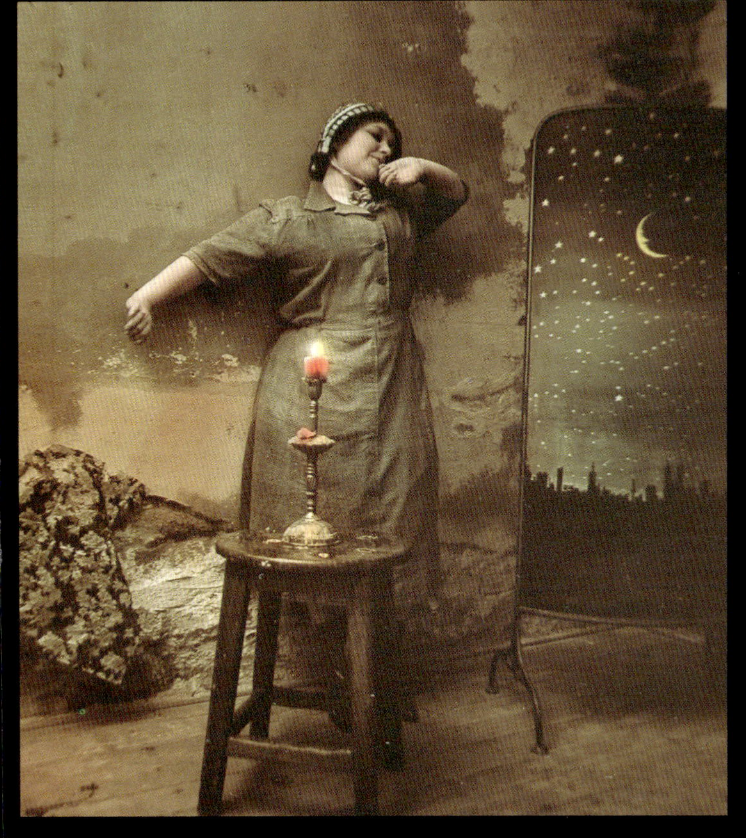
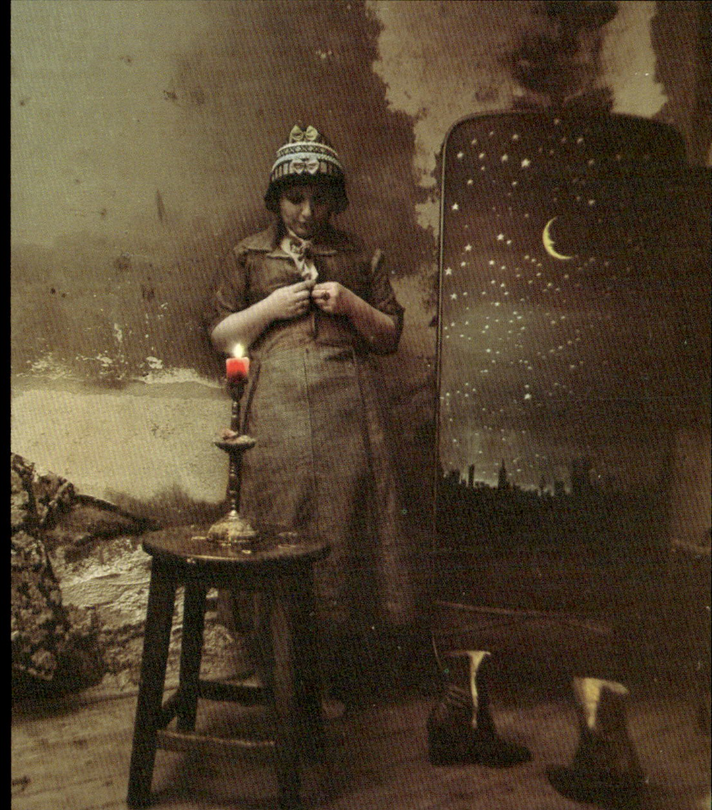
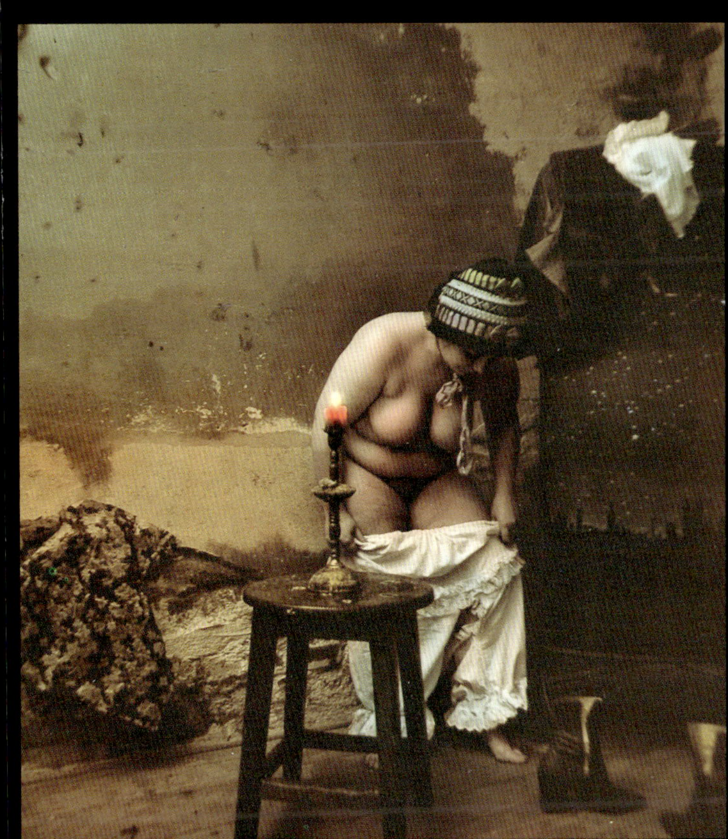
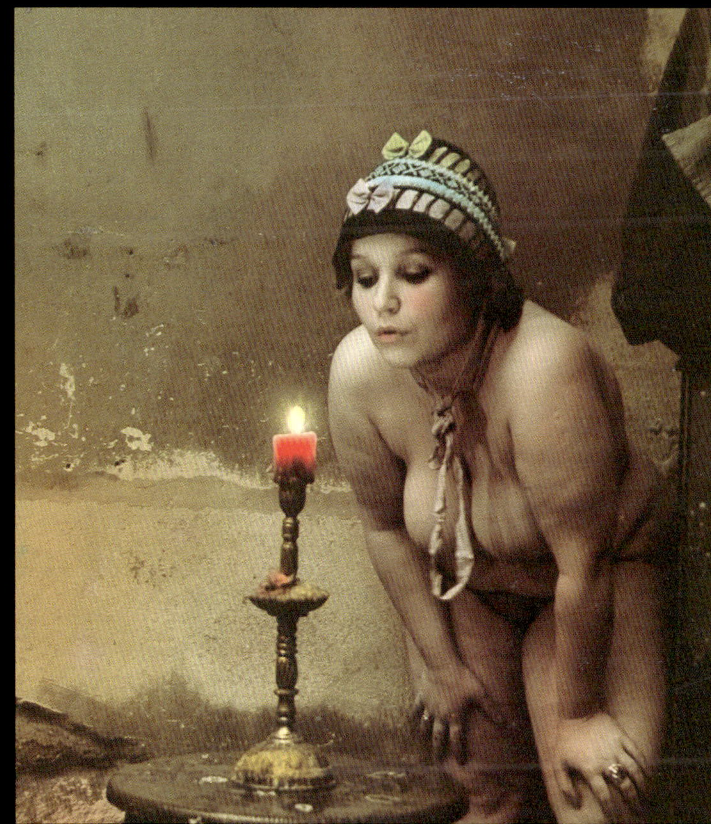

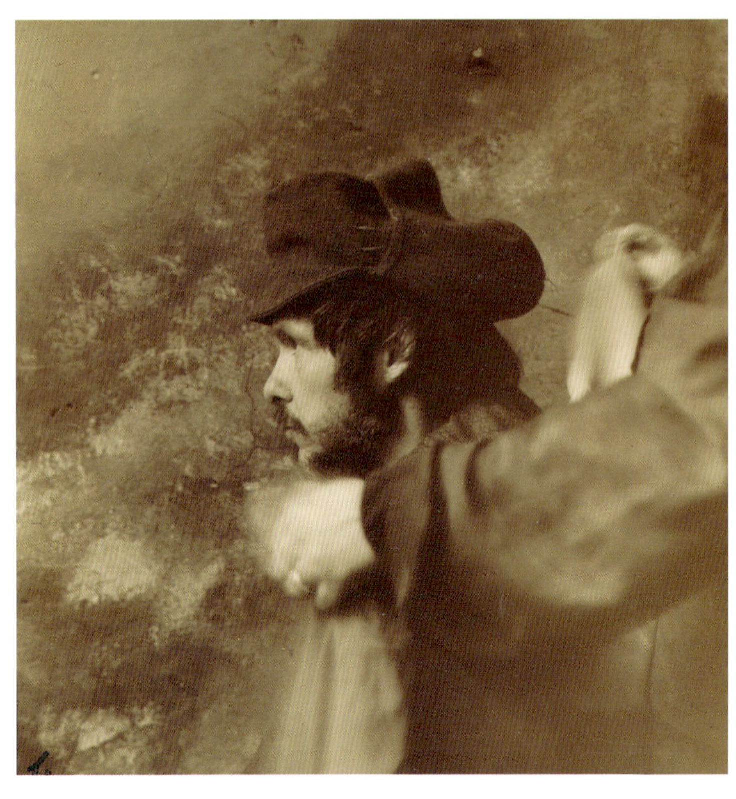

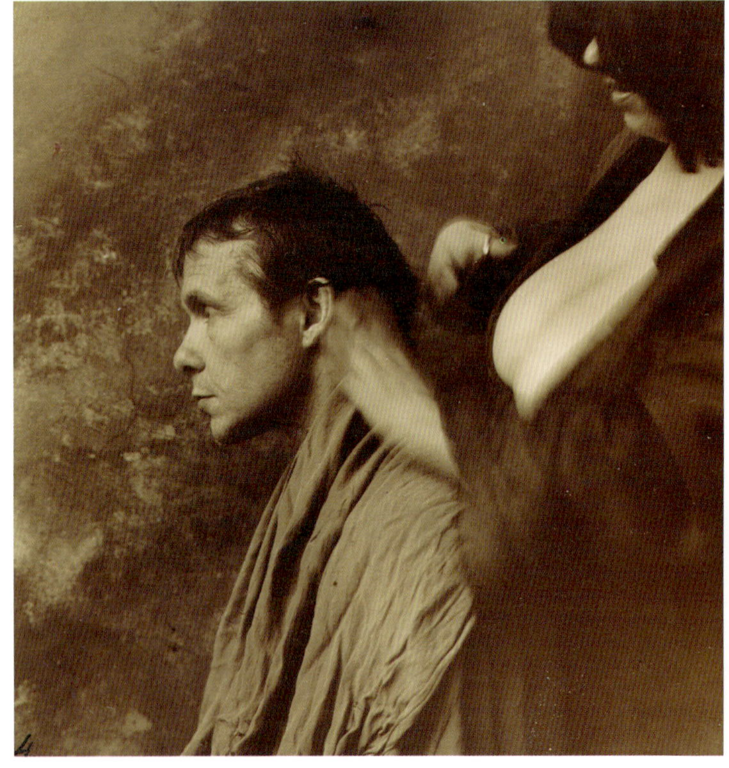

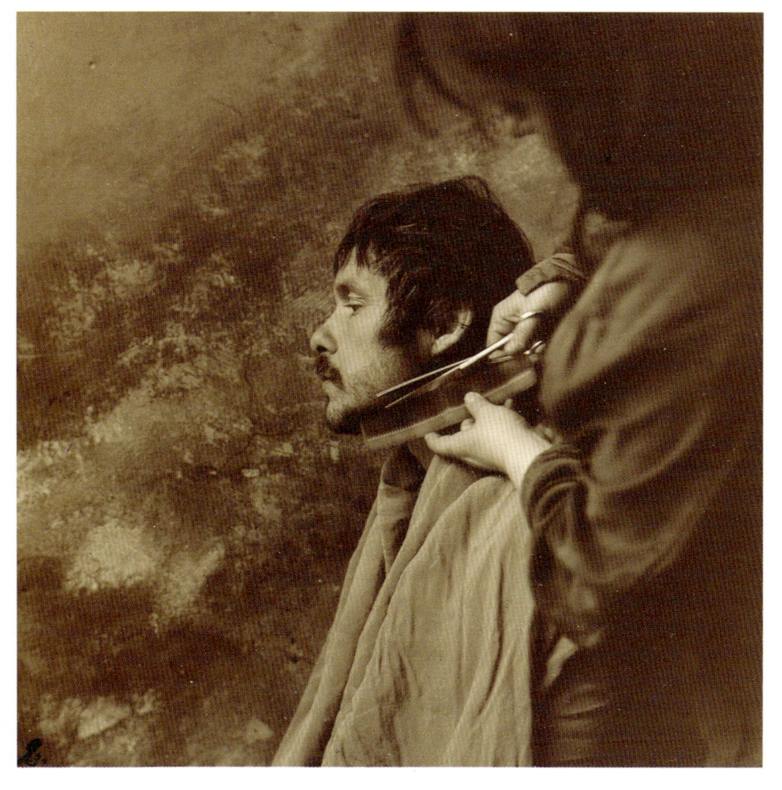

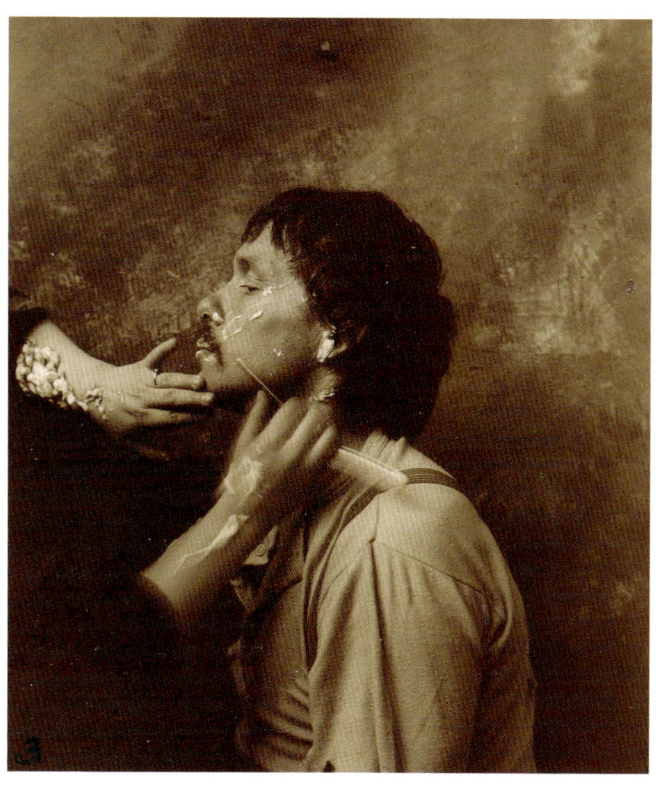

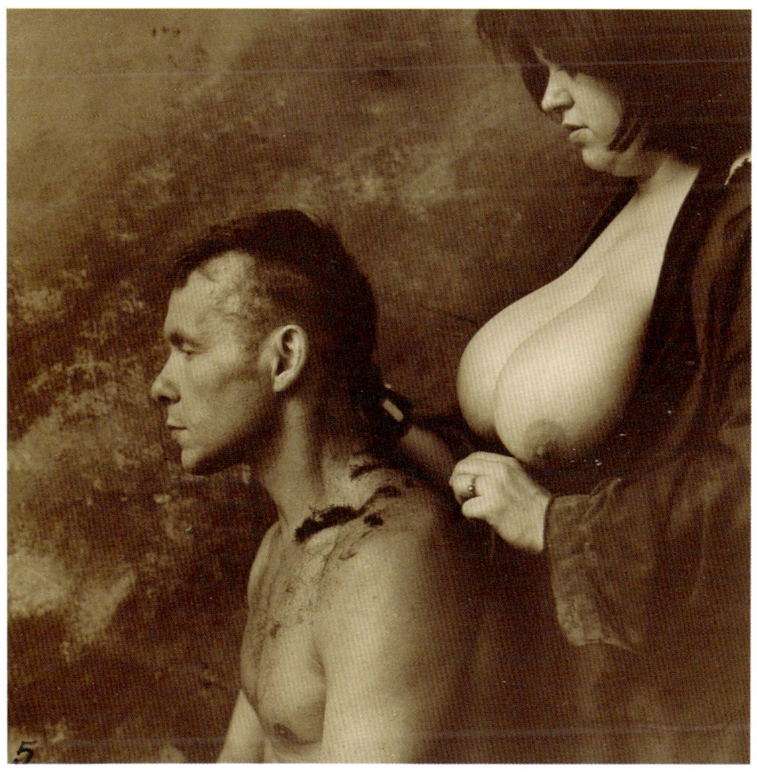
5

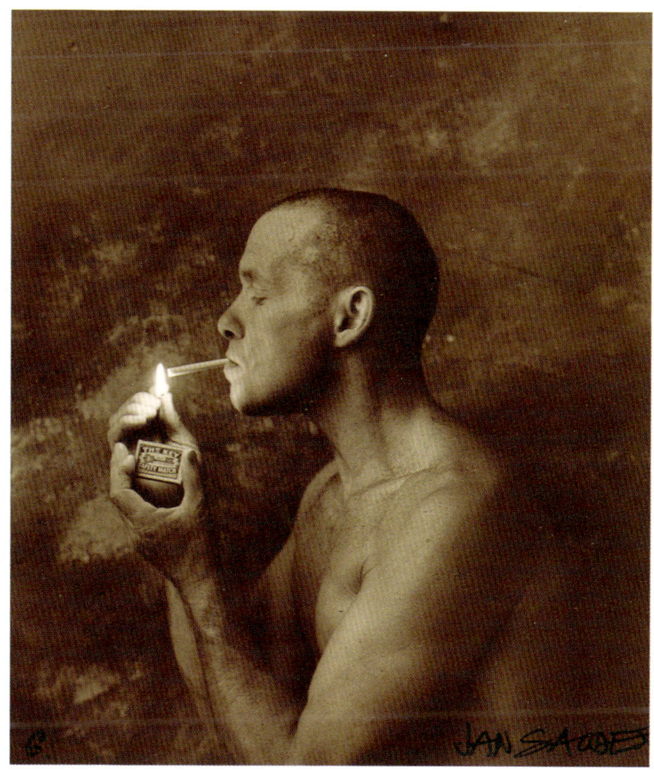
JAN SAUDEK

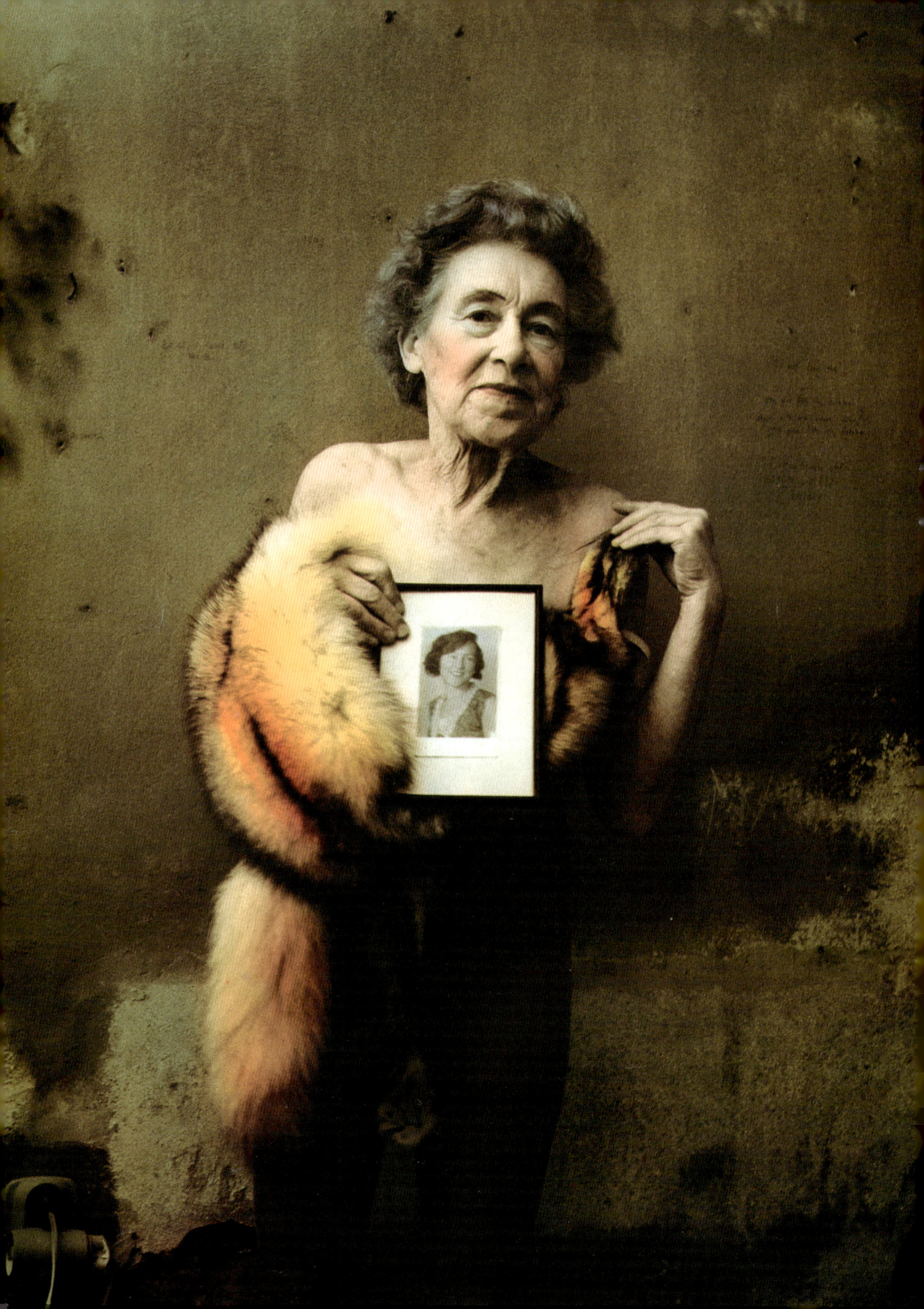

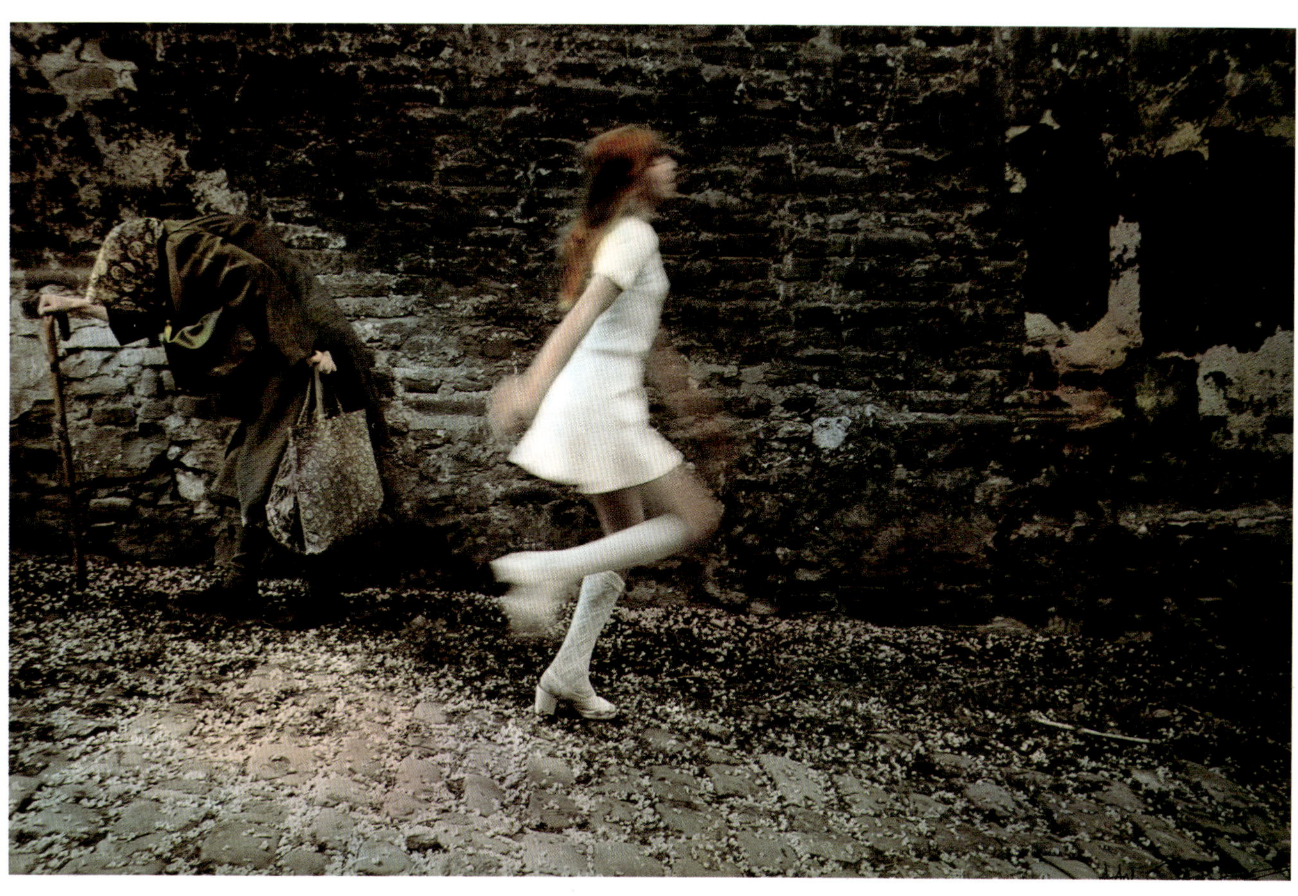

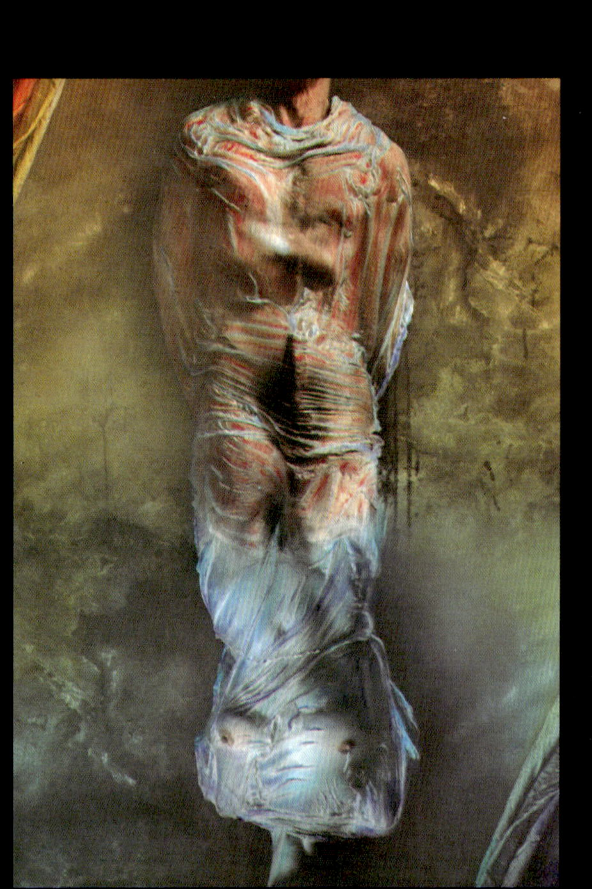

The Battle of the Sexes
Geschlechterkampf
La Lutte des Sexes

There is the world of men and that of women, and war is raging between them – and there'll be no end to it ... as long as planet Earth keeps turning ...

Es gibt ein Land der Männer und ein Land, in dem die Frauen leben, und zwischen diesen beiden Ländern herrscht Krieg – ein endloser Krieg ... bis ans Ende aller Tage ...

Il y a un pays où vivent les hommes et un pays où vivent les femmes, et la guerre fait rage entre les deux – une guerre sans fin ... jusqu'à la fin du monde

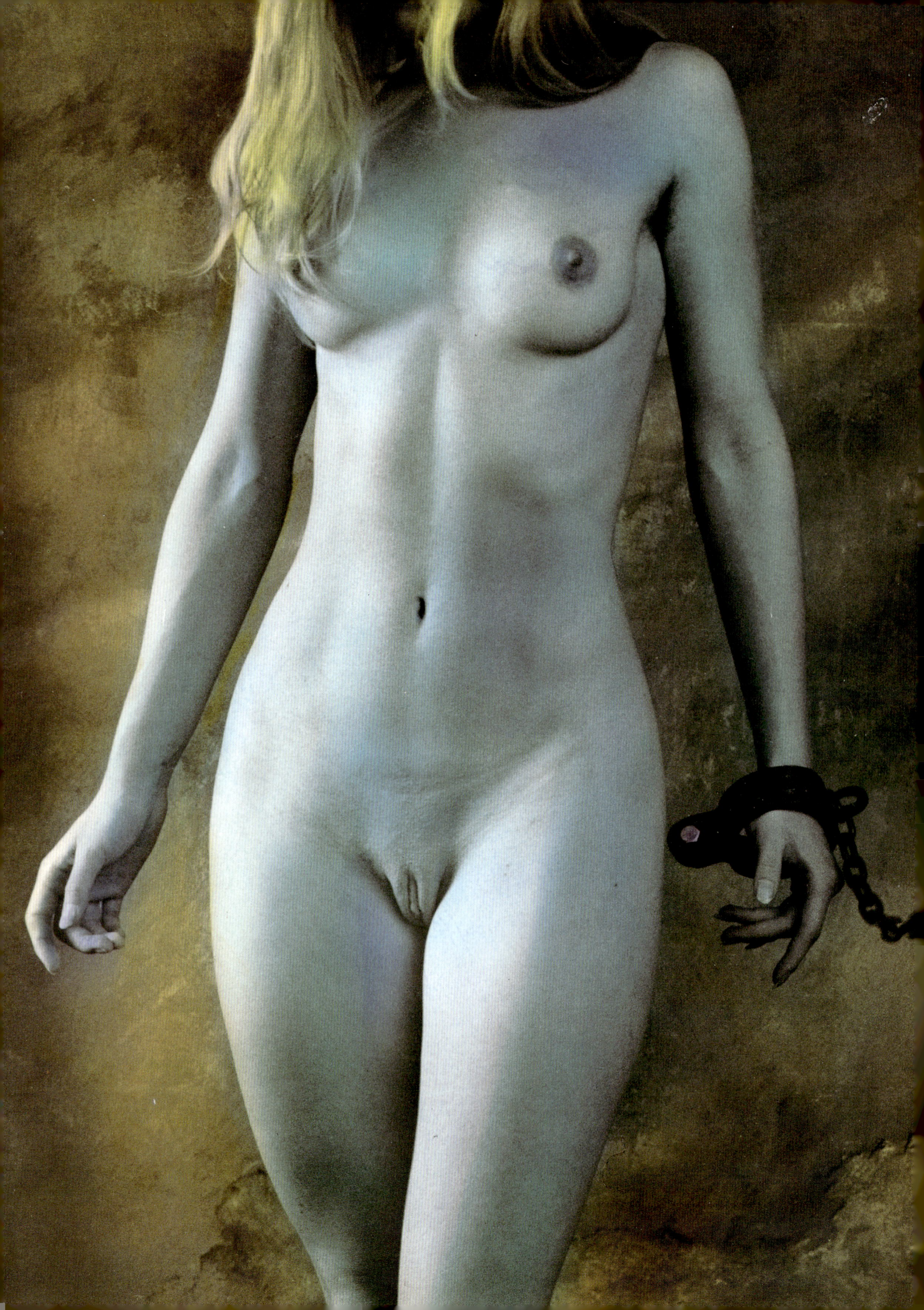

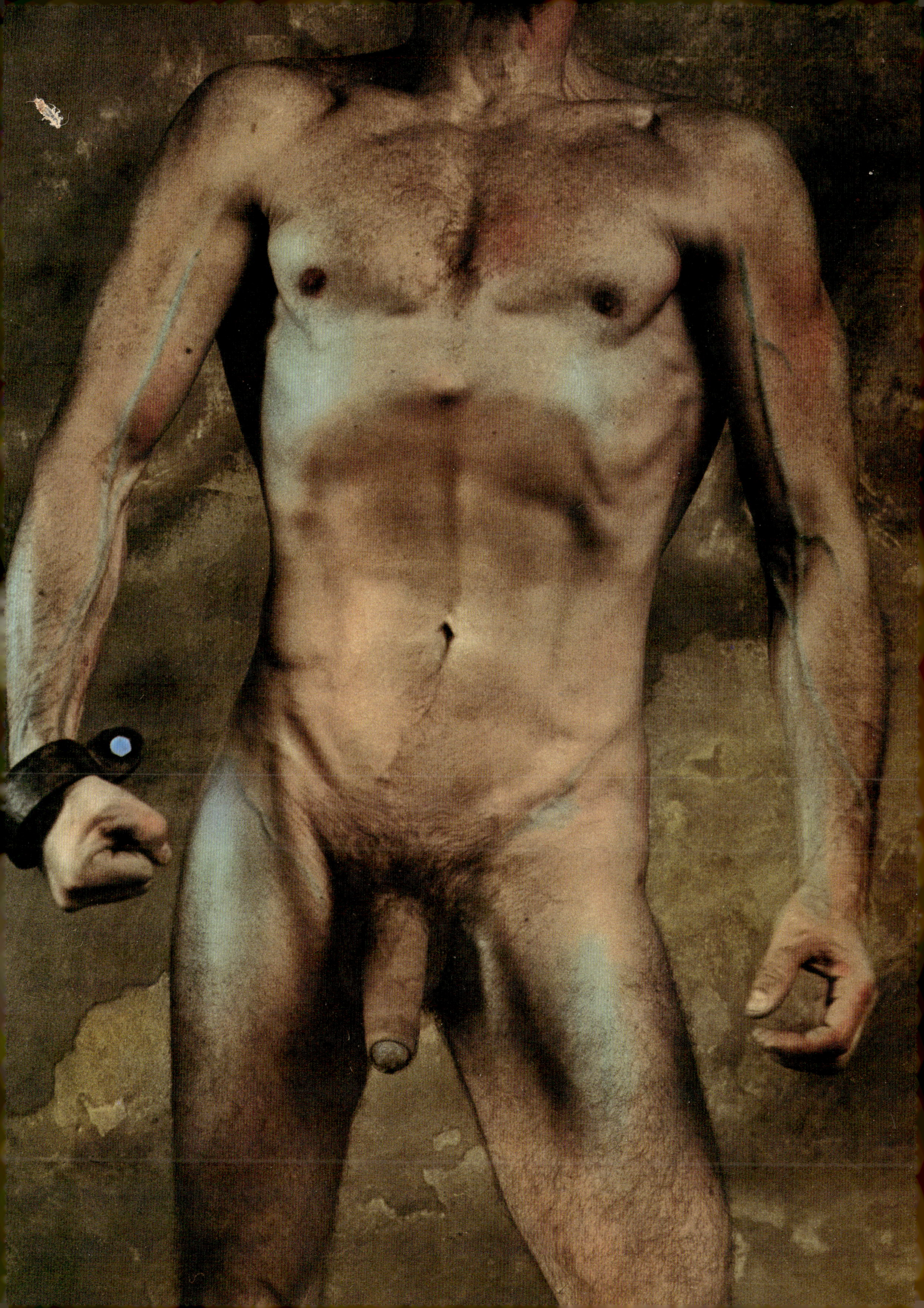

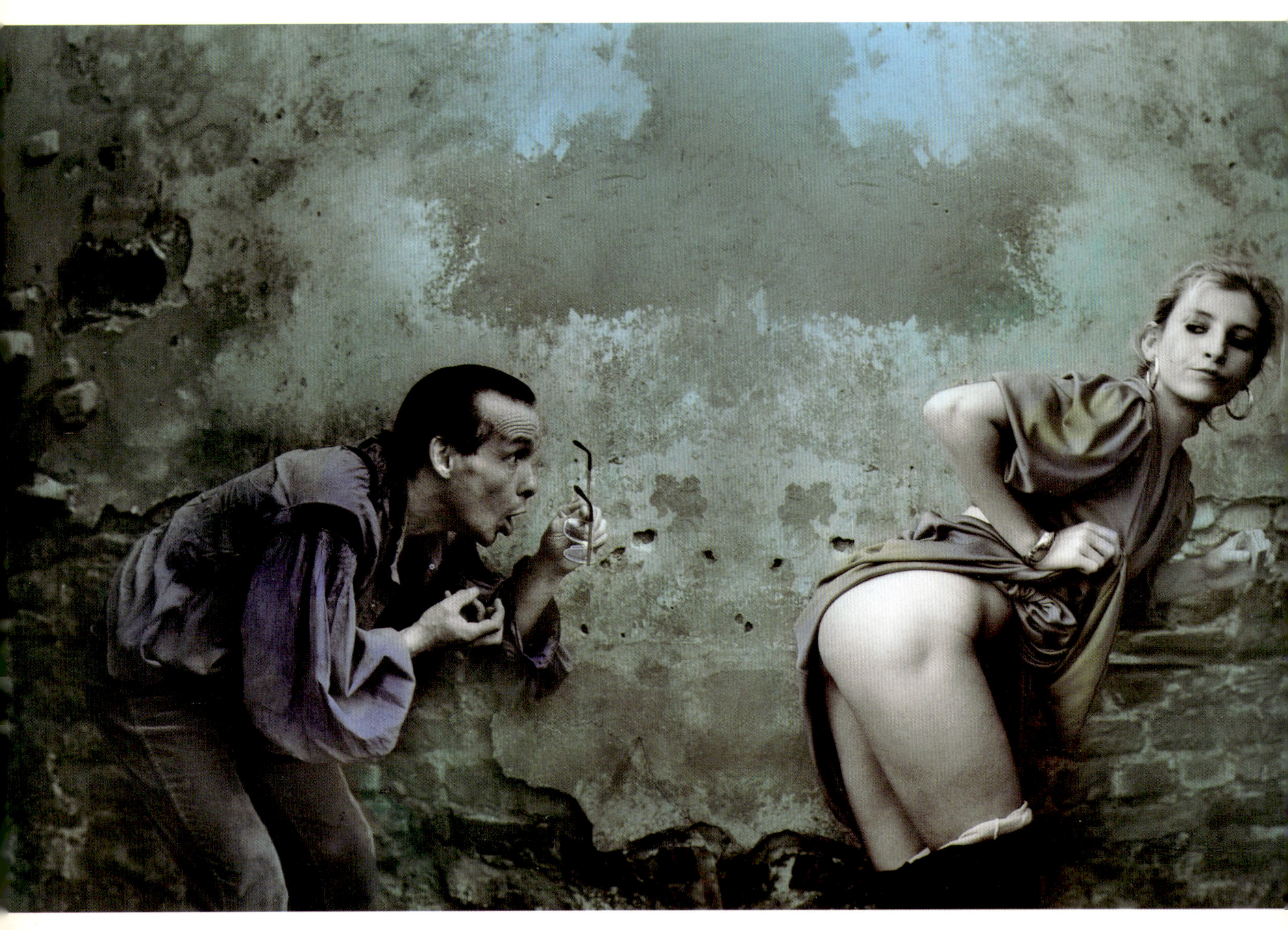

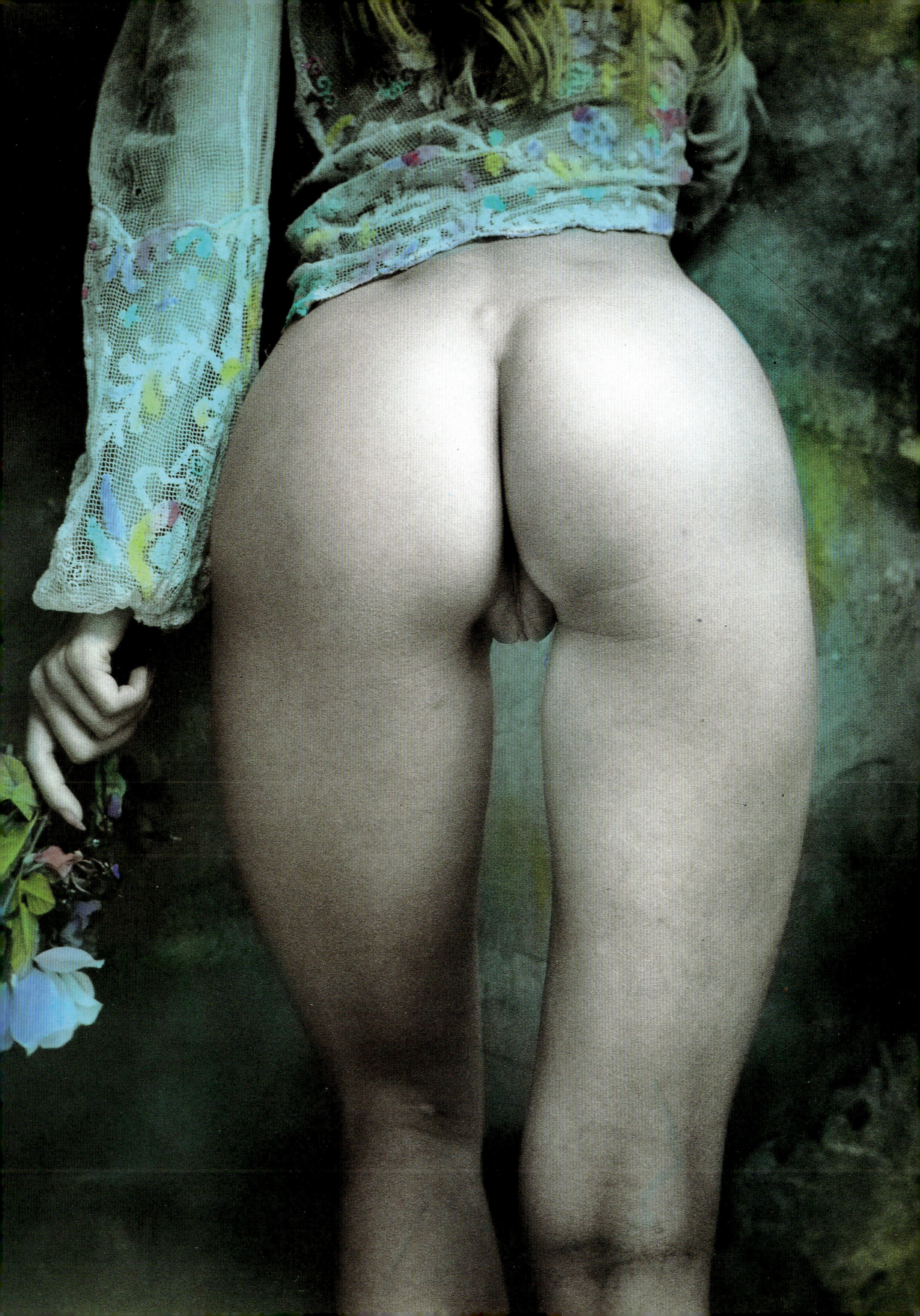

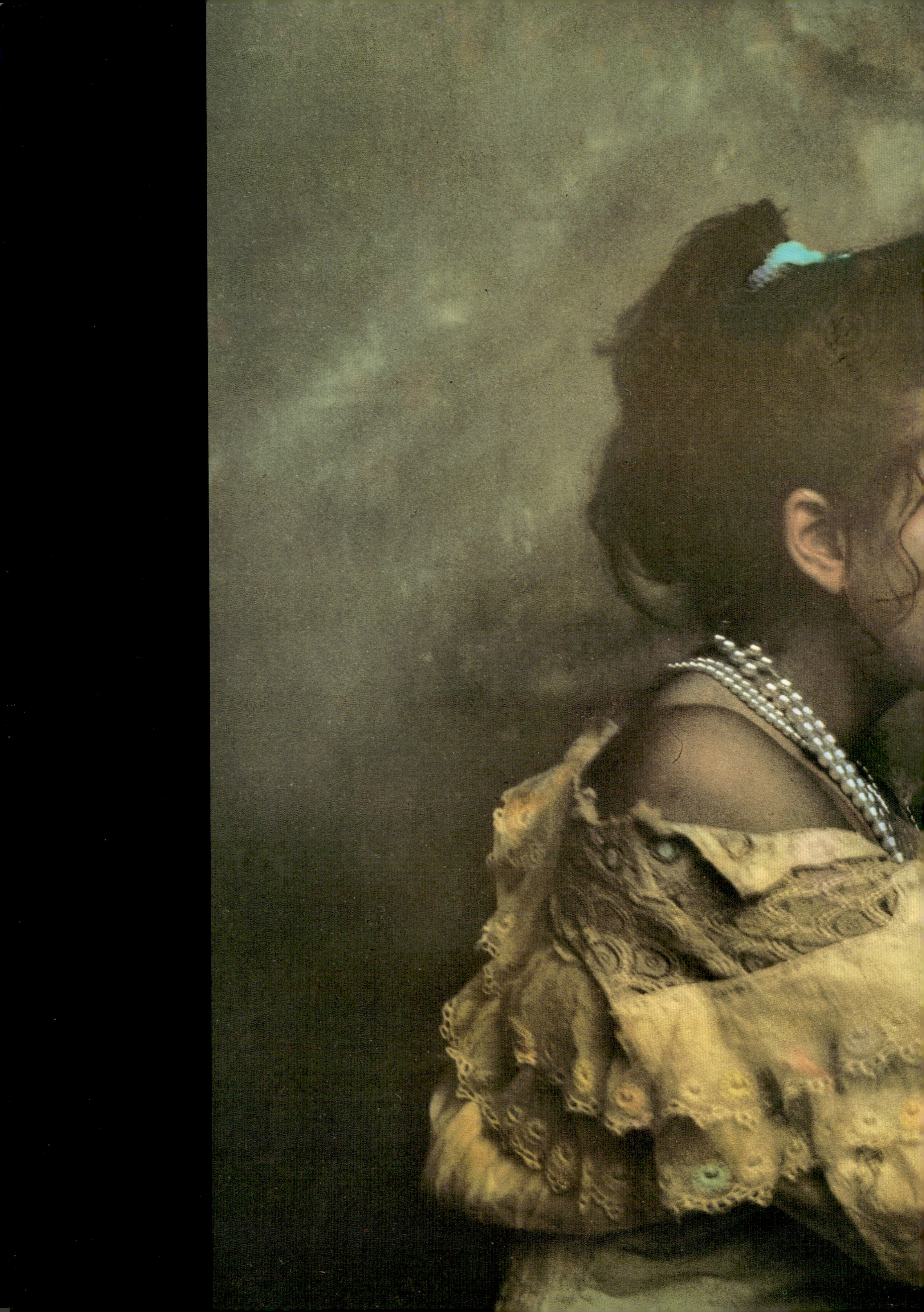

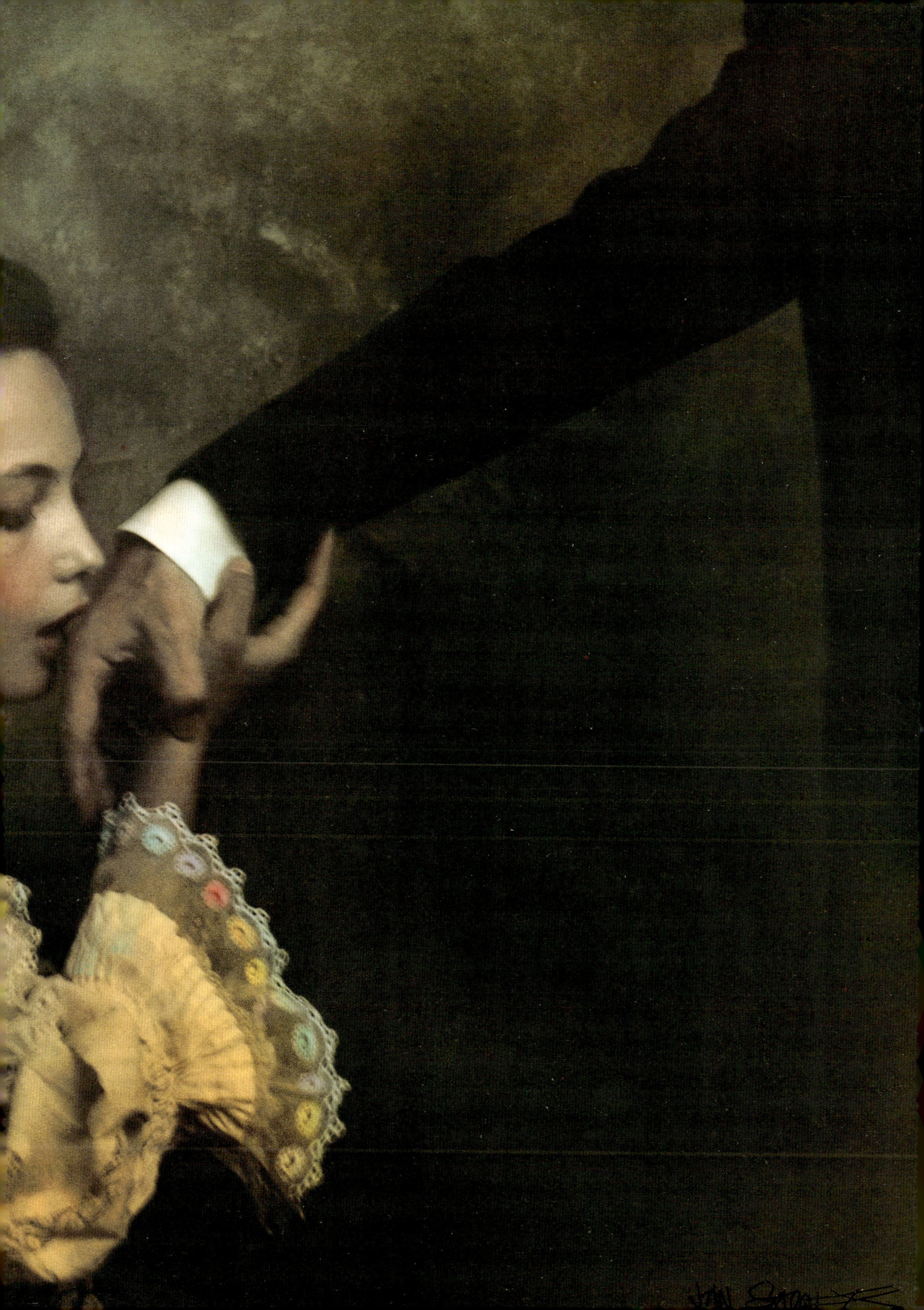

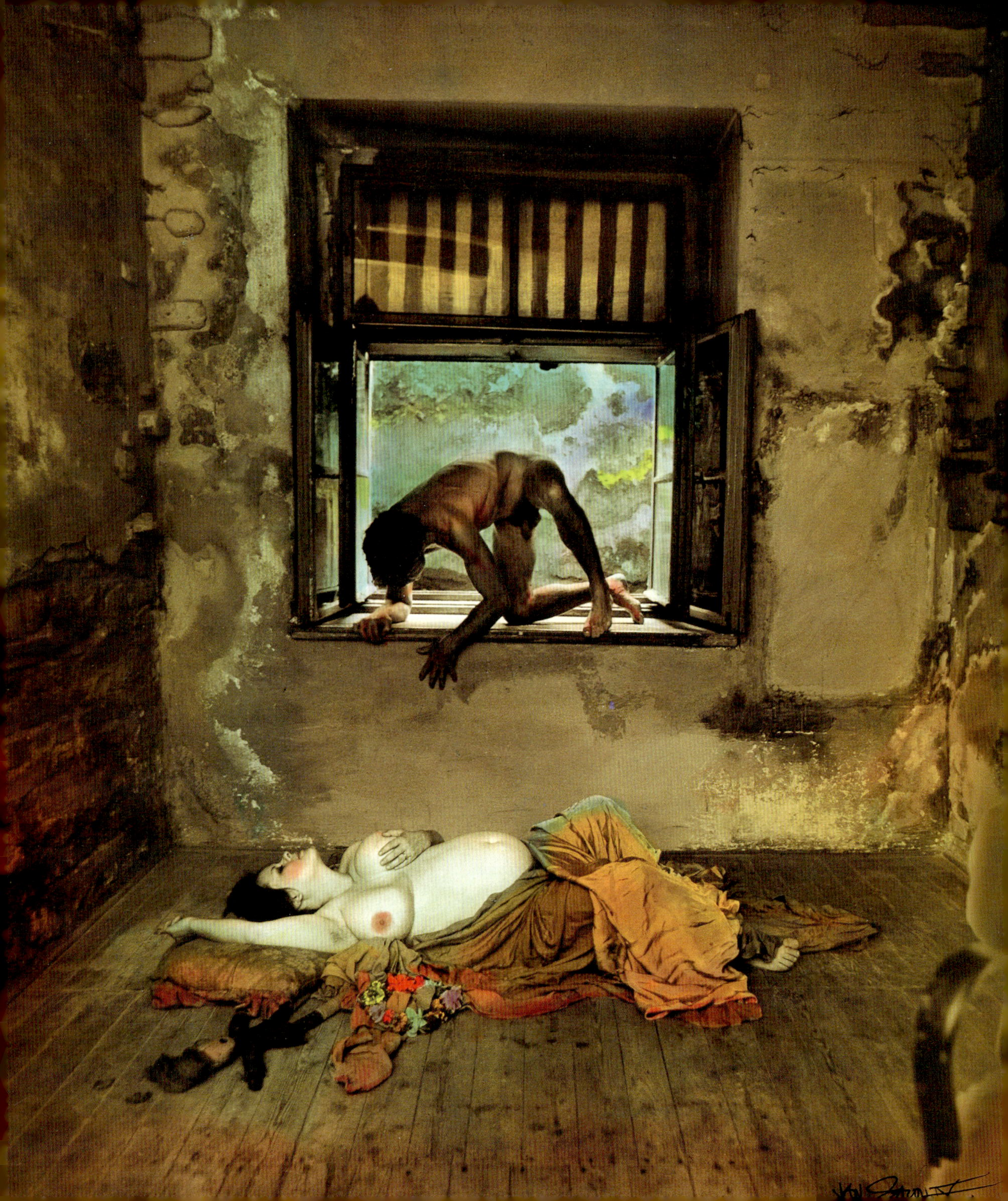

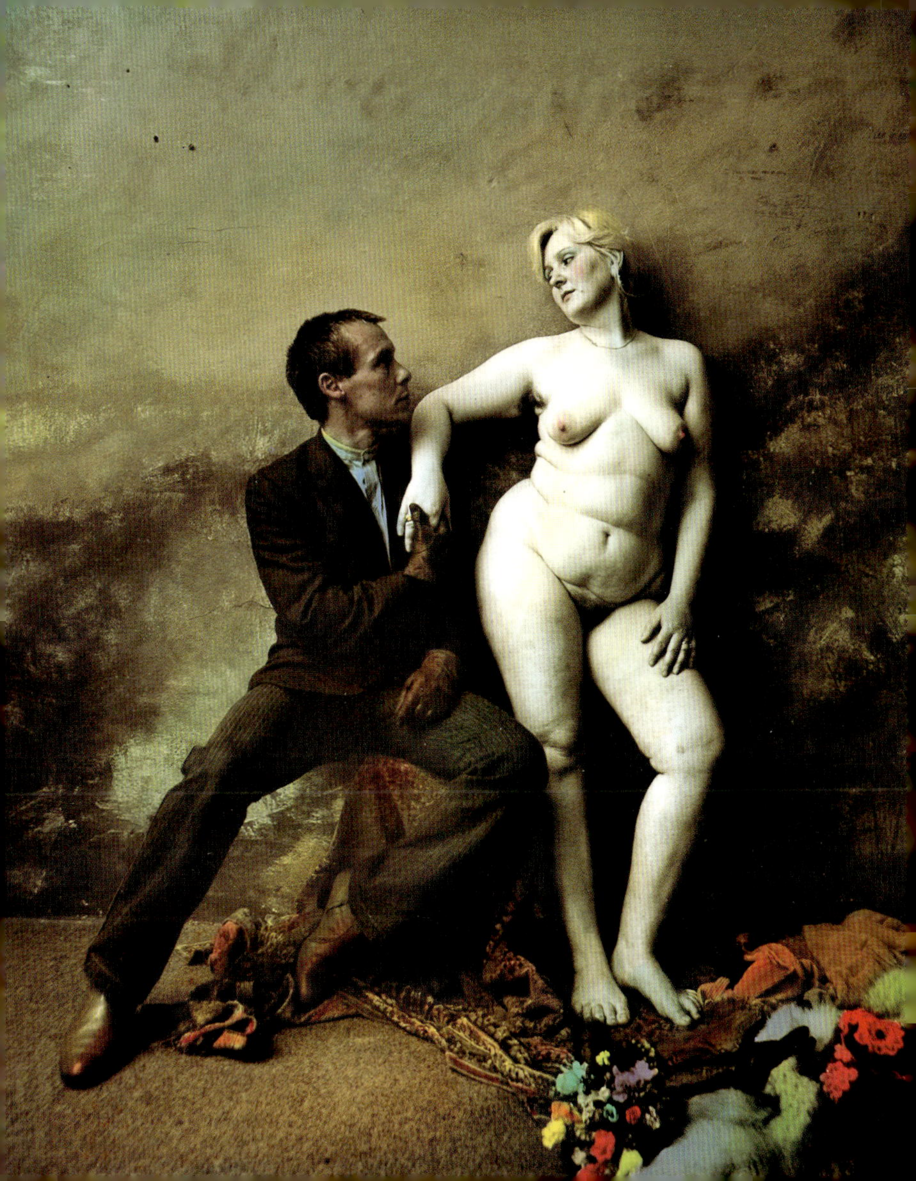

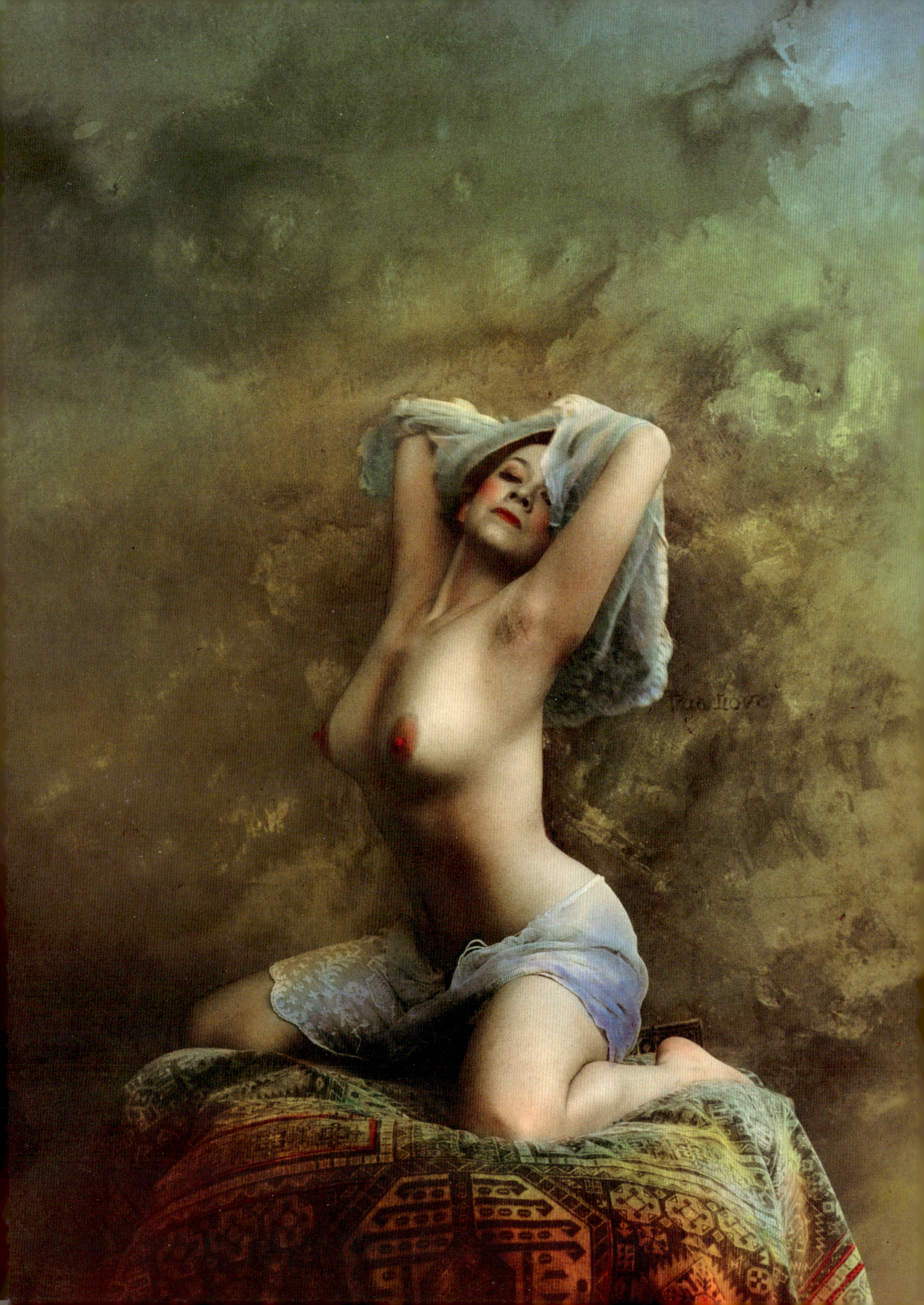

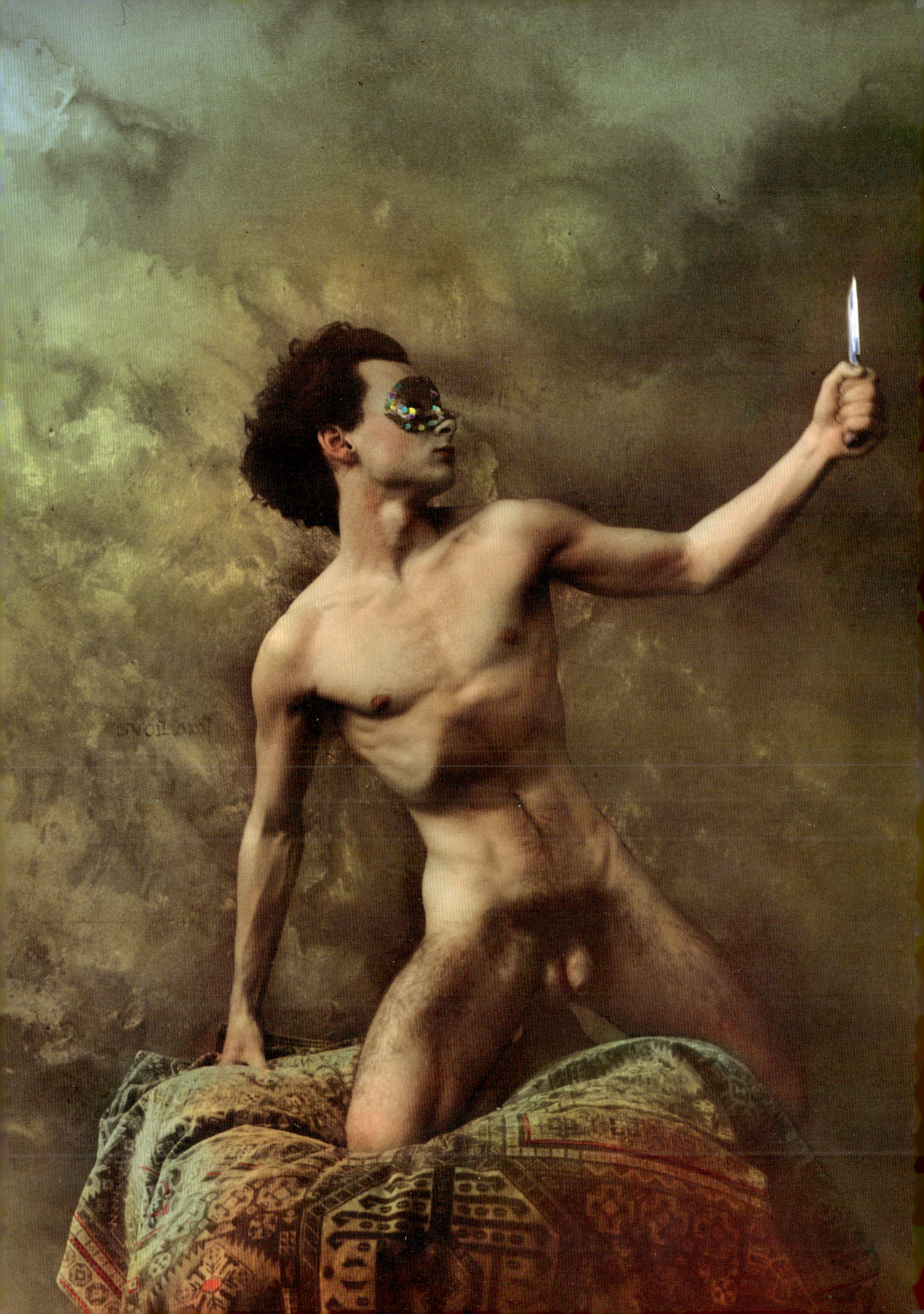

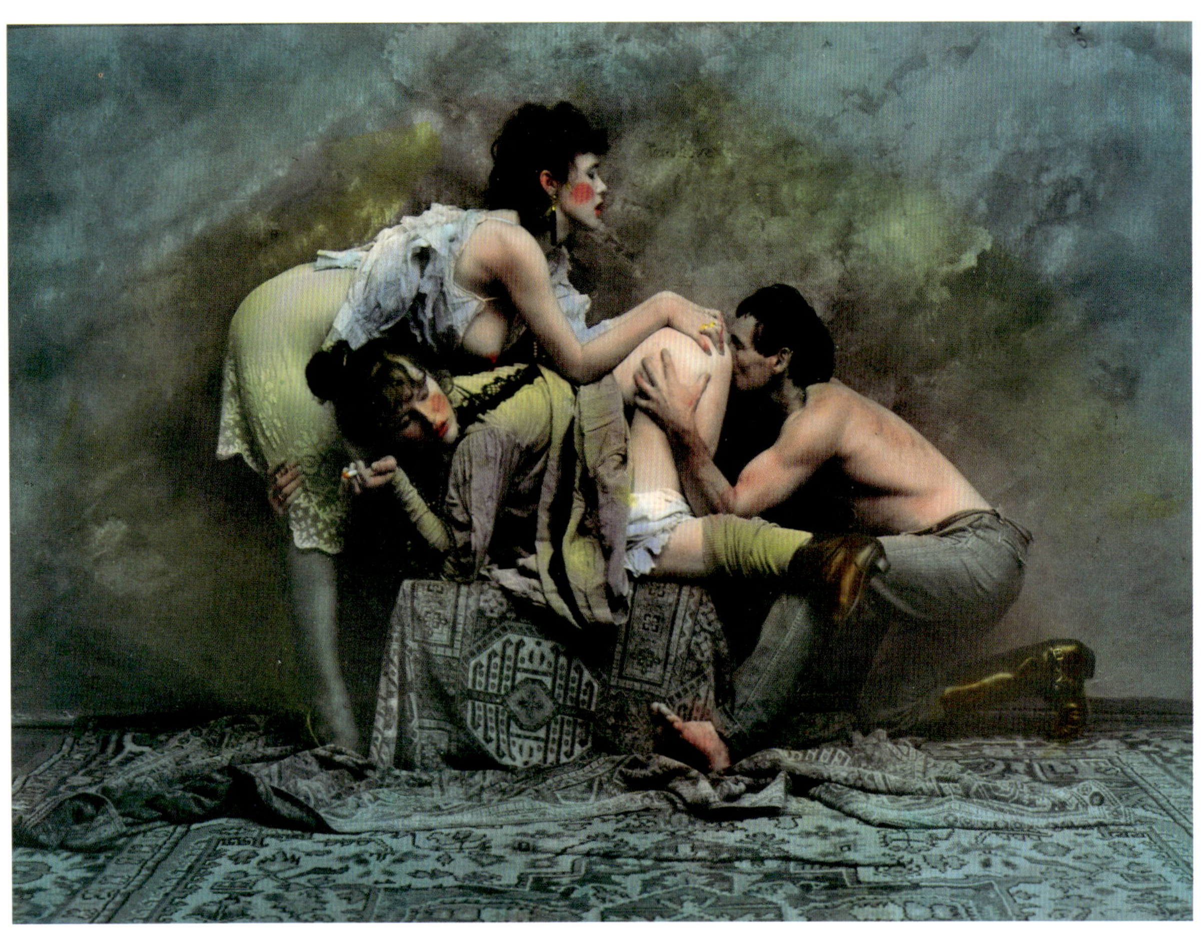

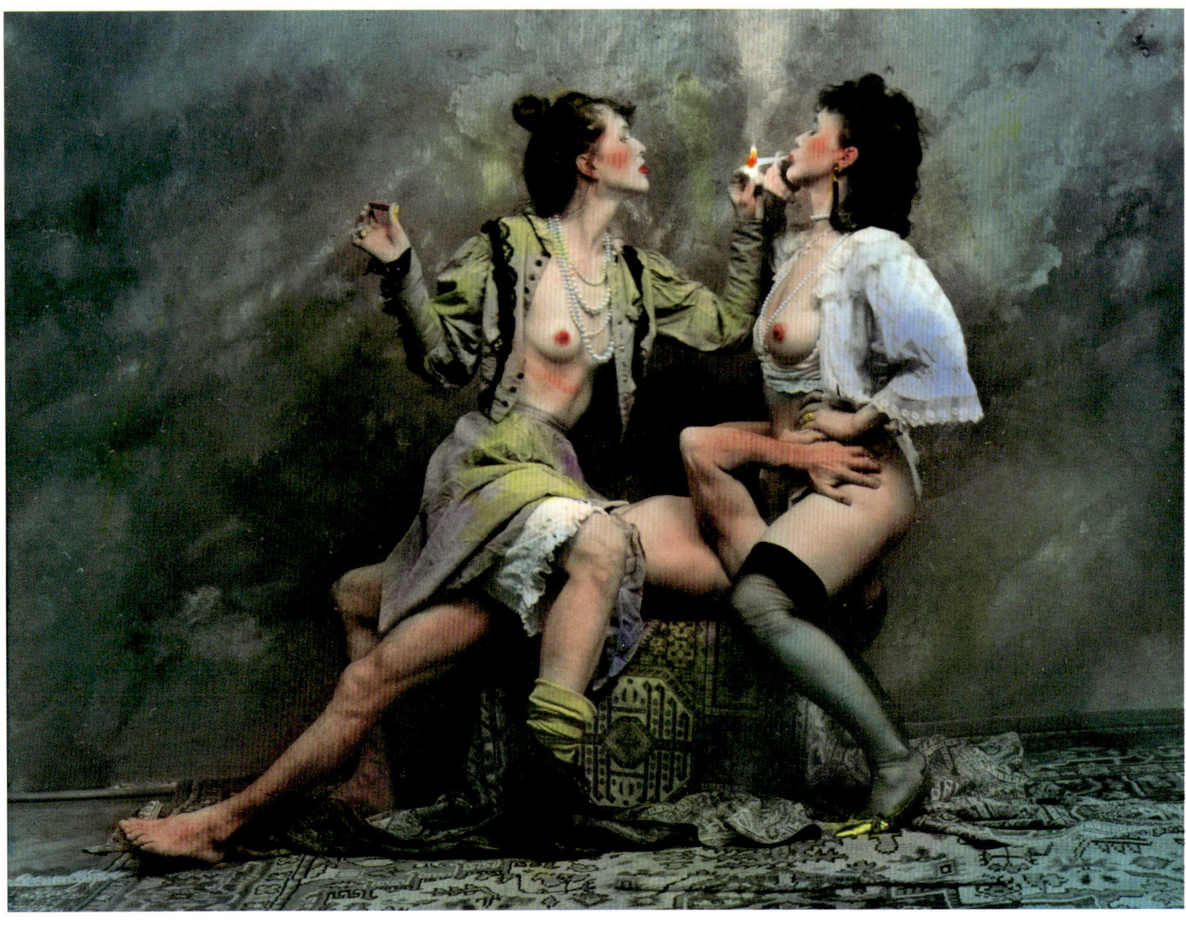

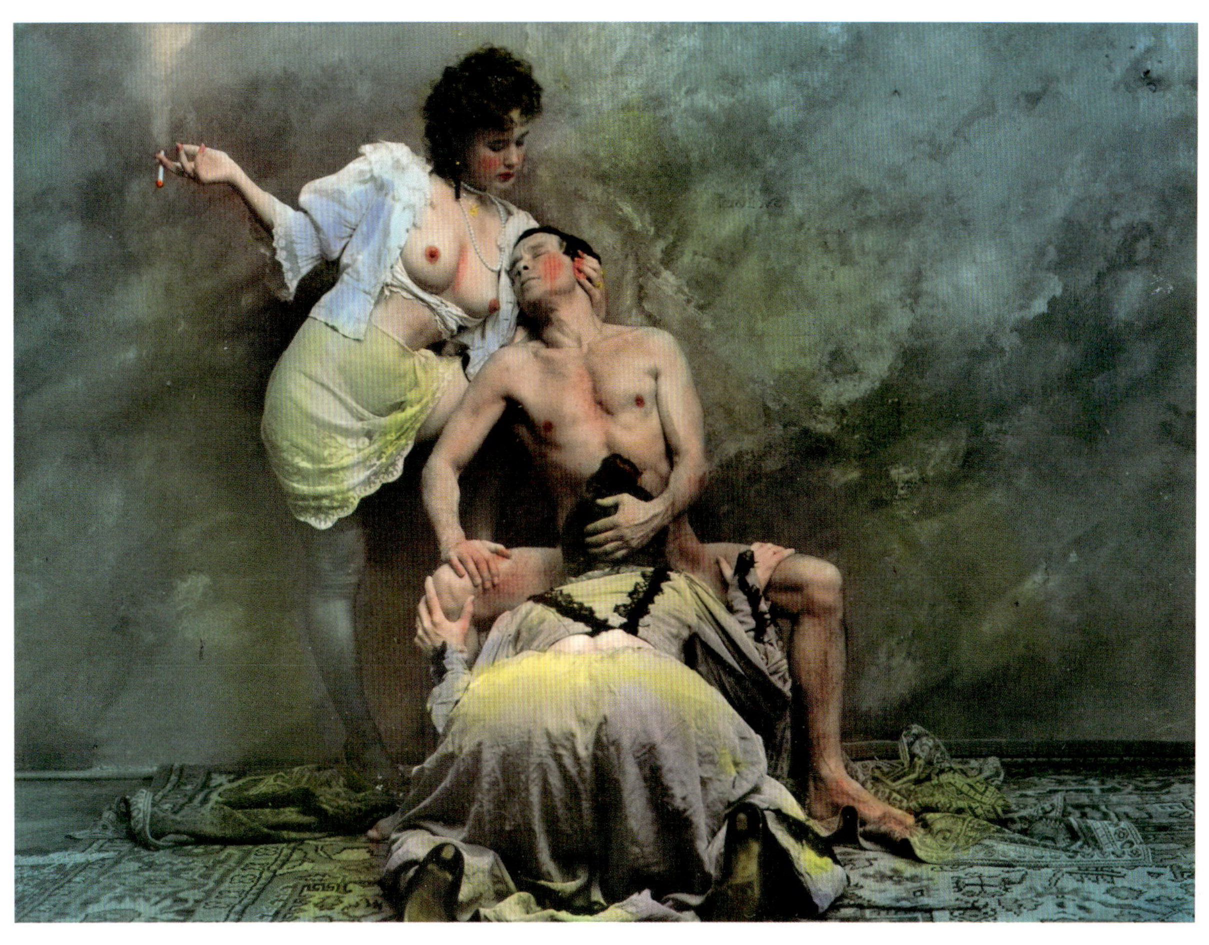

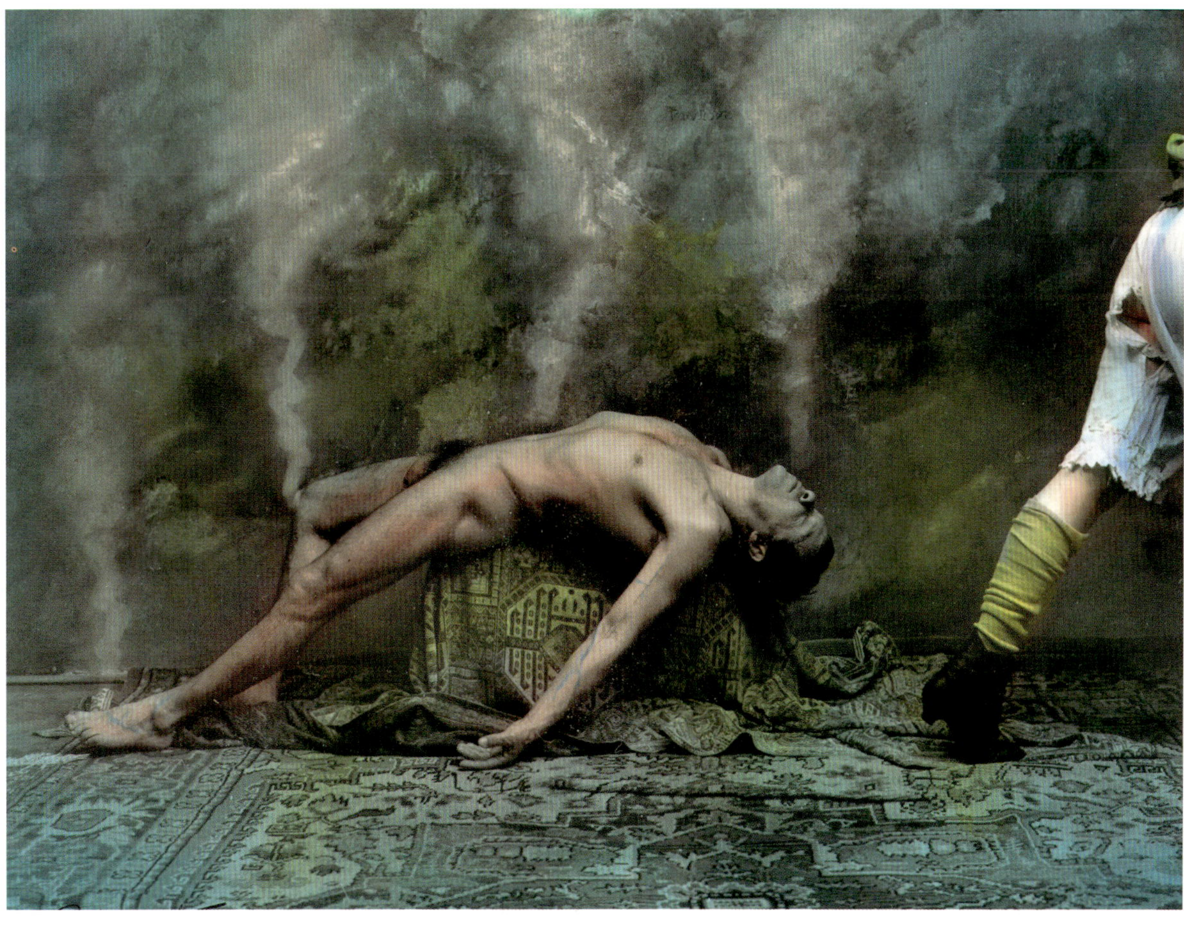

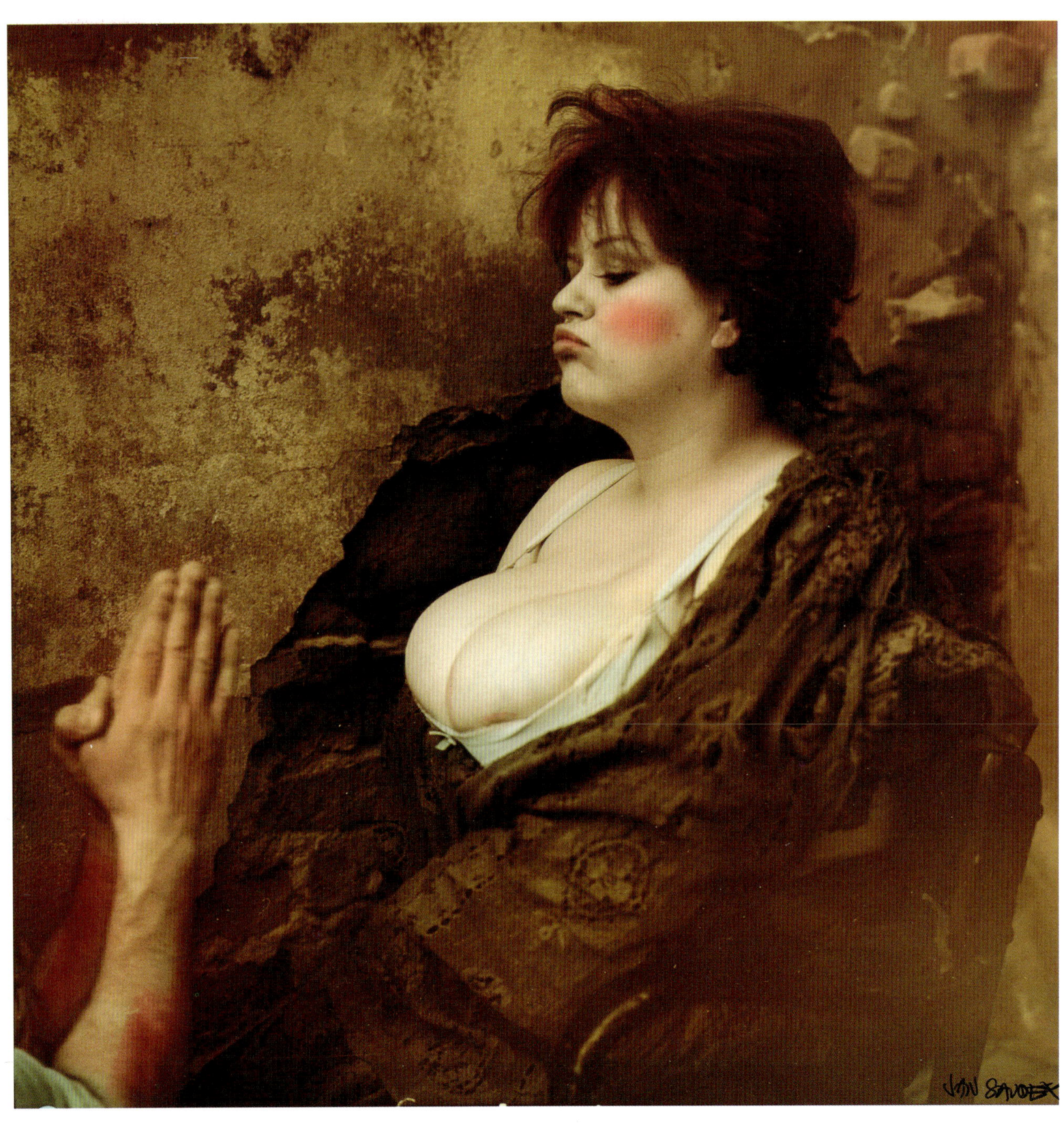

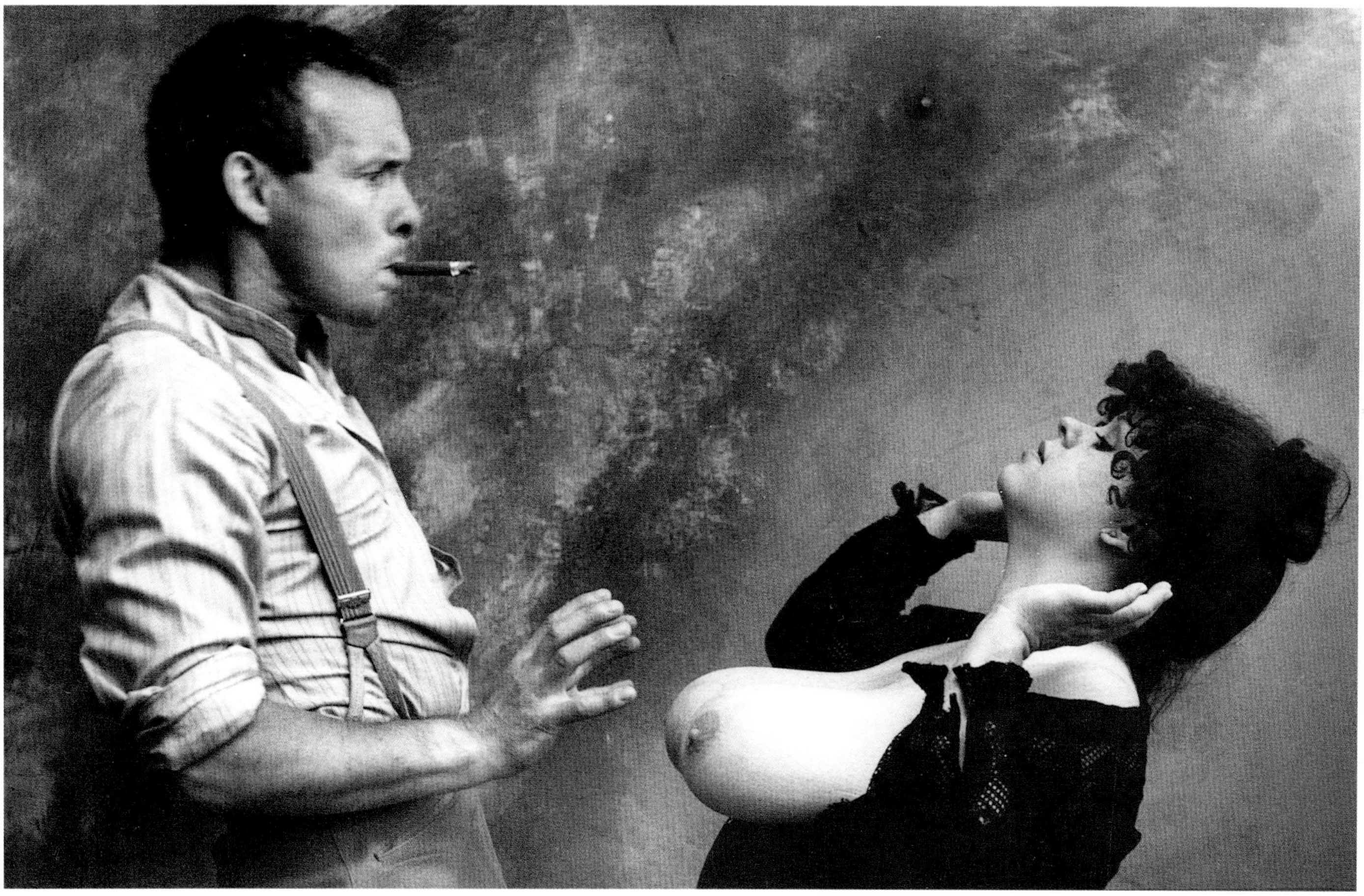

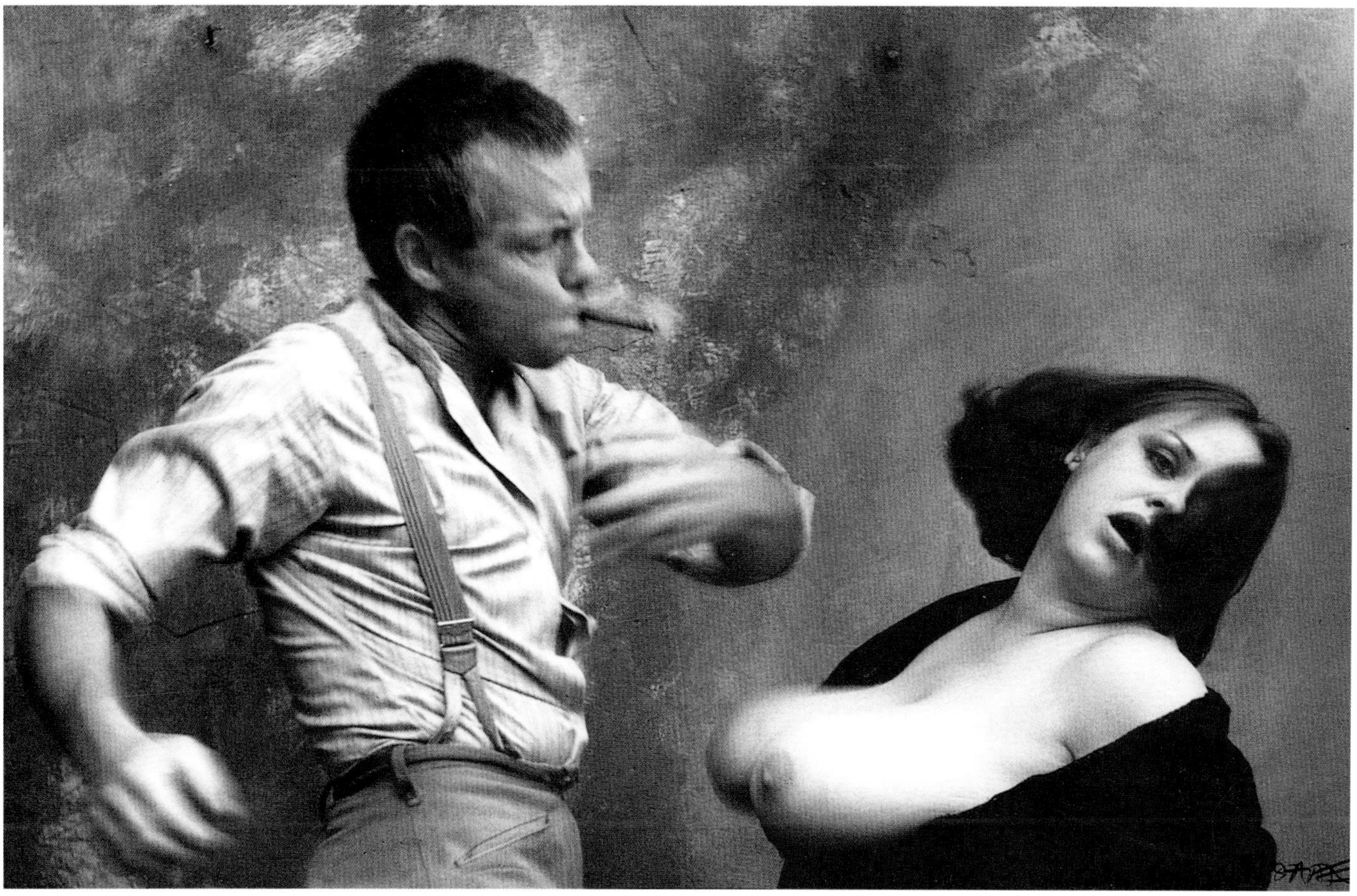

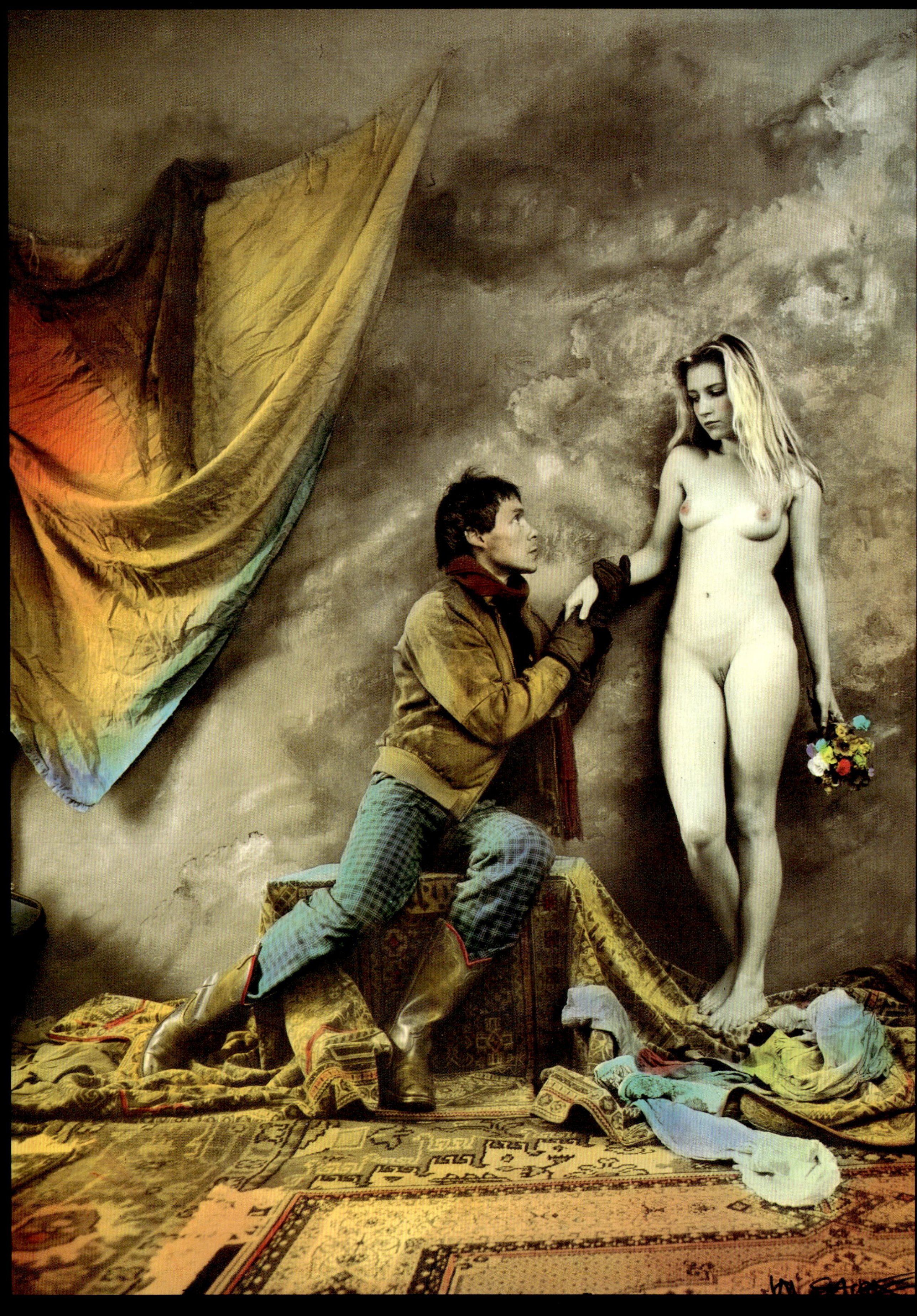

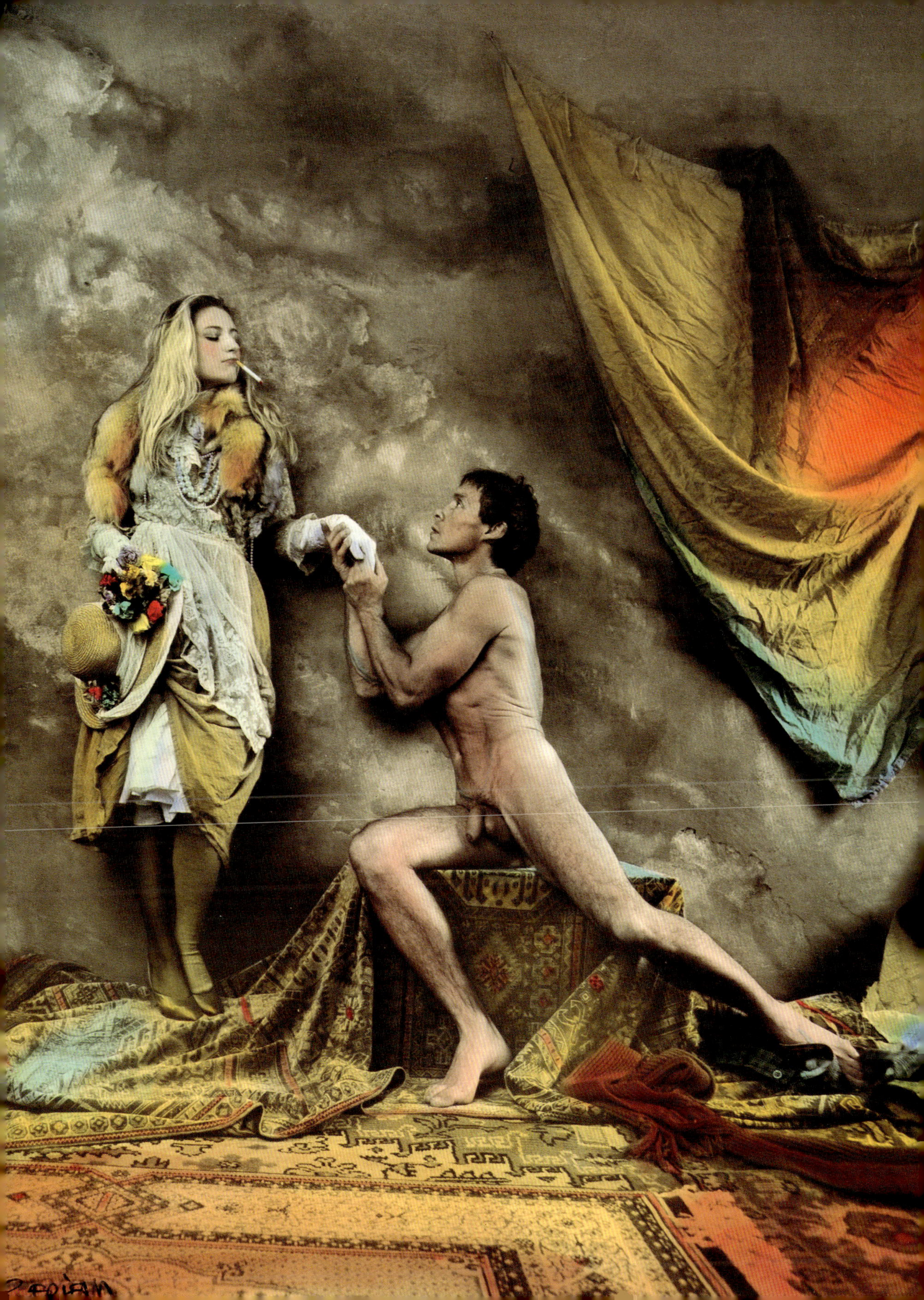

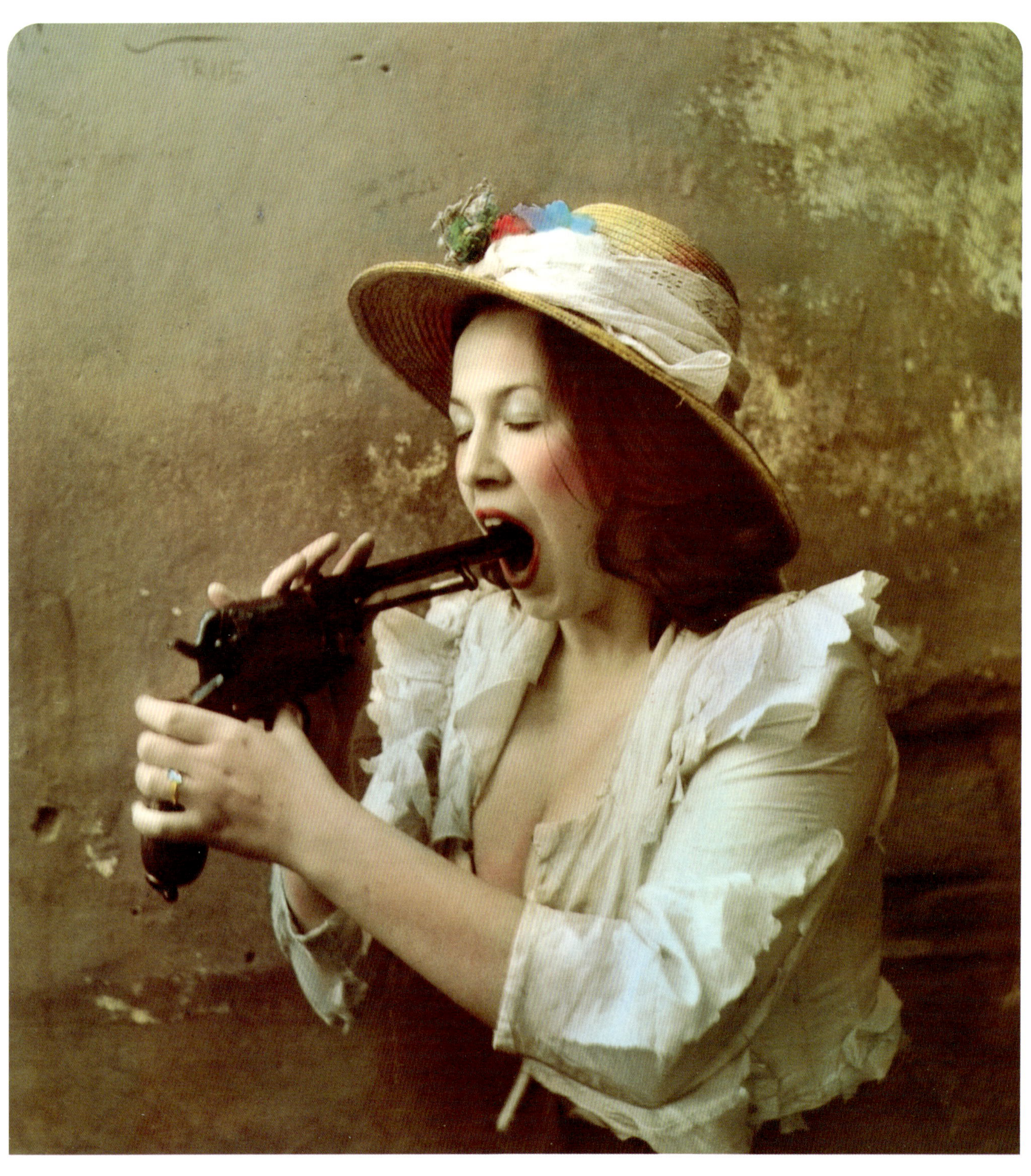

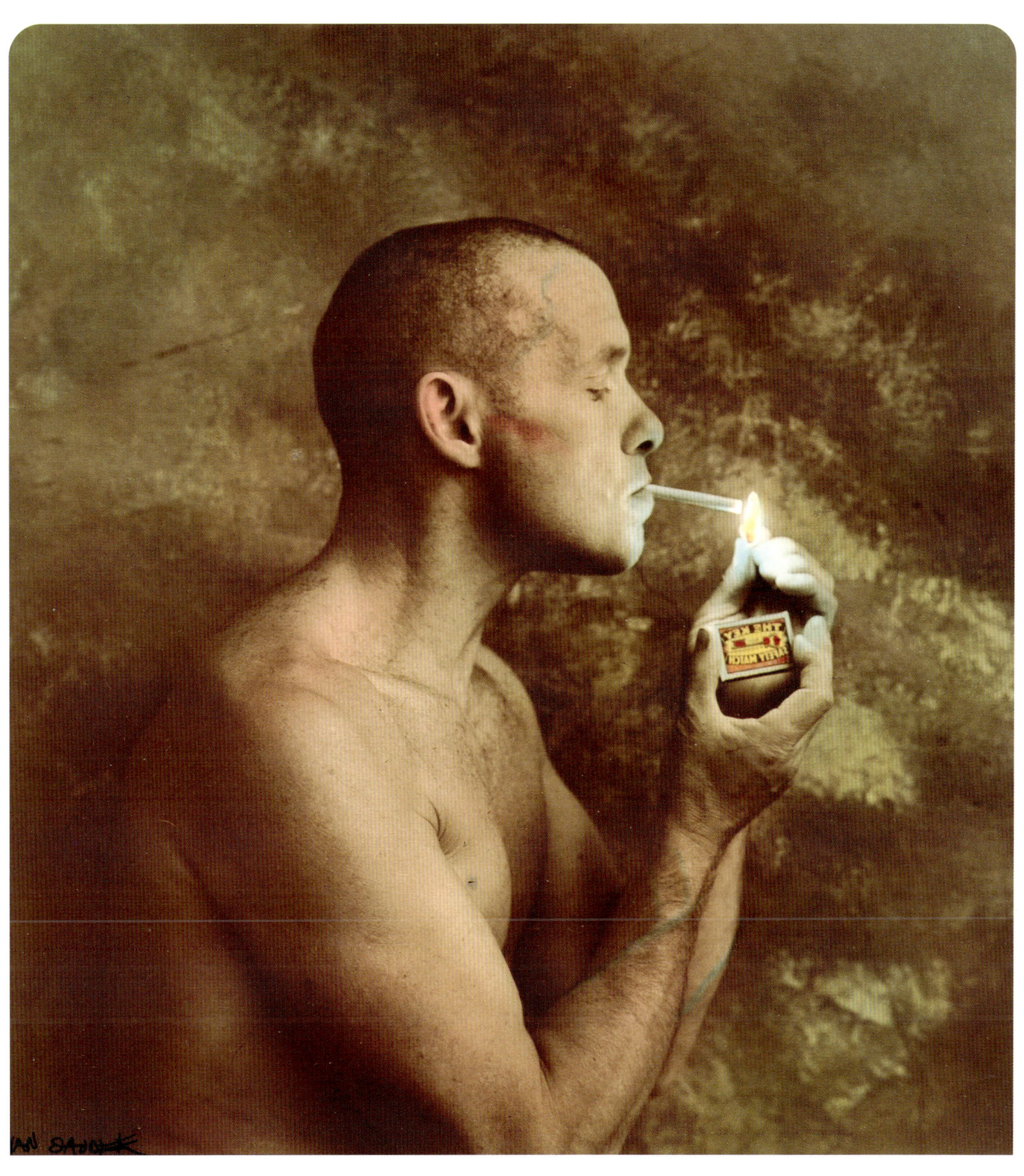

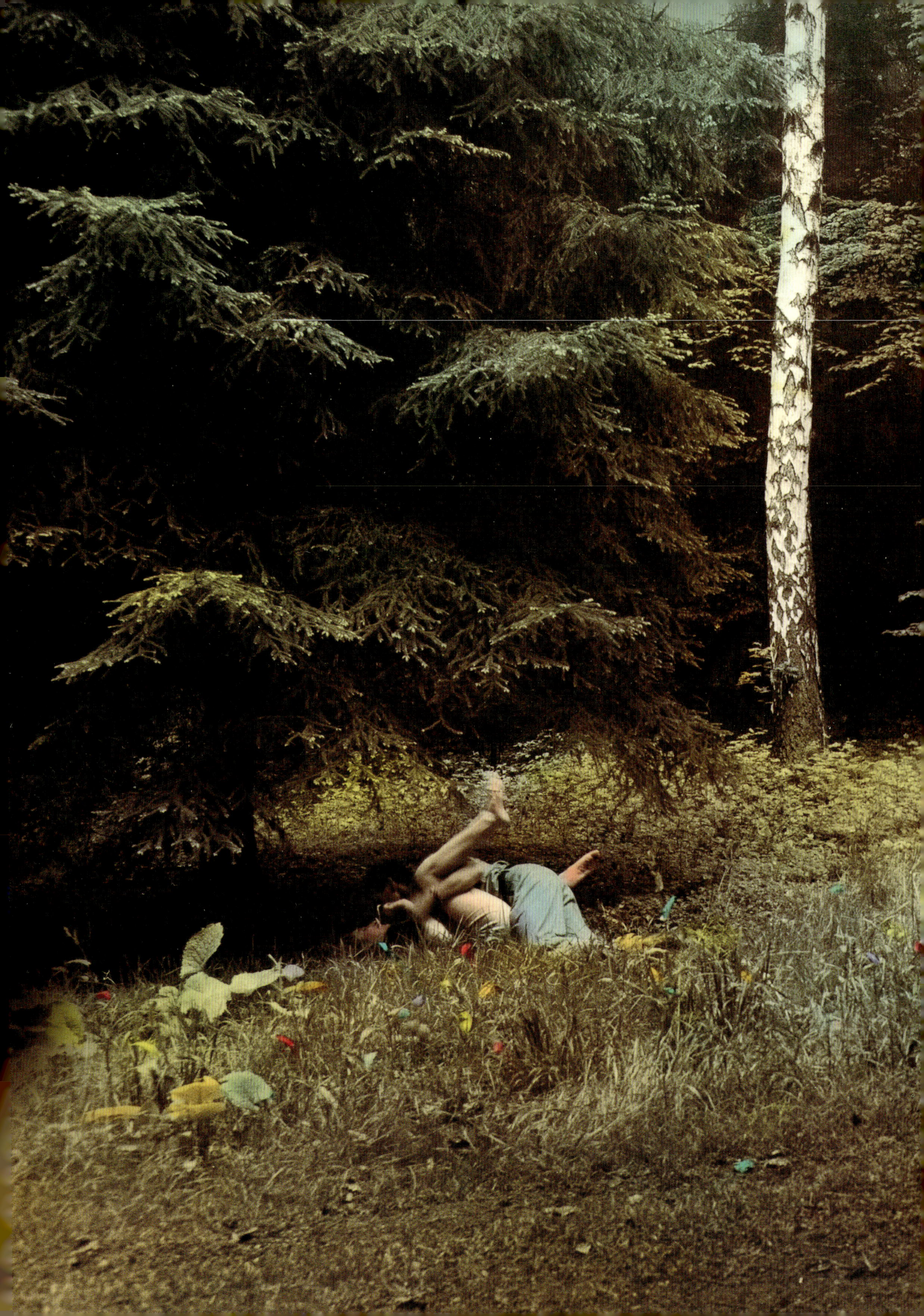

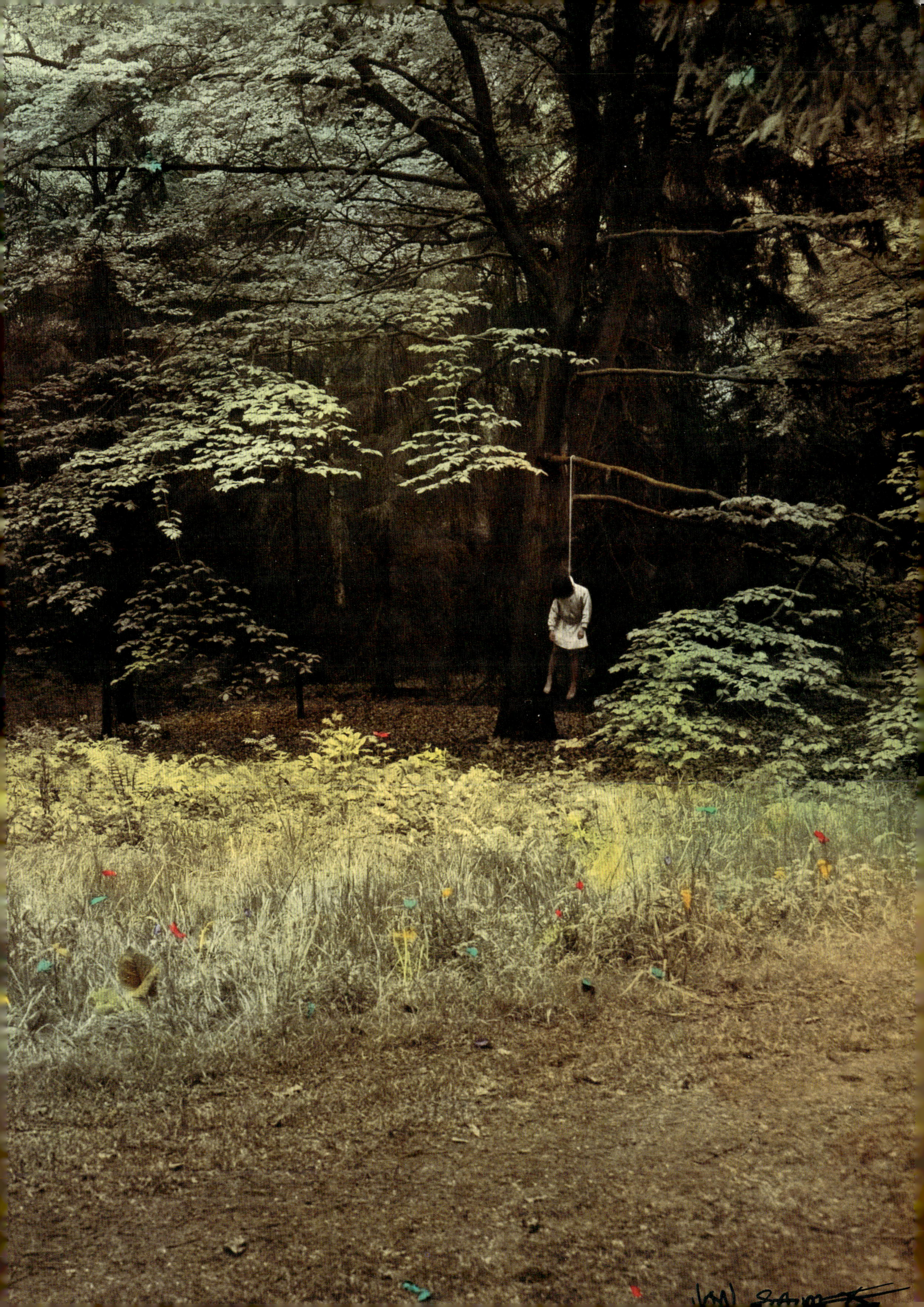

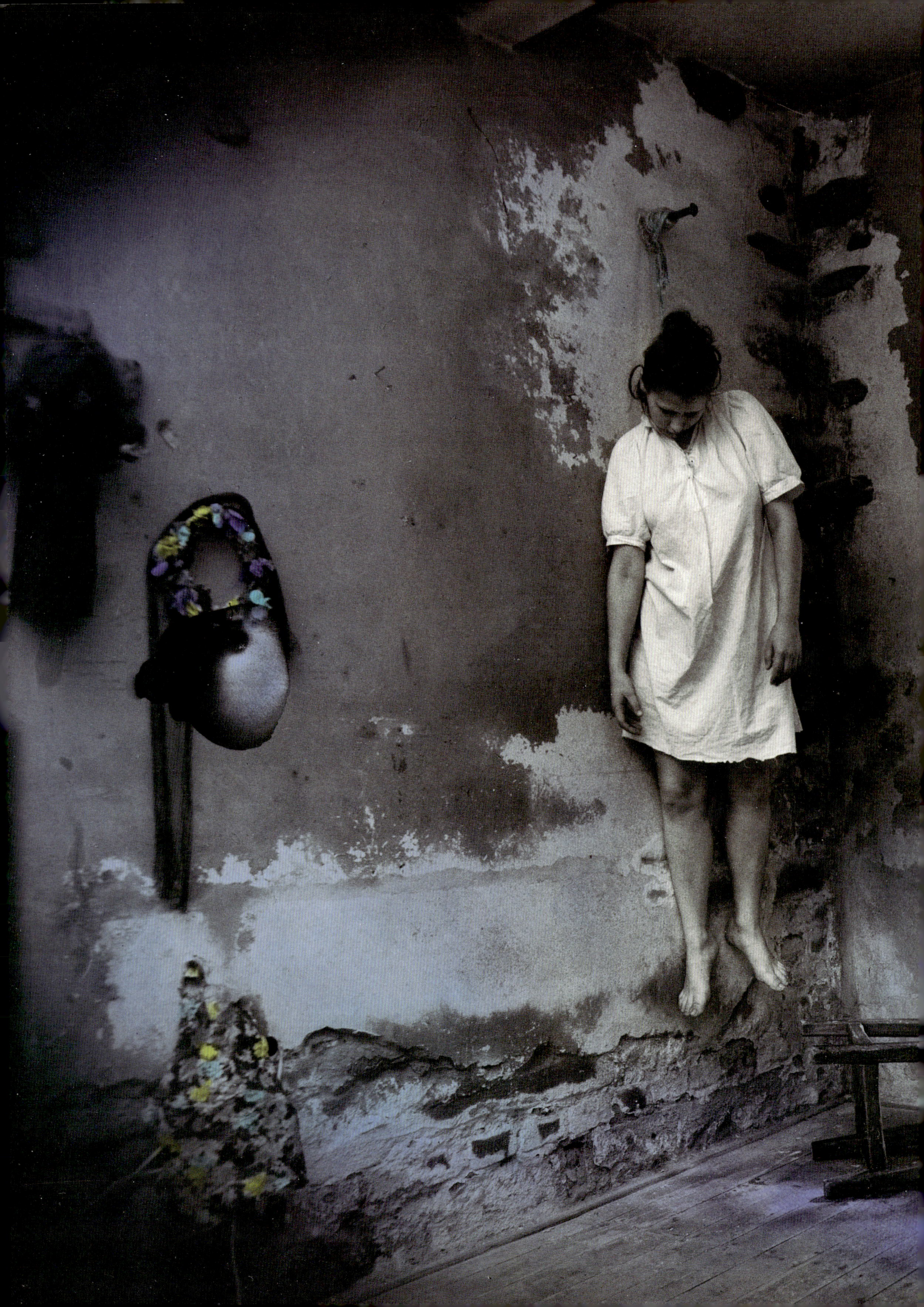

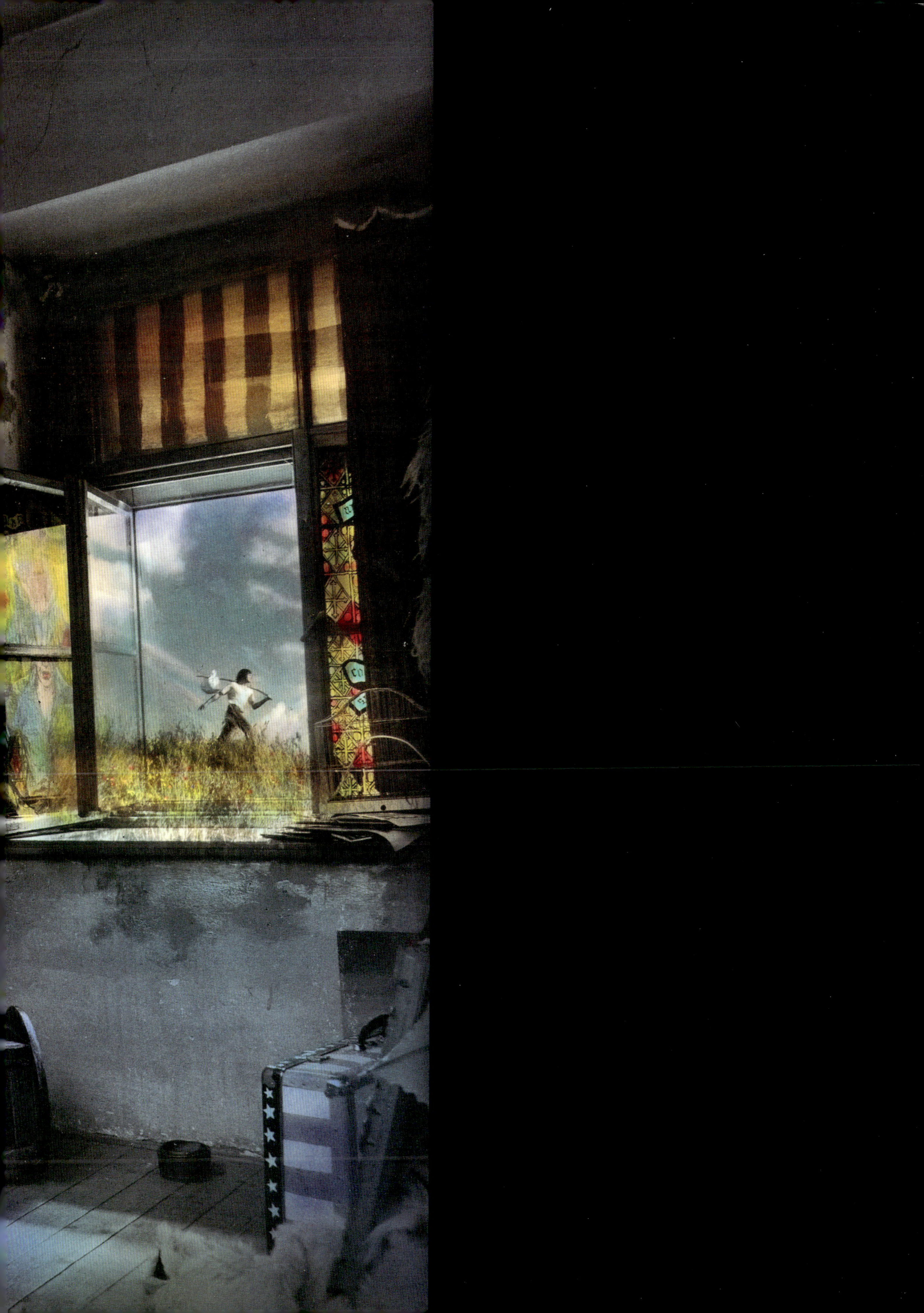

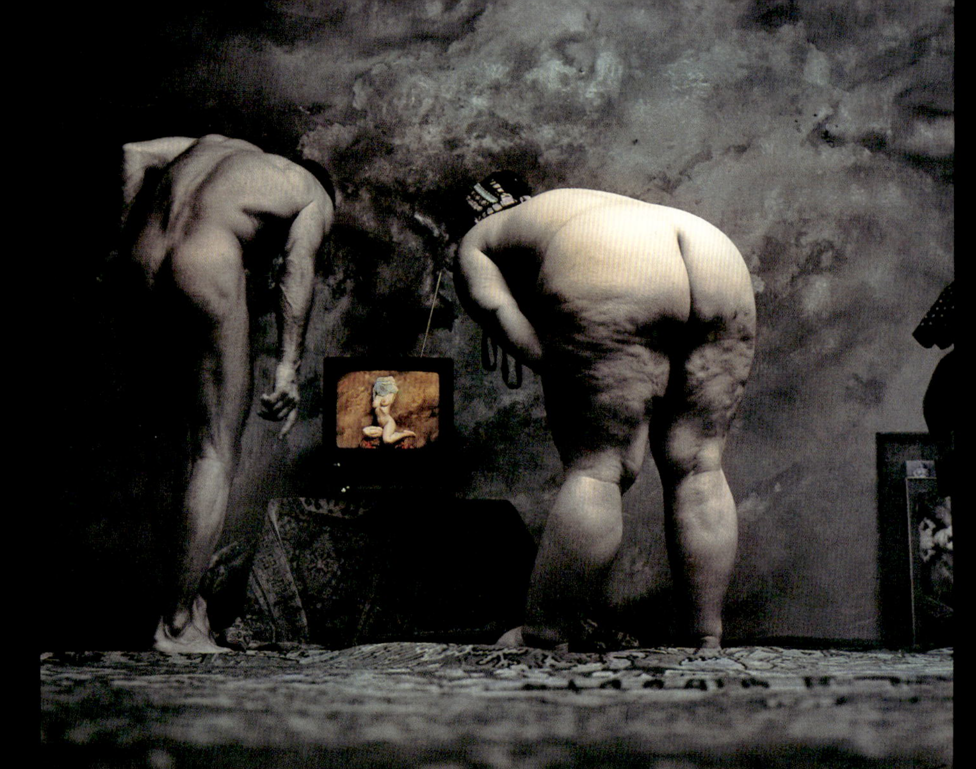

Theatre of Life
Theater des Lebens
Le Théâtre de la Vie

Yes – it's a theatre – and we are viewers and actors at the same time – and it's a funny and sordid performance!

Ja – die Welt ist ein Theater – und wir sind Zuschauer und Darsteller zugleich – in einer Schmierenkomödie!

Oui – la vie est un théâtre – et nous sommes à la fois les spectateurs et les acteurs – d'une comédie sordide !

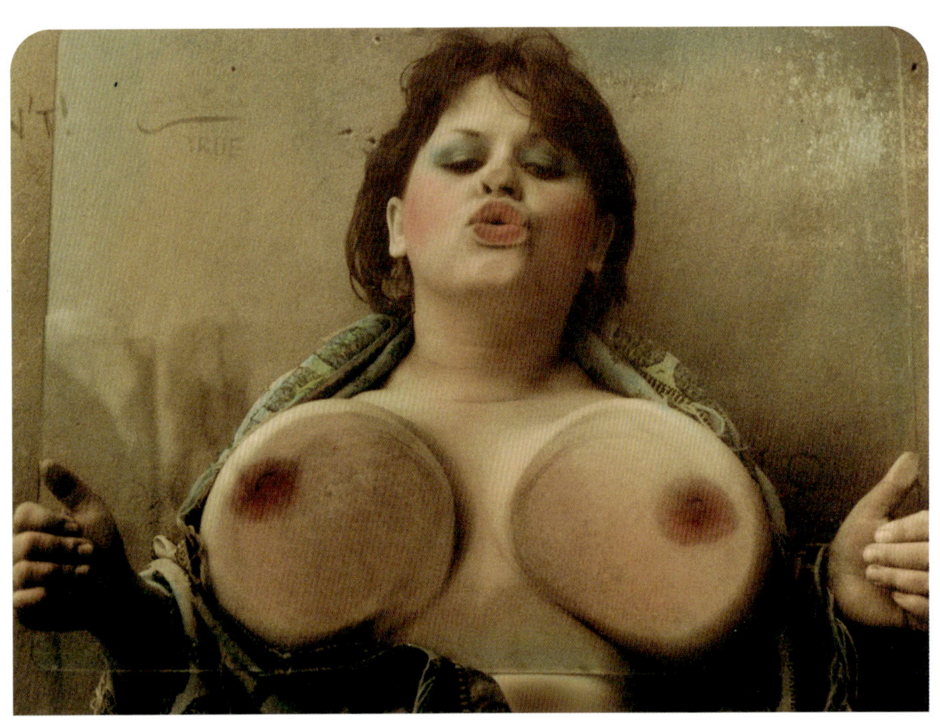

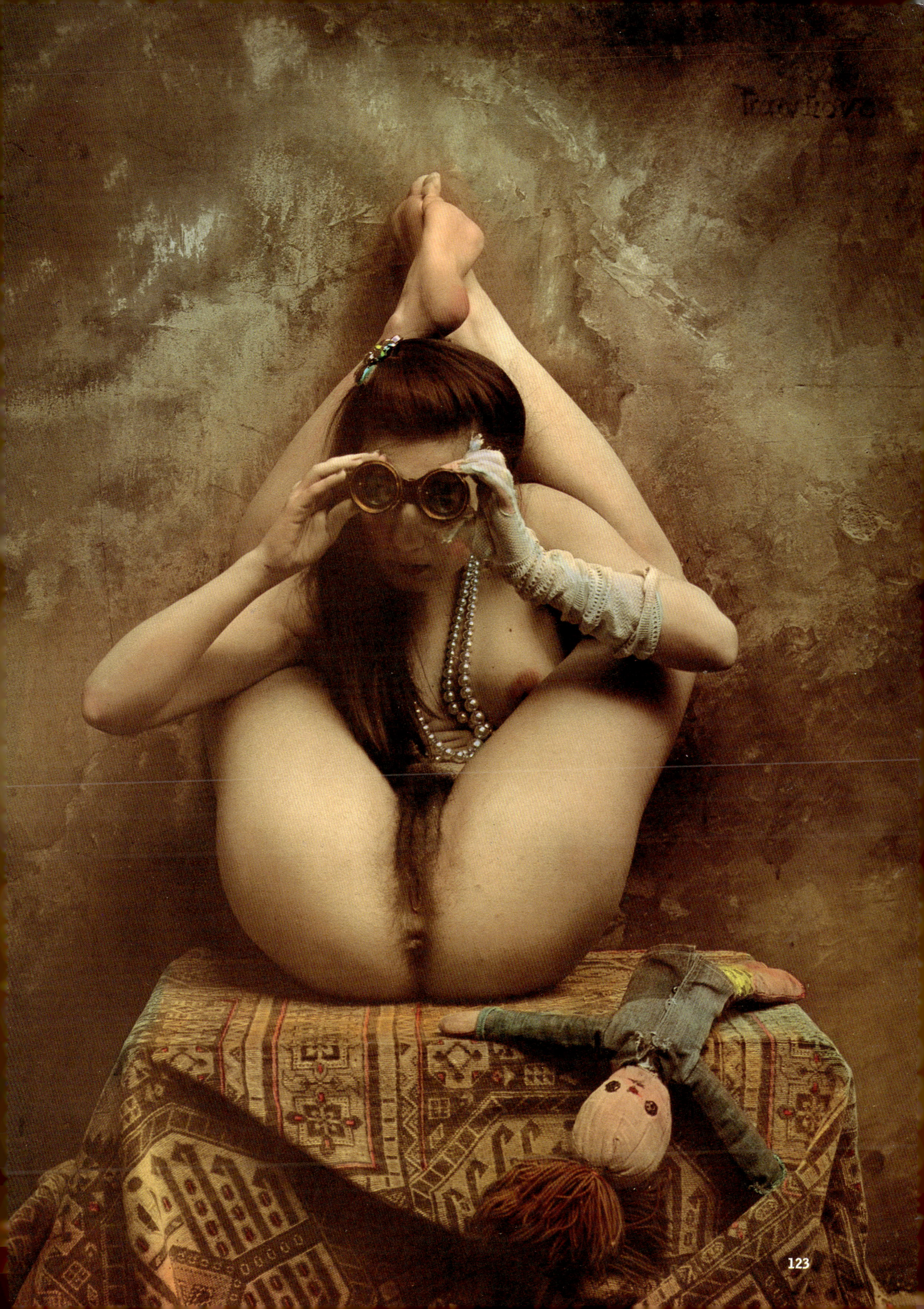

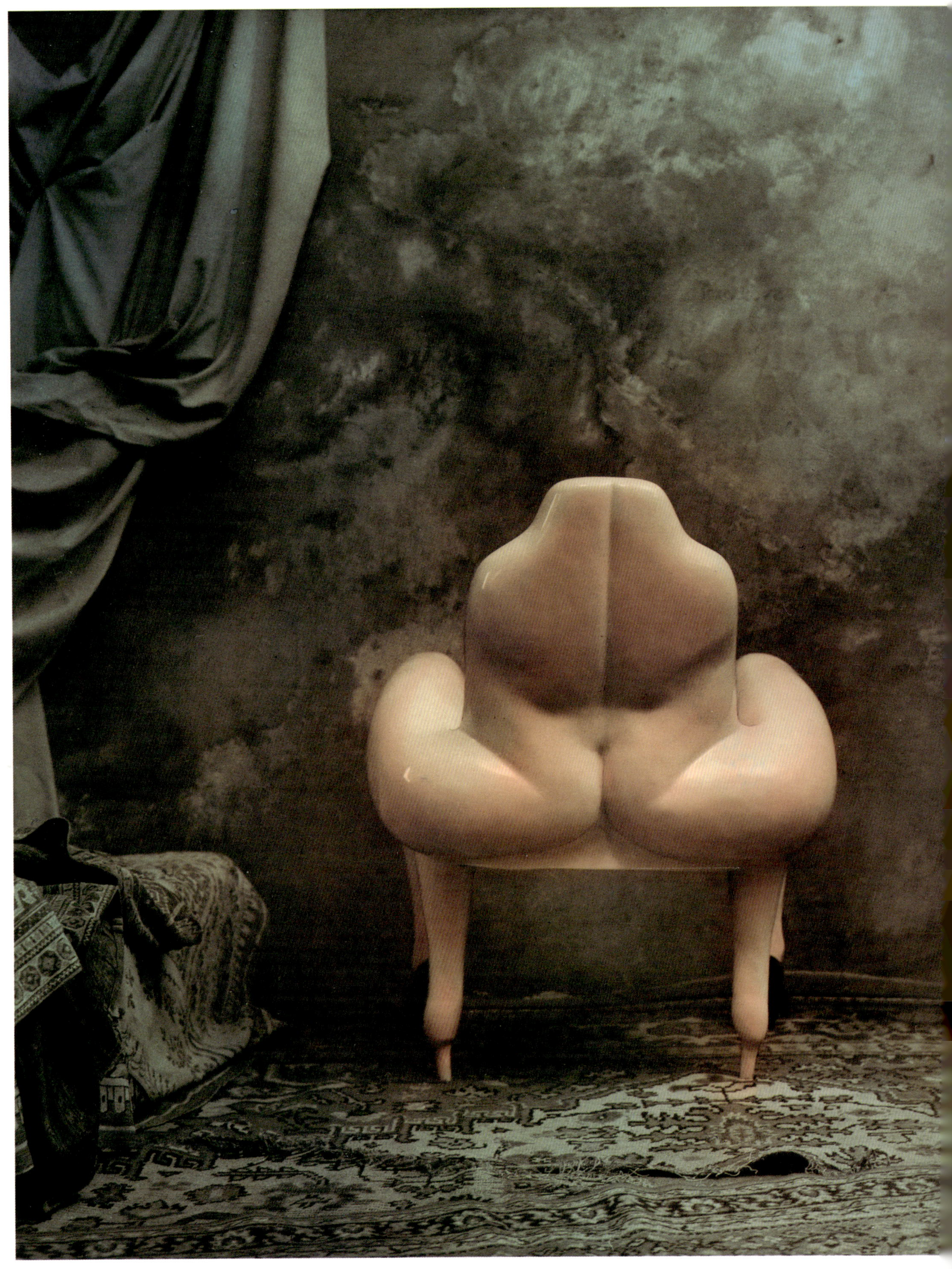

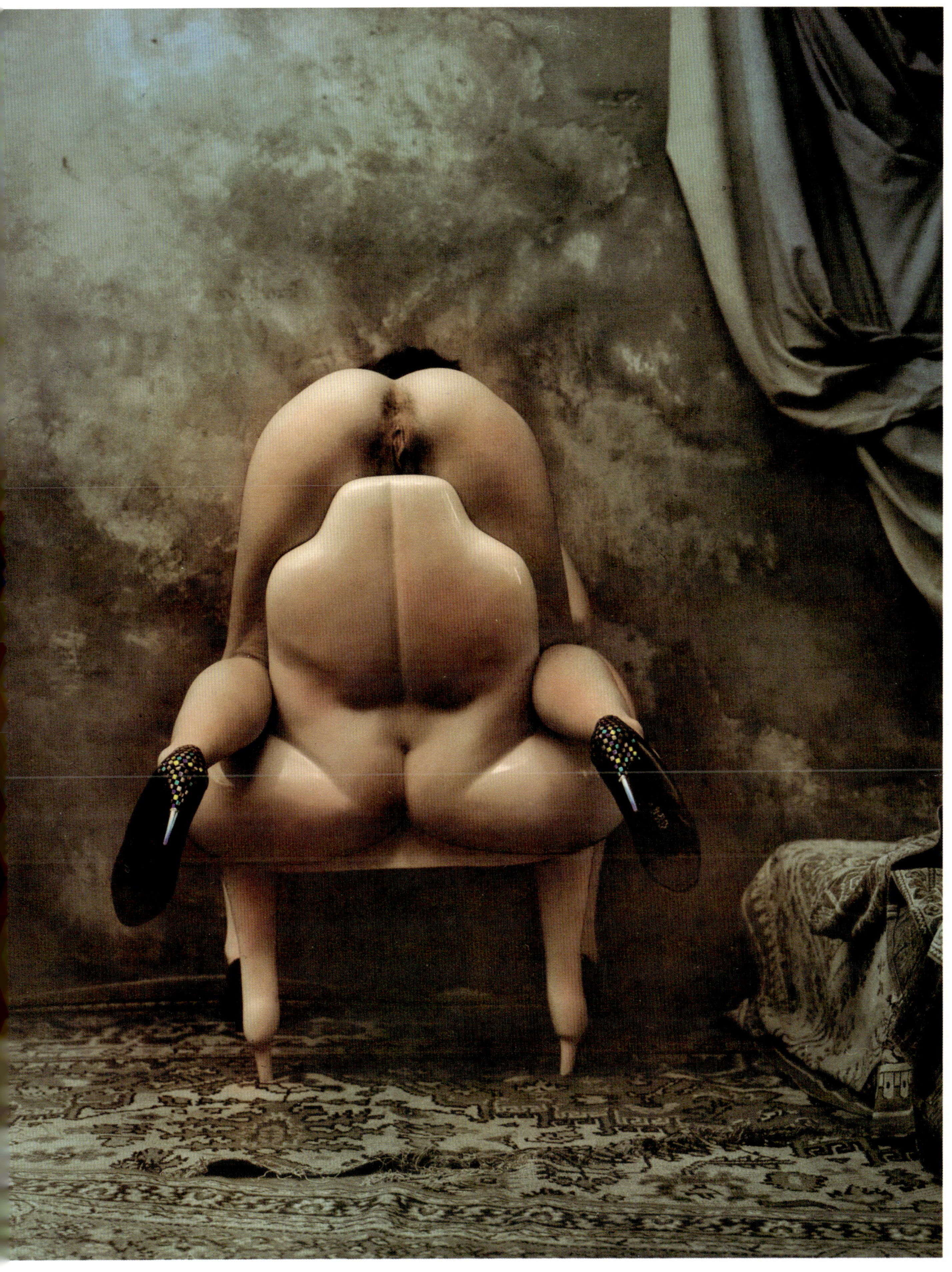

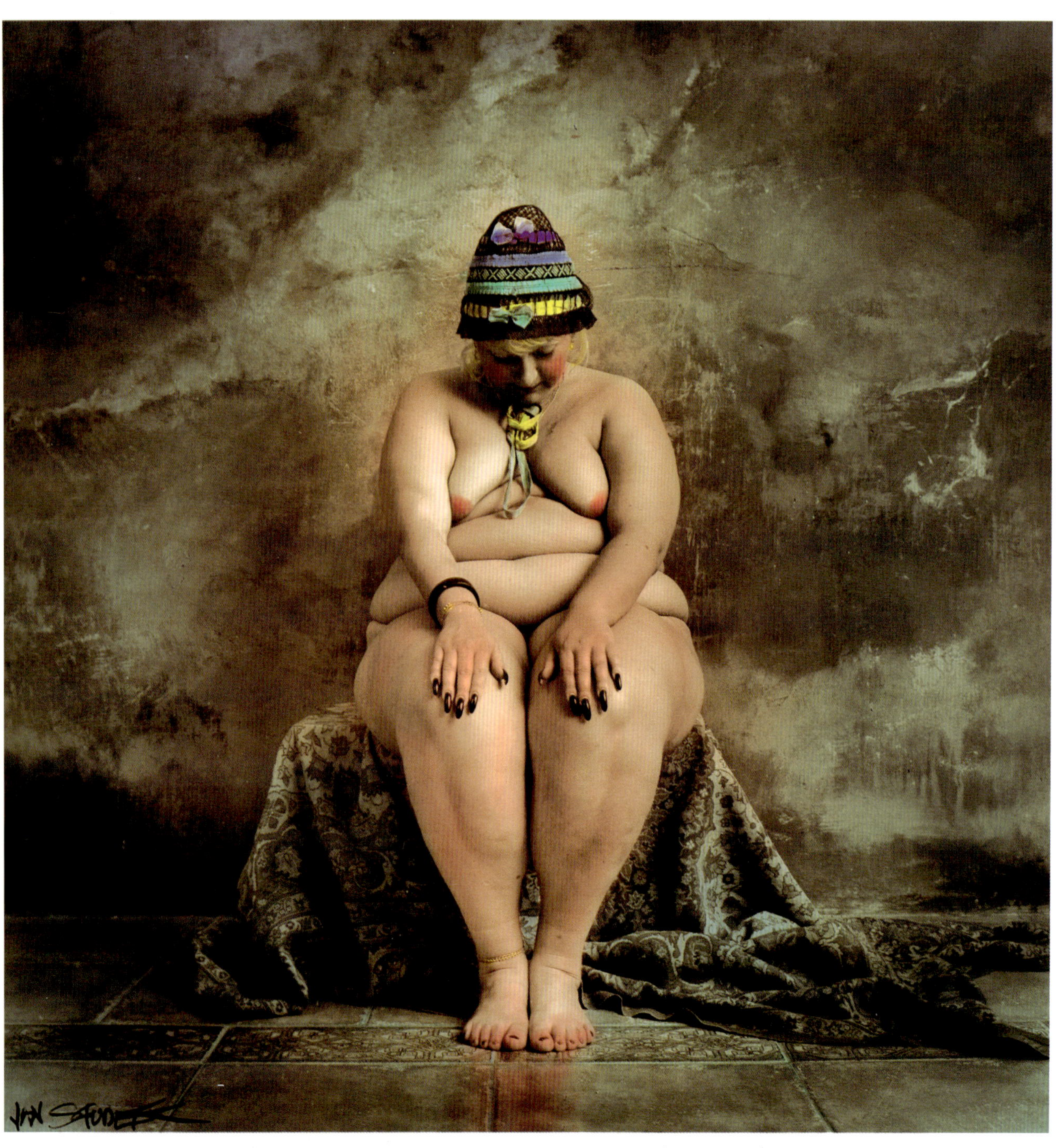

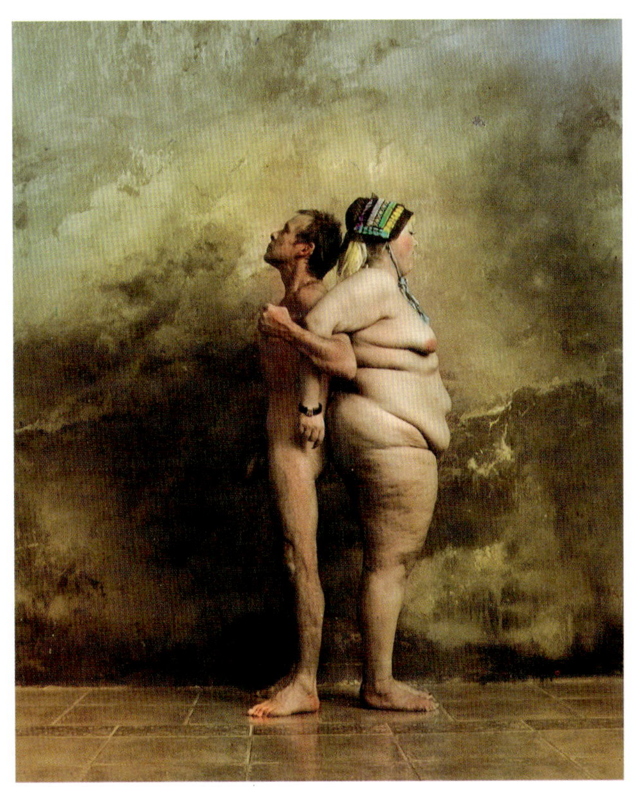
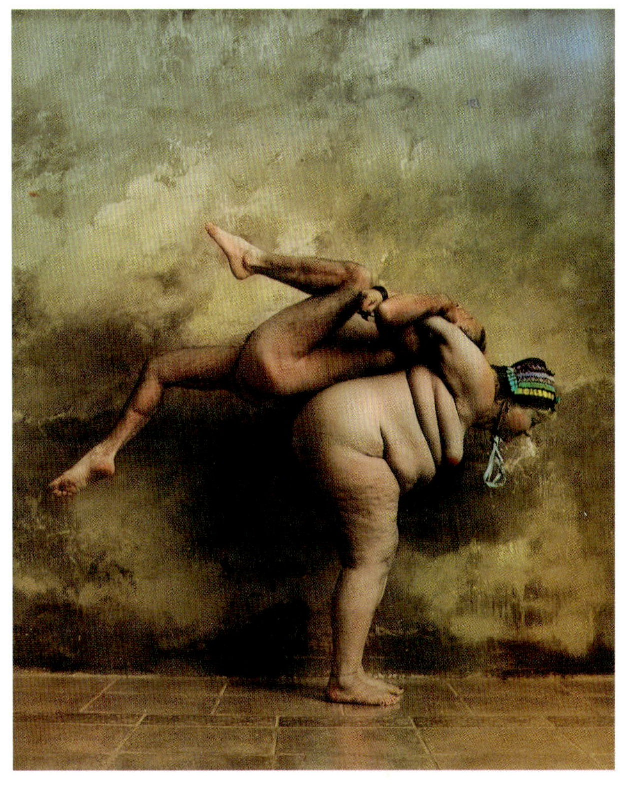
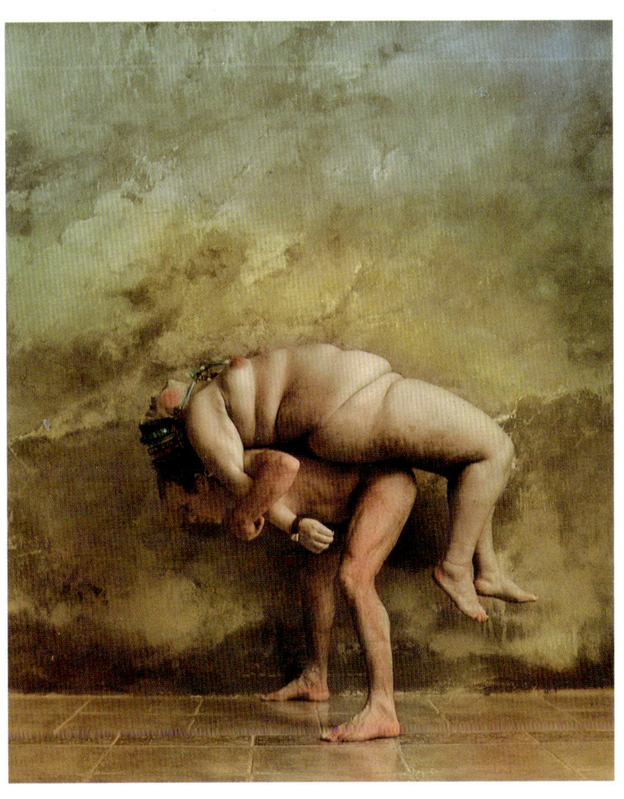
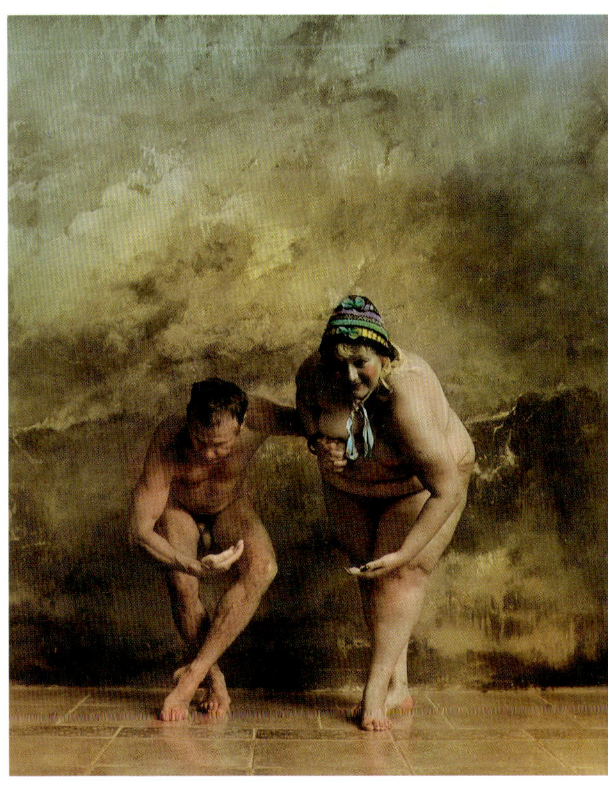

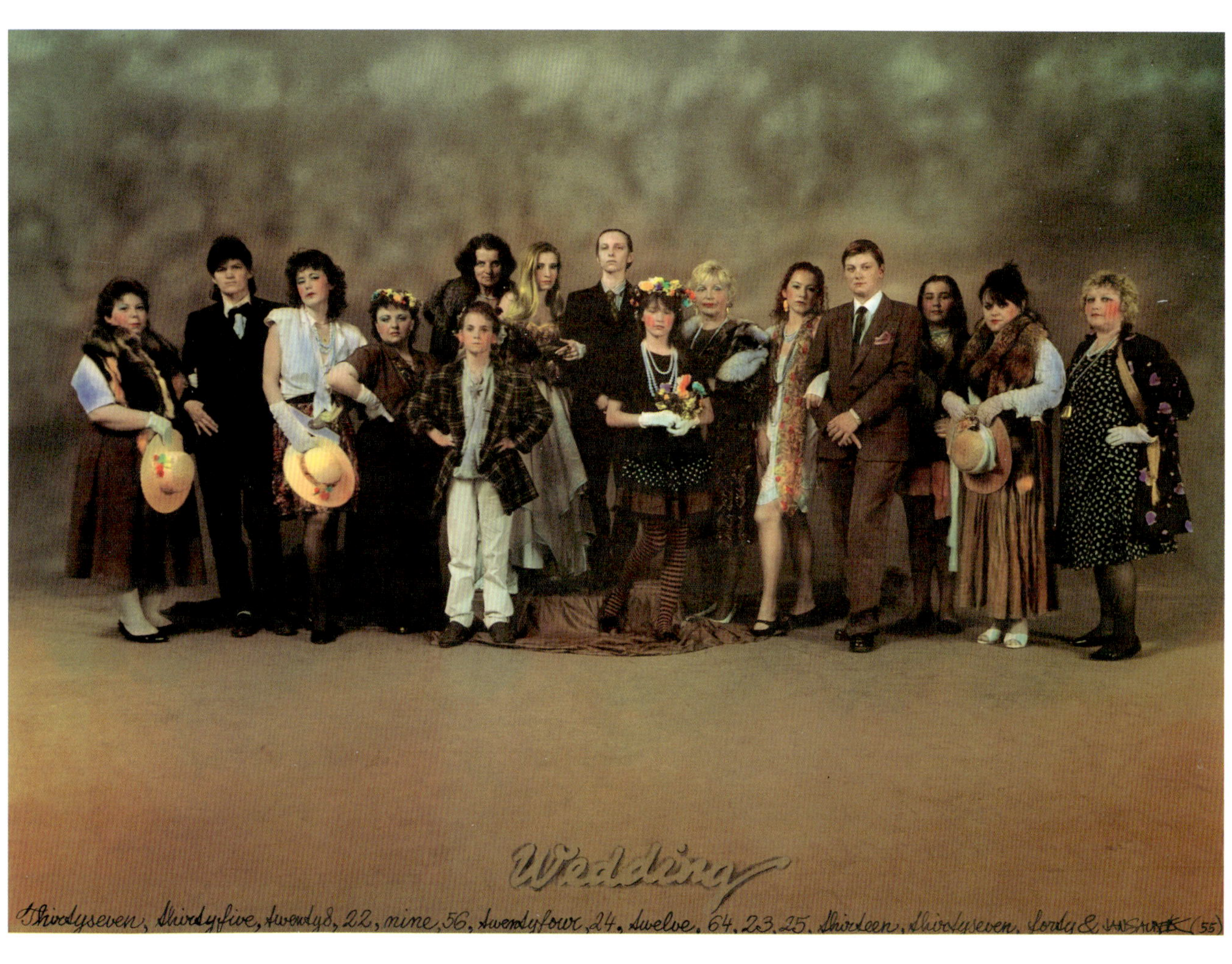
Wedding
Thirtyseven, thirtyfive, twenty8, 22, nine, 56, twentyfour, 24, twelve, 64, 23, 25, thirteen, thirtyseven, forty & JAN SAUDEK (55)

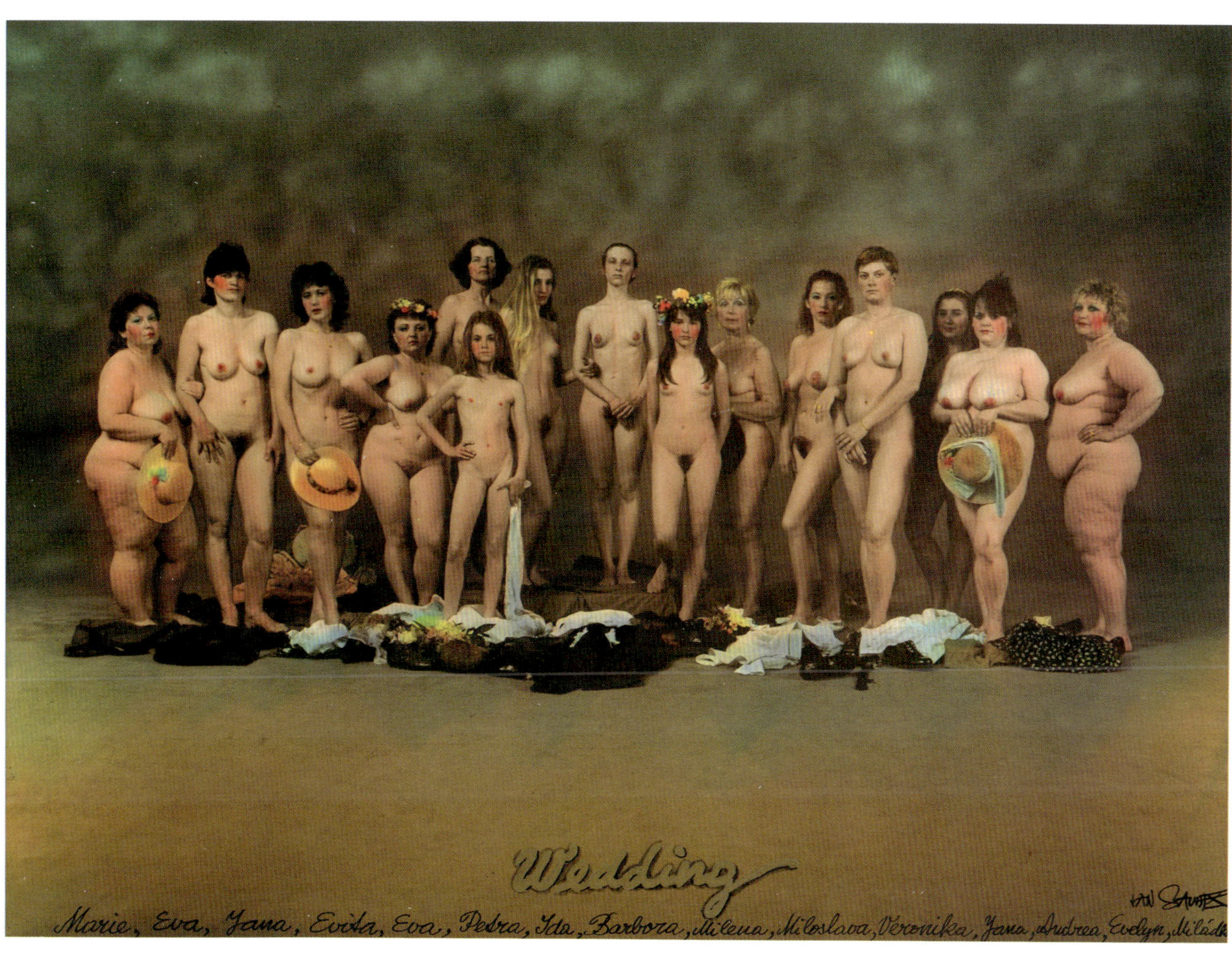
Wedding
Marie, Eva, Jana, Evita, Eva, Petra, Ida, Barbora, Milena, Miloslava, Veronika, Jana, Andrea, Evelyn,

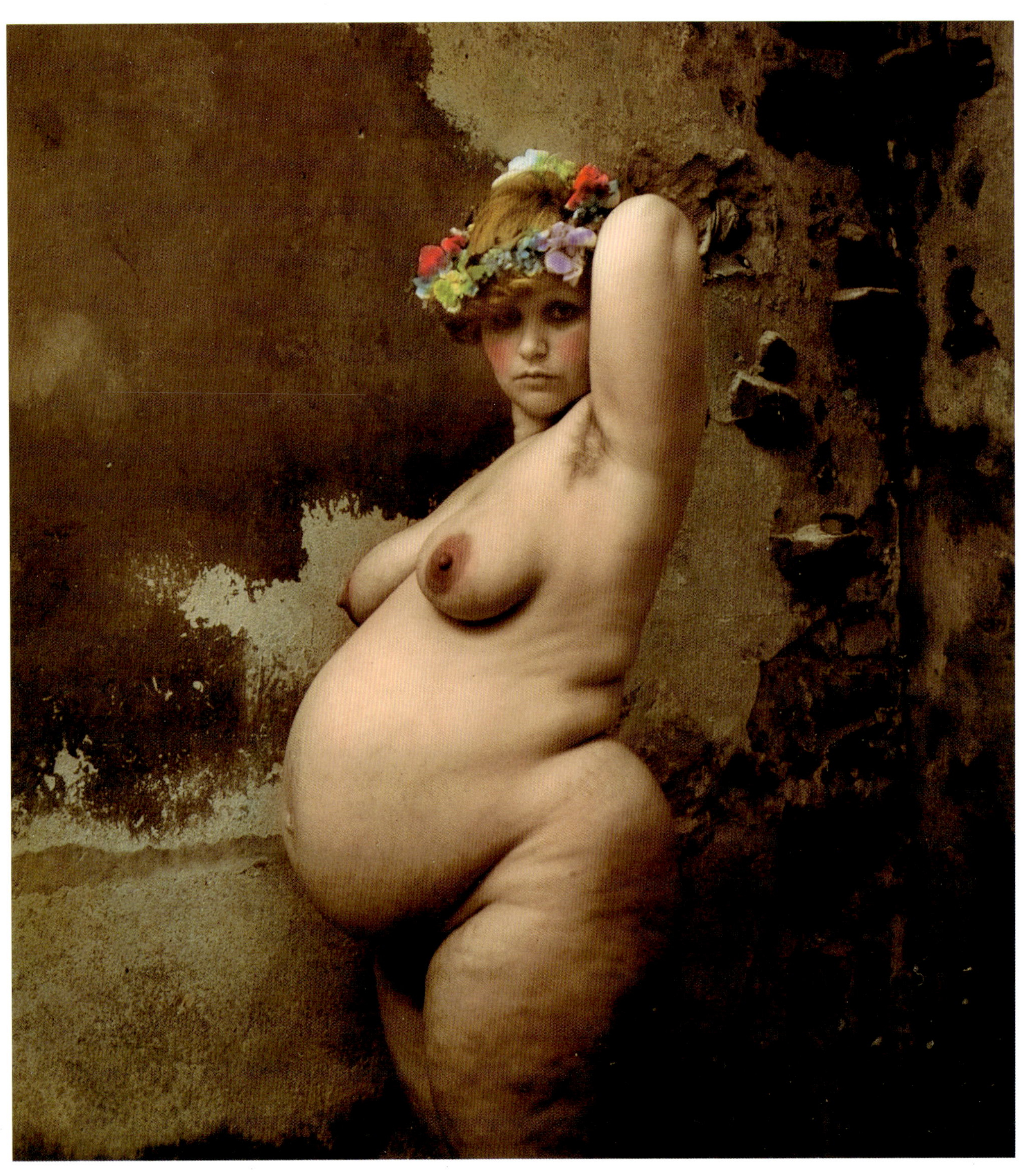

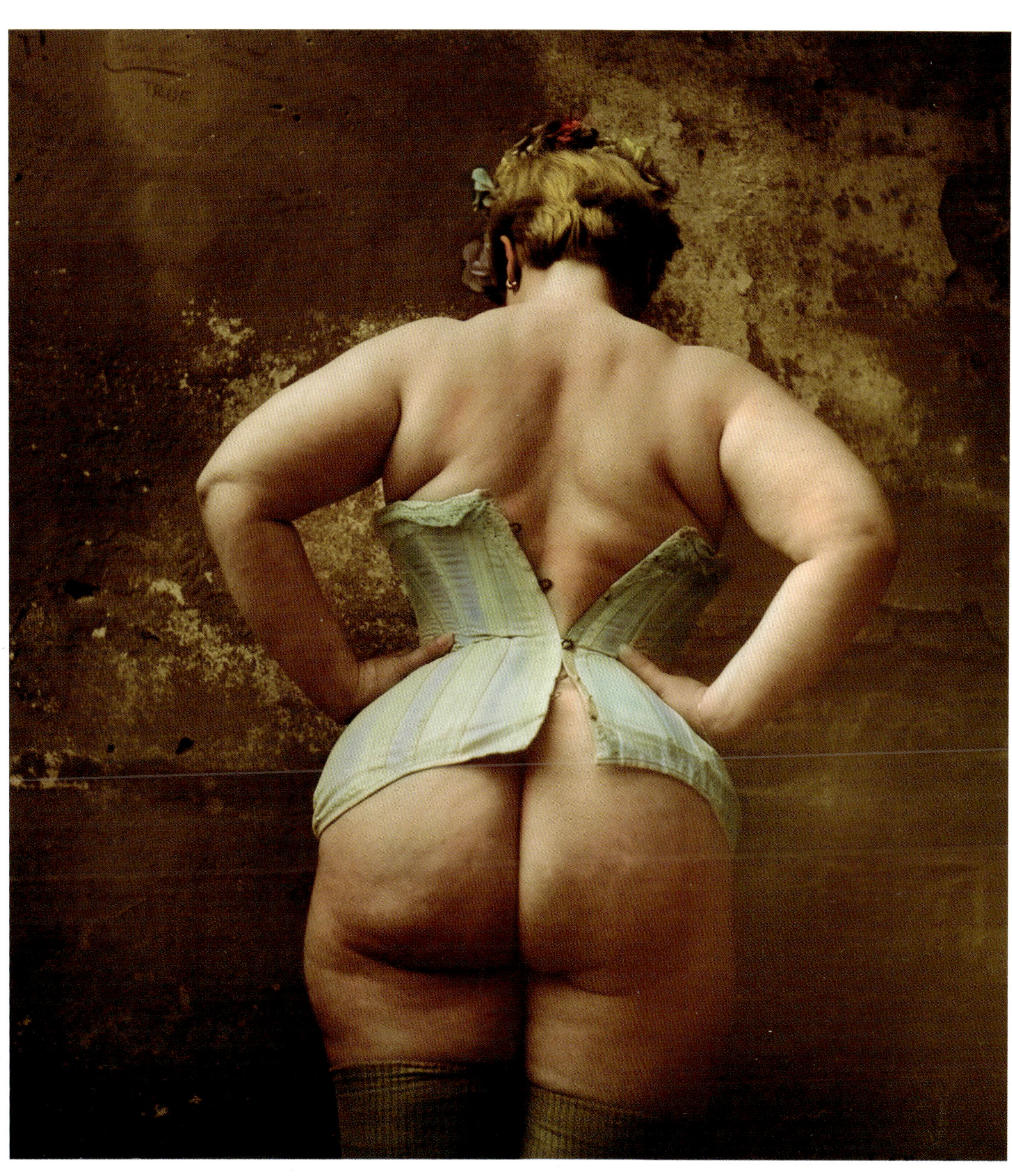

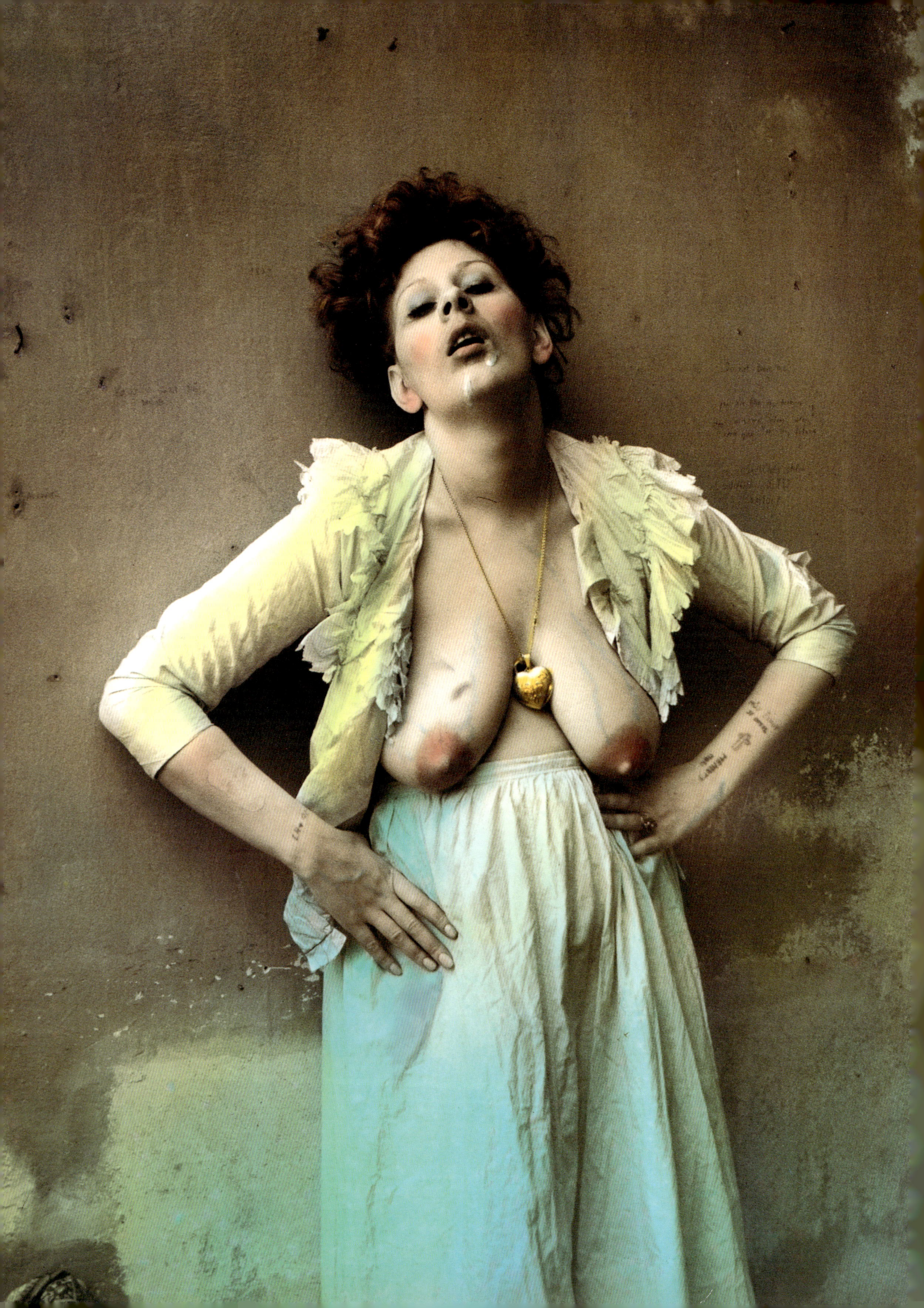

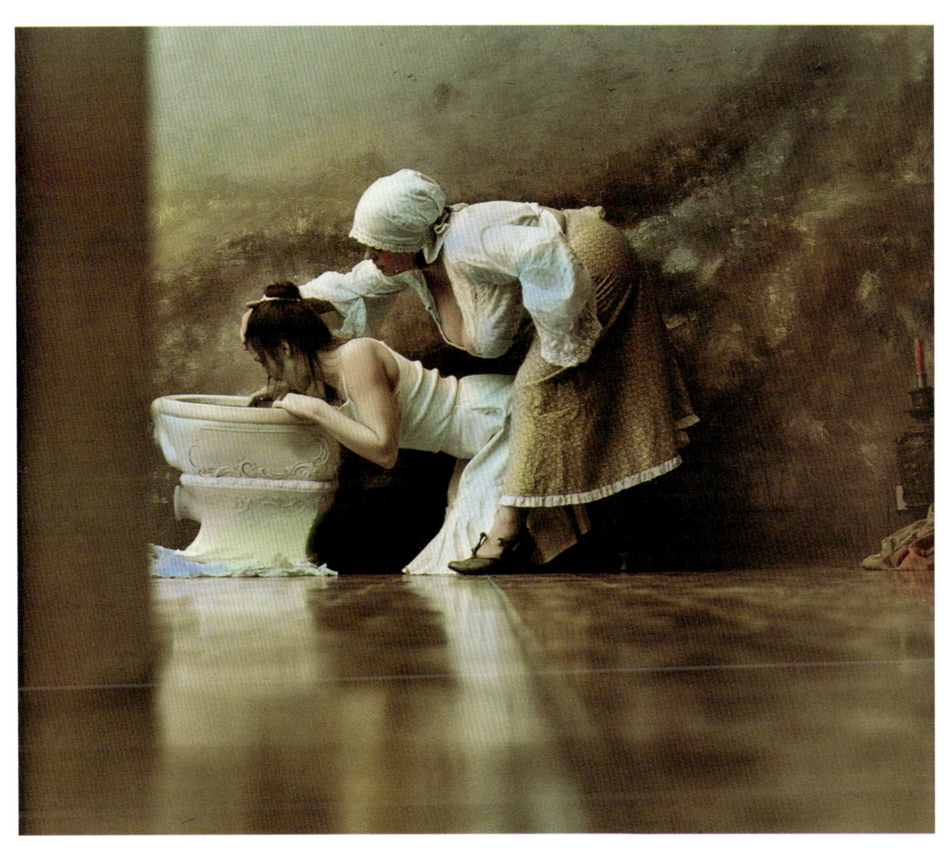

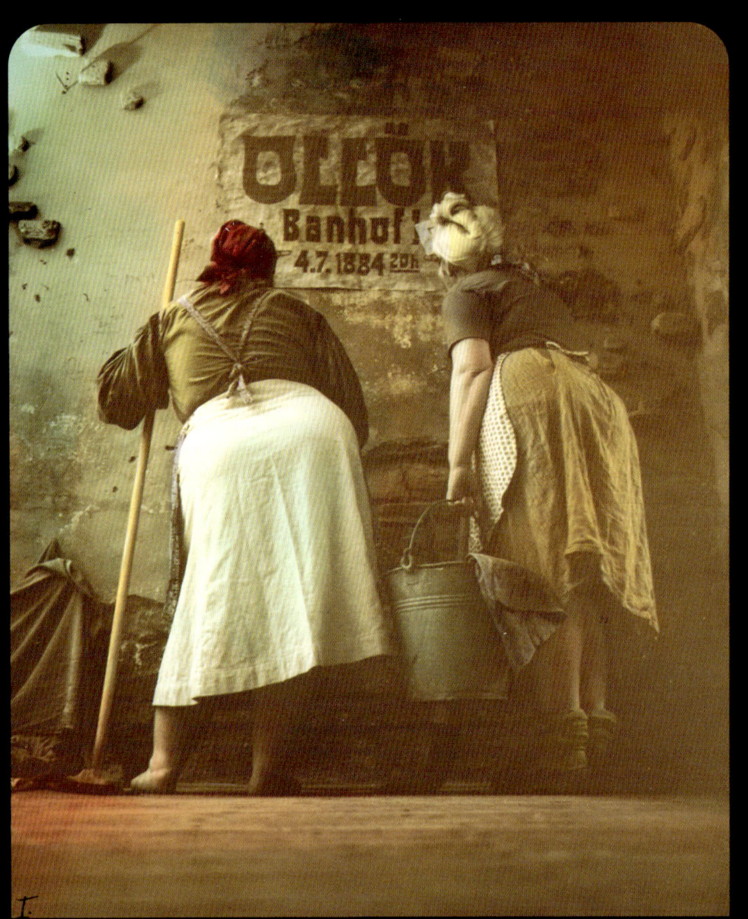
OLLÖK
Banhof!
4.7.1884 20h
I.

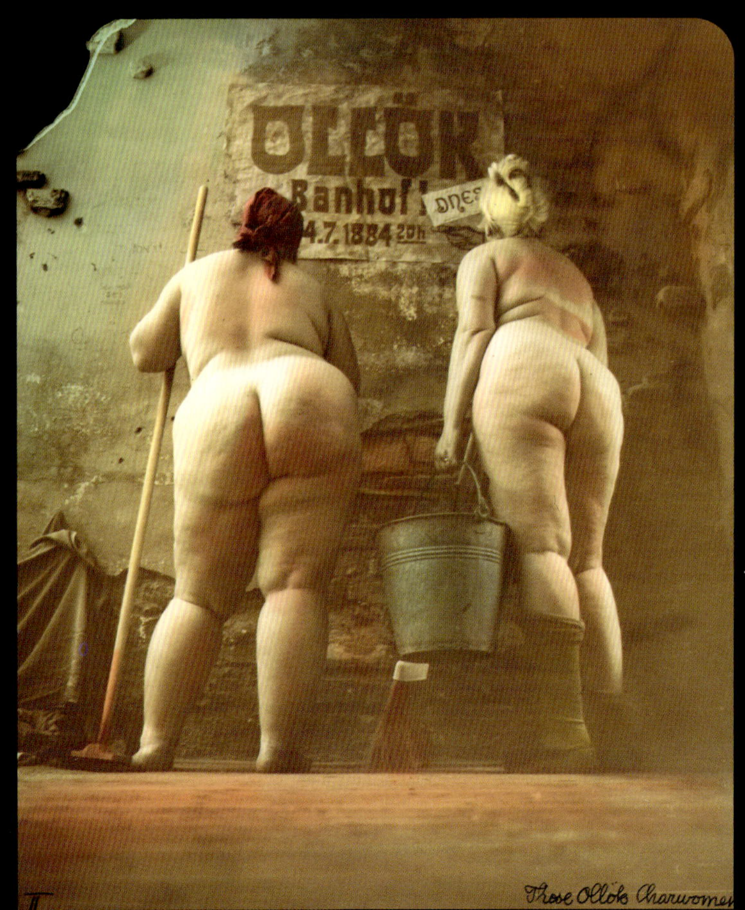
OLLÖK
Banhof!
DNES
4.7.1884 20h
II.
These Ollöks Charwomen

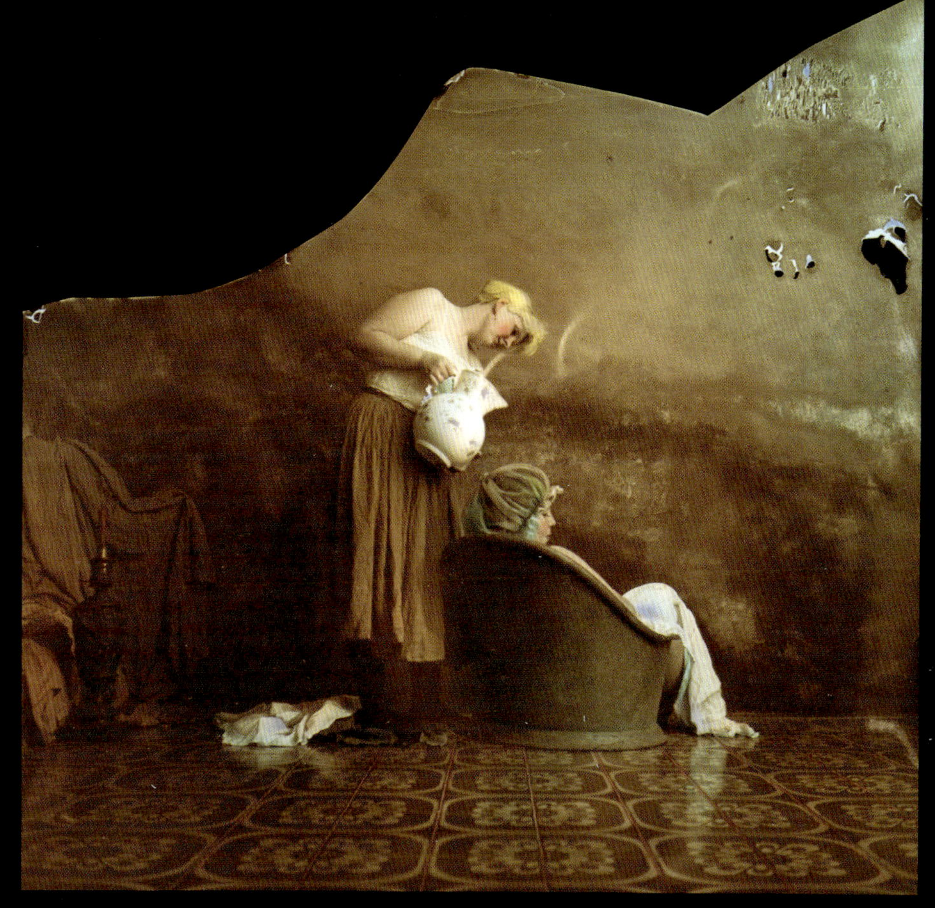

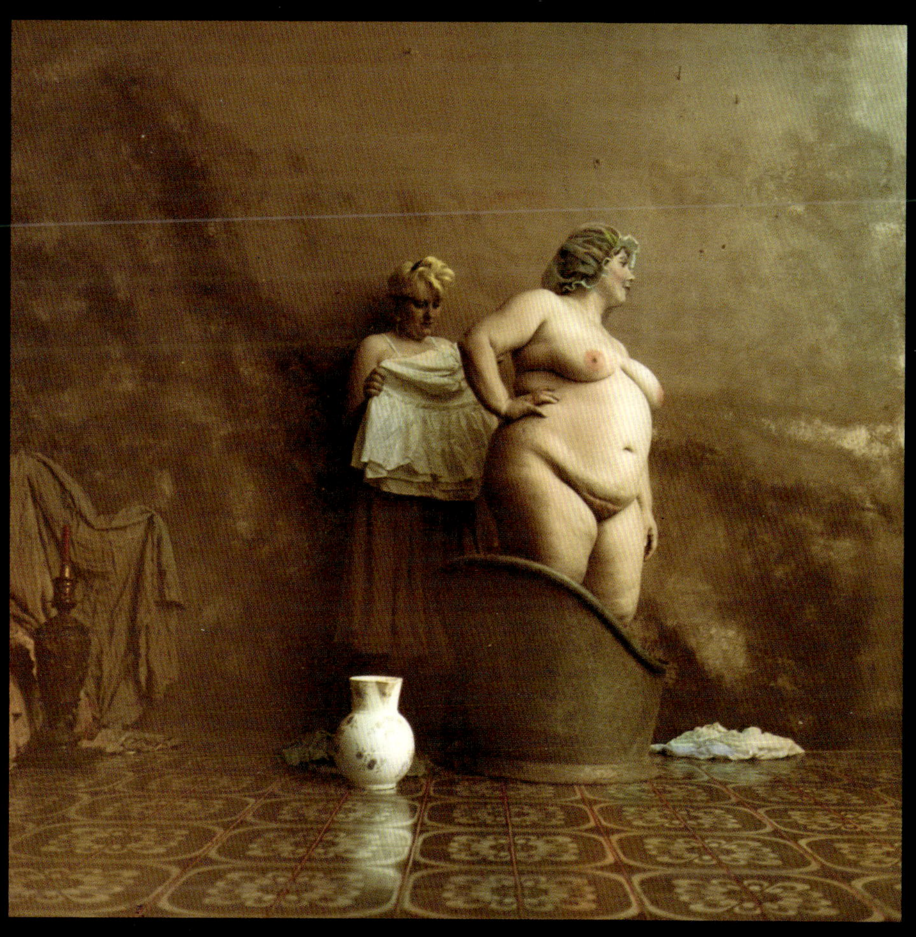

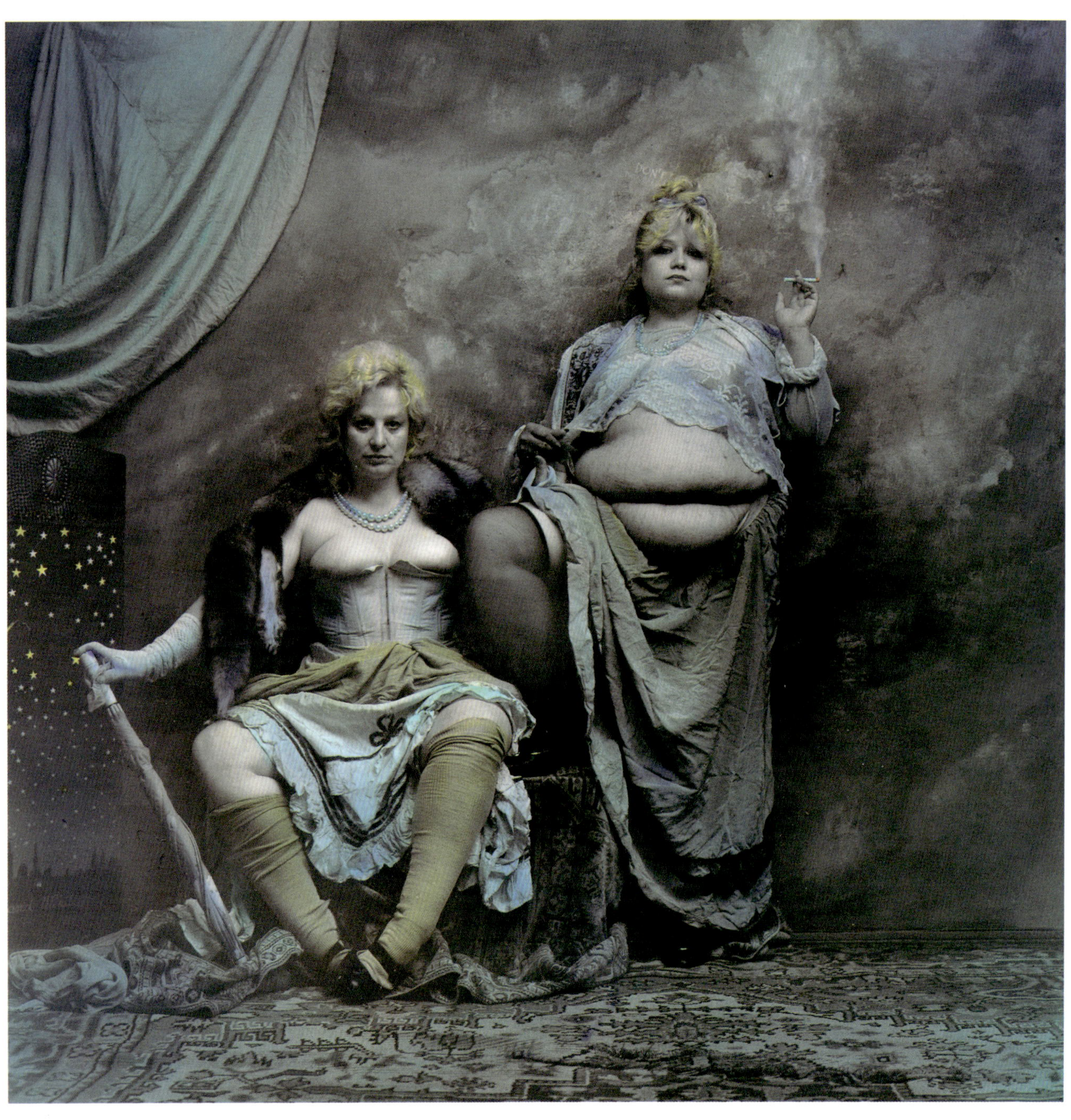

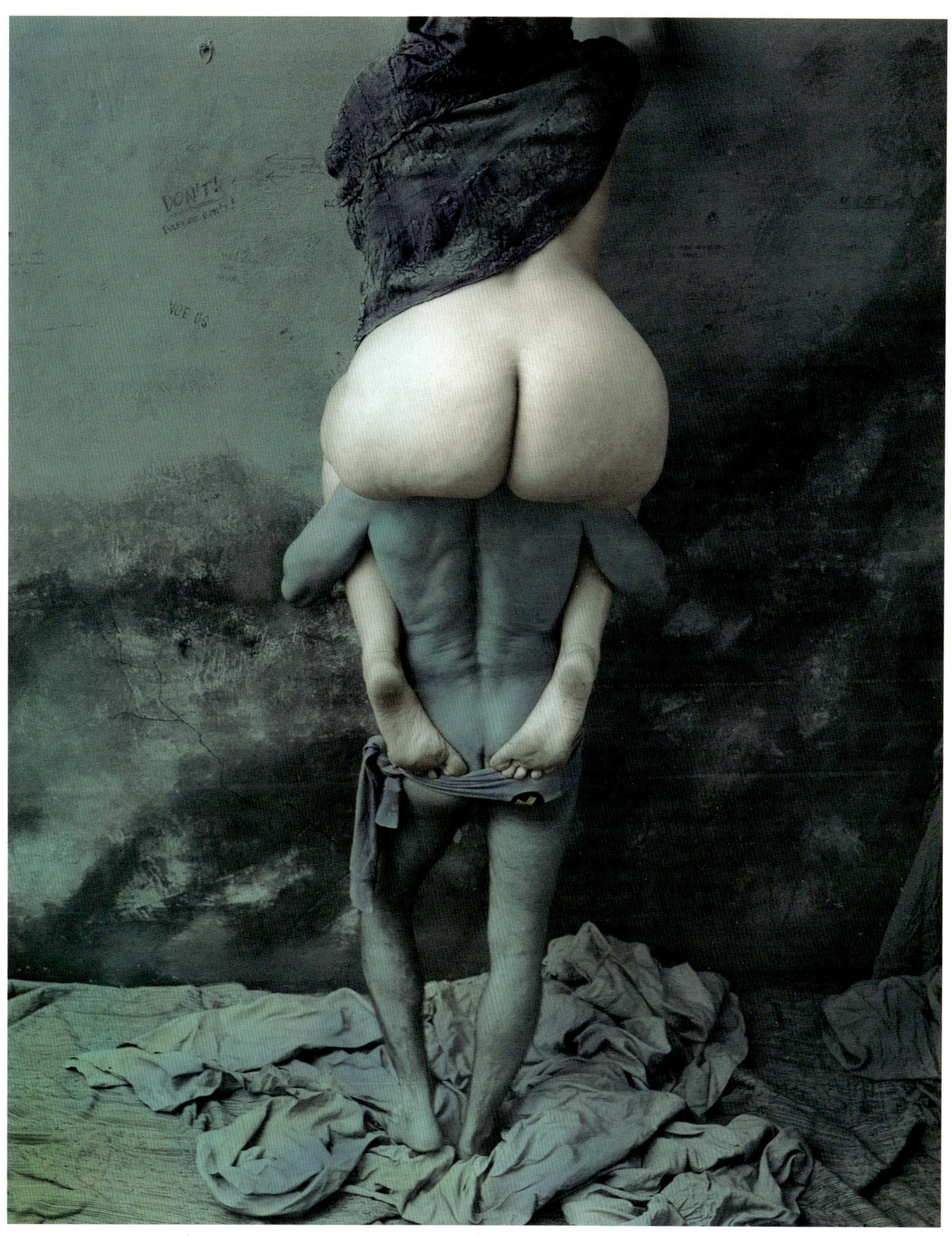
DON'T!

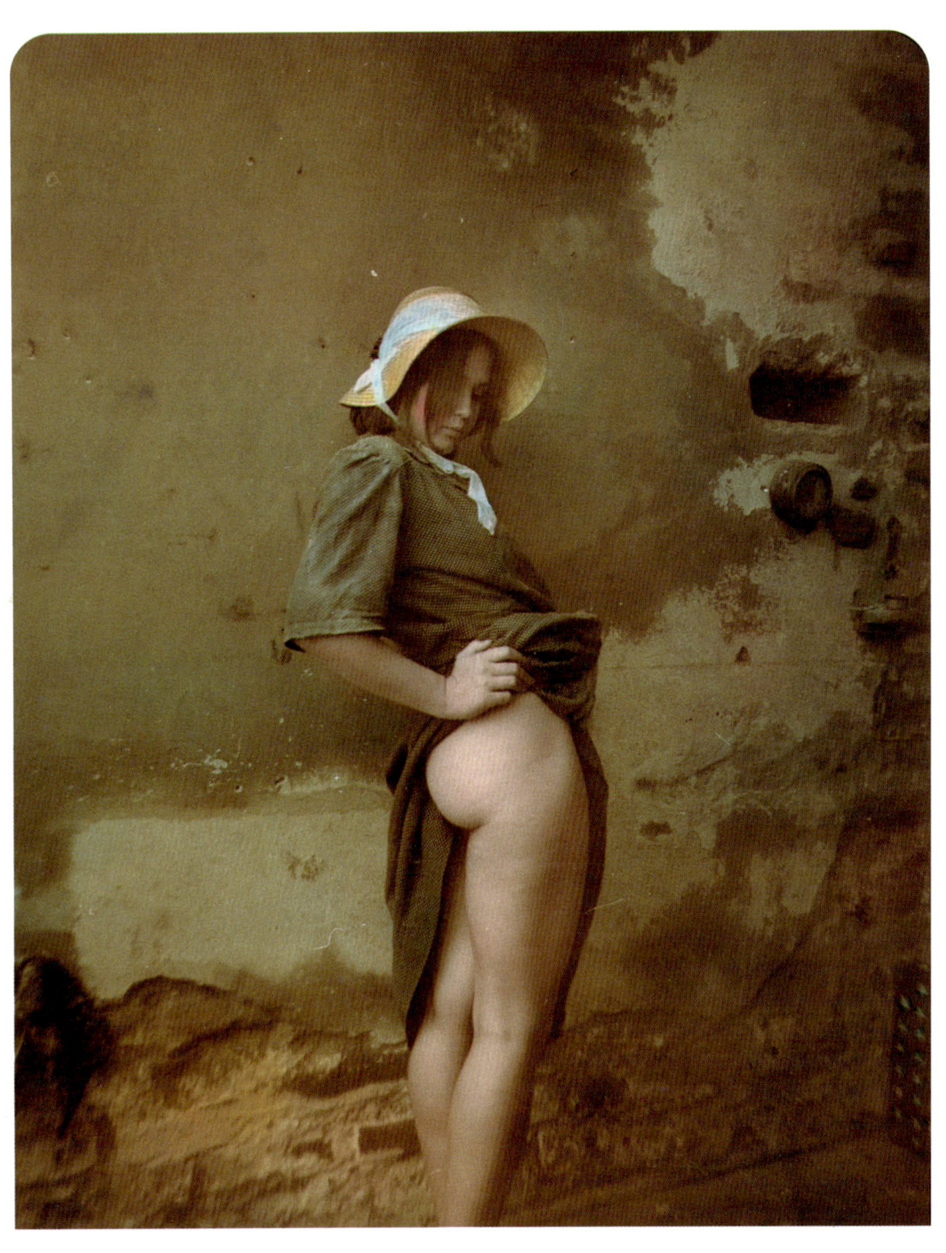

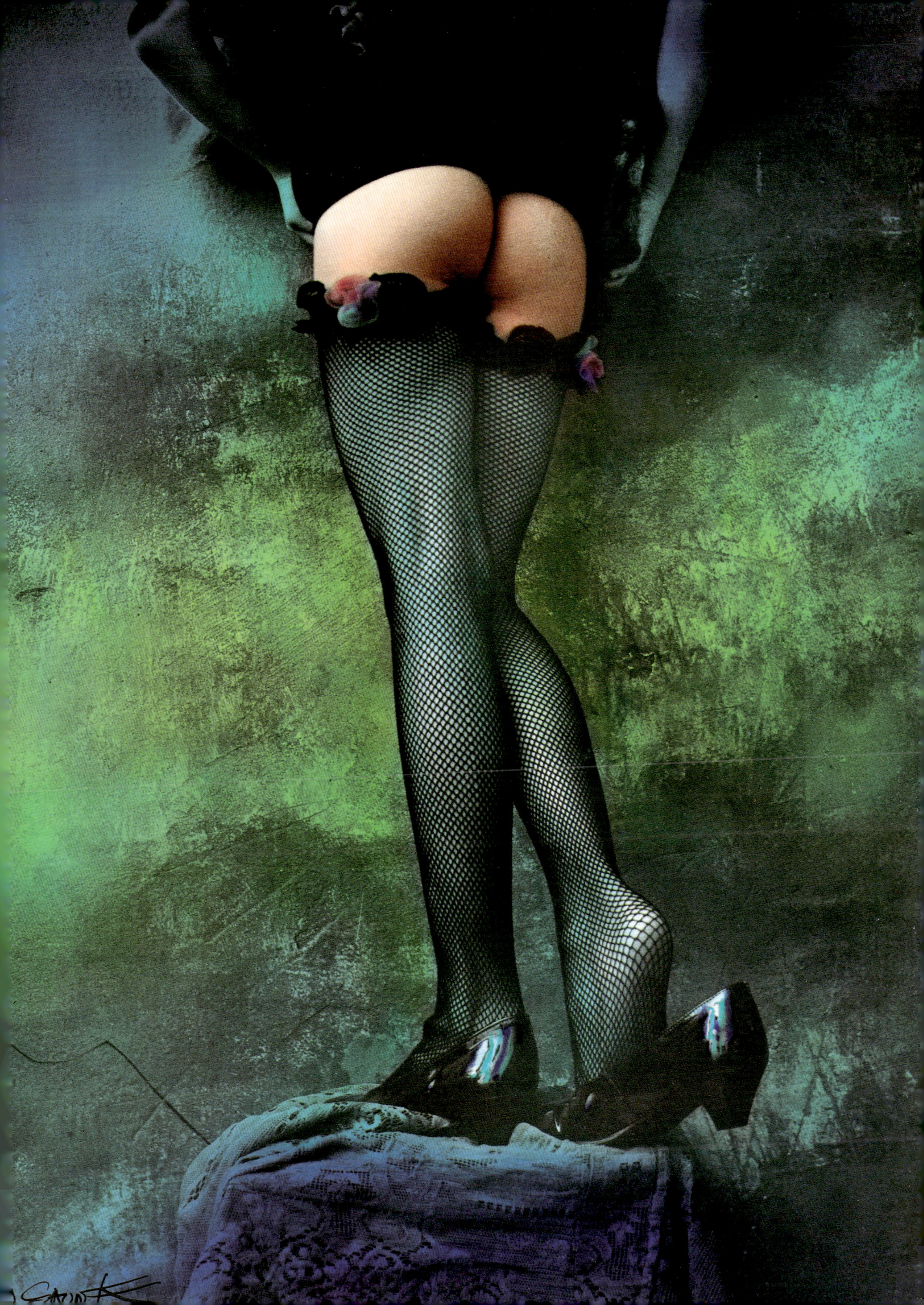

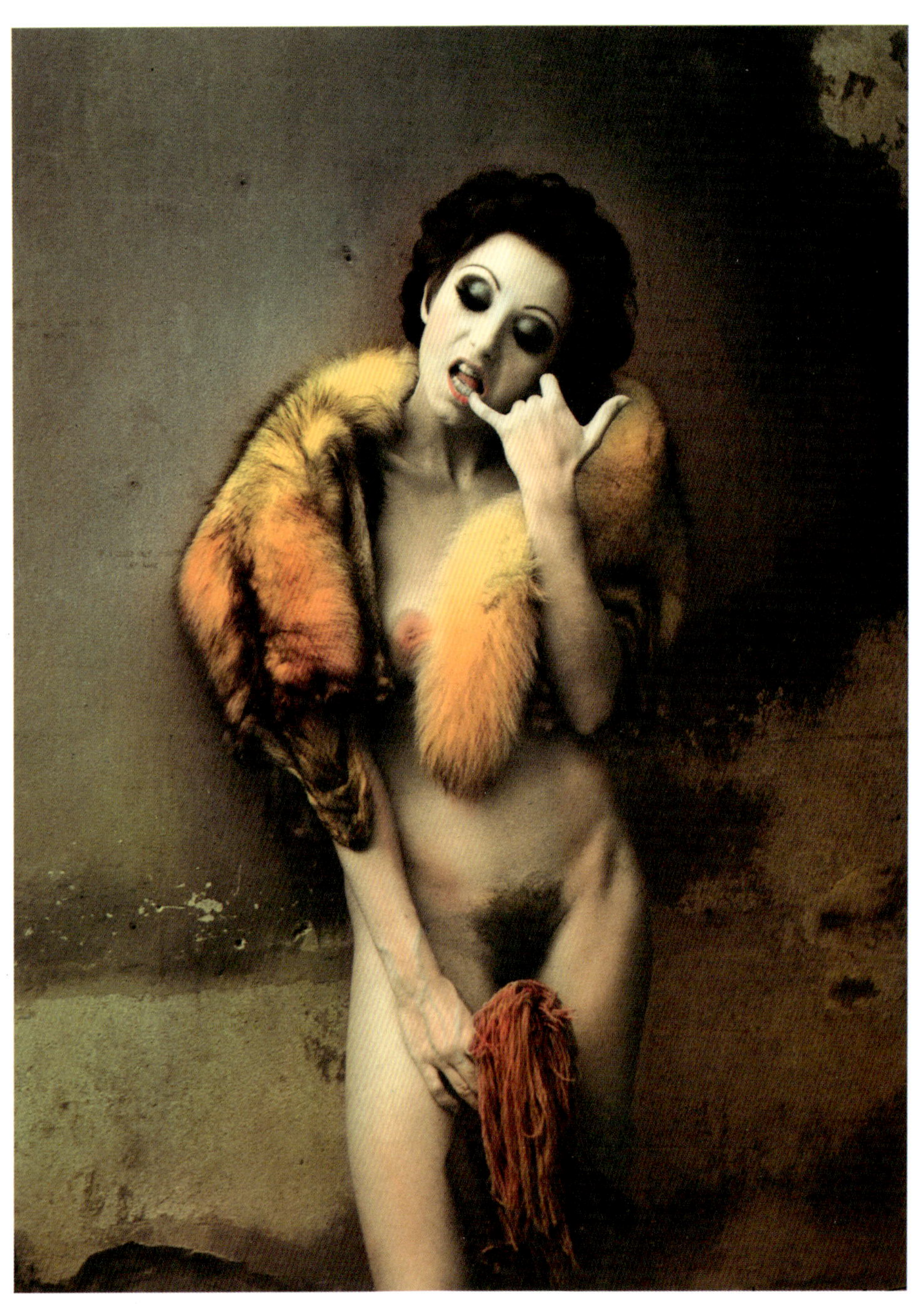

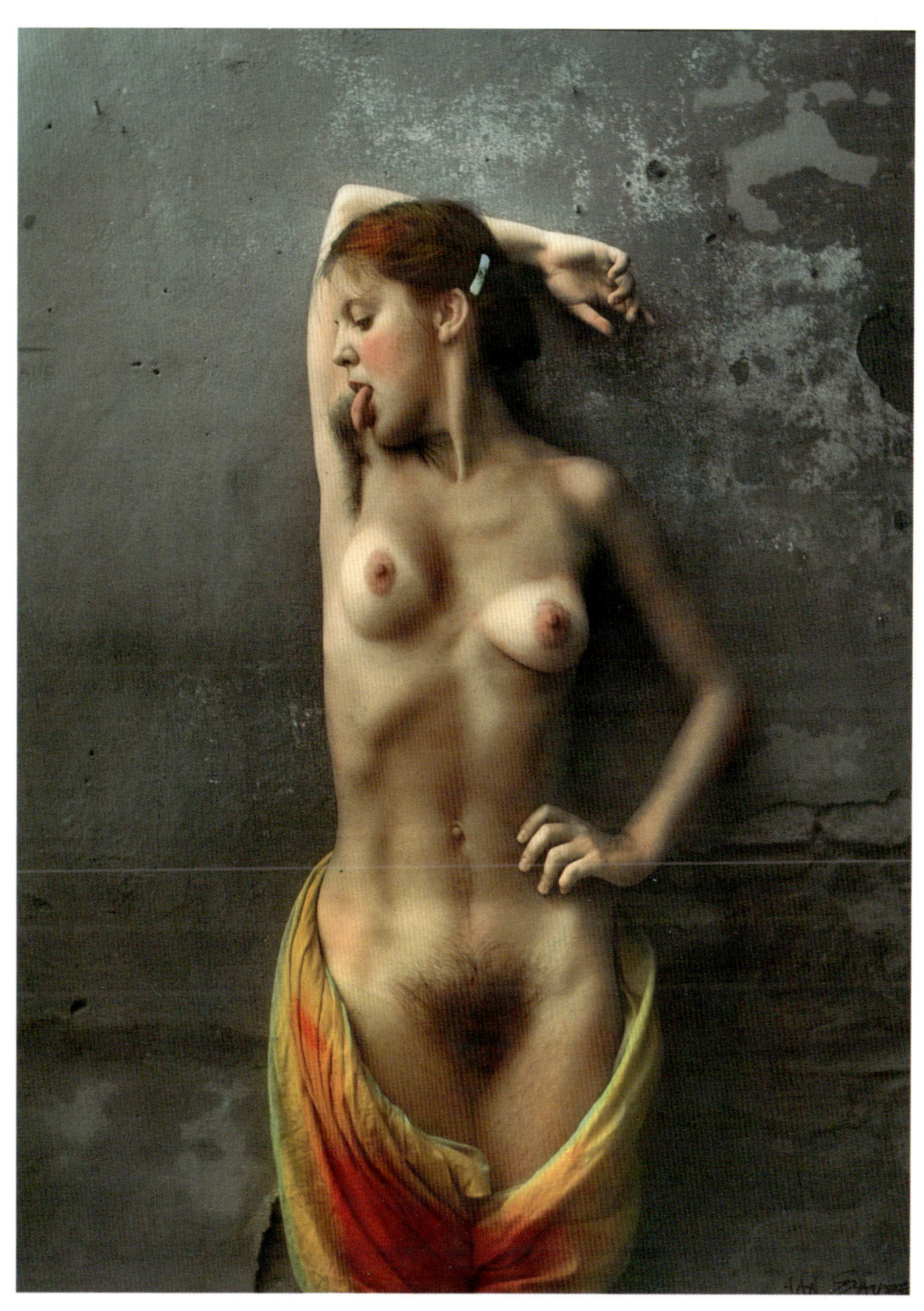

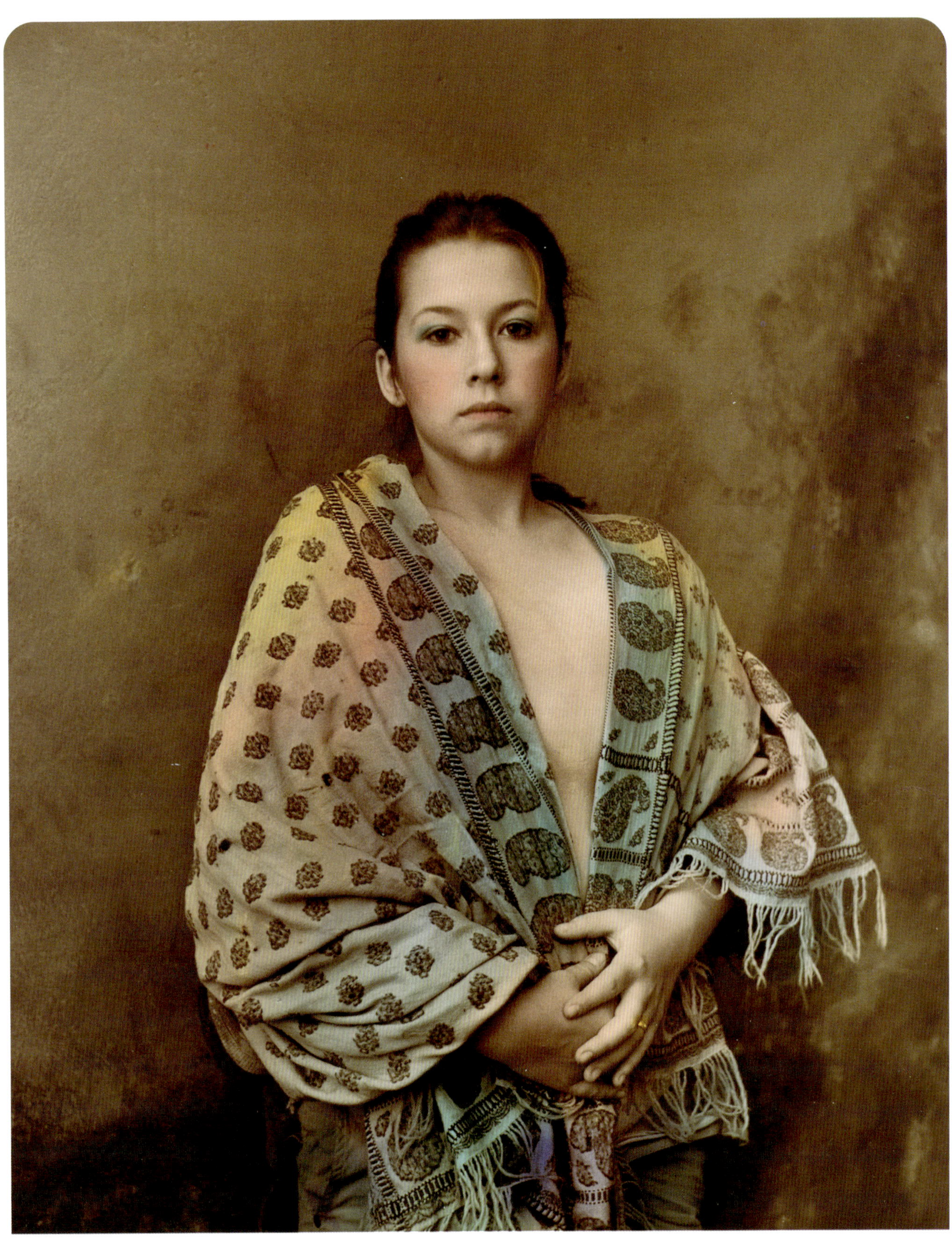

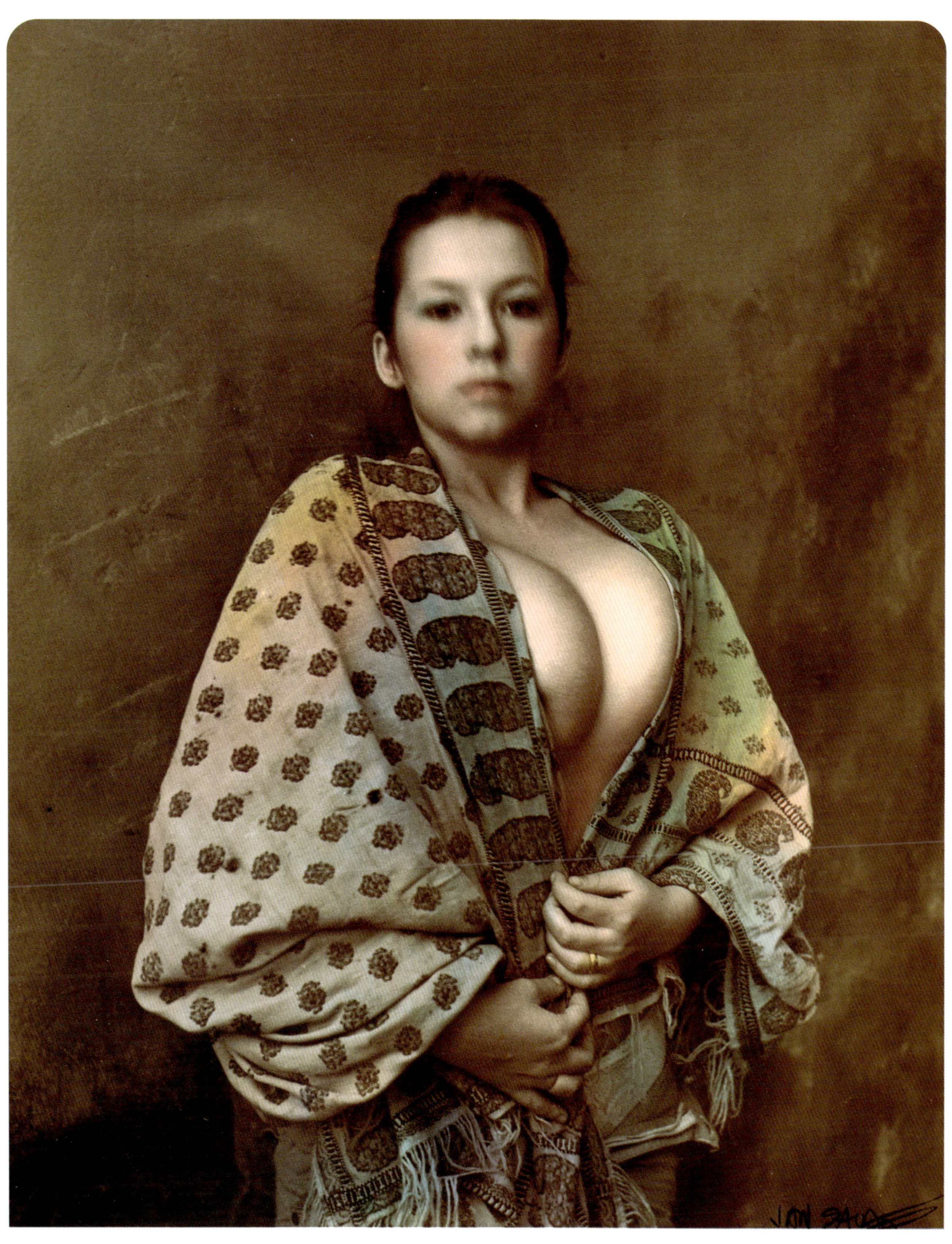

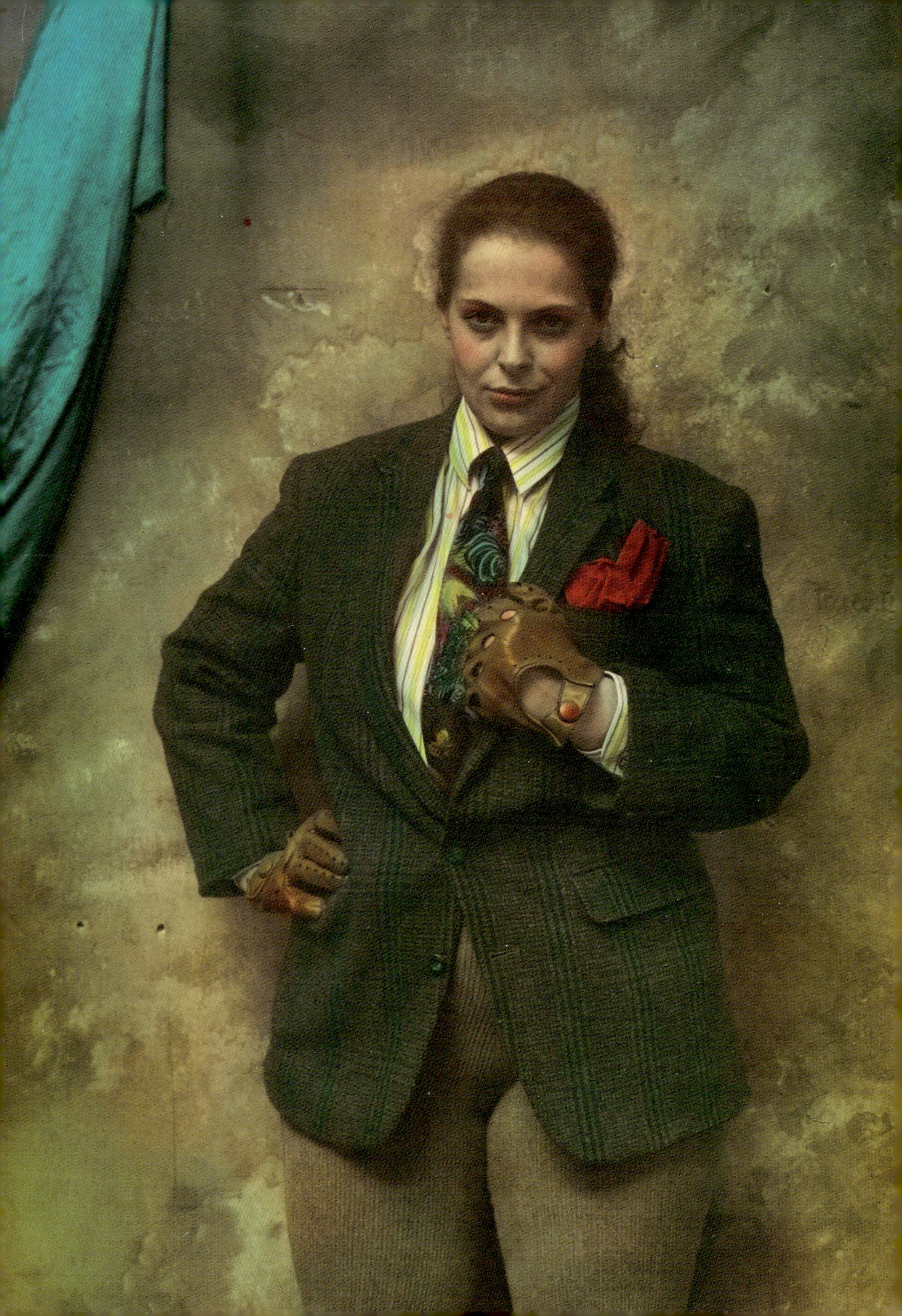

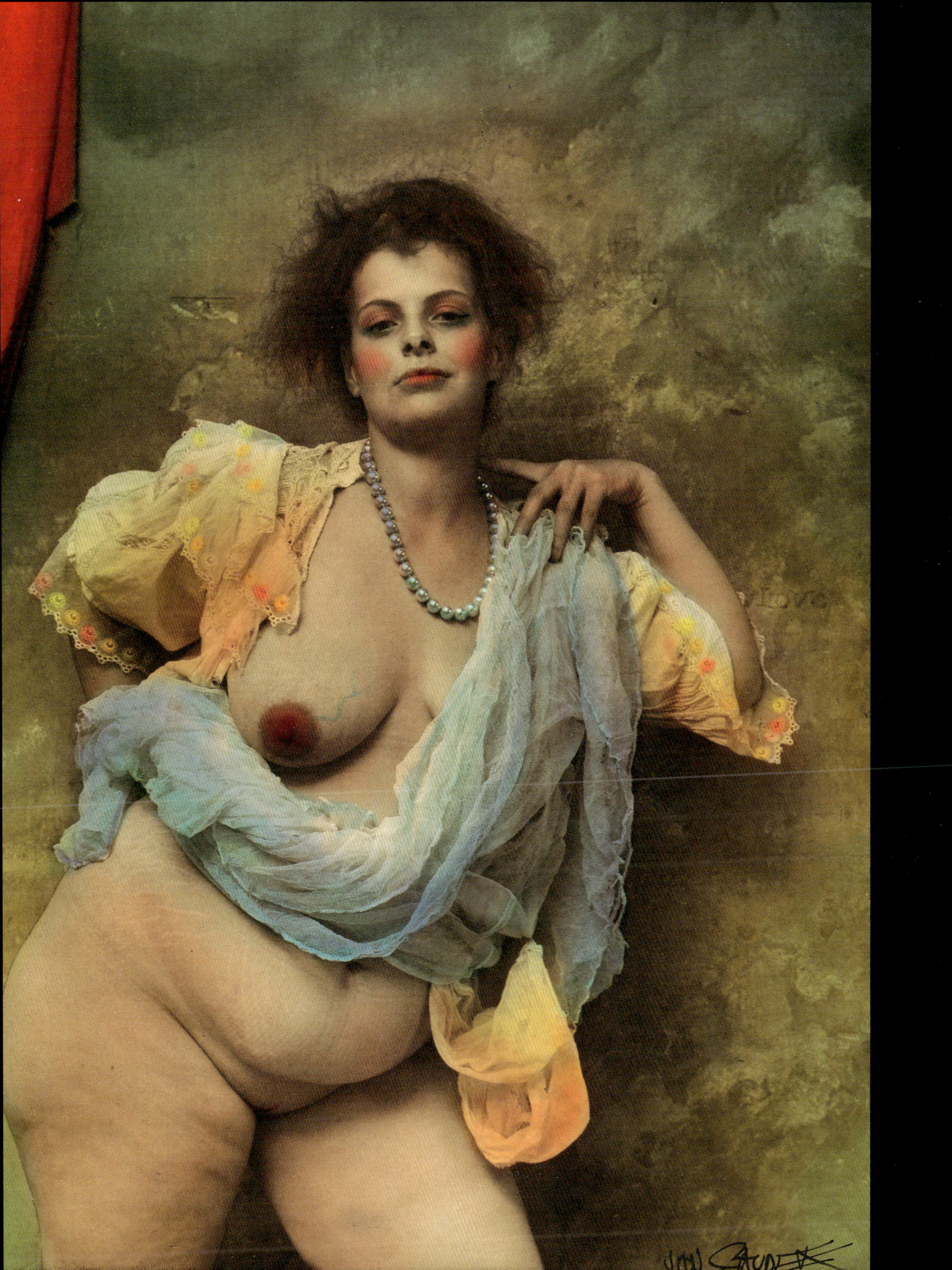
JAN SAUDEK

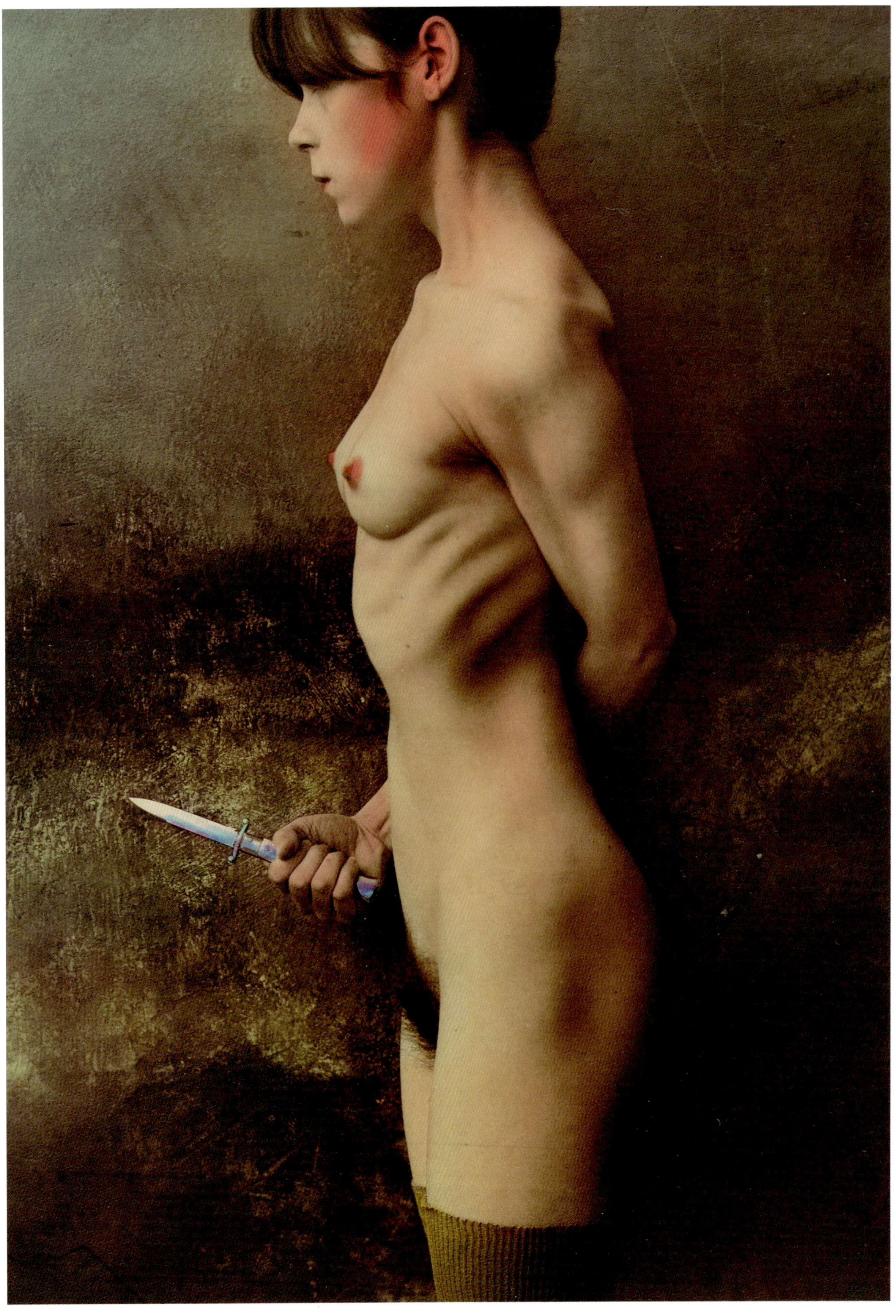

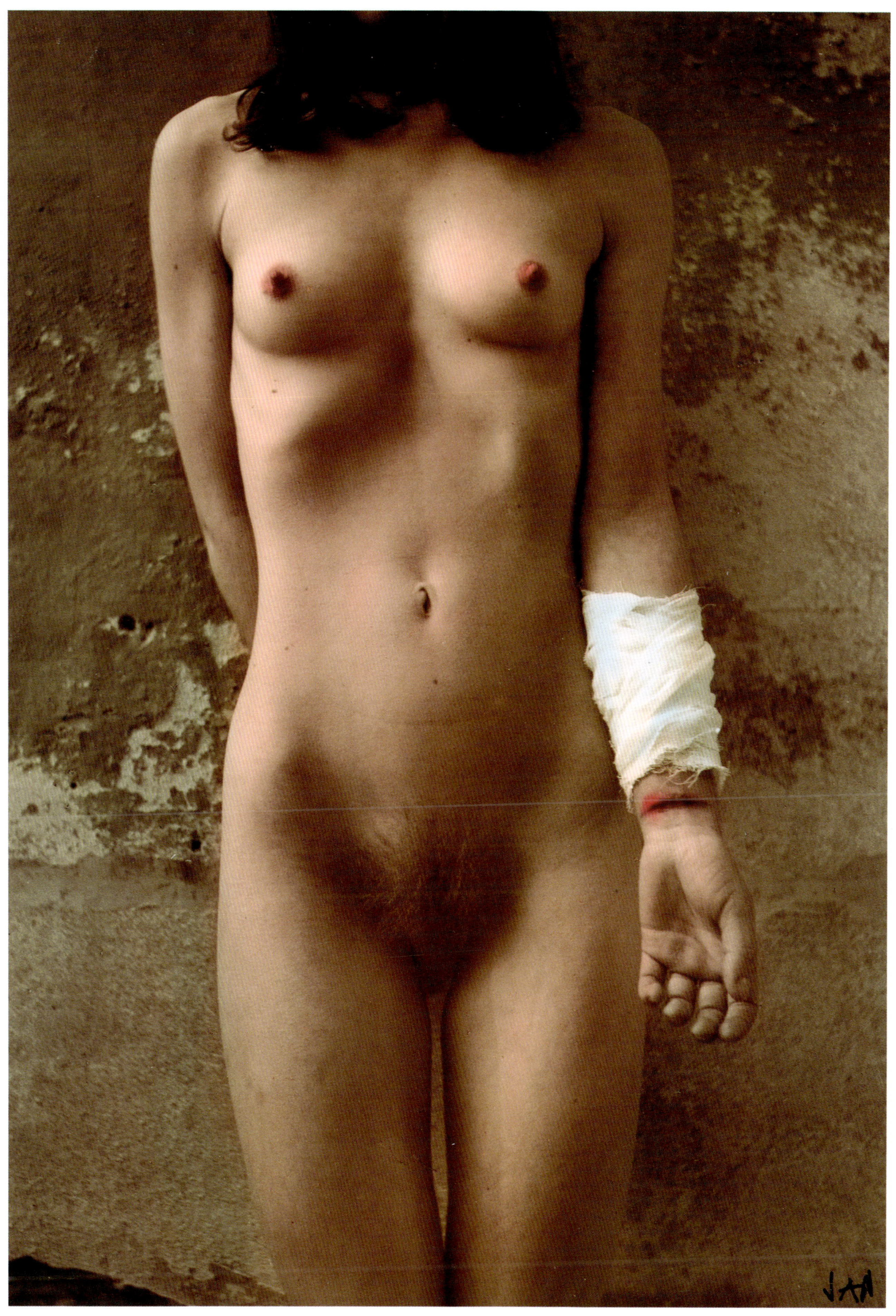

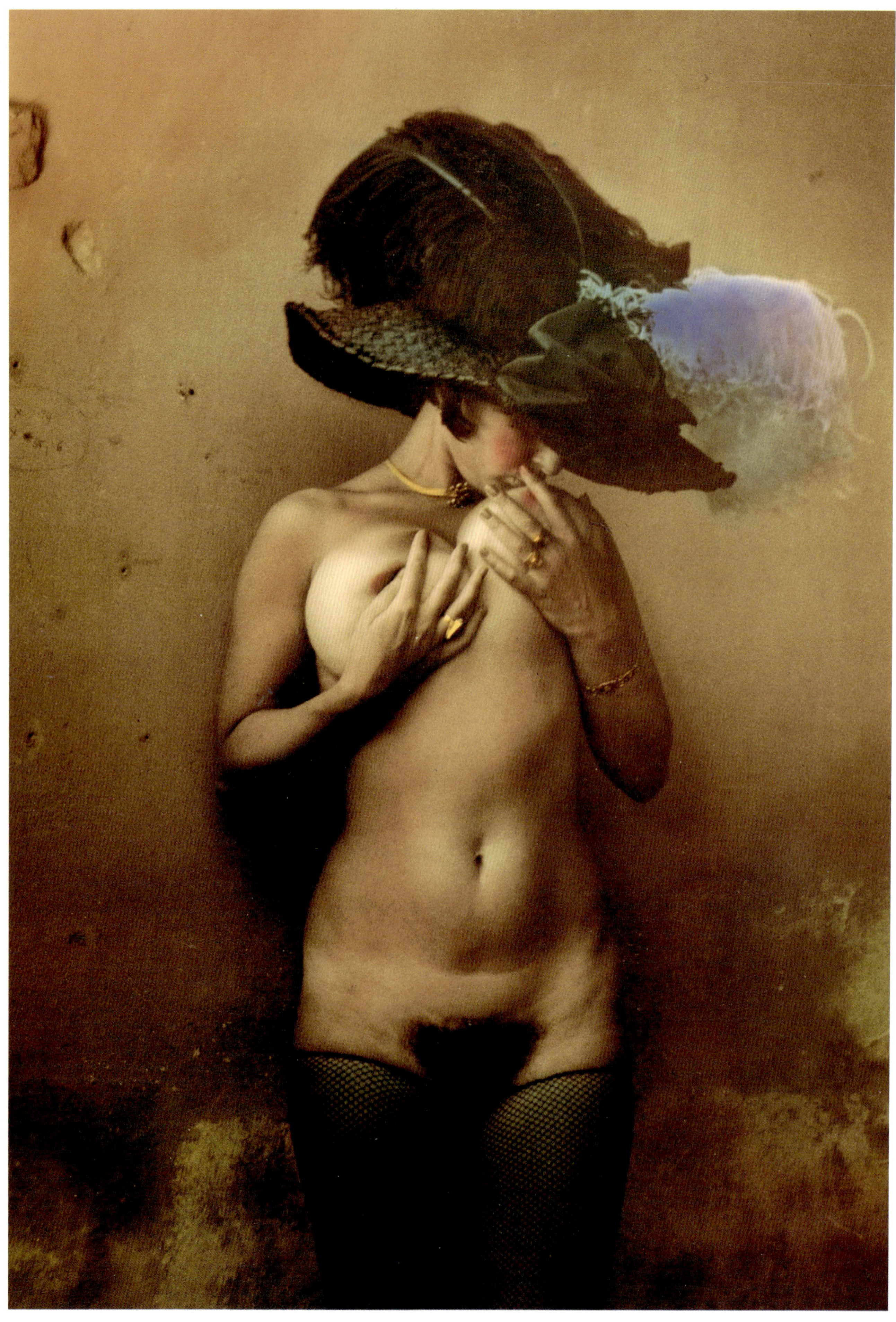

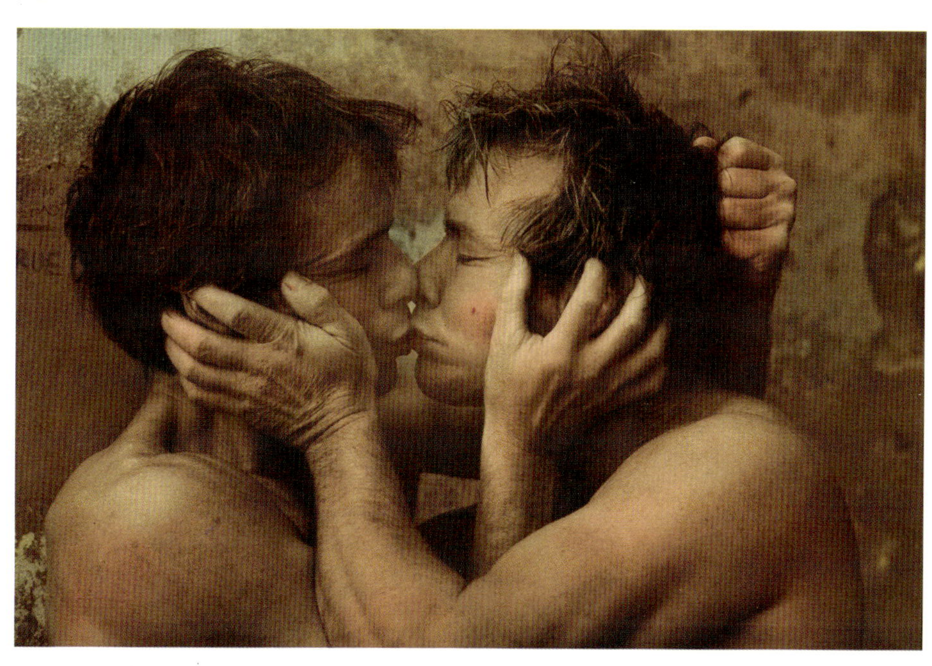

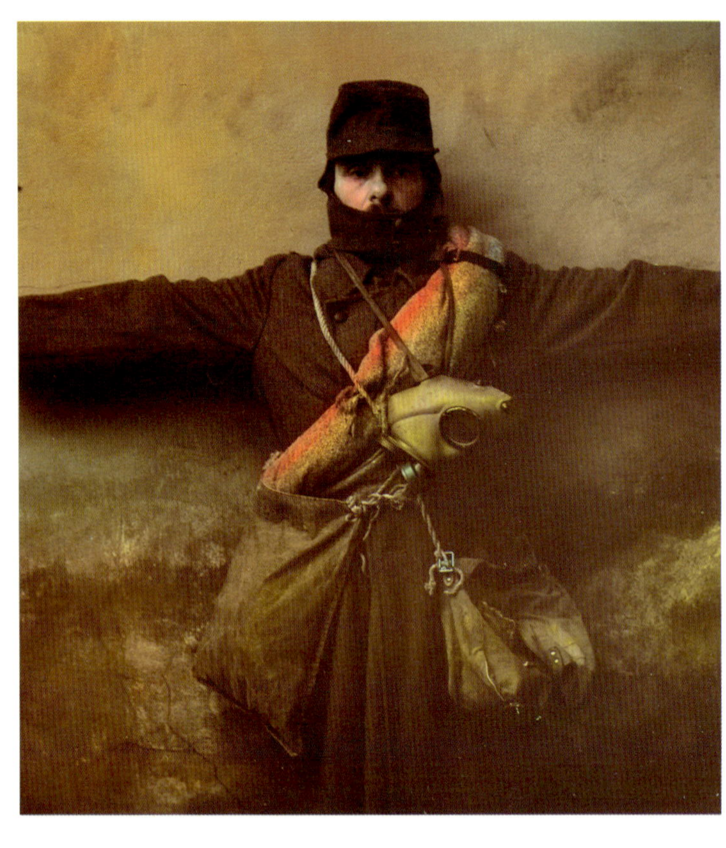

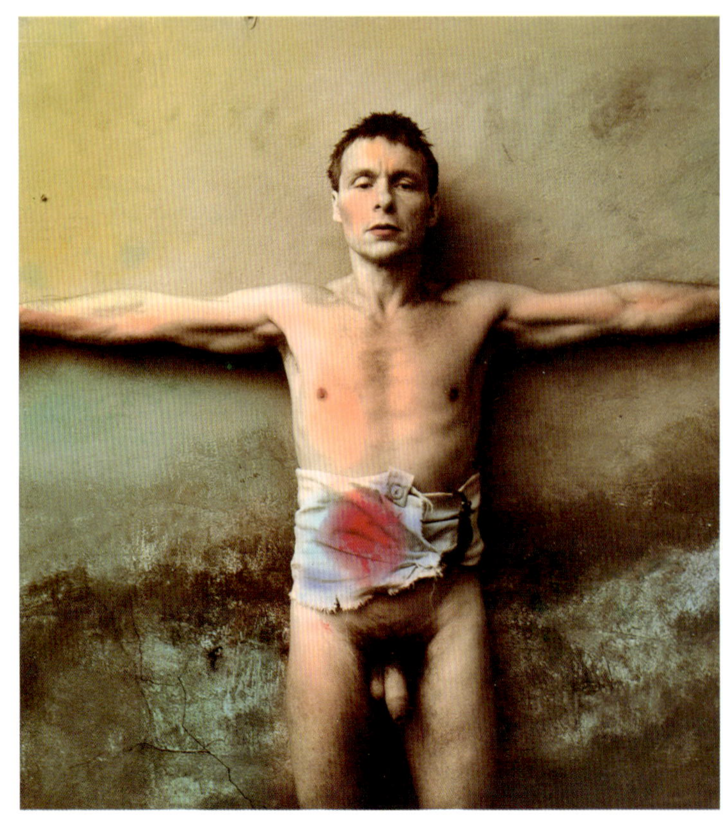

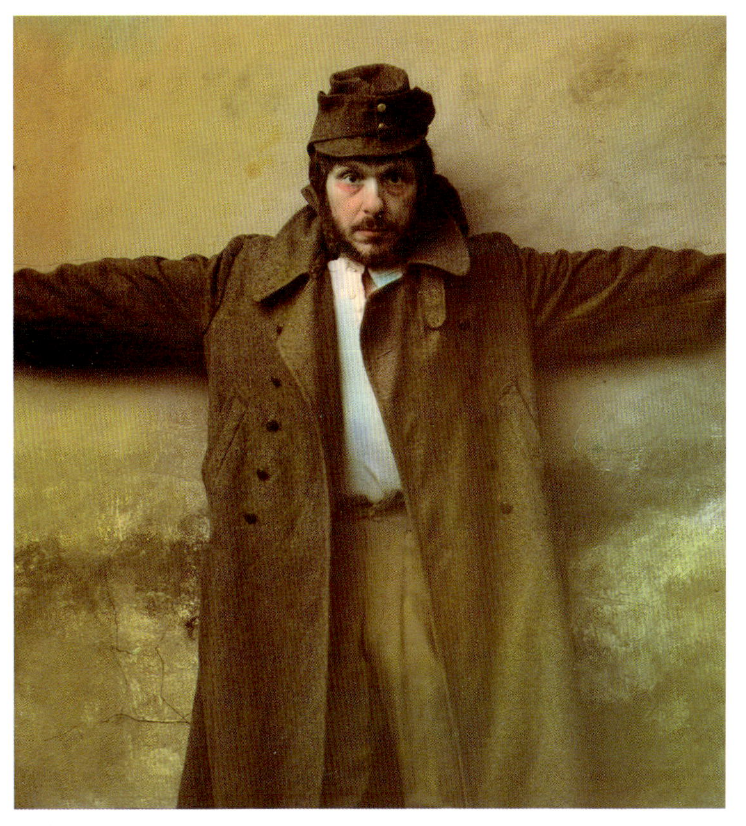

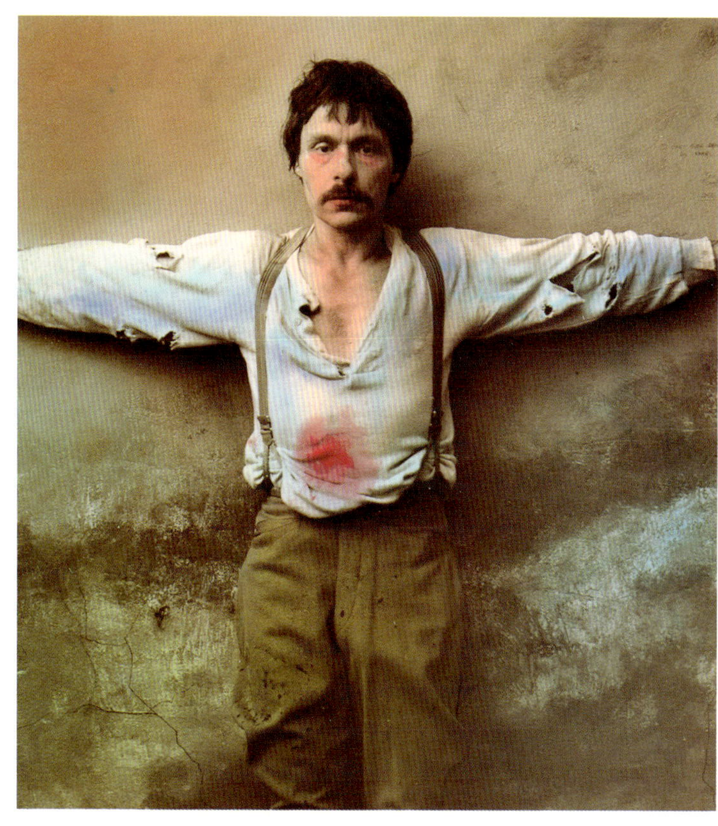

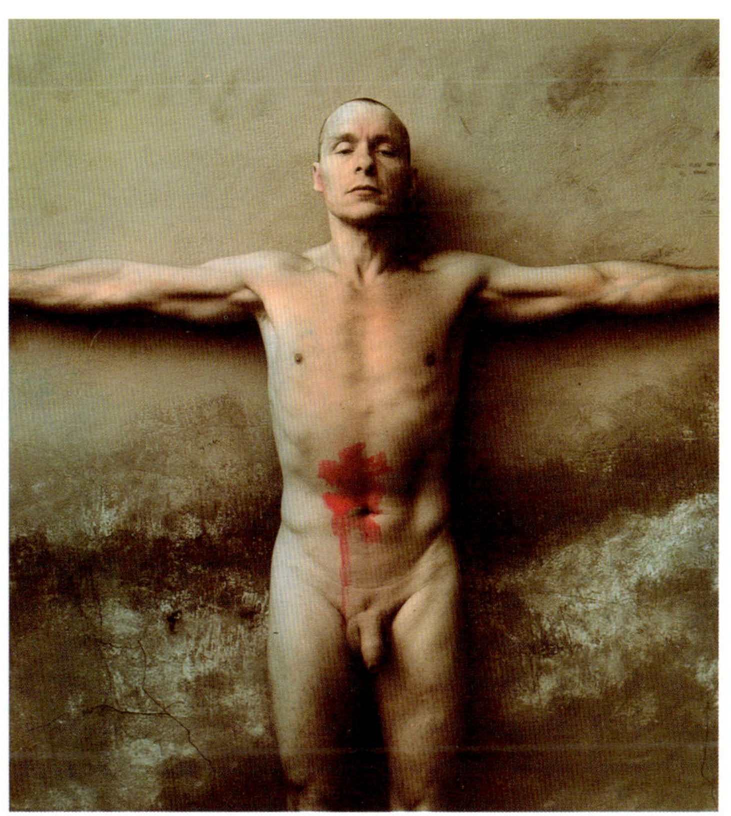

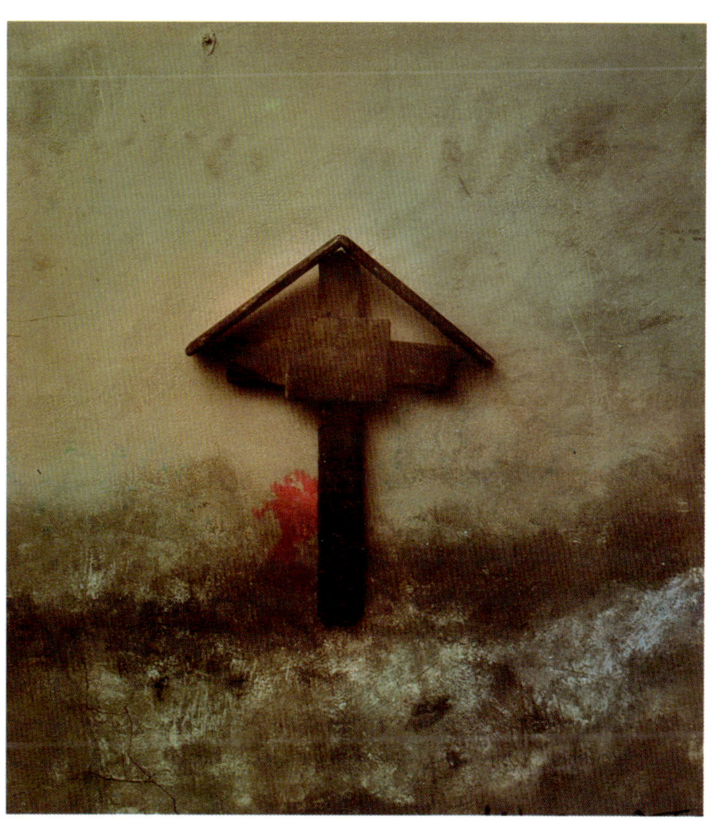

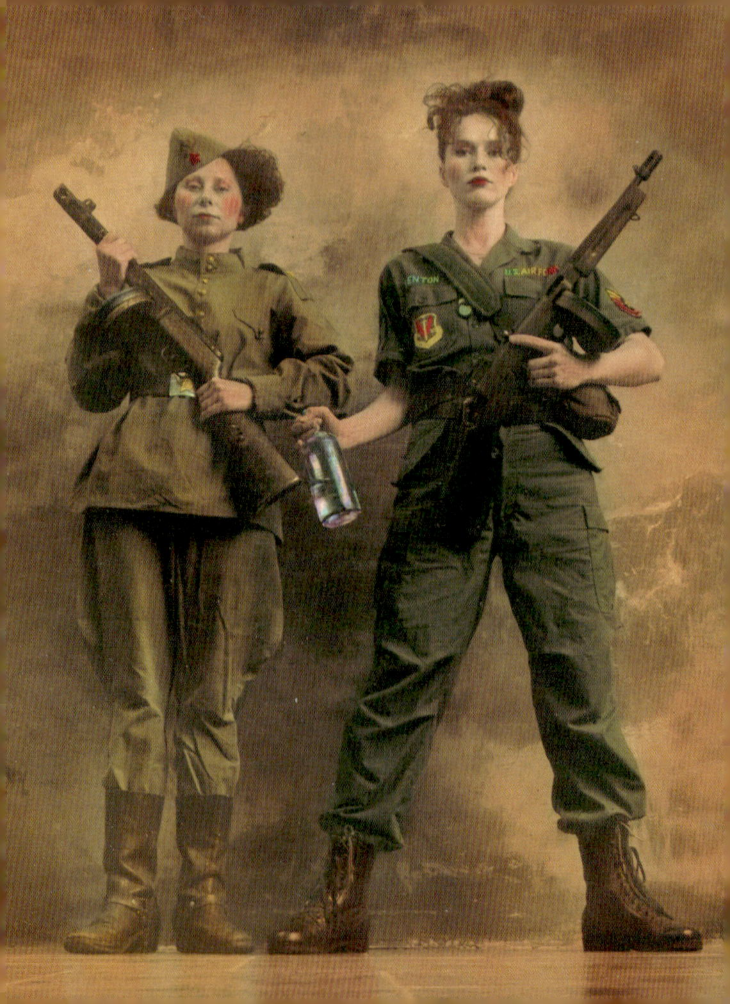

Neben neueren Arbeiten zeigt dieses Kapitel auch einige nach thematischen Gesichtspunkten-ausgewählte Werke aus früheren Jahren.

A côté des œuvres tardives, on trouvera dans ce chapitre quelques travaux plus anciens choisis pour leur sujet.

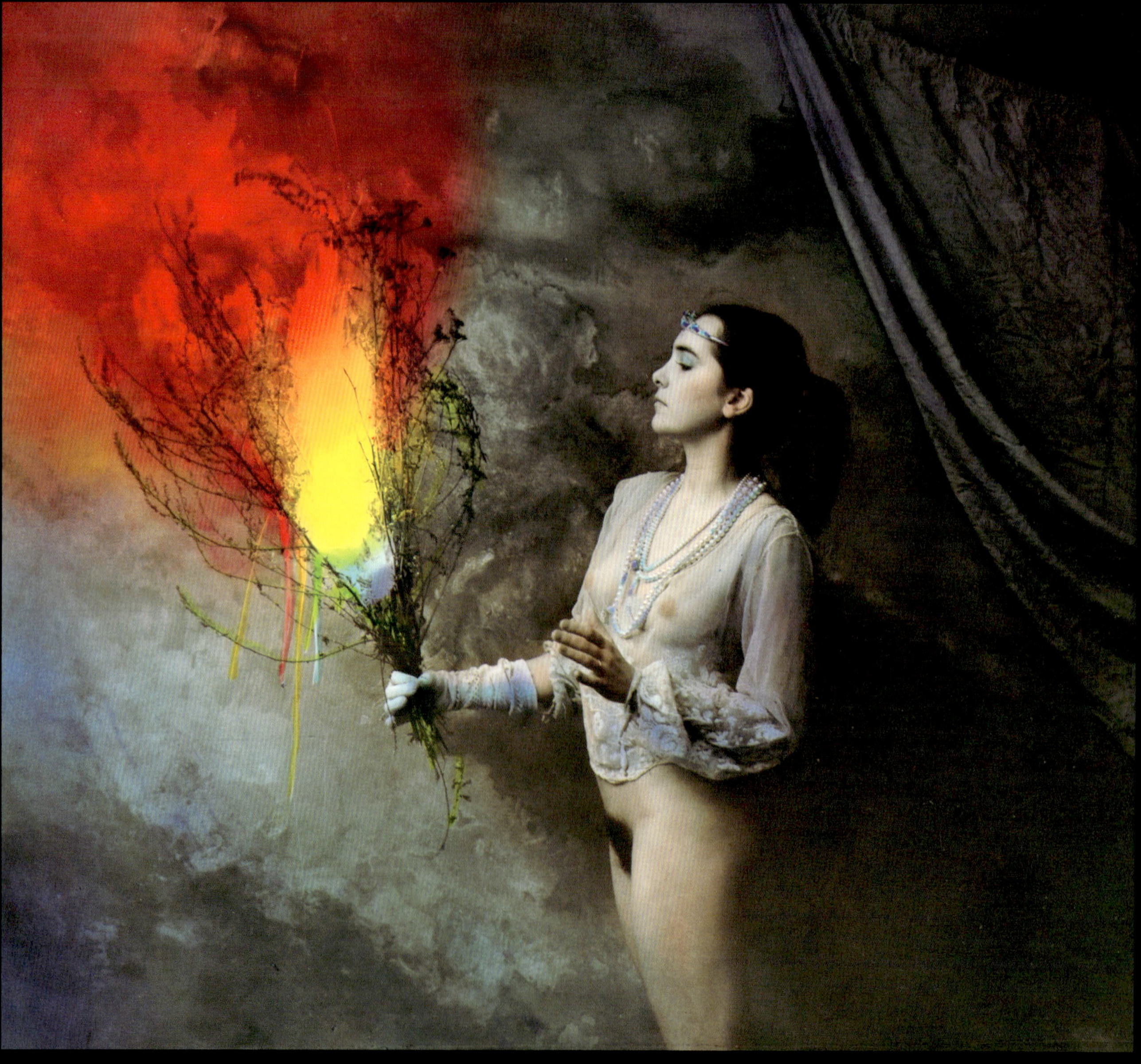

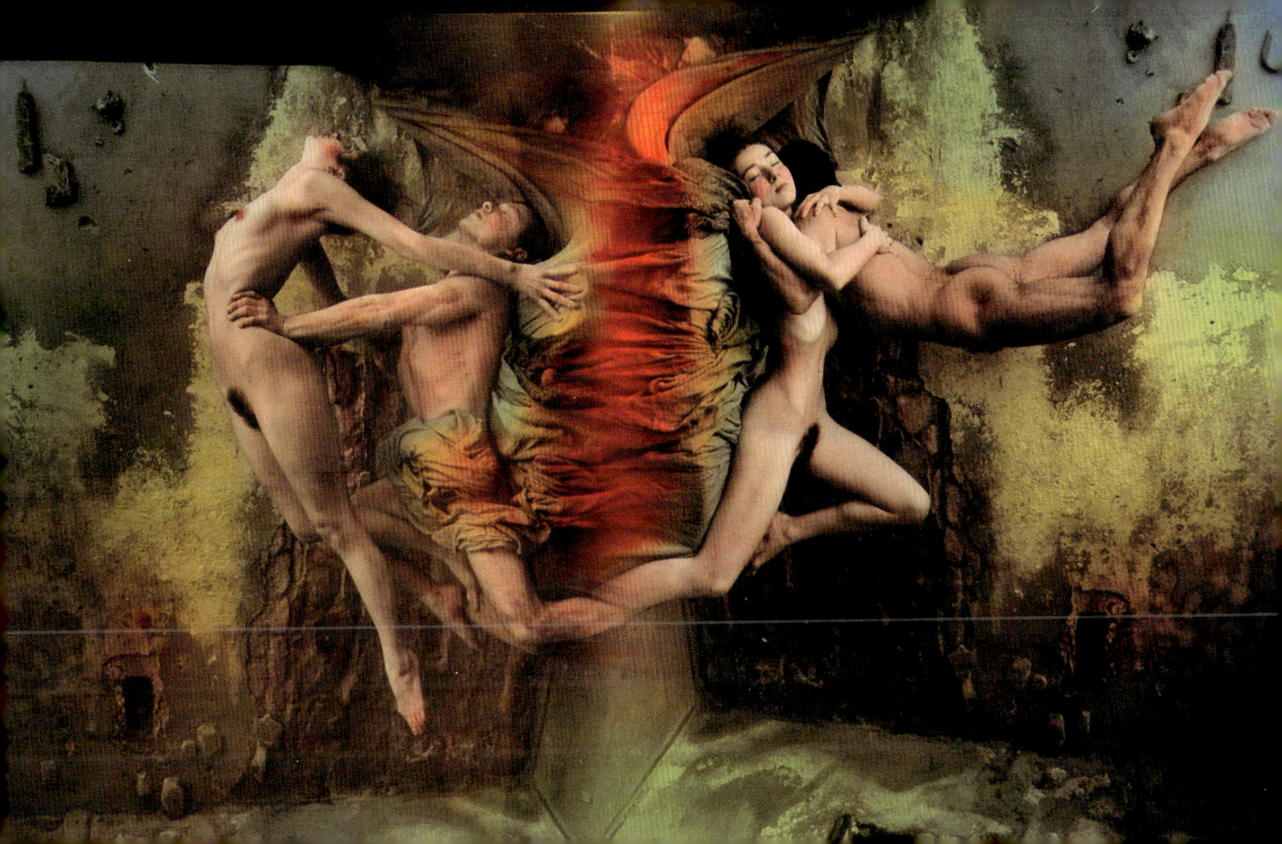

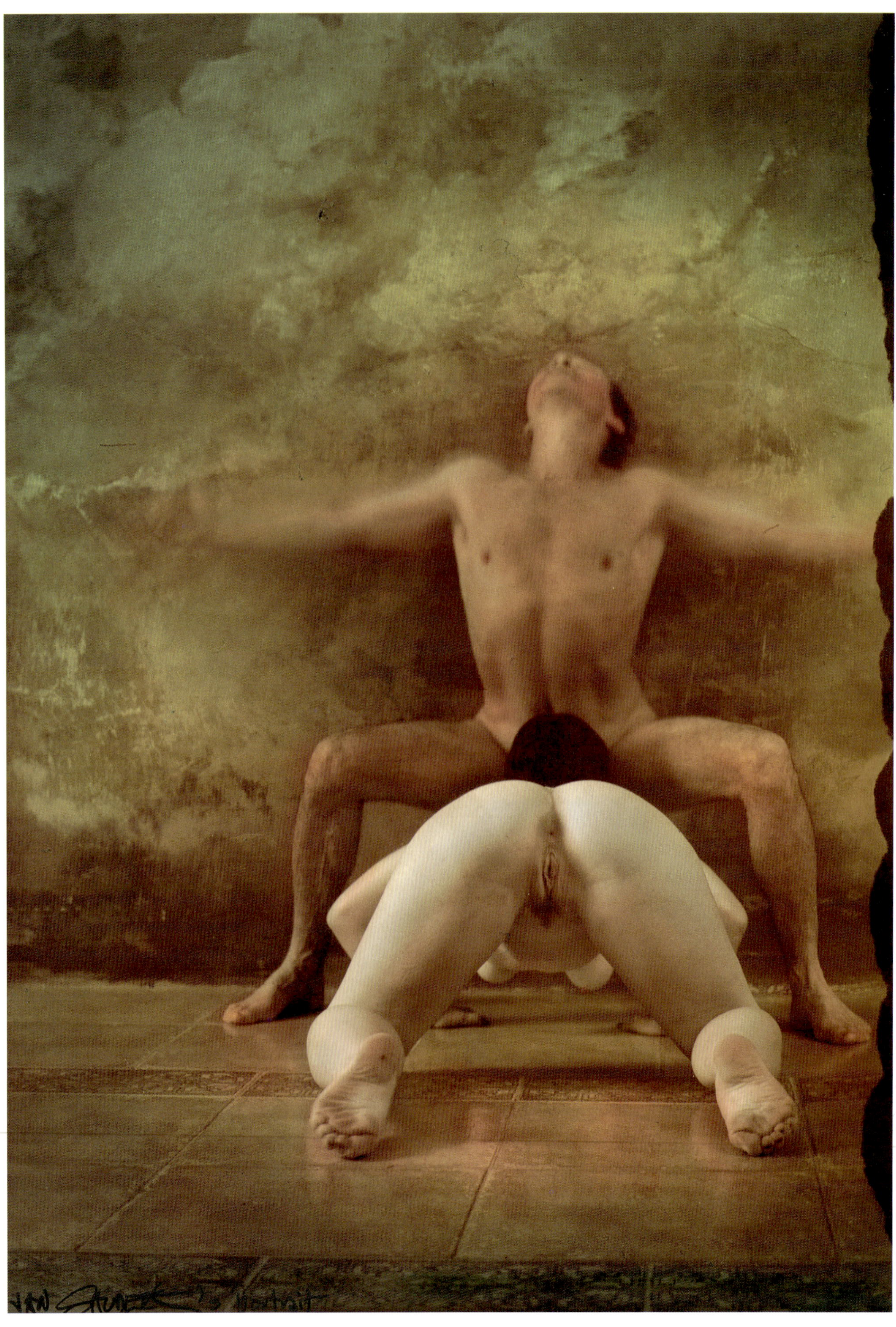

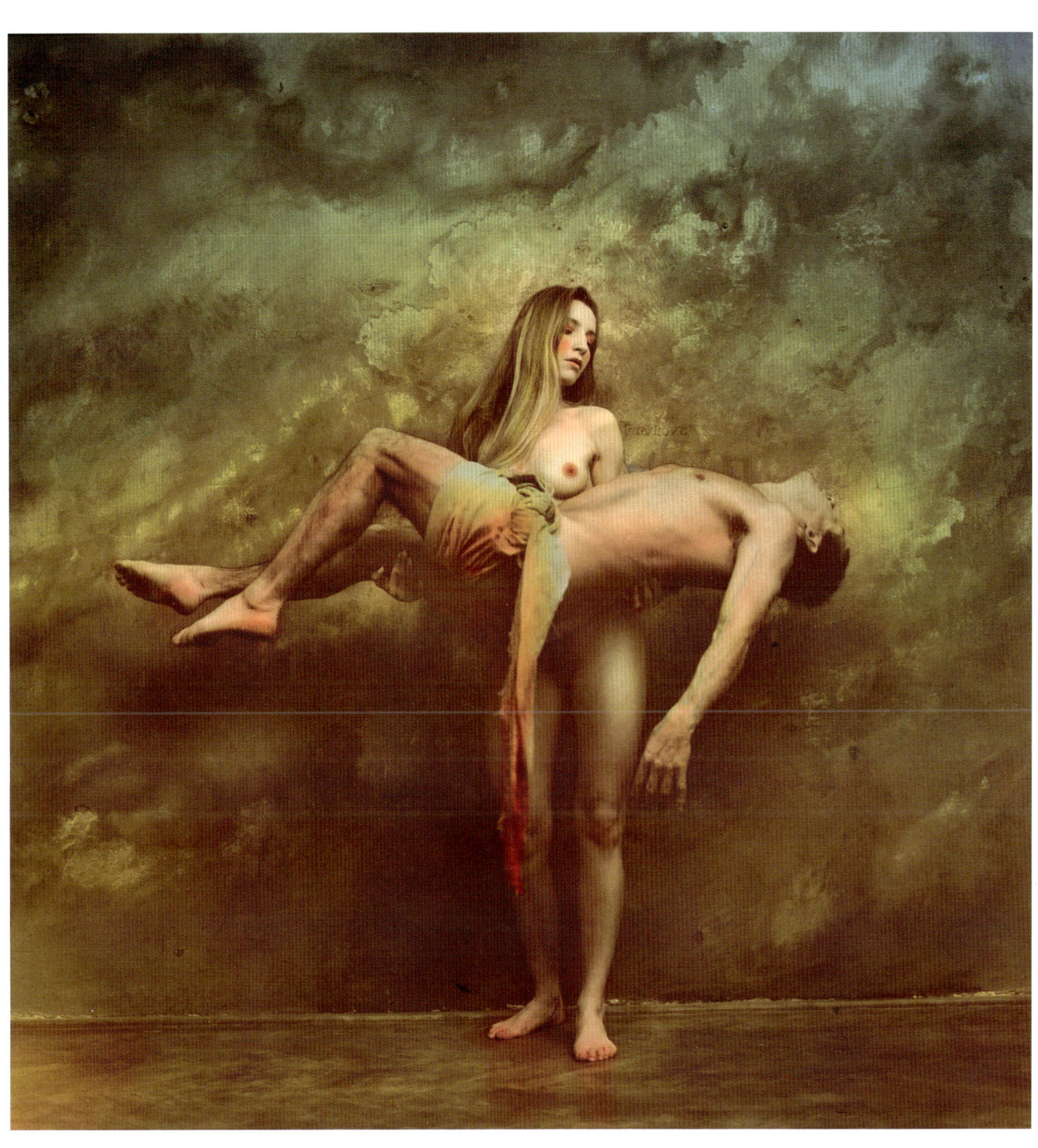

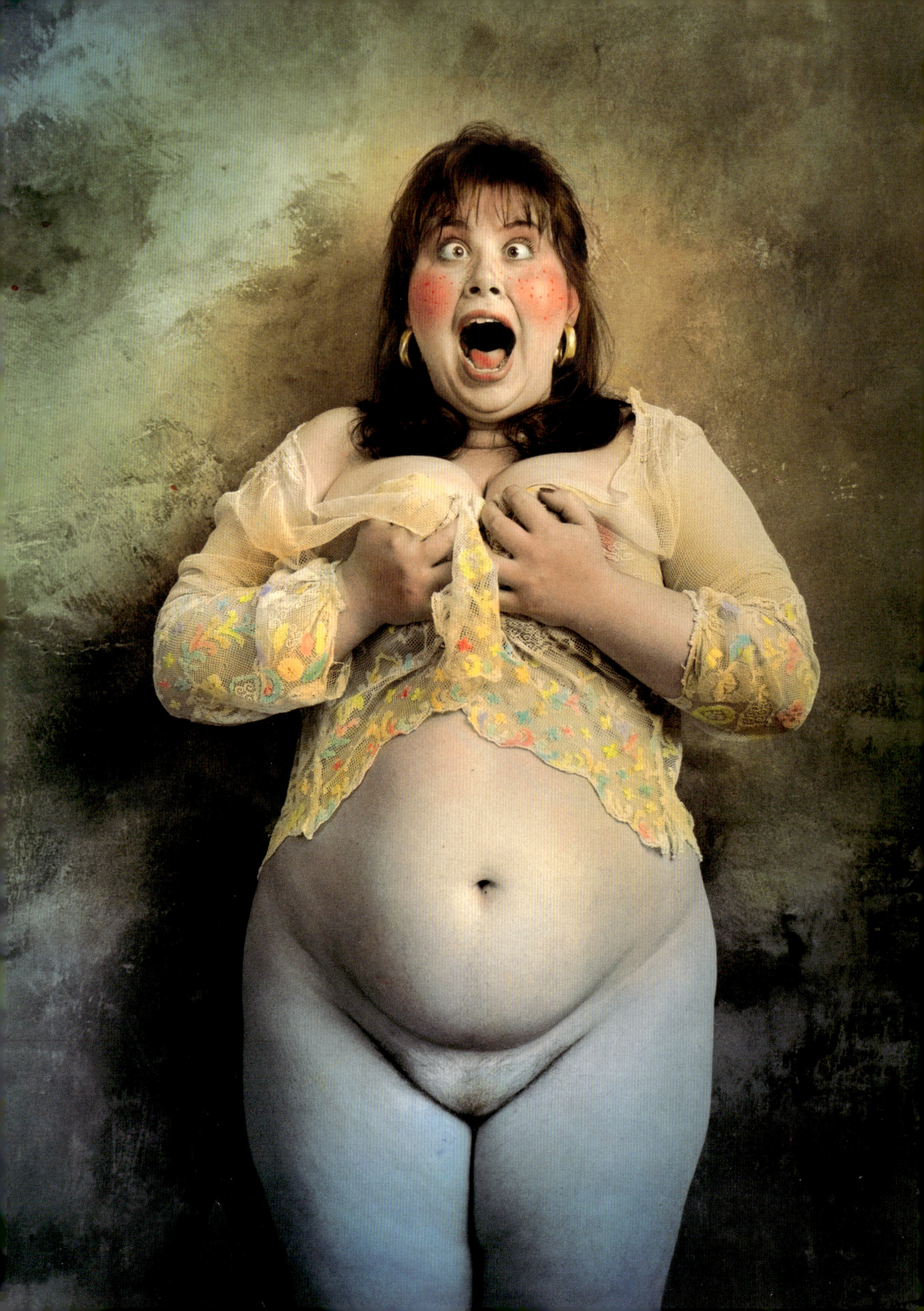

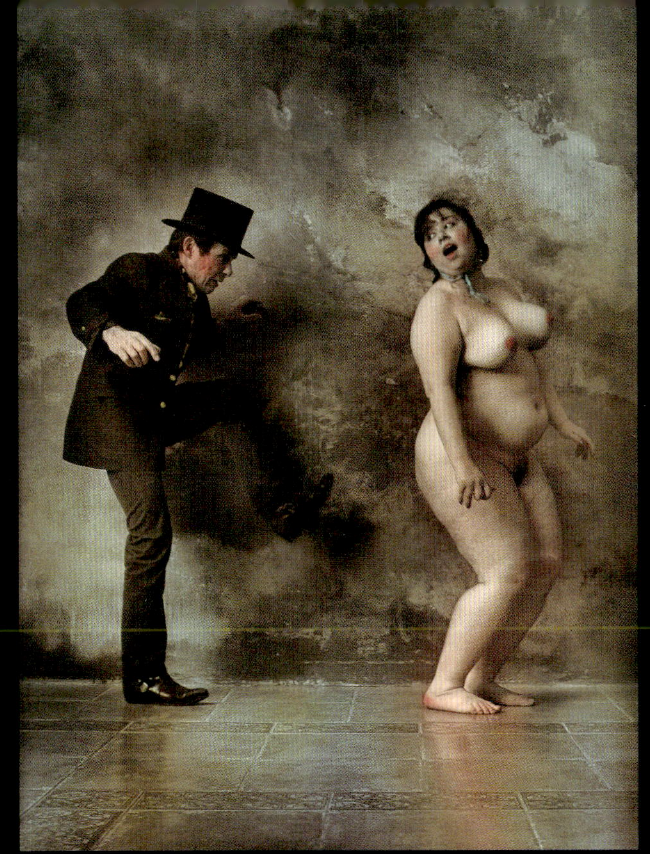

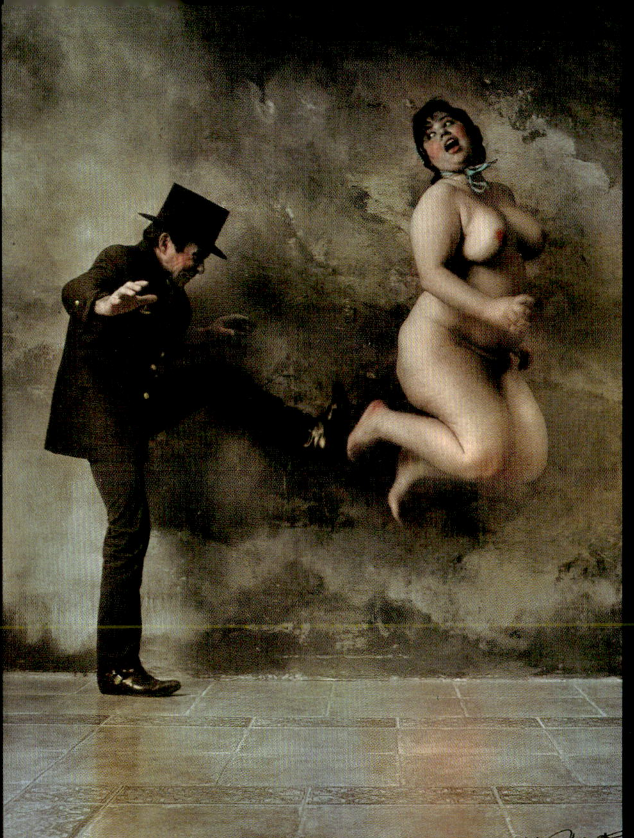

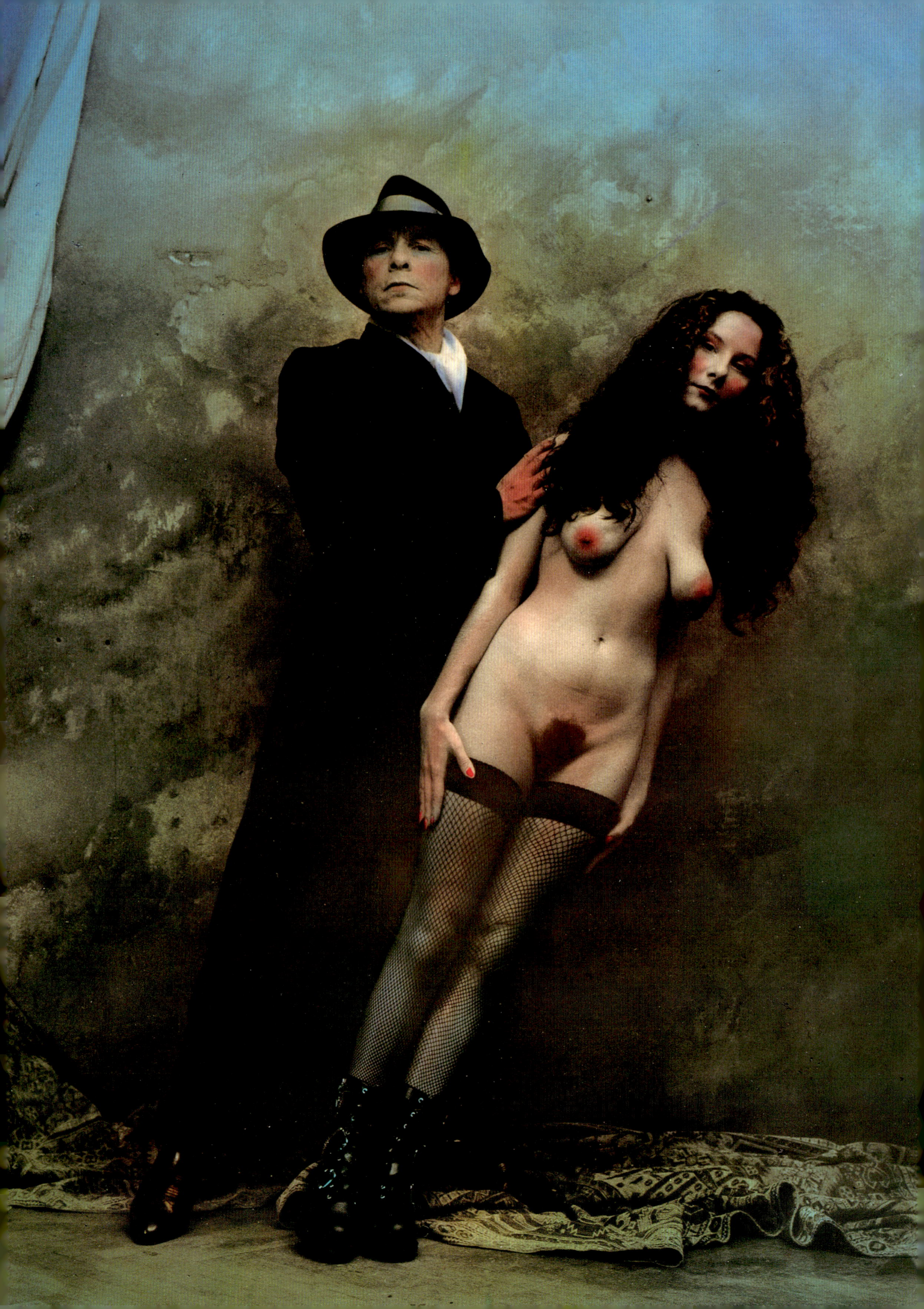

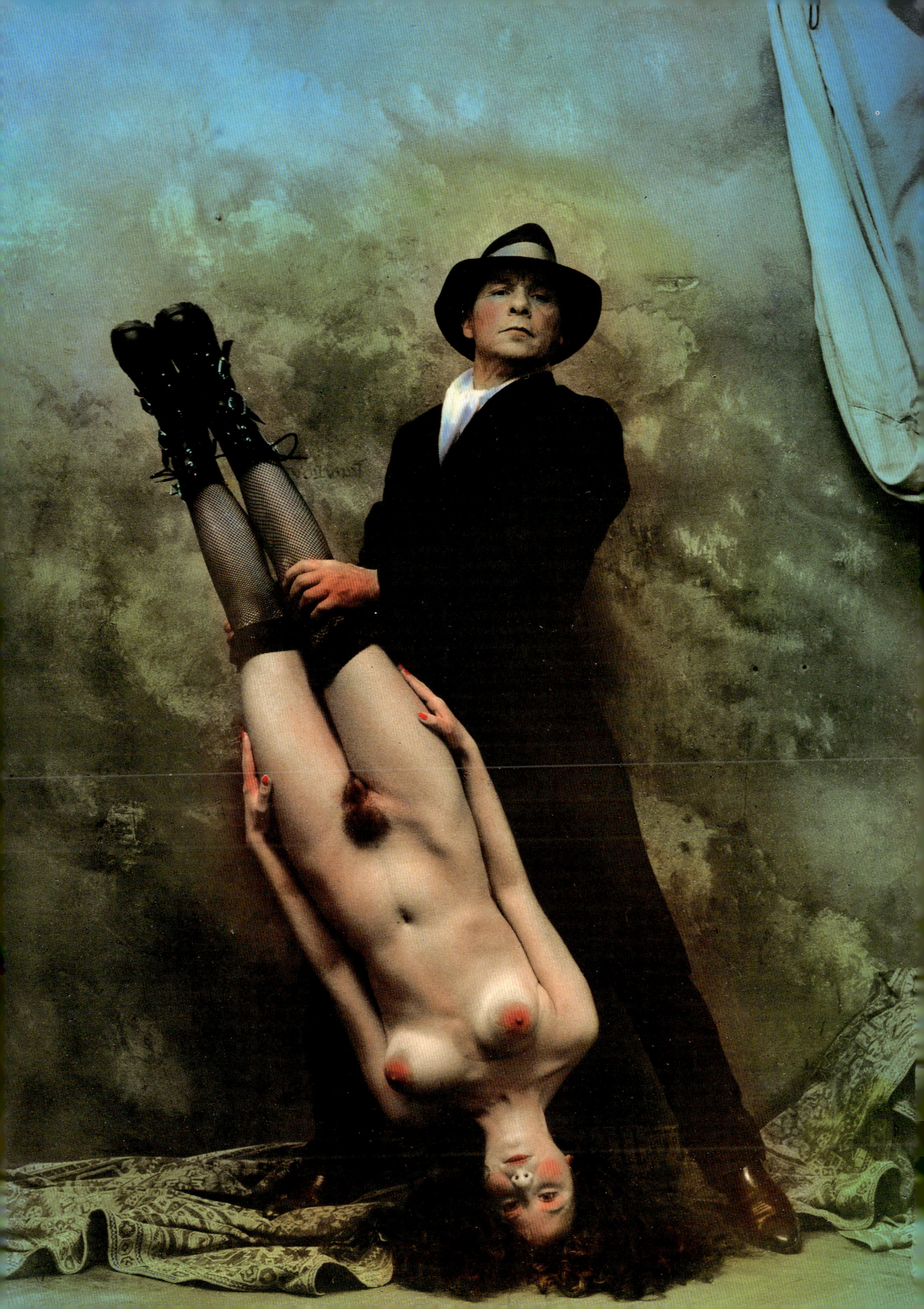

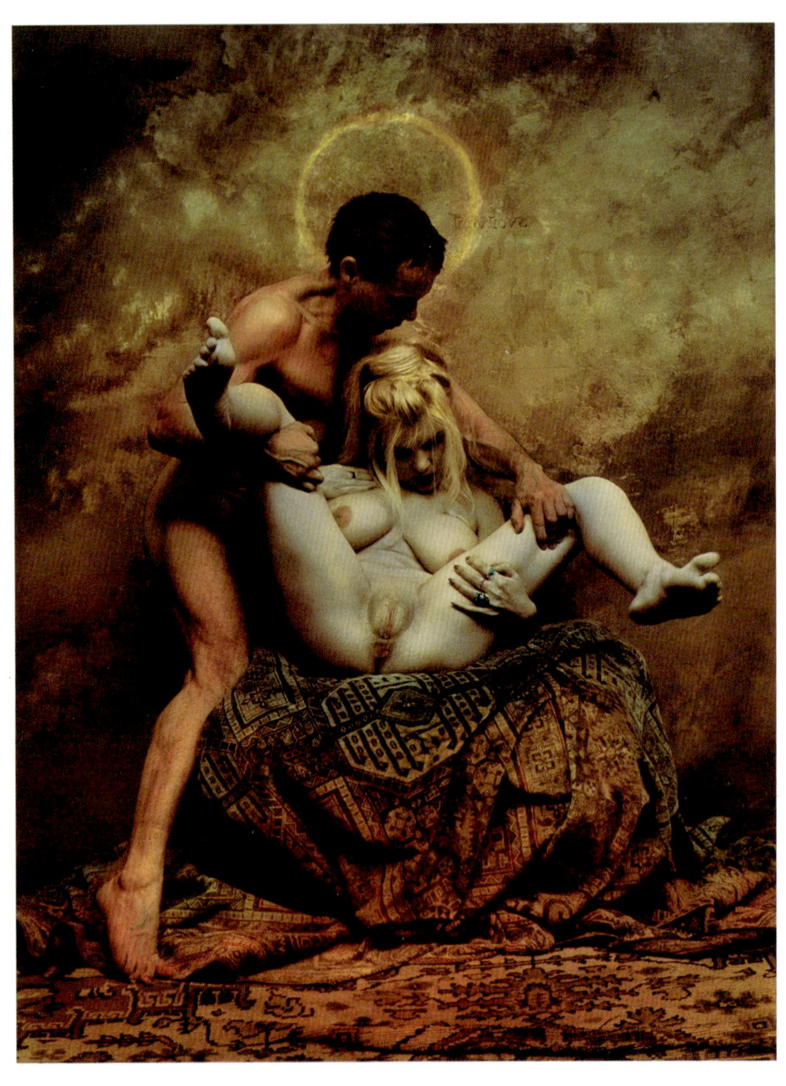

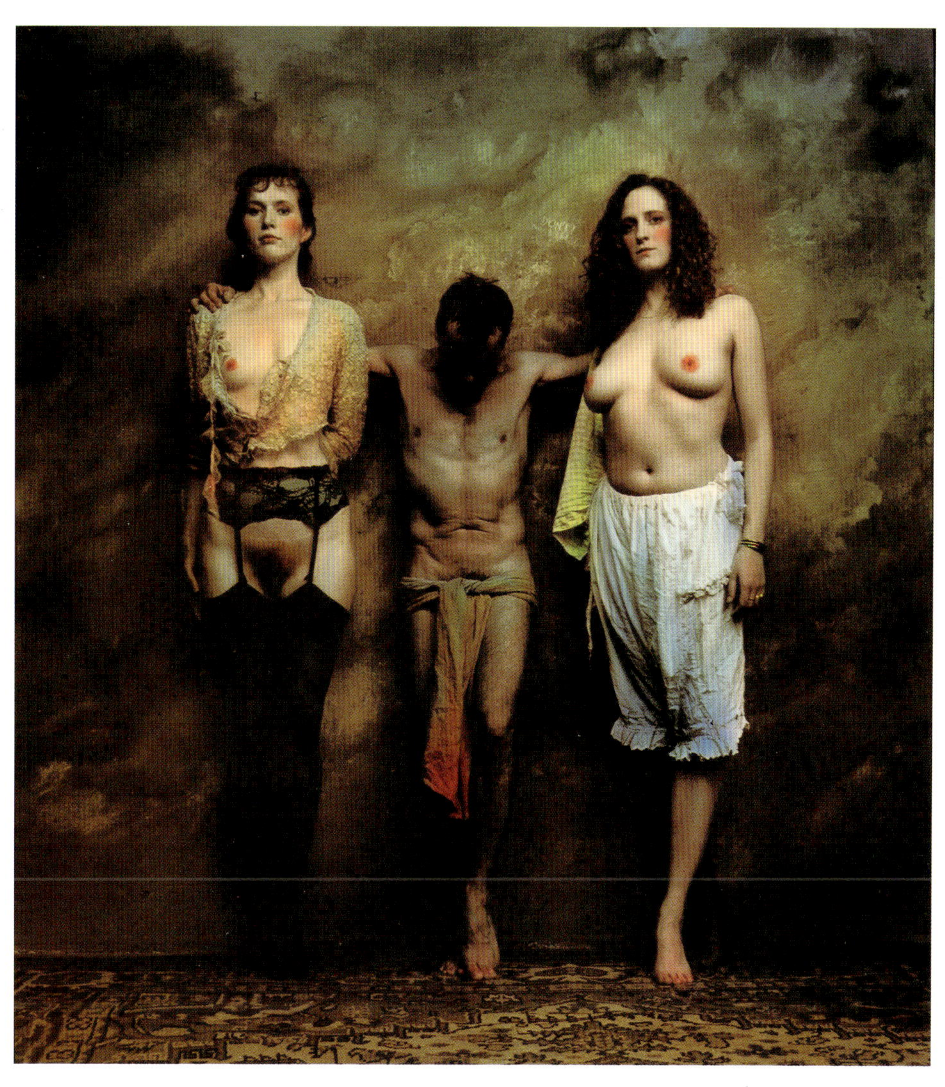

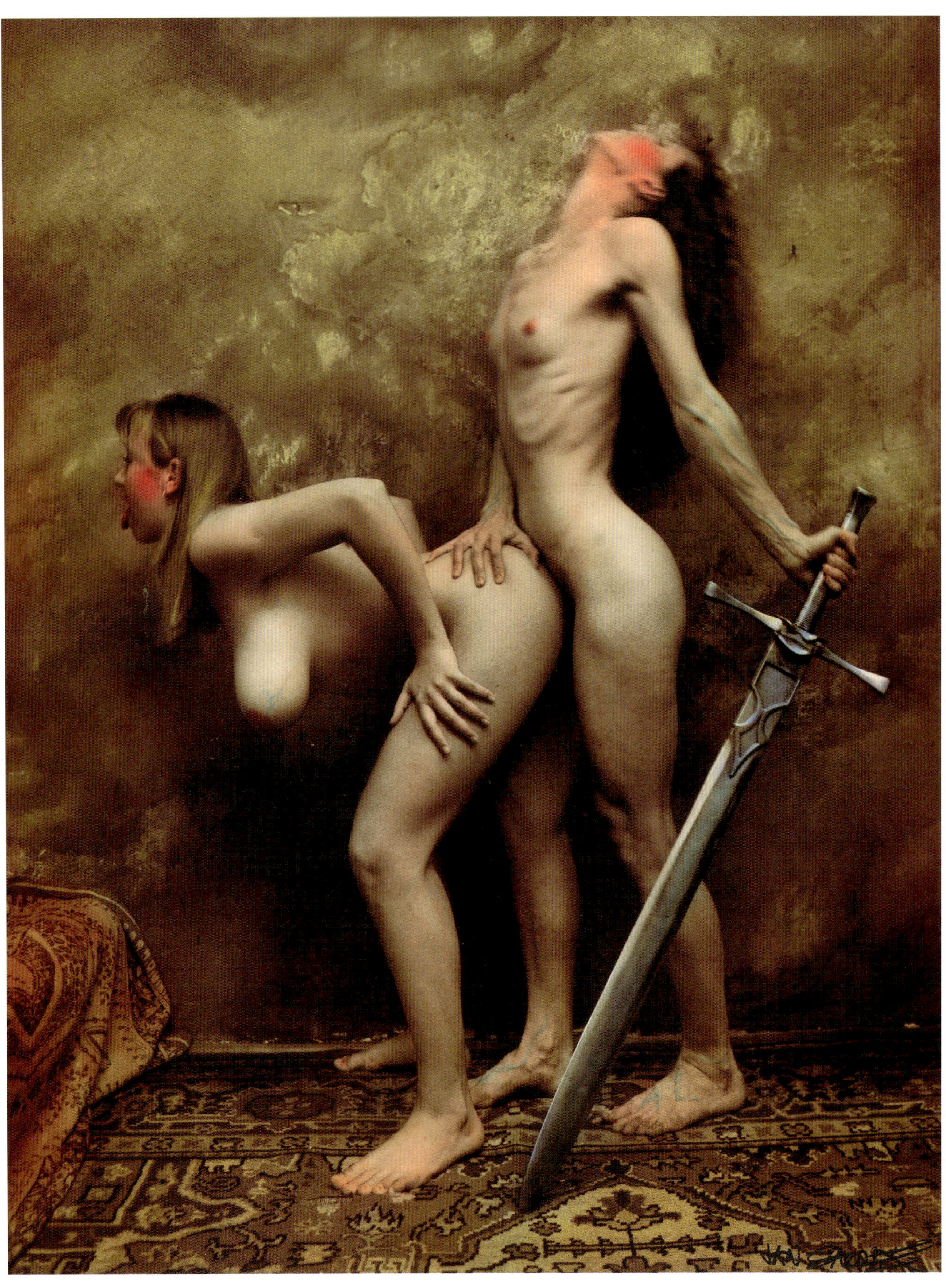

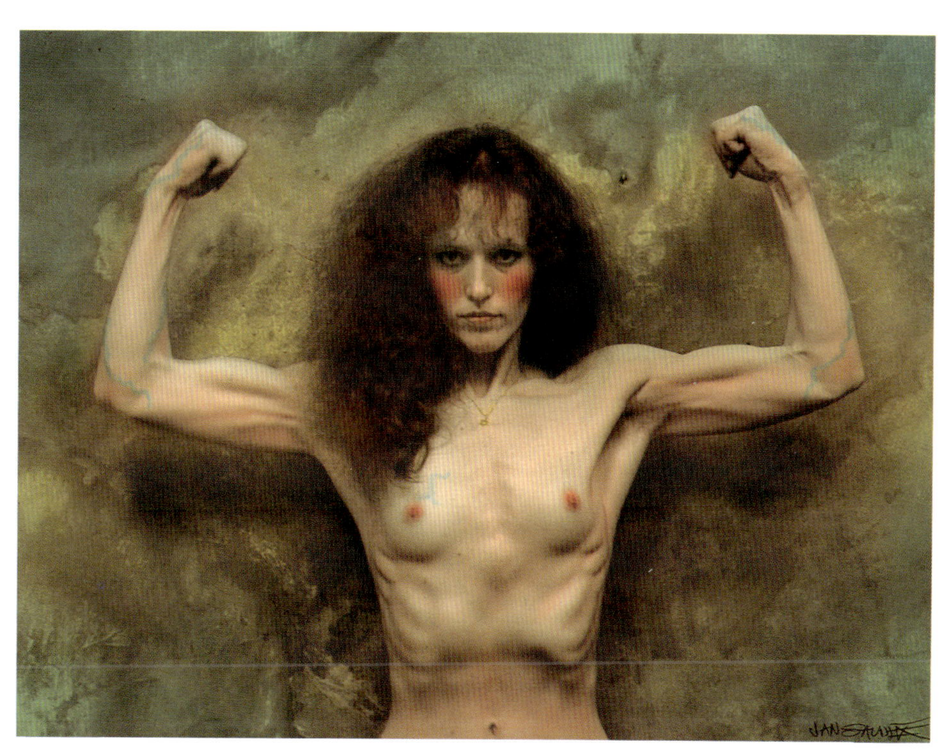

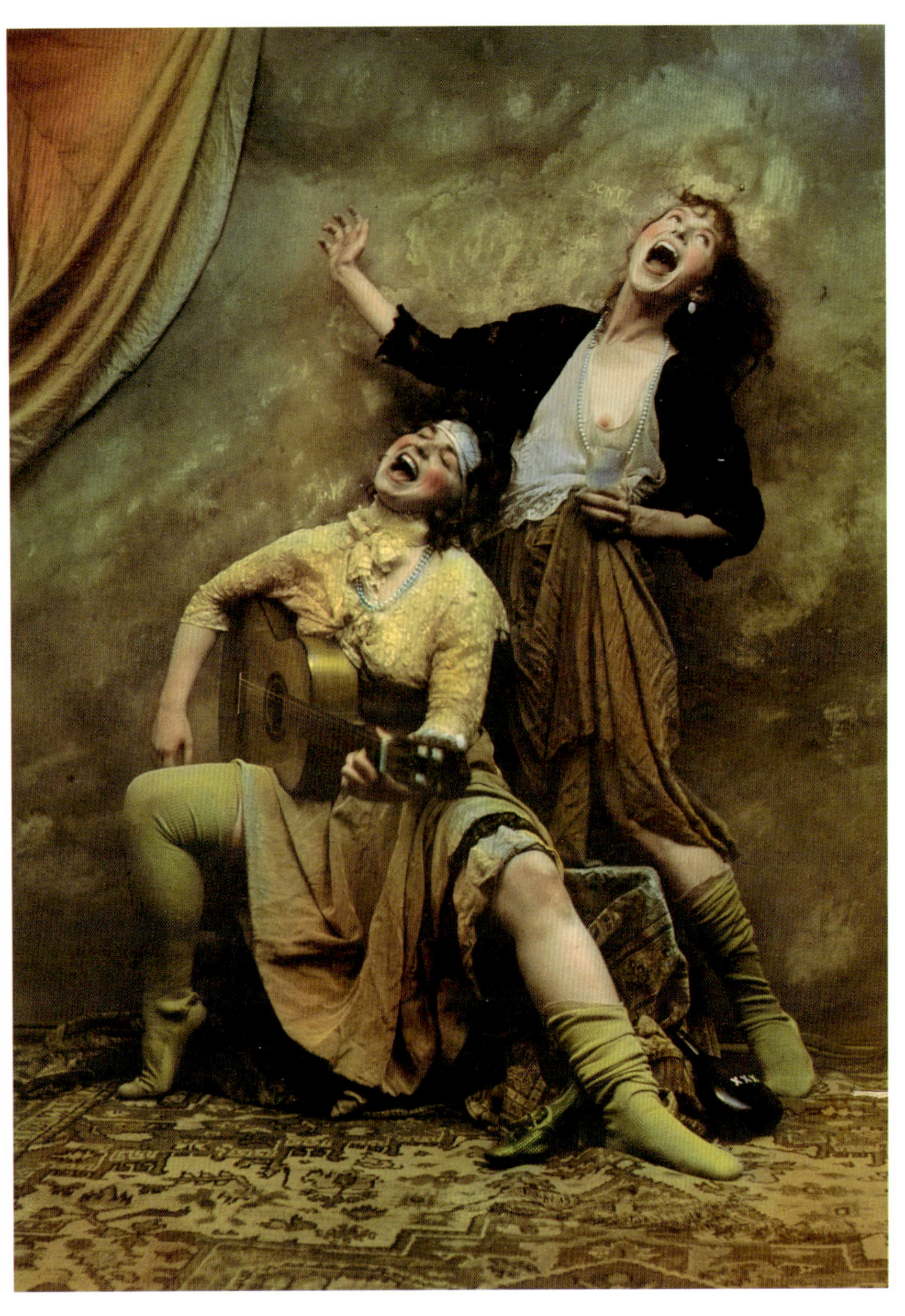

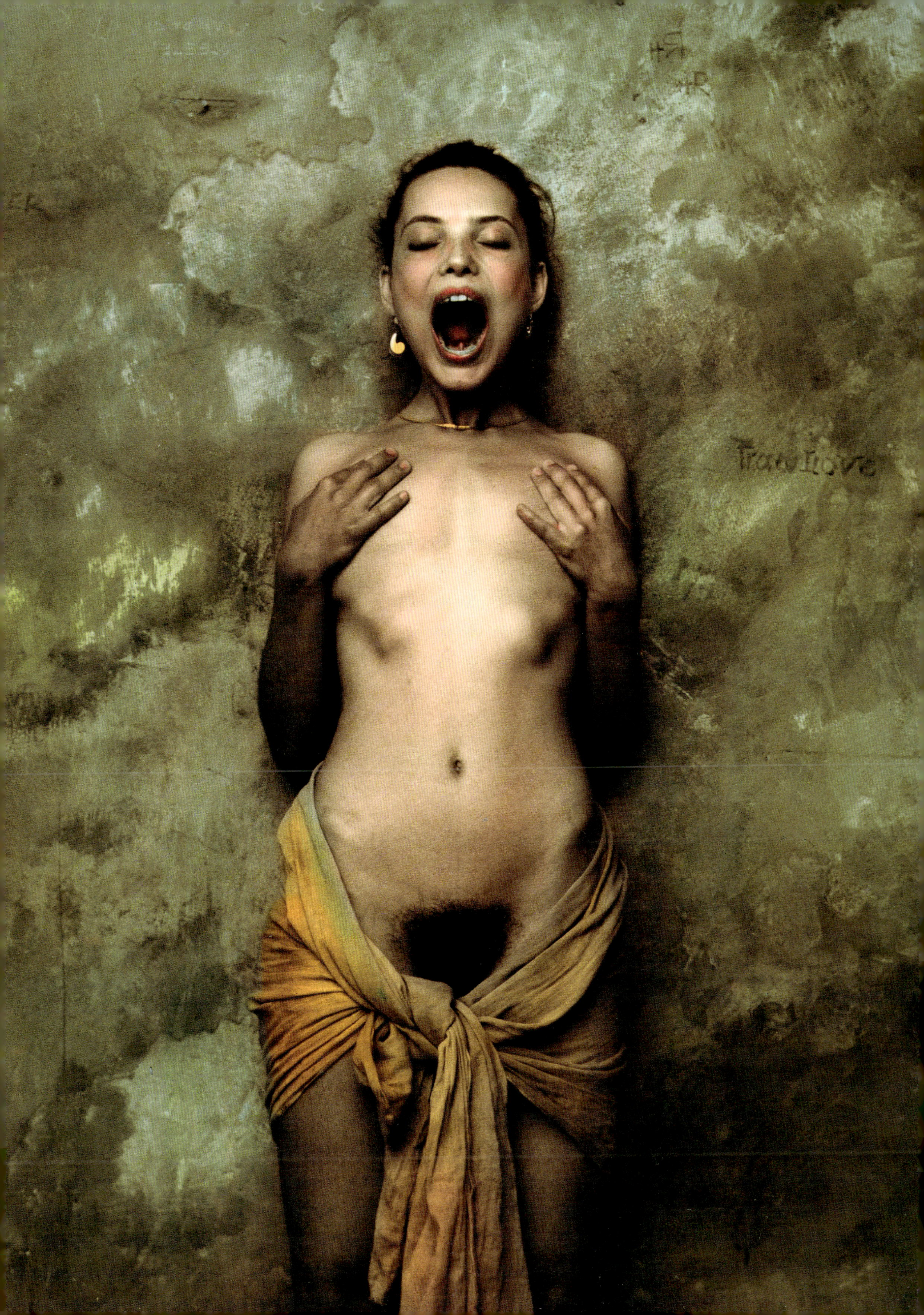

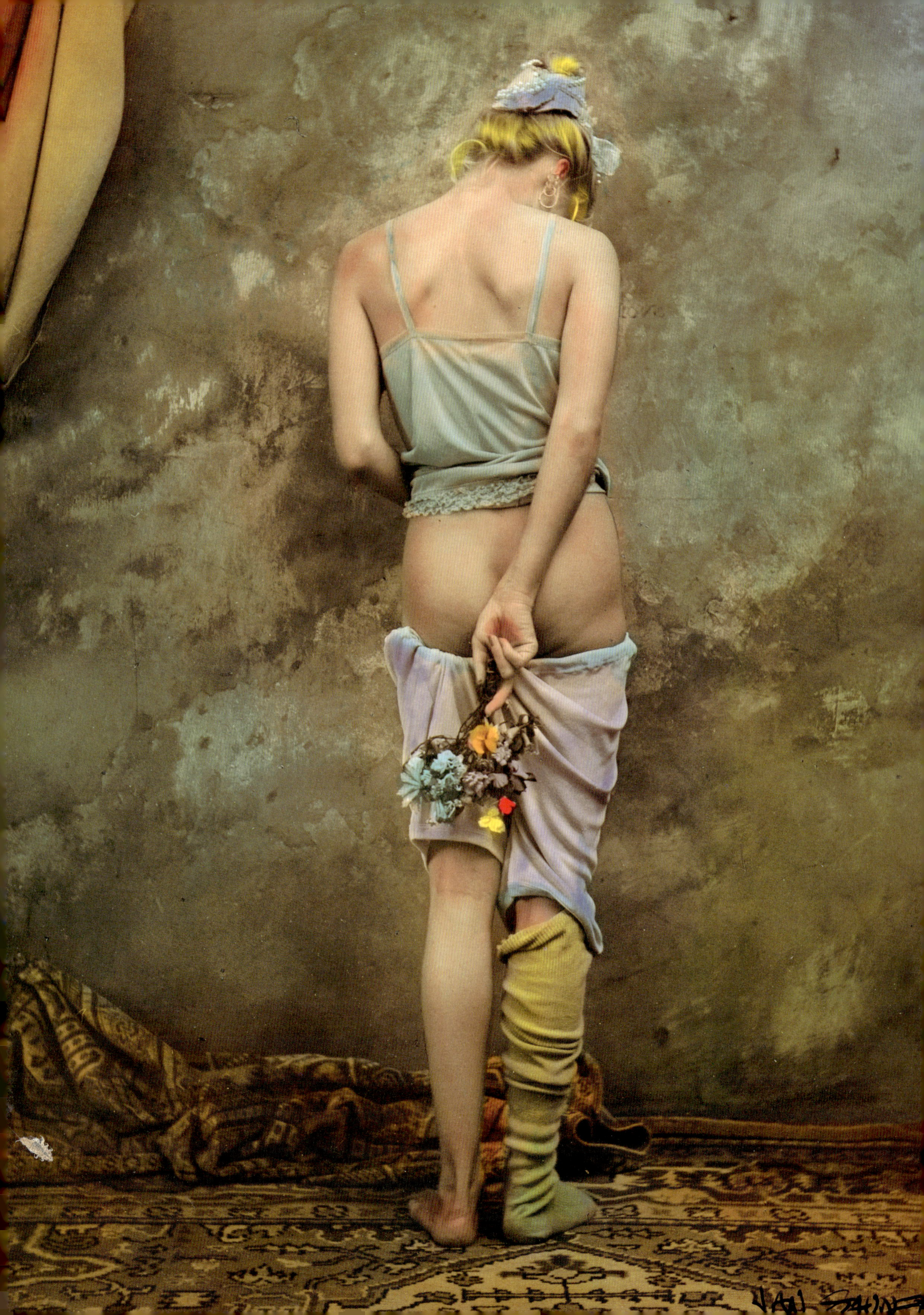

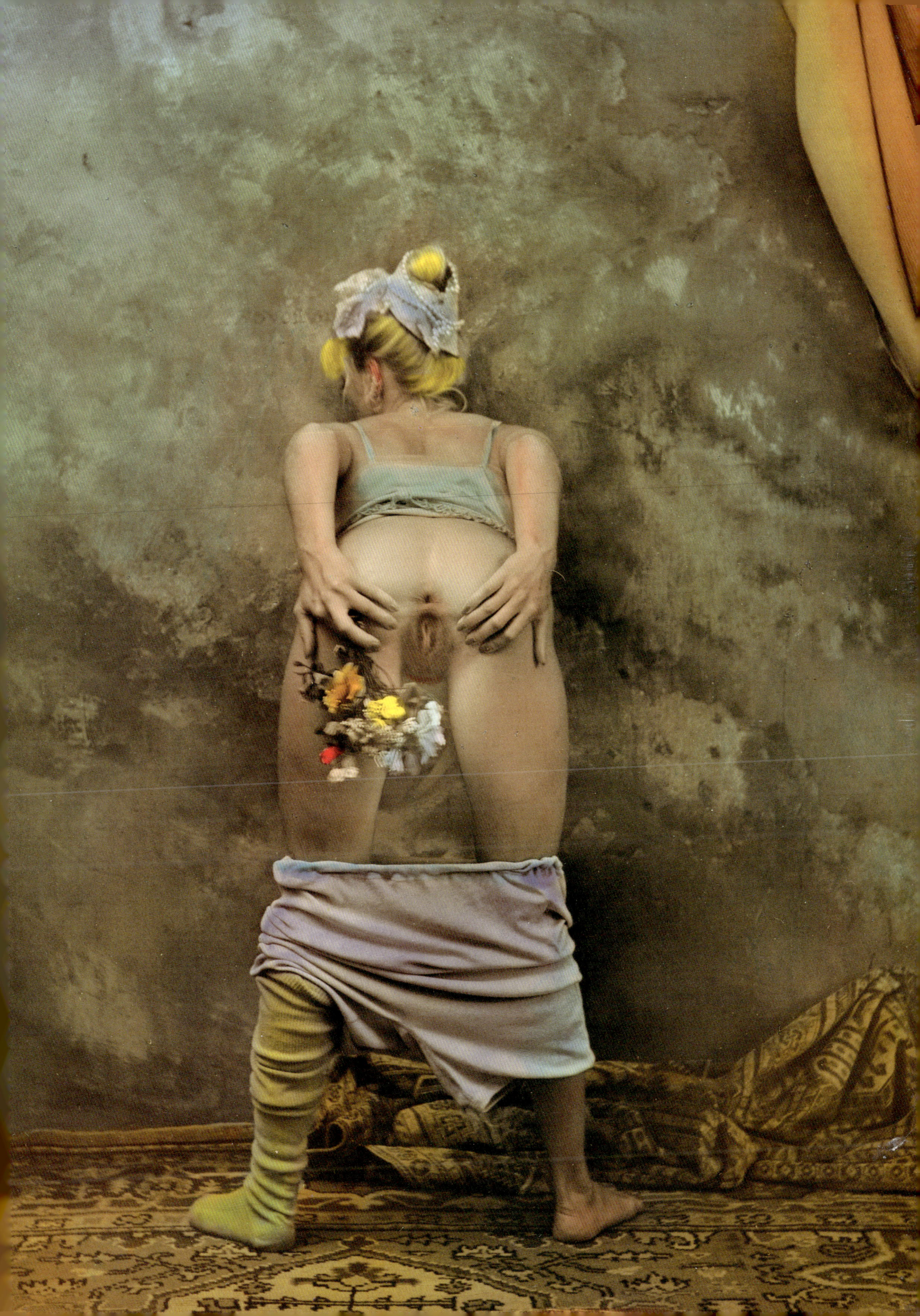

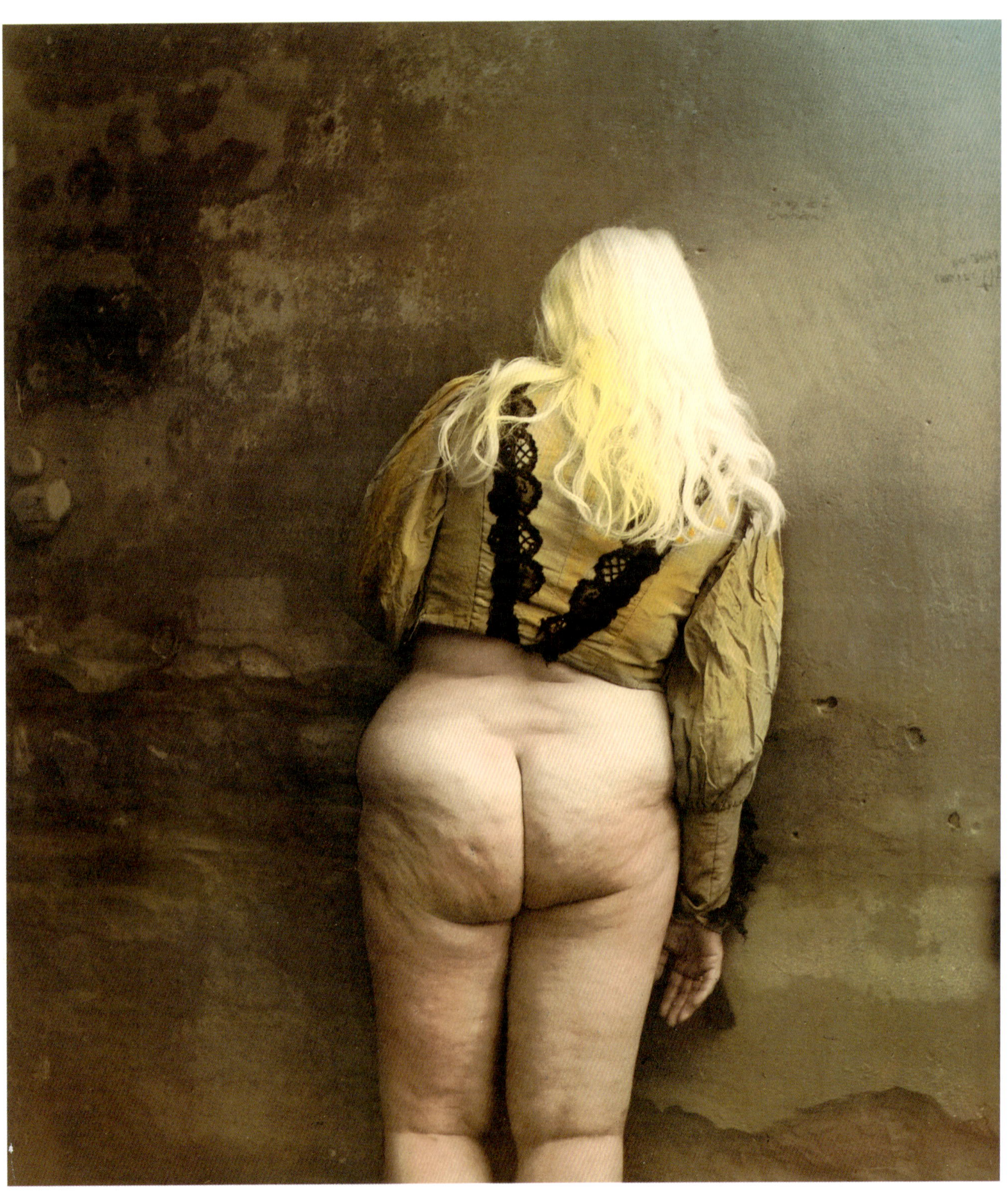

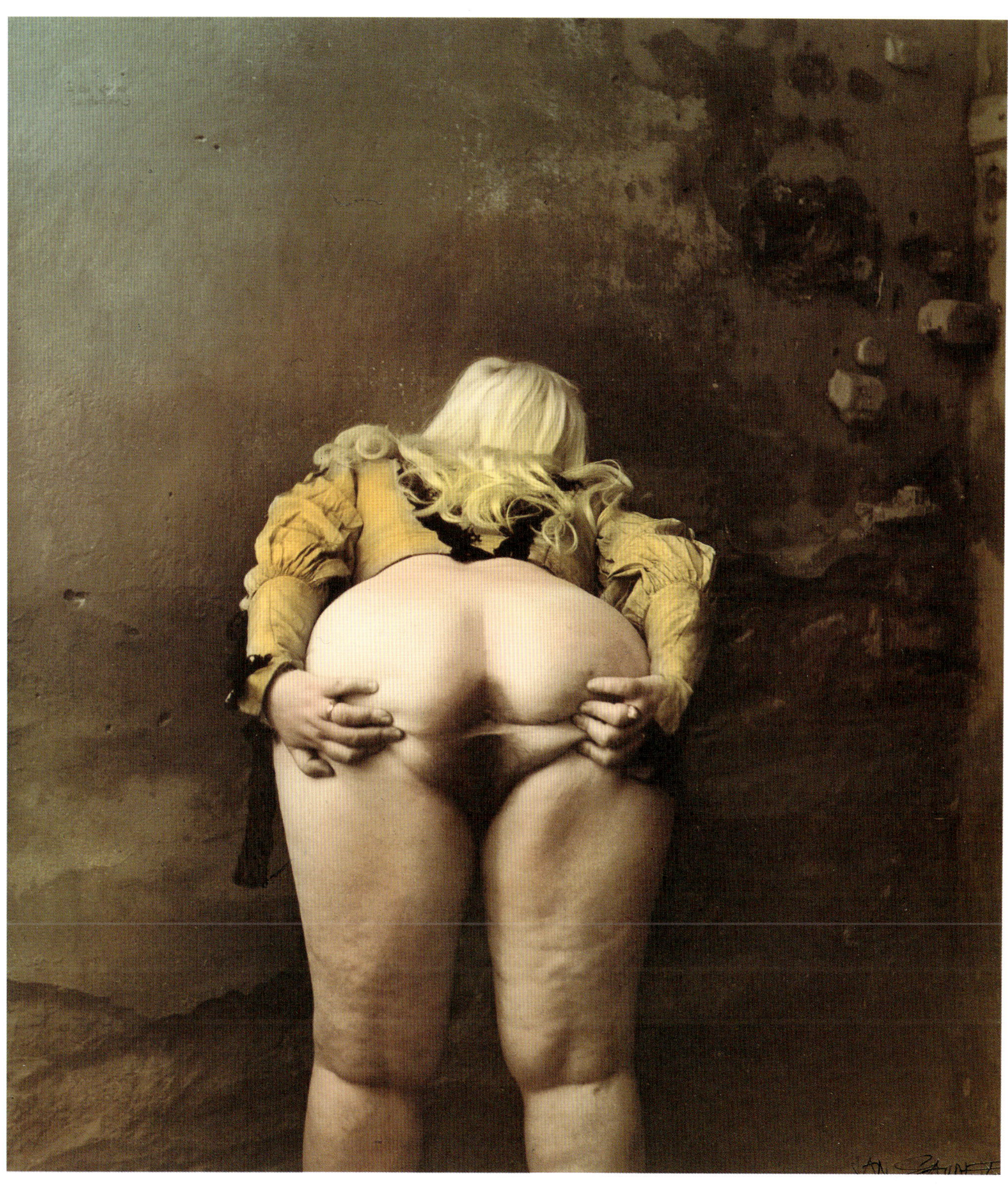

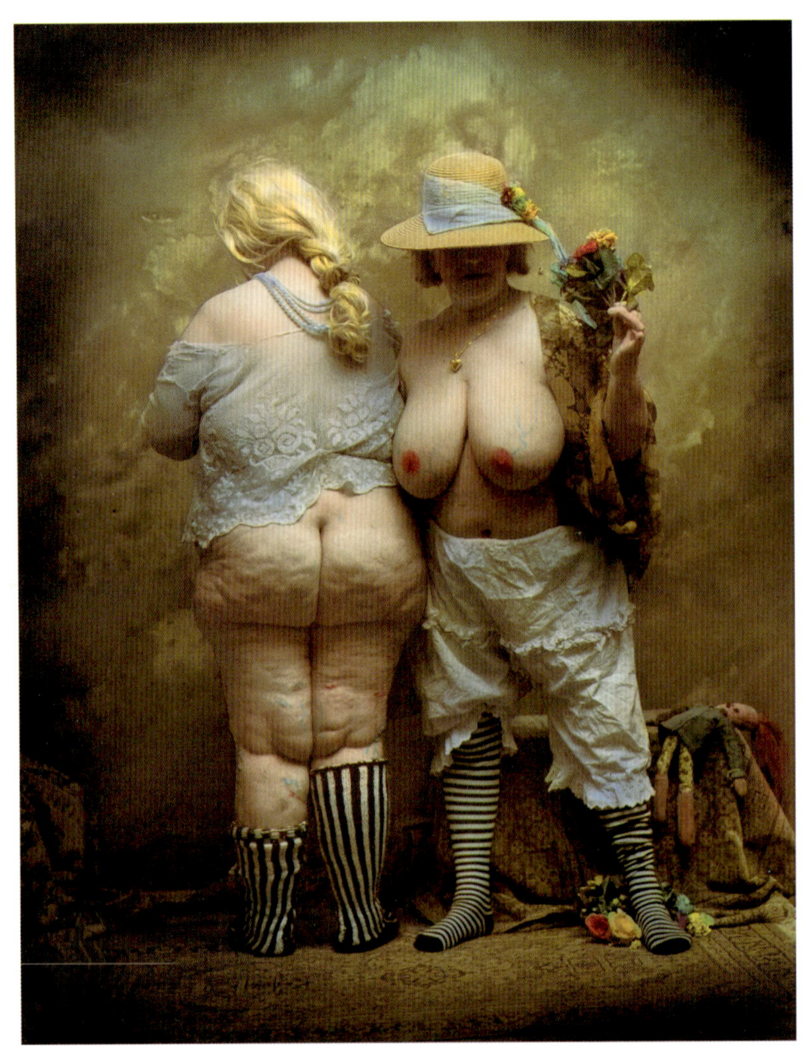

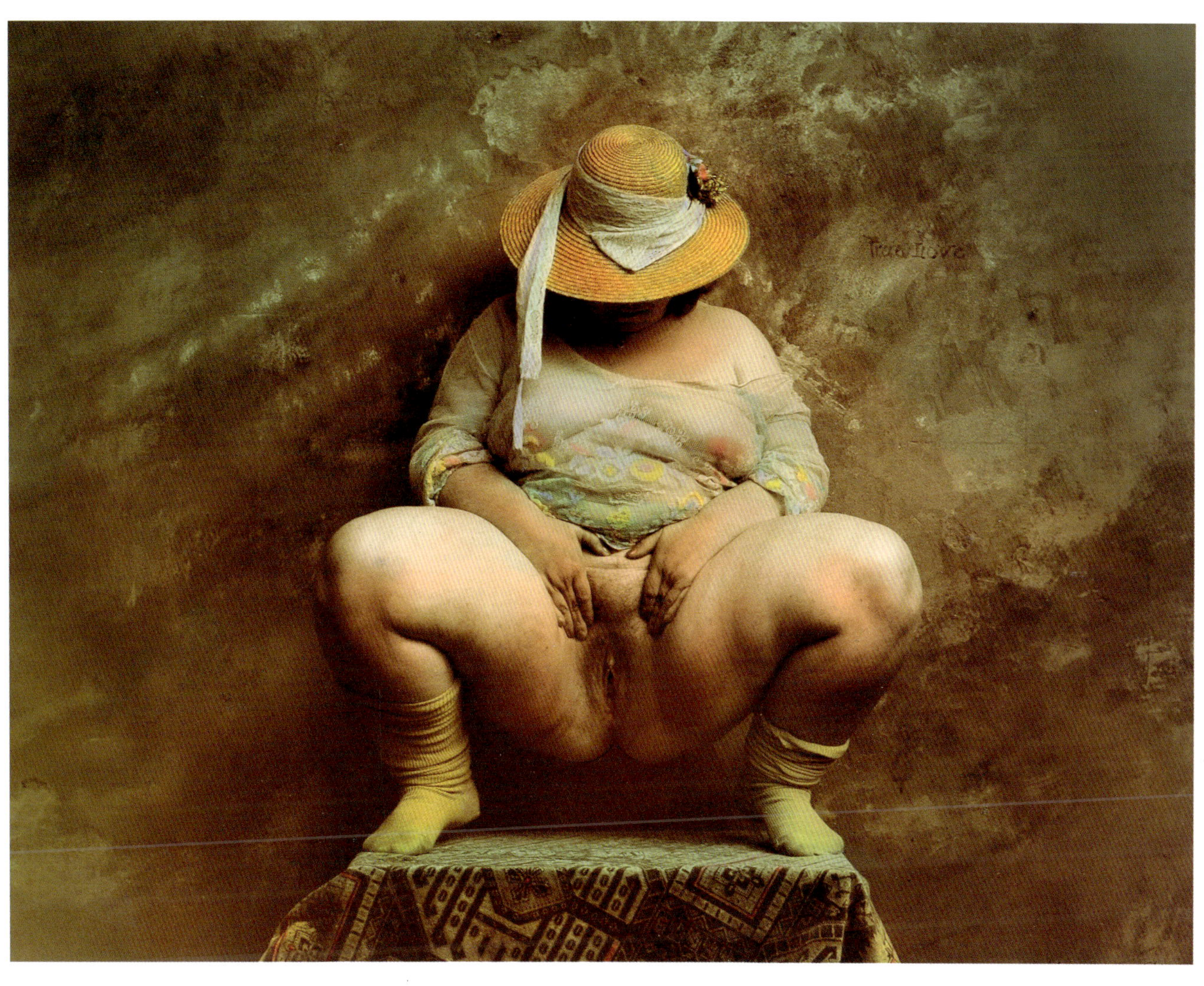

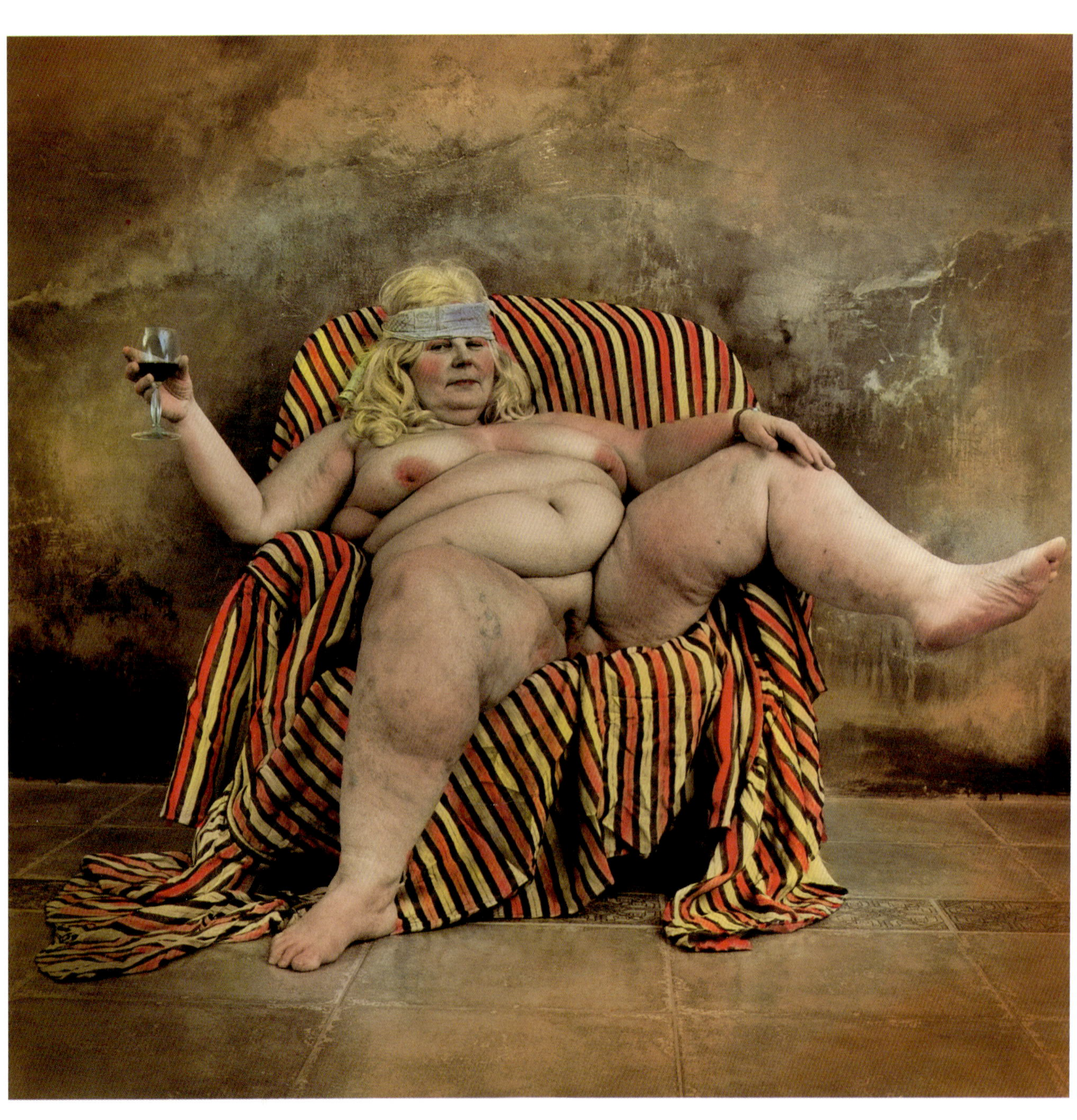

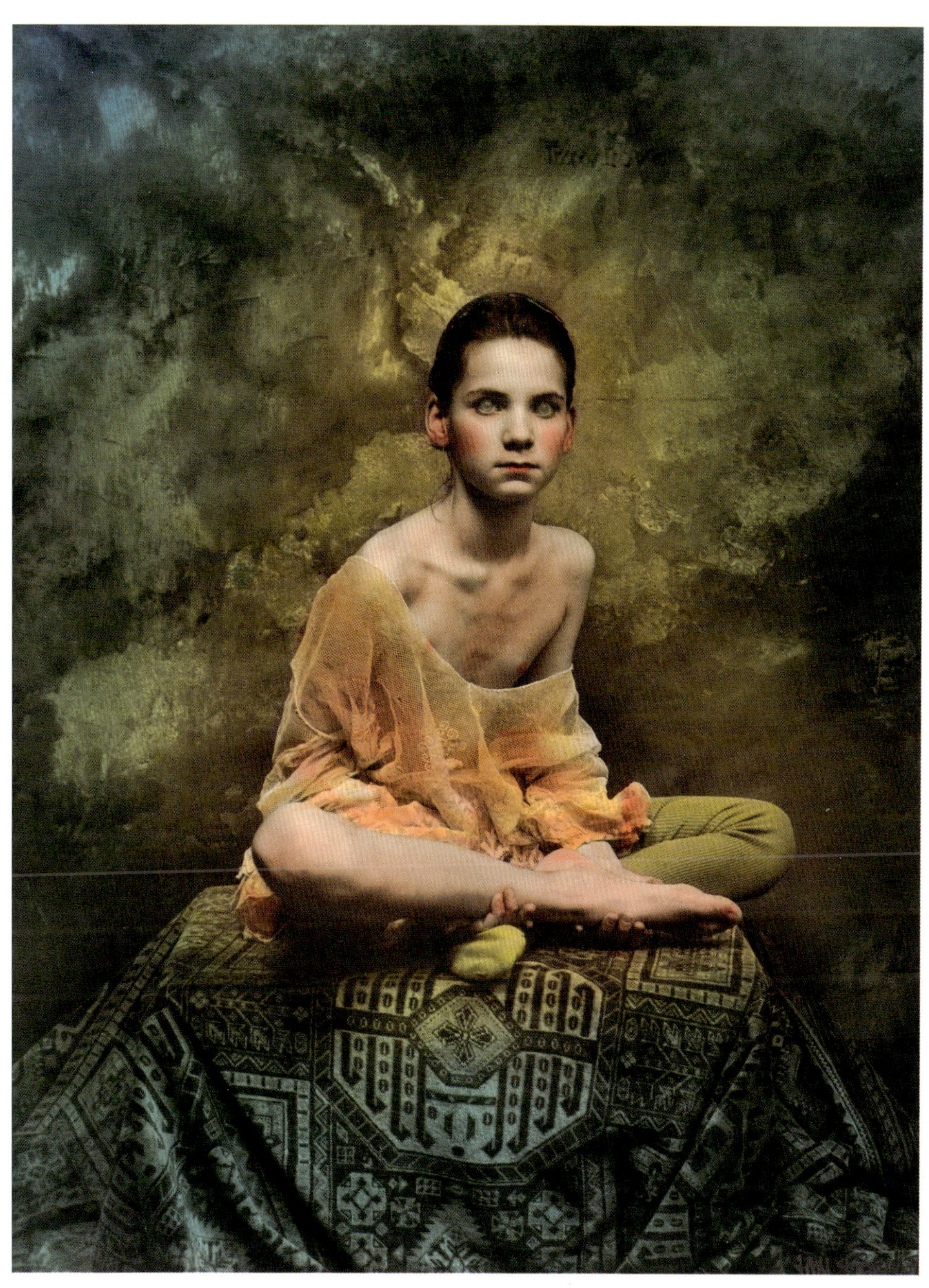

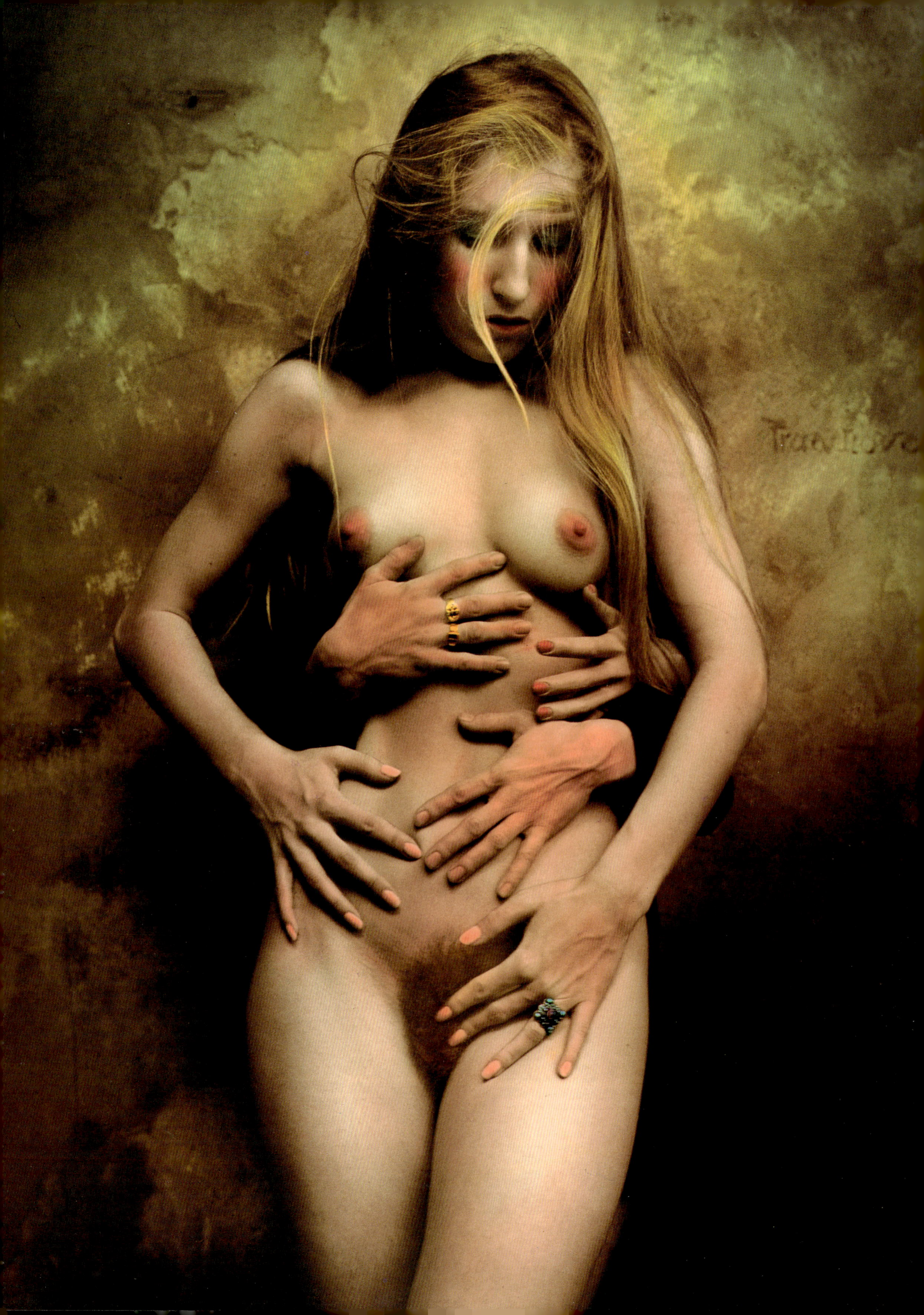

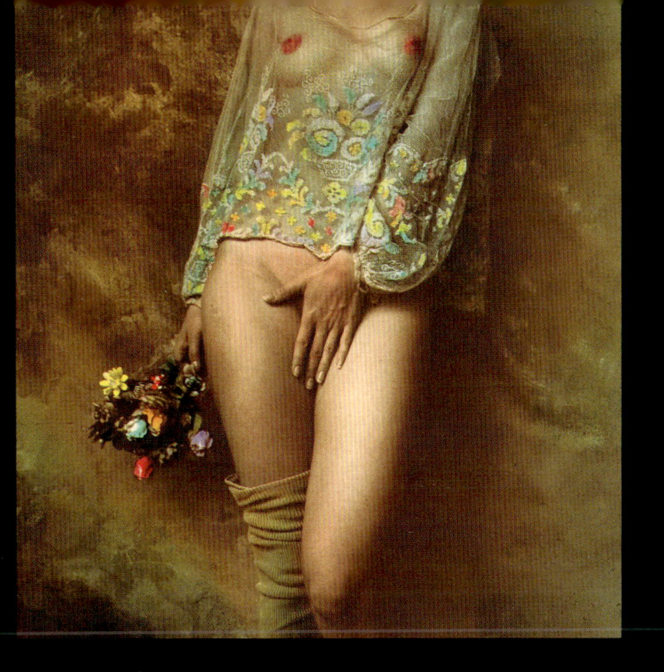

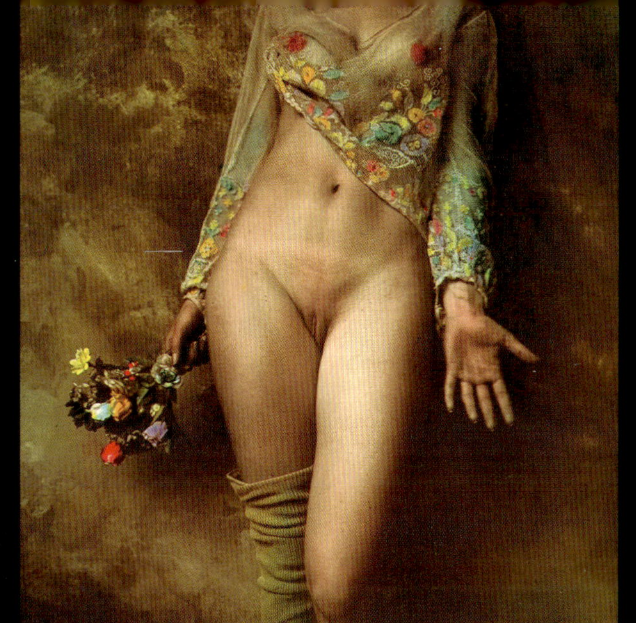

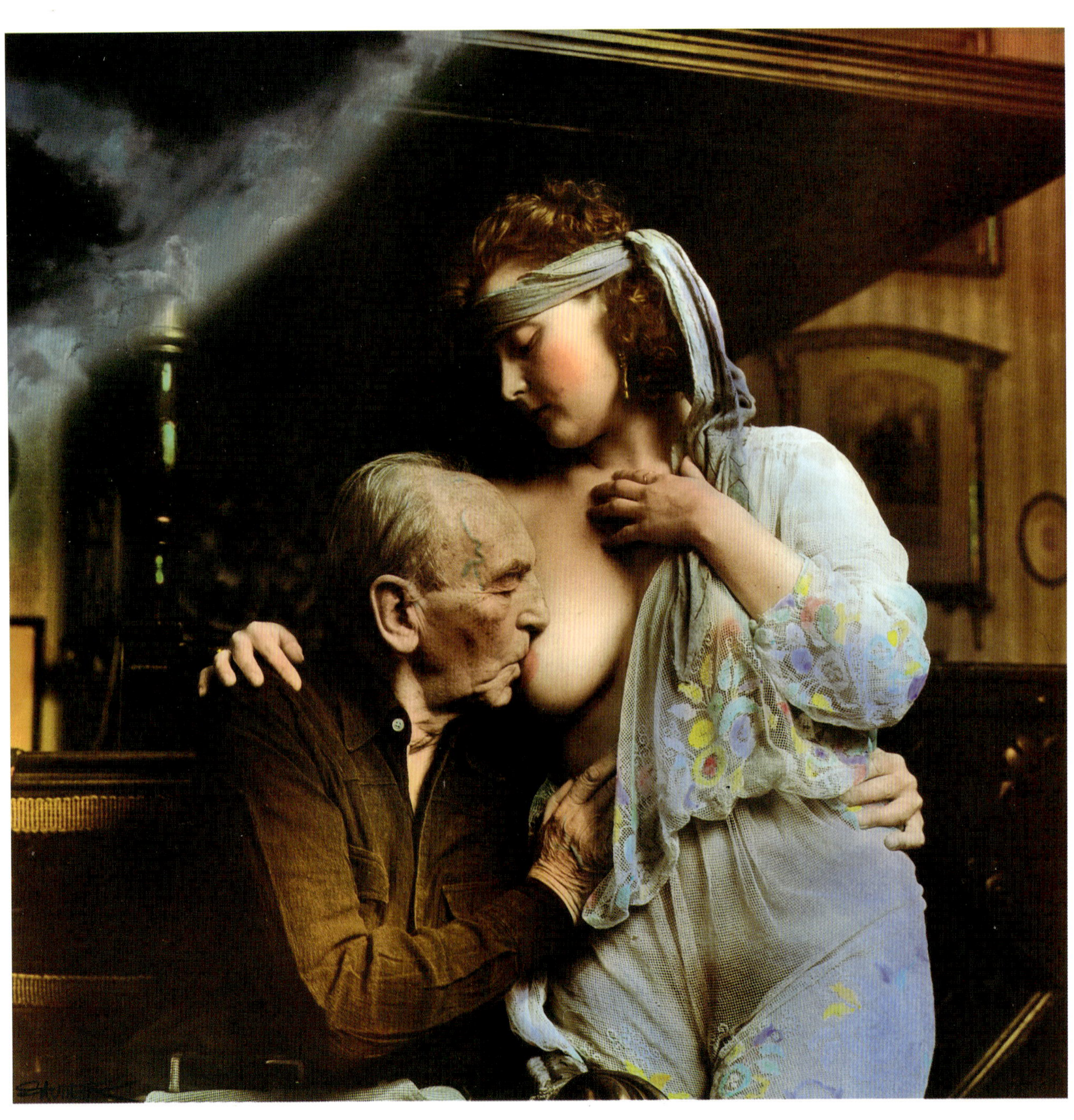

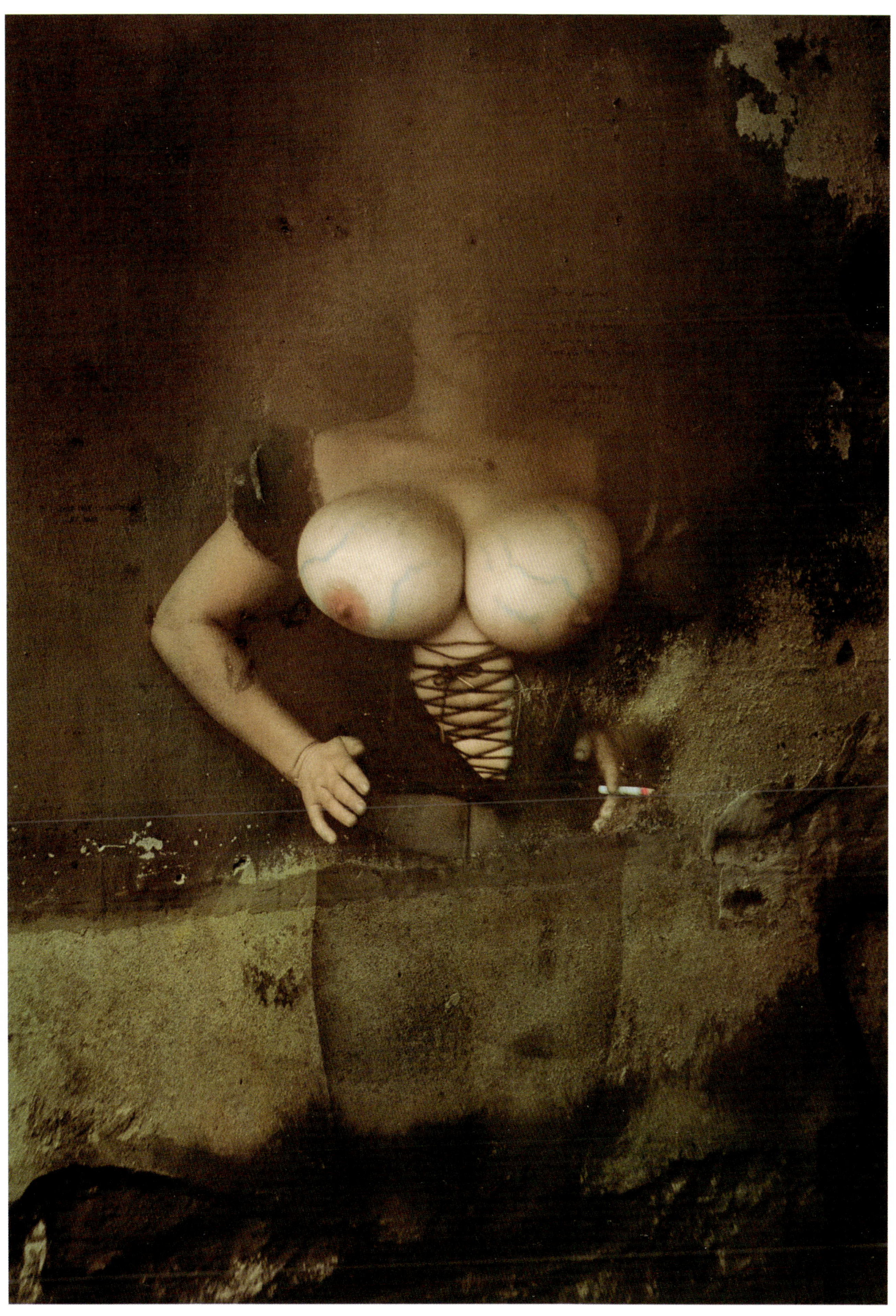

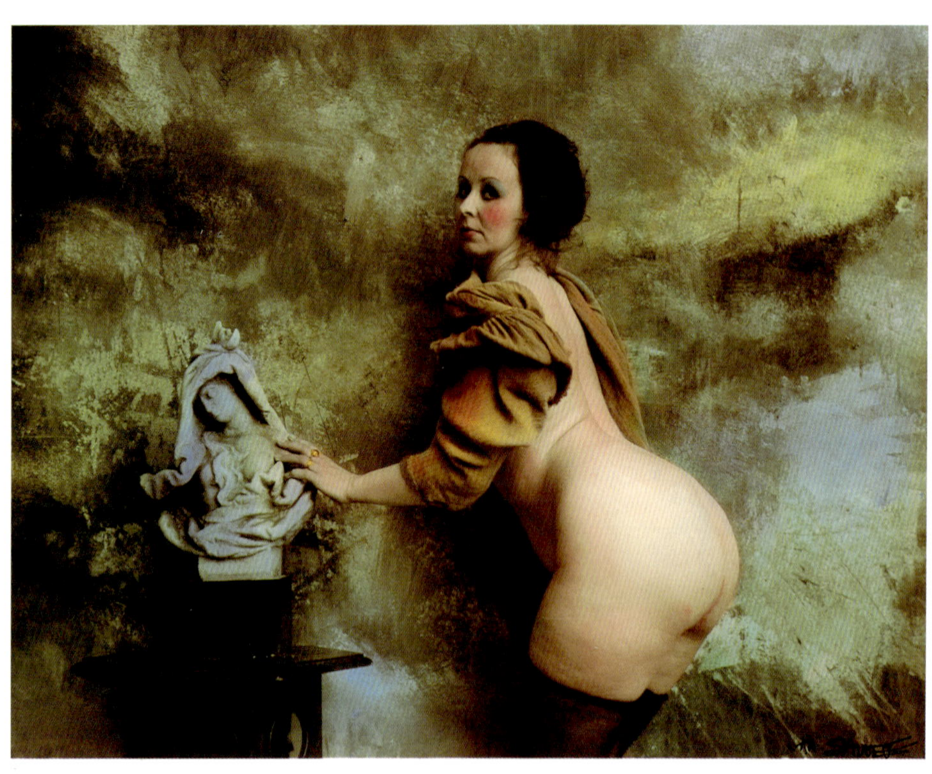

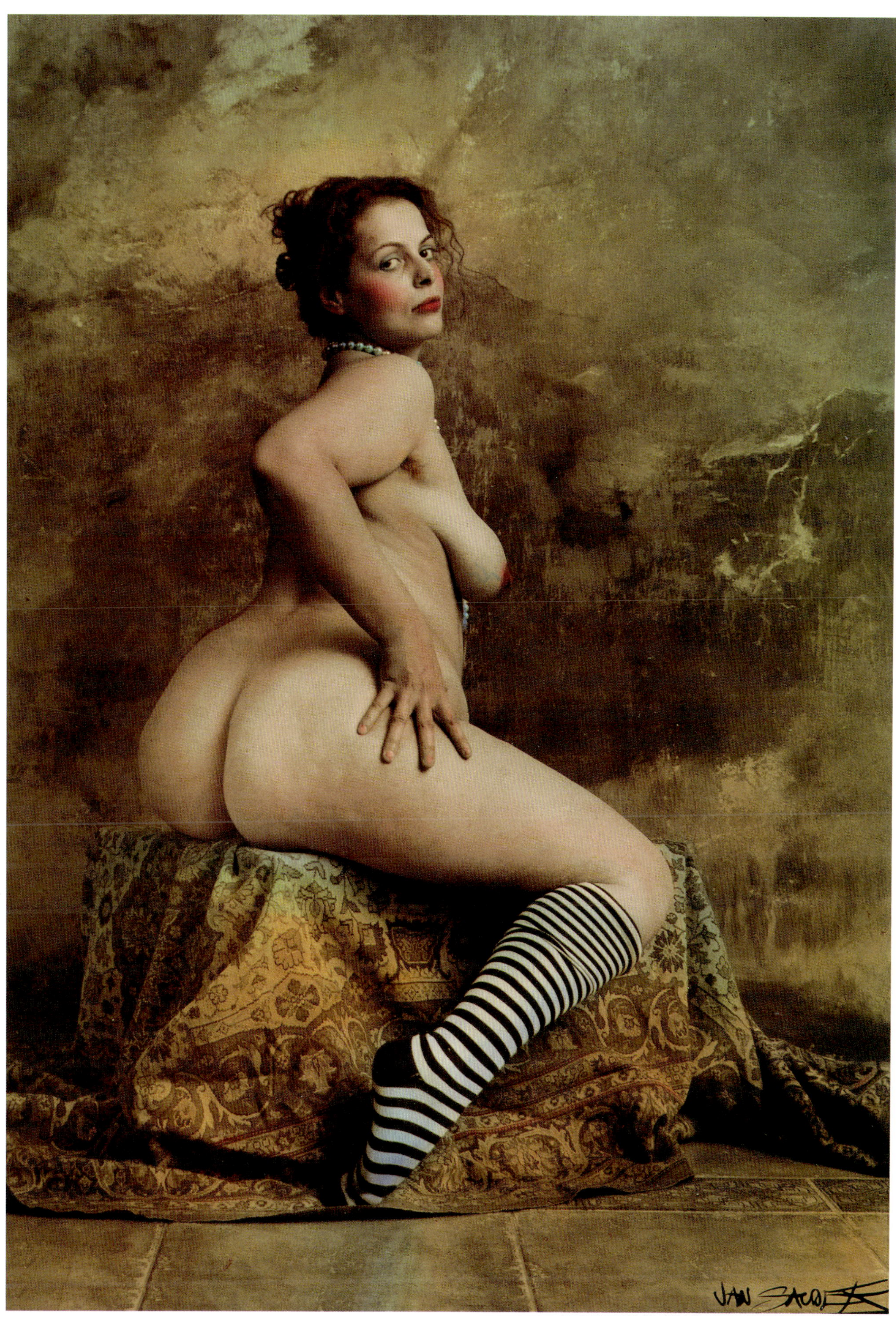

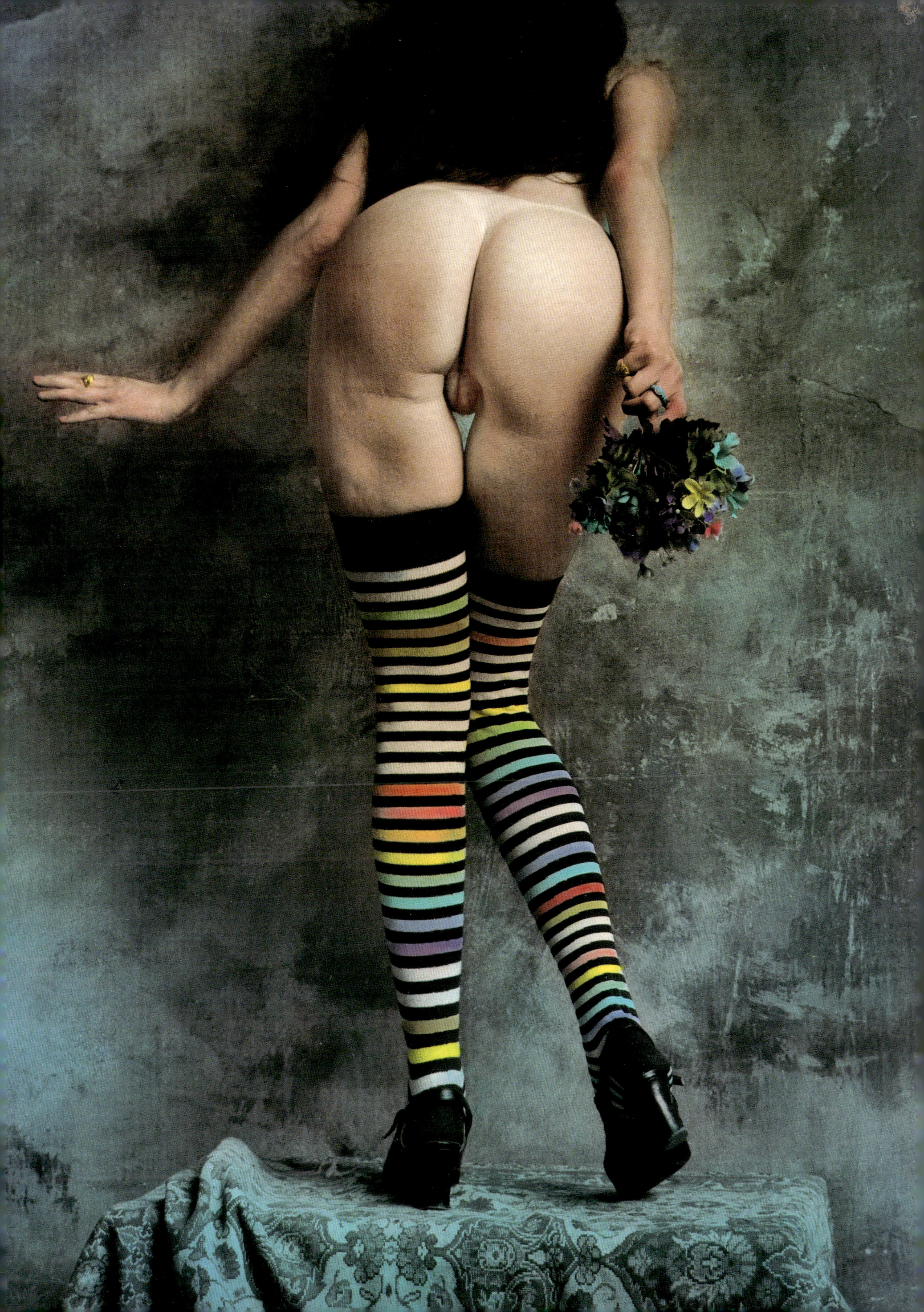

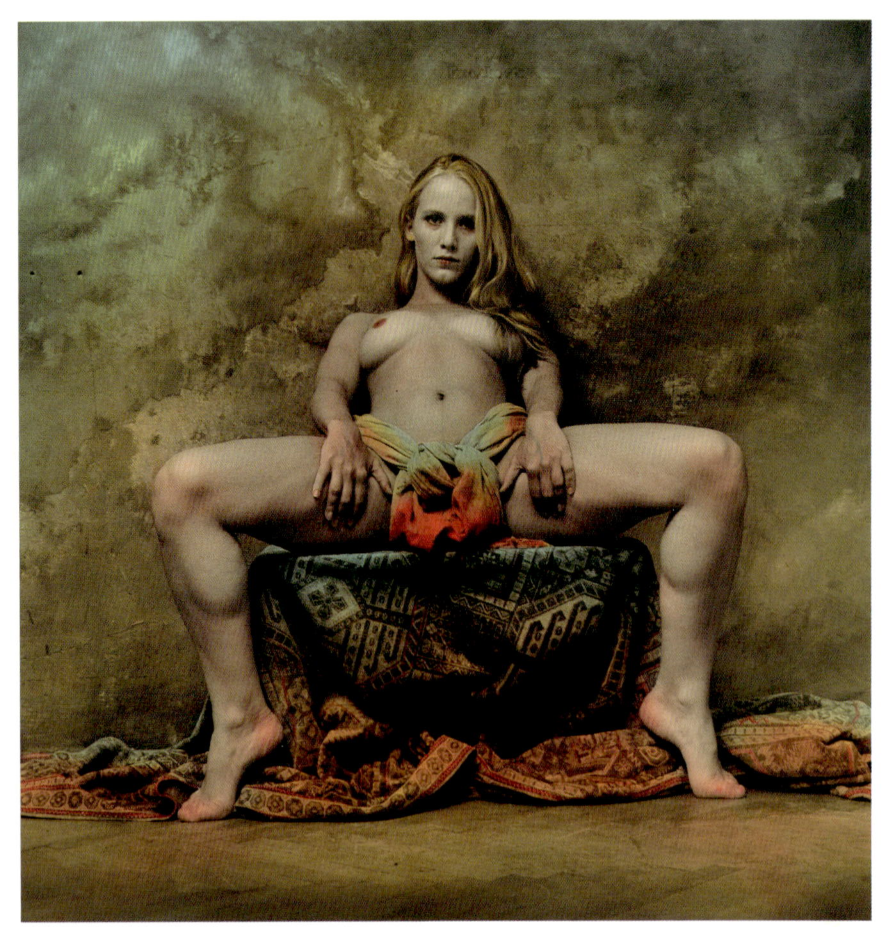

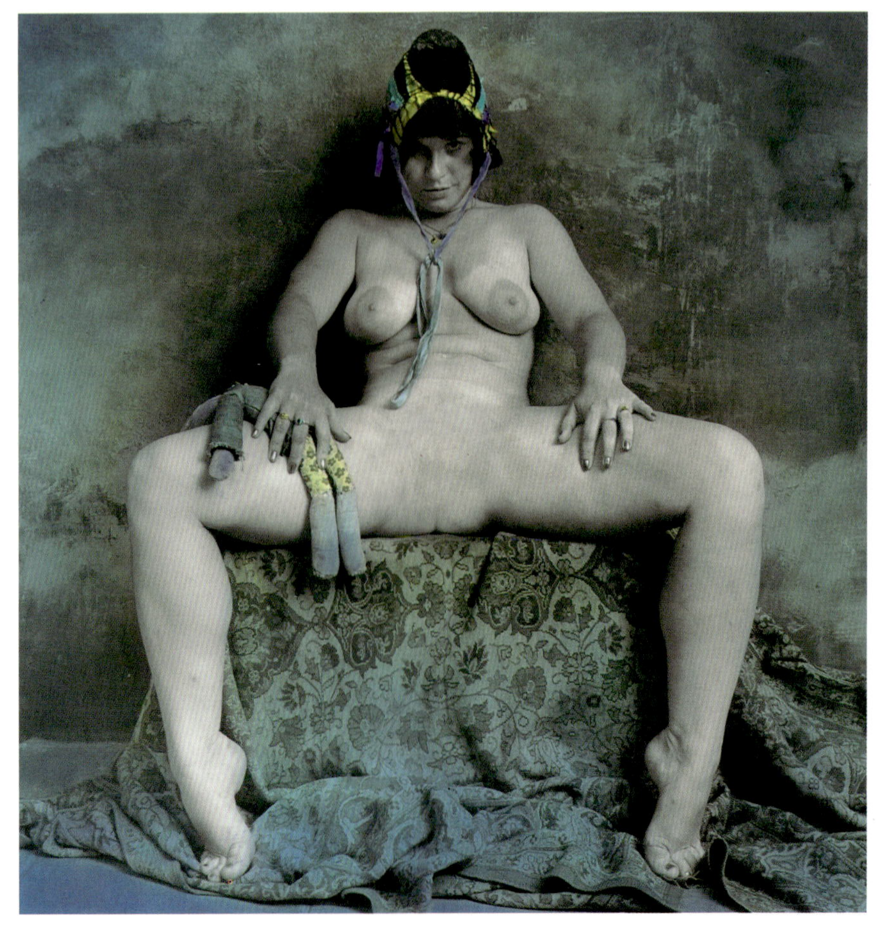

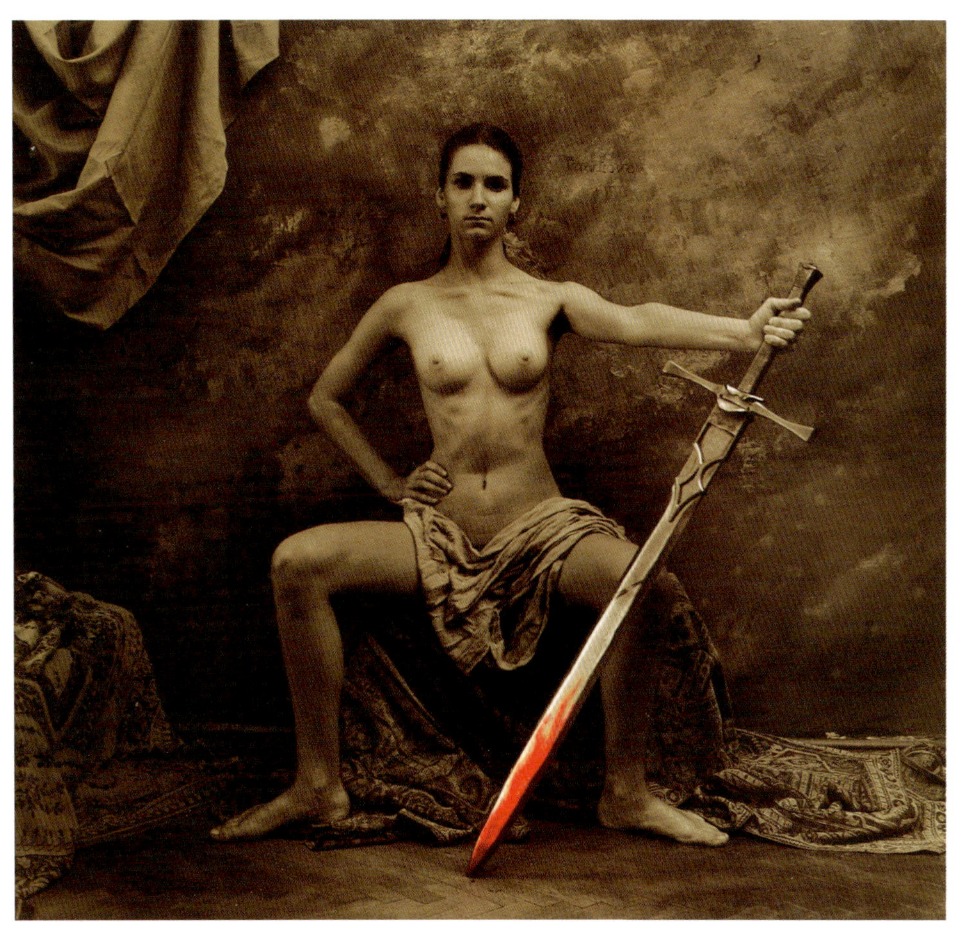

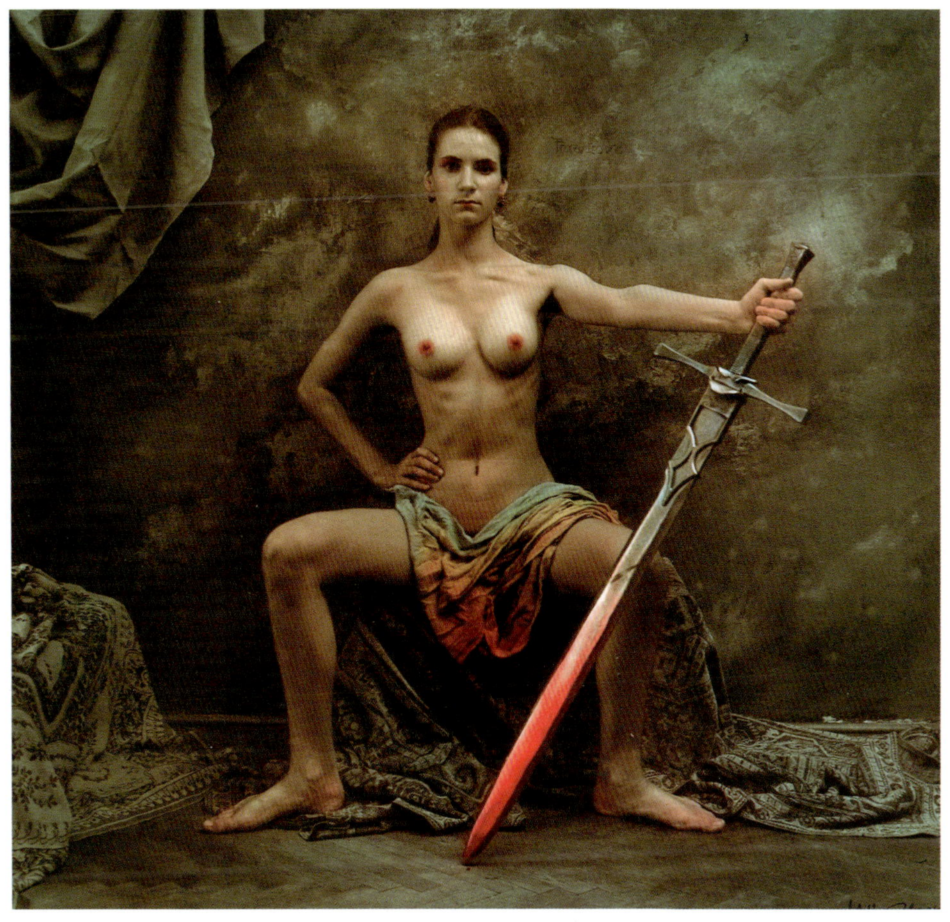

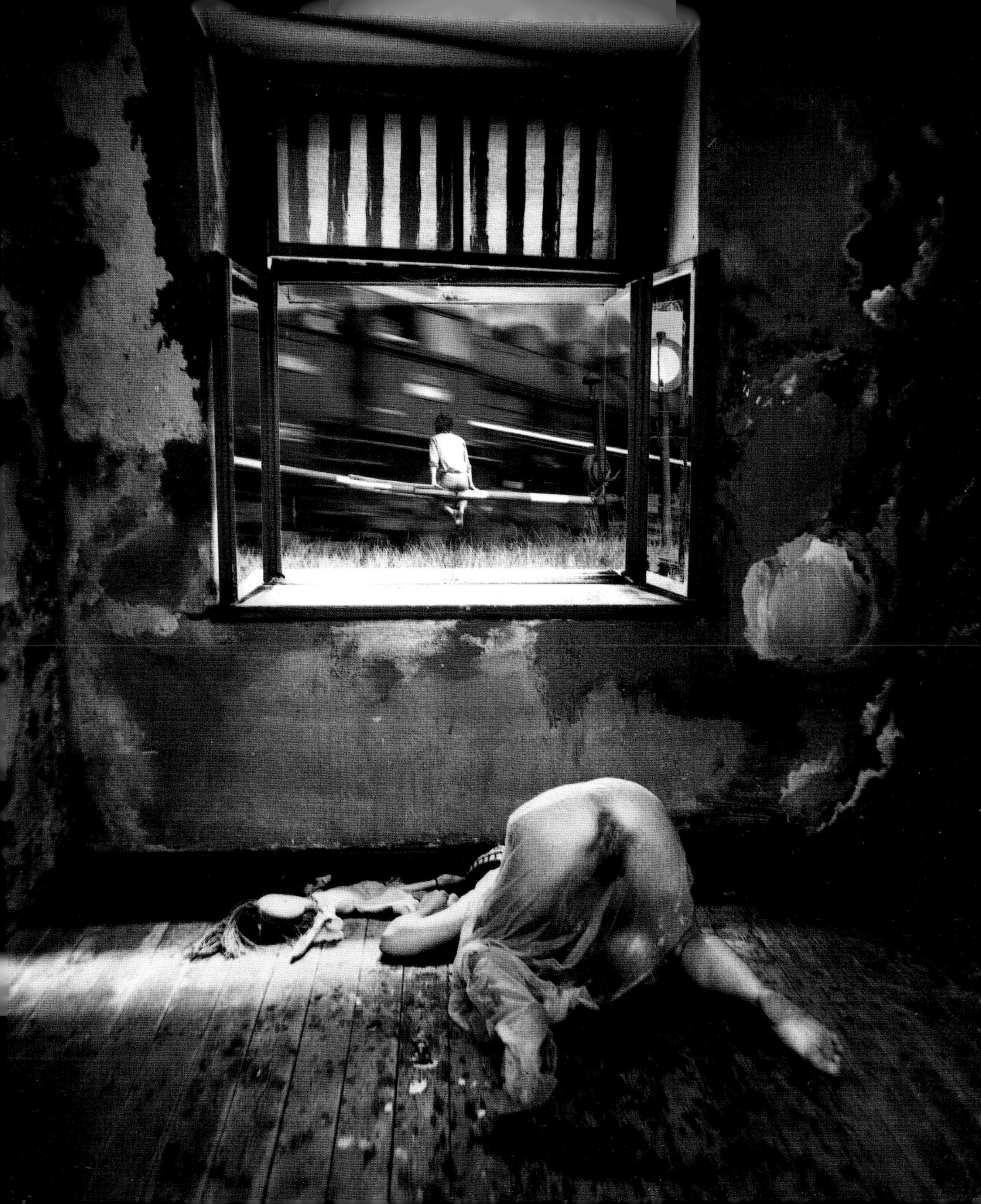

Picture Index
Verzeichnis der abgebildeten Werke
Index des illustrations

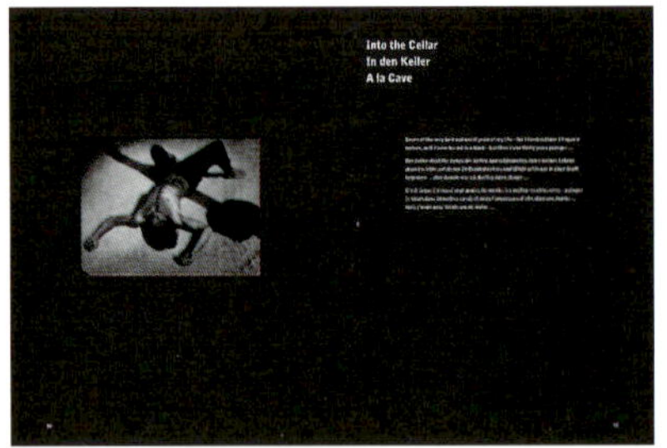

30
My Very First Photograph, 1953
Meine allererste Photographie
Ma toute première photographie

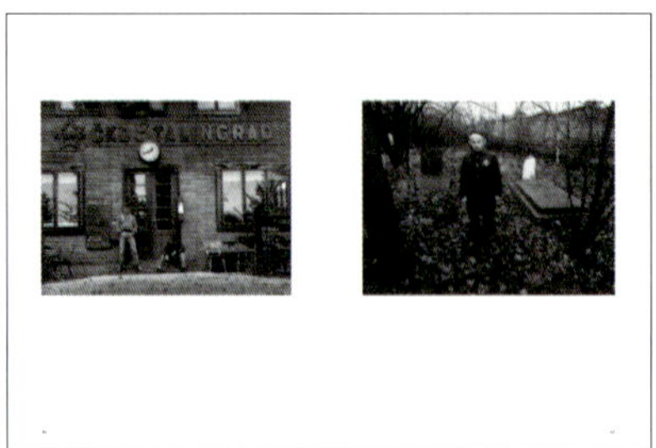

32
Stalingrad, 1956

33
My Father, 1975
Mein Vater
Mon Père

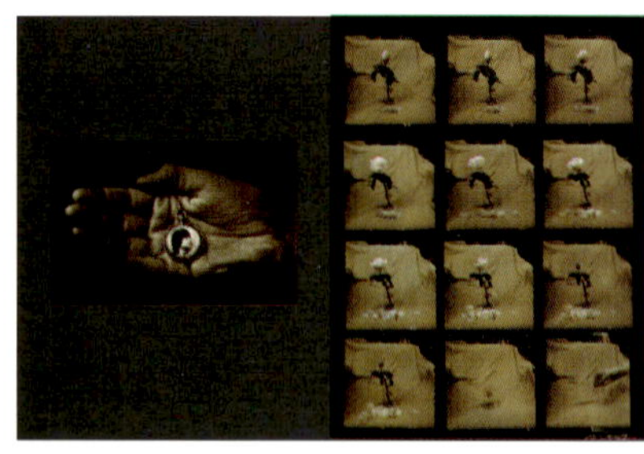

34
Medallion, 1970

35
Love Story, 1974

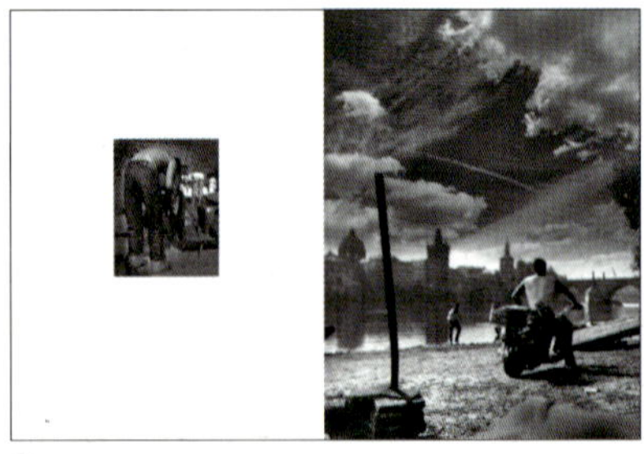

36
Paul Pollack Repairs My Brother's Scooter, 1963
Paul Pollack repariert den Motorroller meines Bruders
Paul Pollack répare le scooter de mon frère

37
Hey, Joe!, 1959

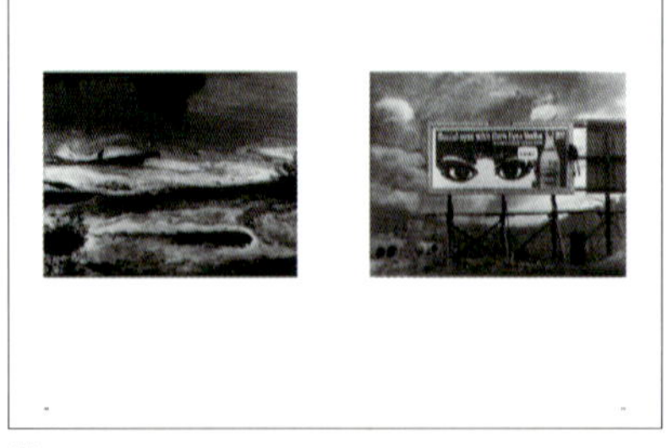

38
The River, 1962
Der Fluß
La Rivière

39
Social-eyes with Dark Eyes Vodka, 1969

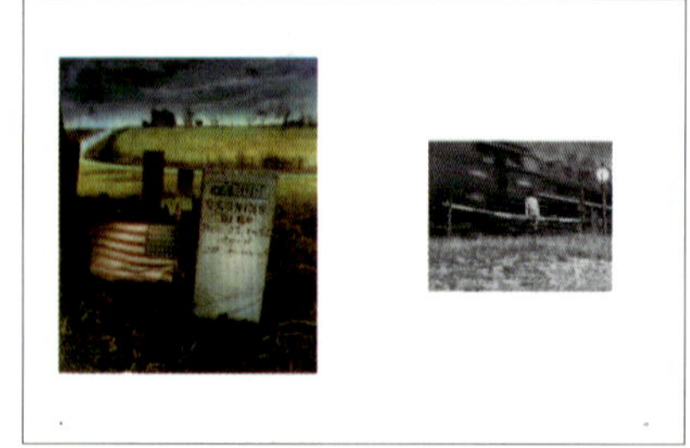

40
U.S.A., 1969

41
120 km/hr, 1975

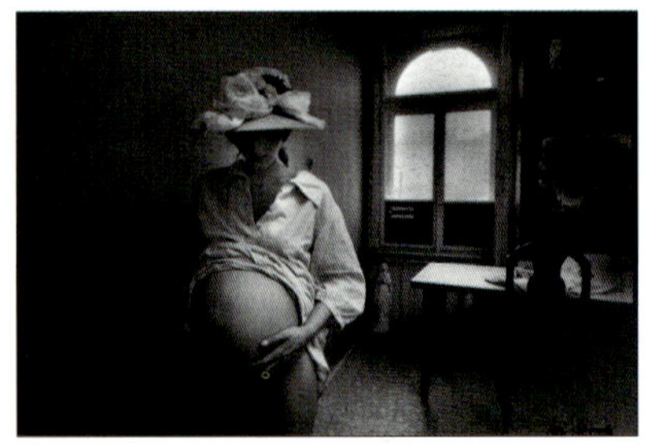

42/43
Last Summer's Sweet Memories, 1974
Süße Erinnerungen an den letzten Sommer
Doux Souvenirs de l'été dernier

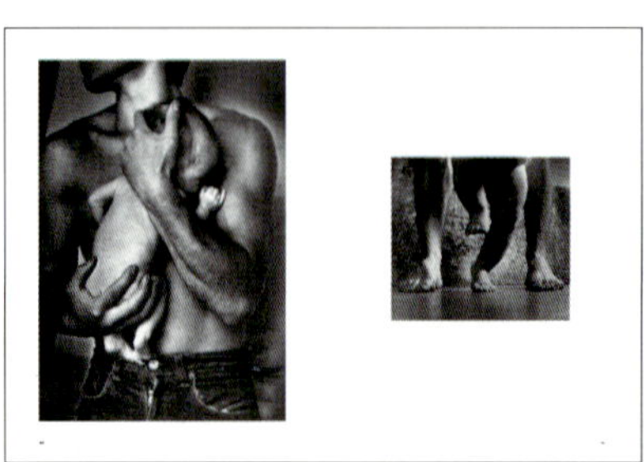

44
Life, 1966
Leben
Vie

45
First Steps, 1963
Erste Schritte
Premiers pas

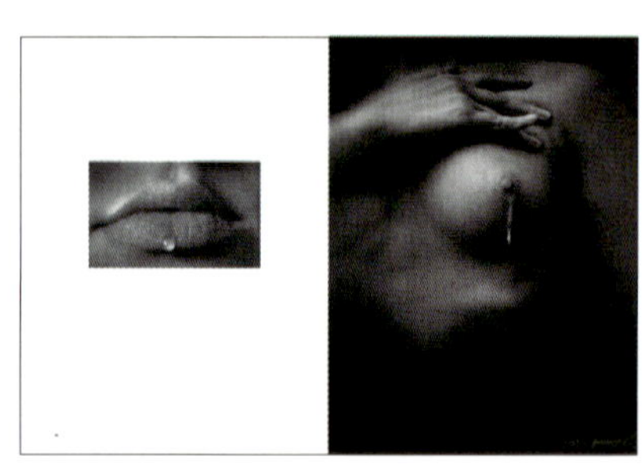

46
Marie no. 1, 1974

47
The Mother, c. 1986
Die Mutter
La Mère

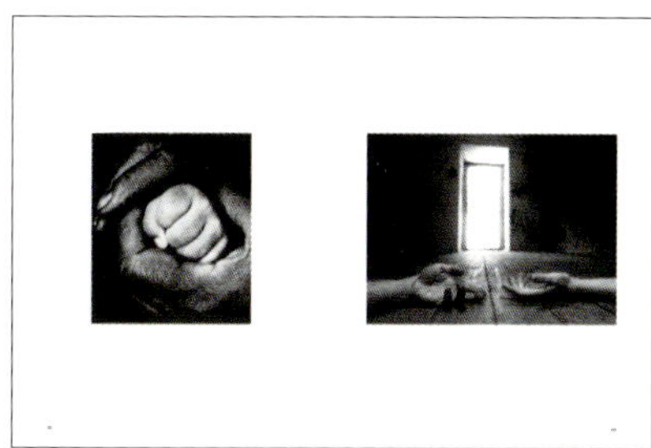

48
The Shelter, 1963
Die Zuflucht
Le Refuge

49
Hungry for Your Touch, 1971
Hungrig nach deiner Berührung
Faim de tes caresses

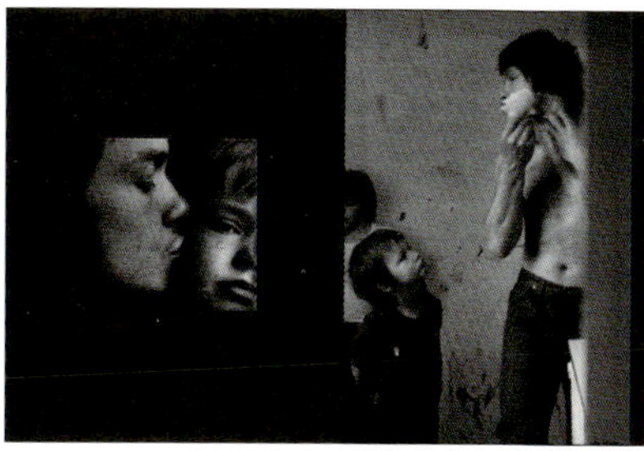

50
Kissing the Tears Away, 1967
Küsse gegen Tränen
Des baisers pour sécher les larmes

51
The World of Men, 1969
Die Welt der Männer
Le Monde des Hommes

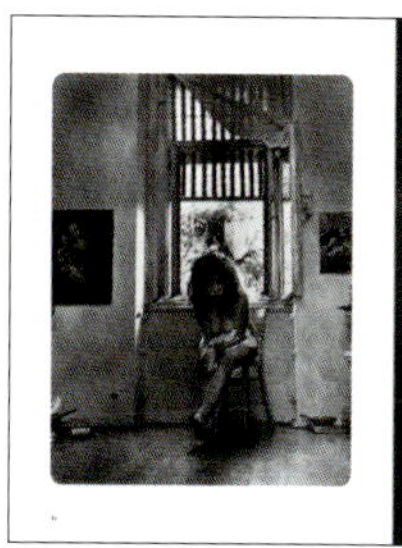

52
Maid's Morning, 1963
Der Morgen des Dienstmädchens
Le Matin de la bonne

53
Those days of the Sixties, 1965
In jenen Tagen der sechziger Jahre
Ces jours des années soixante

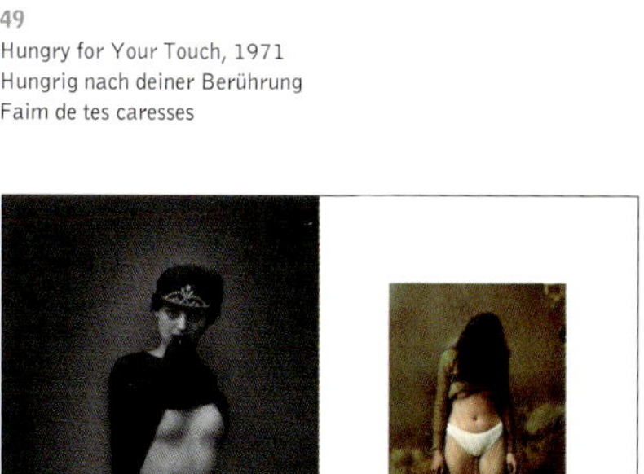

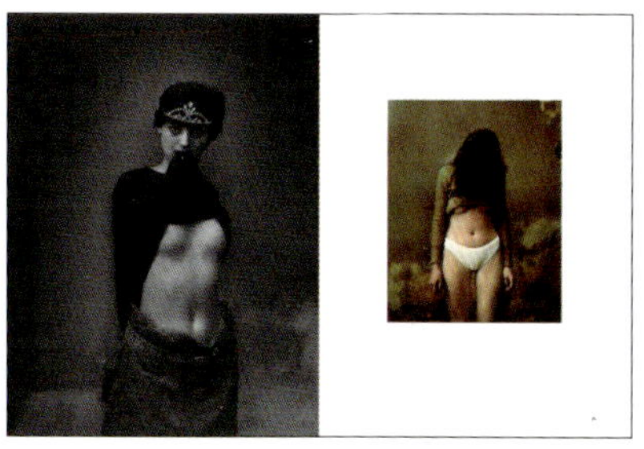

54
Marie no. 142, 1972

55
Agnes, 1973

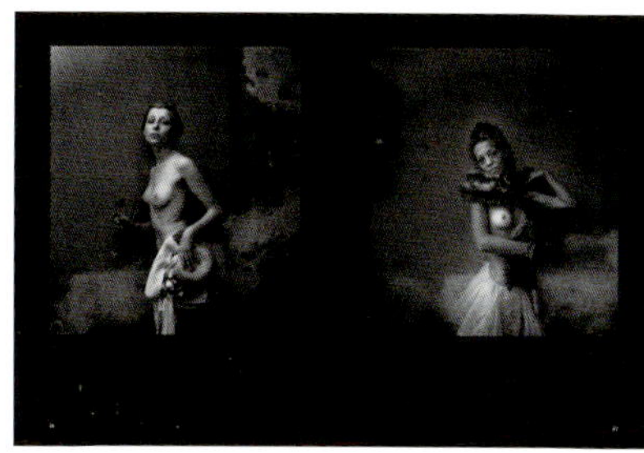

56
What's-her-name Girl, 1973
Wie hieß sie noch gleich?
Comment s'appelle-t-elle déjà?

57
Ballerina, 1973
Ballerine

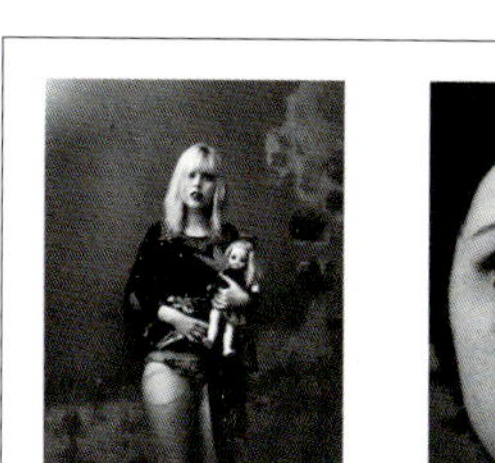

58
The Dolls, 1975
Die Puppen
Les Poupées

59
Lágrimas Negras (Black Tears), 1973
Schwarze Tränen
Larmes noires

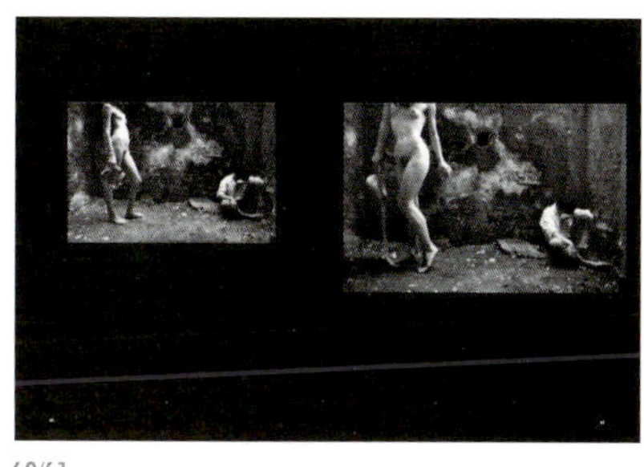

60/61
The Temptation, 1992–1996
Die Versuchung
La Tentation

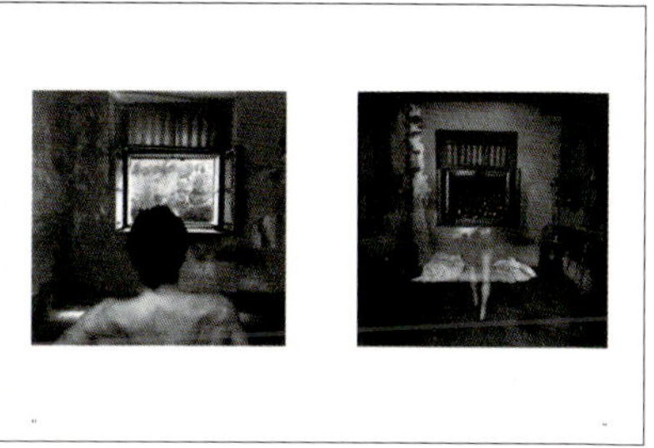

62
I Look Through My Window, 1984
Ich schaue durch mein Fenster
Je regarde à travers ma fenêtre

63
Going Downtown, 1976
Auf dem Weg in die Stadt
Sur le chemin de la ville

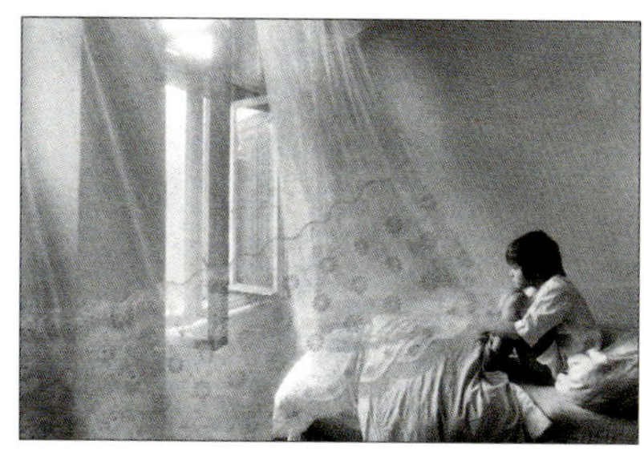

64/65
The Morning, 1970
Der Morgen
Le Matin

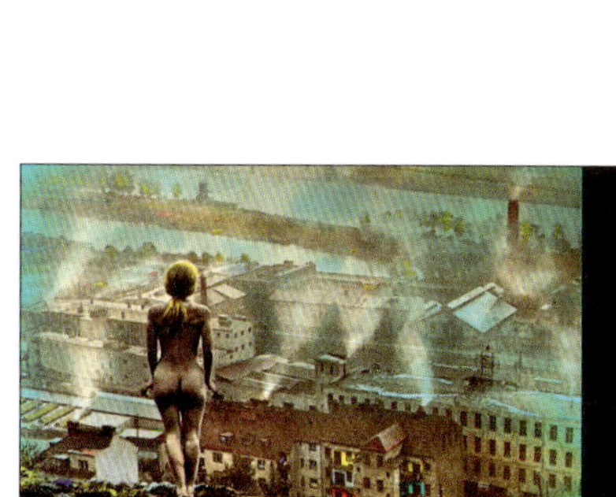

66/67
Early in the Morning, 1960
Früh am Morgen
Tôt le matin

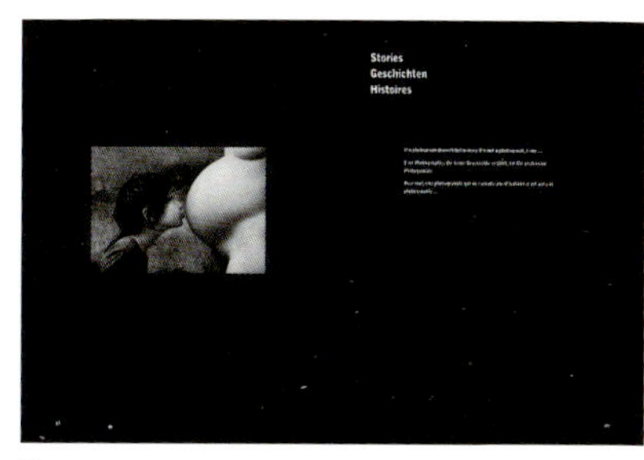

68
The First Kiss for a Little Brother, 1983
Der erste Kuß für einen kleinen Bruder
Le premier baiser à un petit frère

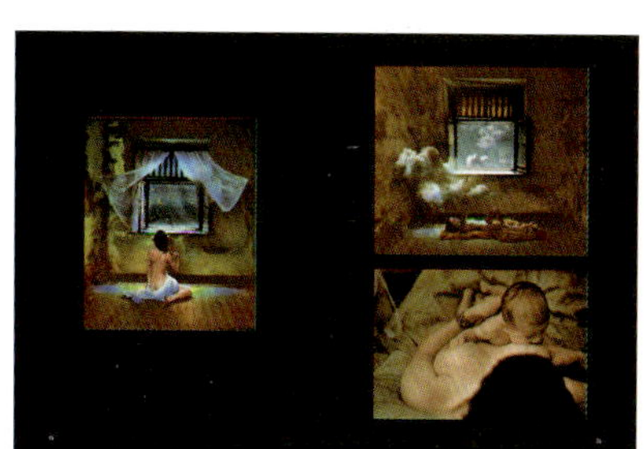

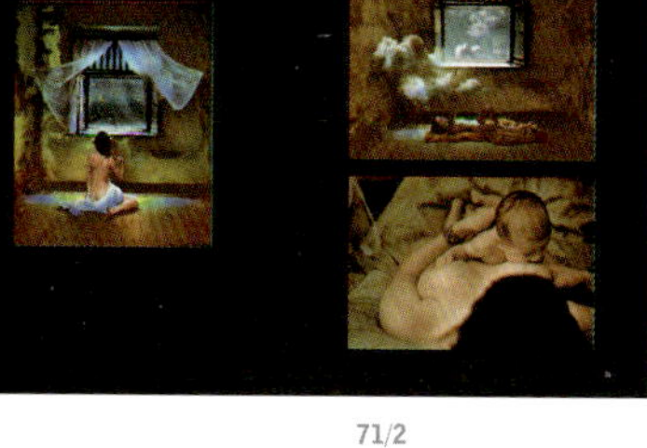

70
Zuzanka's Night Window, 1979
Zuzankas Nachtfenster
La Fenêtre de nuit de Zuzanka

71/1
Catching the Breeze, 1984
Eine kühle Briese
Une petite brise

71/2
The Mother or Love, 1973
Die Mutter oder Die Liebe
La Mère ou L'Amour

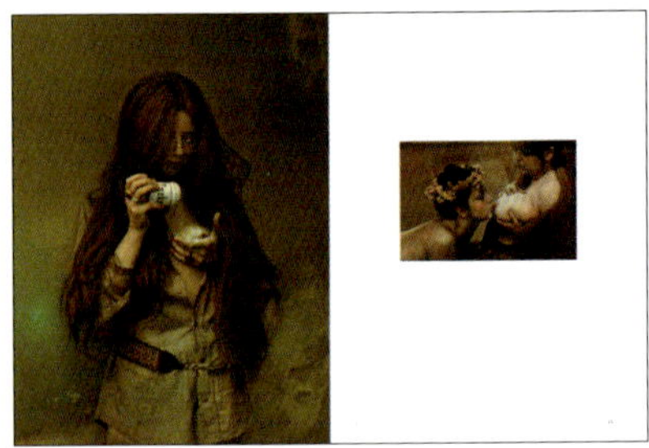

72
Sugar, 1975
Zucker
Sucre

73
It Touches My Very Soul, 1985
Es berührt mich in tiefster Seele
Ça me touche au plus profond de mon âme

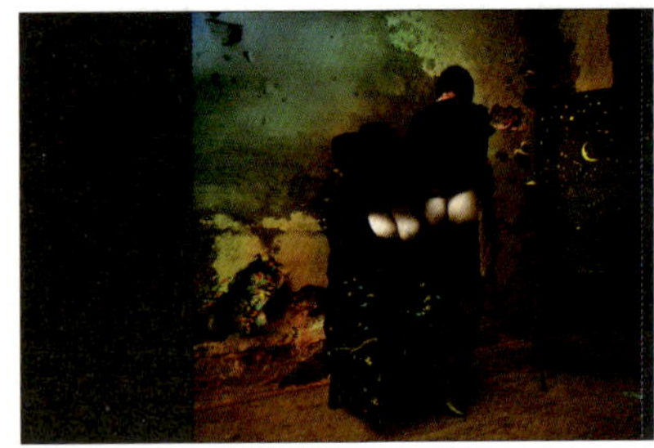

74/75
2 Big 4 You, 1981

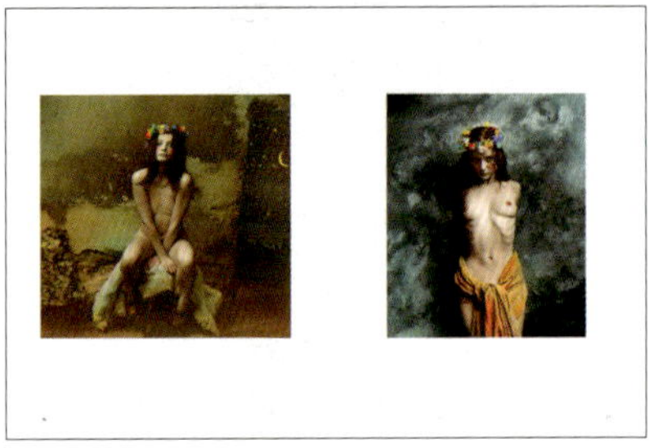

76
Zuzanka no. 1905, 1978

77
Oh, That Virgin Els!, 1985
Oh, diese Jungfrau Els!
Oh, cette pucelle Els!

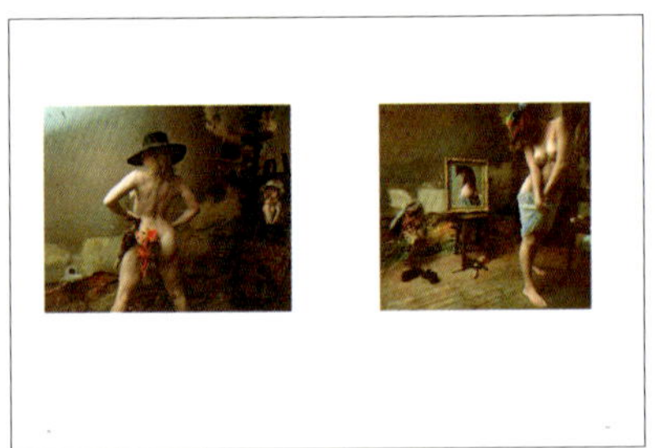

78
Susanna, 1978

79
Tell Me, Mirror, 1978
Spieglein, Spieglein an der Wand ...
Dis-moi, gentil miroir ...

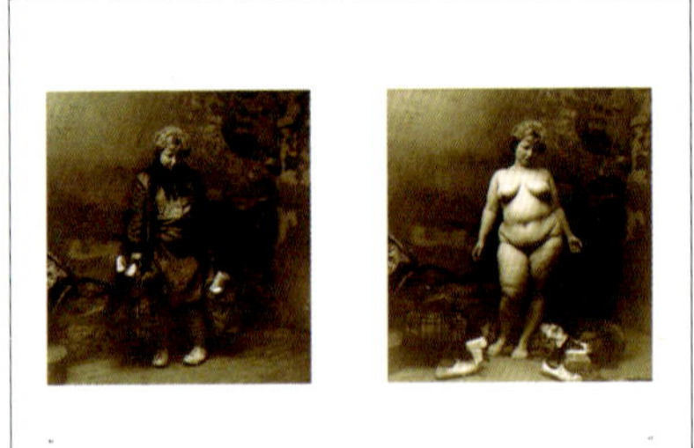

80/81
Housewife, 1984
Hausfrau
Femme au foyer

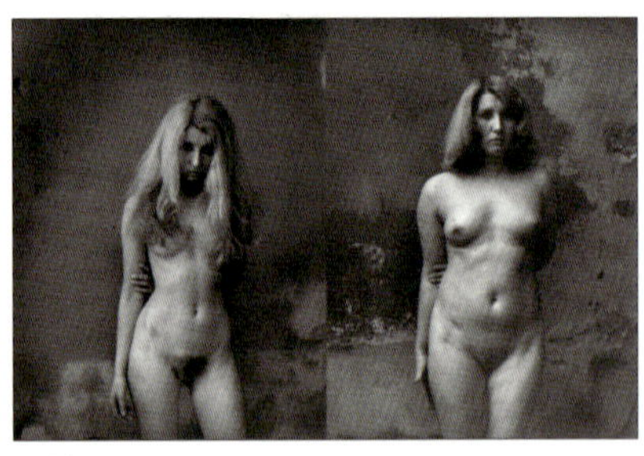

82/83
Five Years in the Life of My Veronika, 1970–1975
Fünf Jahre im Leben meiner Veronika
Cinq ans de la vie de ma Veronika

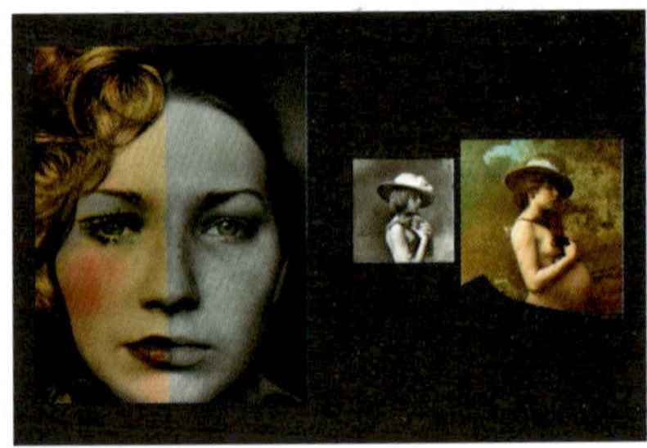

84
Mirka 2 Face, 1974

85
12 Years in the Life of Miroslava, 1973–1985
12 Jahre im Leben Miroslavas
12 ans de la vie de Miroslava

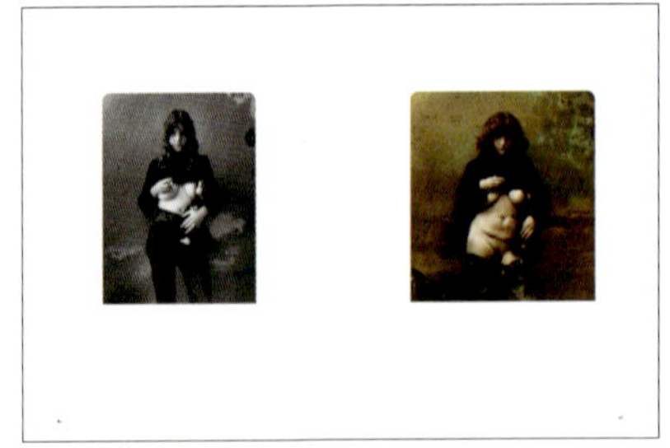

86/87
Ten Years of My Girl Markéta, 1971–1981
Zehn Jahre meines Mädchens Markéta
Dix ans de mon amie Markéta

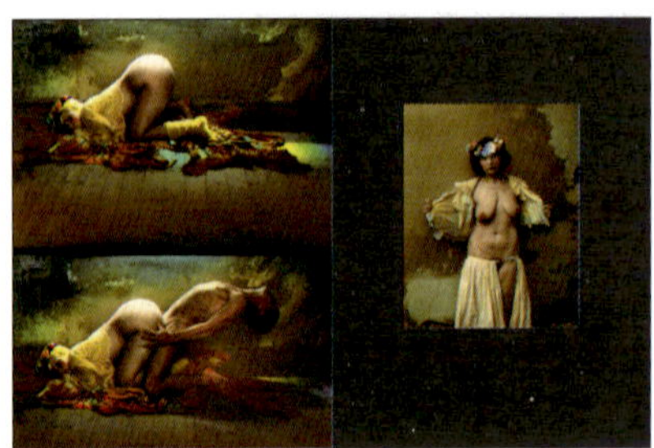

88
Jan's Heaven, 1988
Jans Himmel auf Erden
Le Paradis de Jan

89
The Mother, 1976
Die Mutter
La Mère

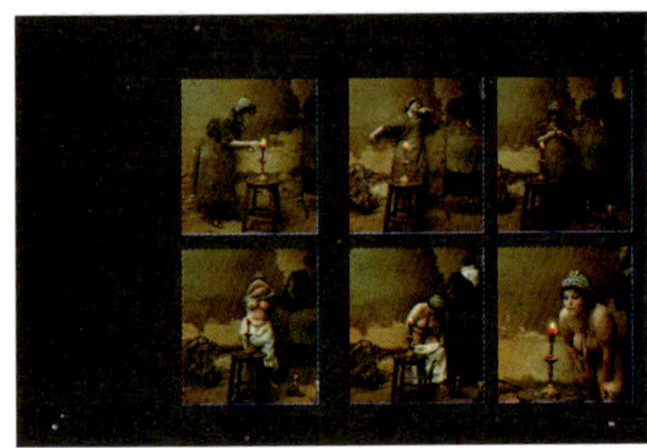

90/91
Maid's Evening, 1980
Der Abend des Dienstmädchens
La Soirée de la bonne

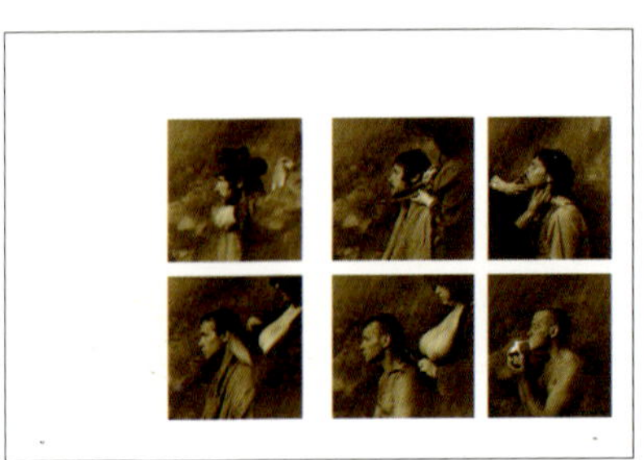

92/93
The Story of the Haircut of a Soldier, 1984
Die Geschichte des Haarschnitts eines Soldaten
L'Histoire de la coupe de cheveux d'un soldat

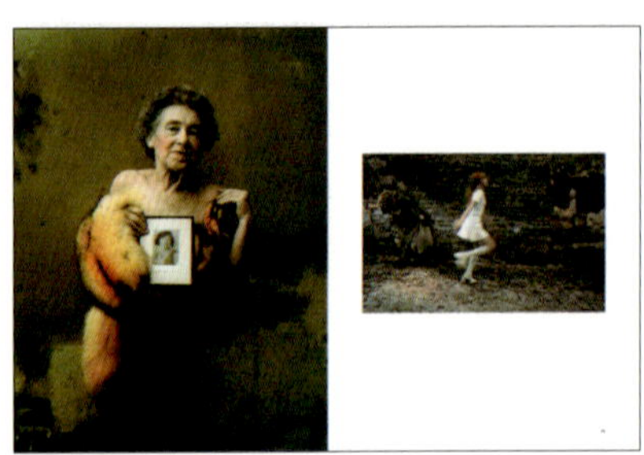

94
My Mother, 1979
Meine Mutter
Ma Mère

95
Two Women, 1974
Zwei Frauen
Deux Femmes

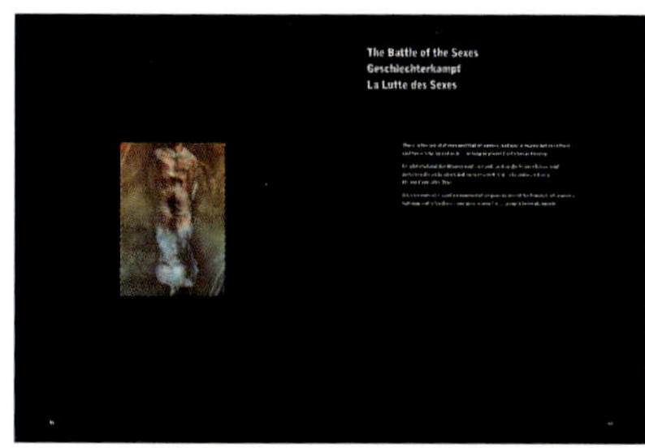

96
Fire and Rain, 1988
Feuer und Regen
Feu et Pluie

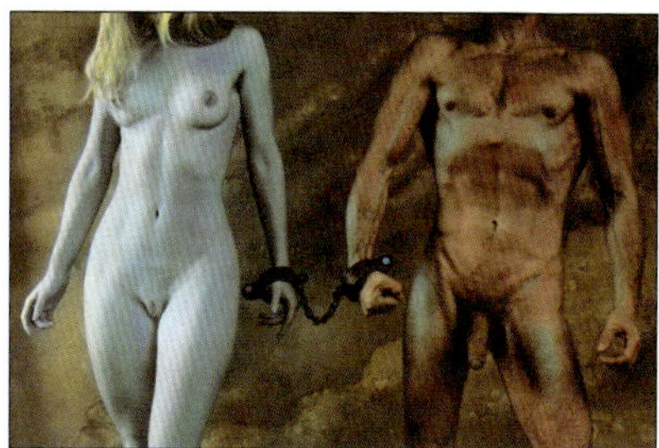

98/99
Chains of Love, 1987
Fesseln der Liebe
Les Liens de l'Amour

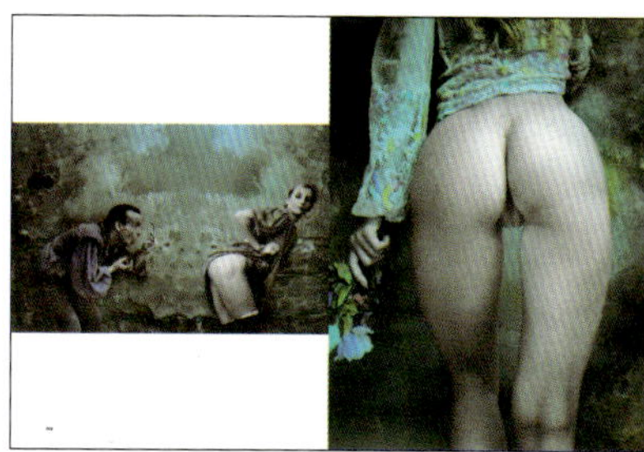

100
At the Waterfront, 1987
An den Gestaden
Sur le Rivage

101
Ida, 1988

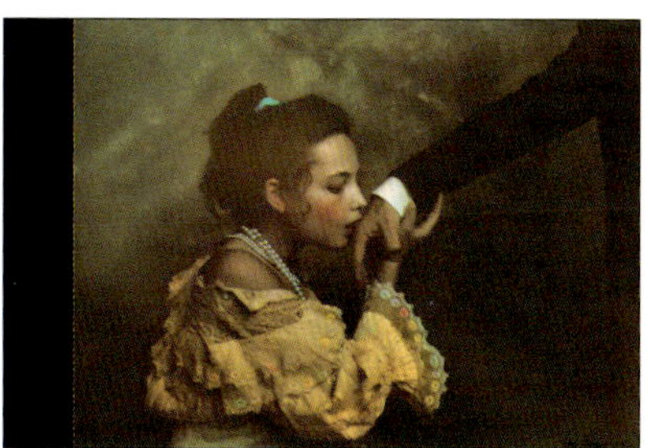

102/103
Deep Devotion, 1988
Tiefe Hingabe
Profonde Dévotion

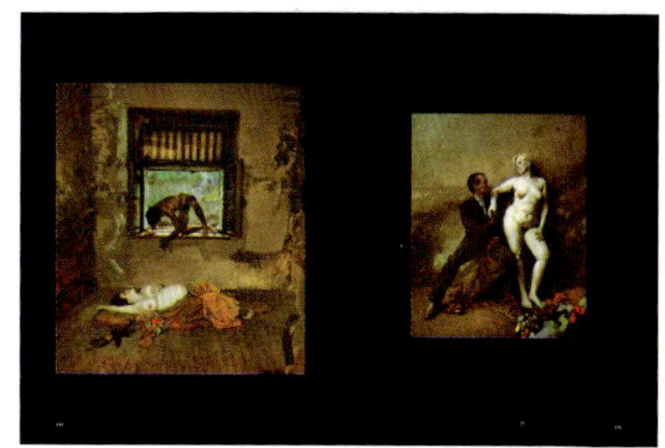

104
The Nightmare, 1983
Der Alptraum
Le Cauchemar

105
White Woman, 1982
Weiße Frau
Femme blanche

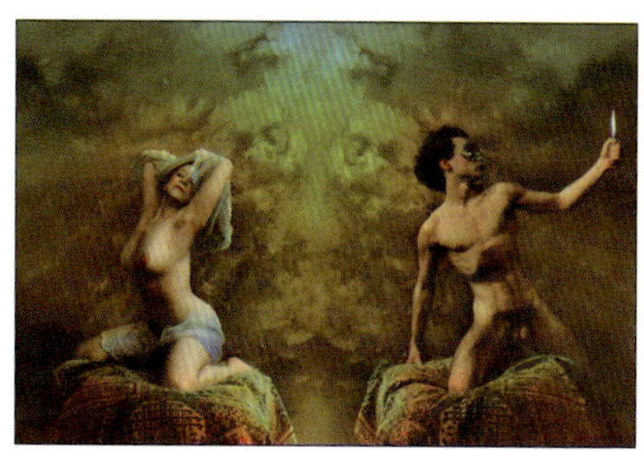

106/107
Weapons of Women and Men, 1989
Die Waffen der Frauen und der Männer
Les Armes des Femmes et des Hommes

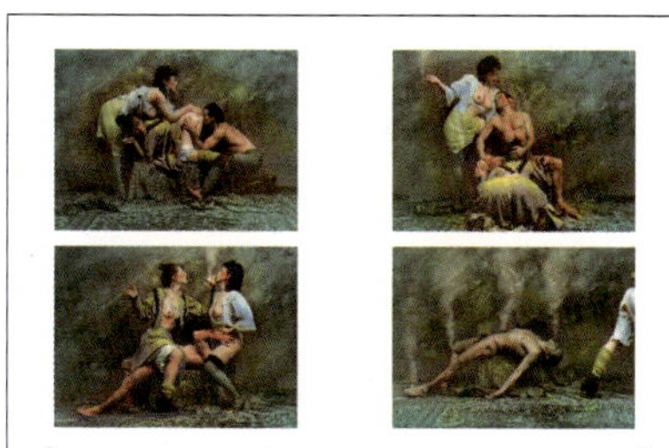

108/109
Pornographer, 1991
Der Pornograph
Le Pornographe

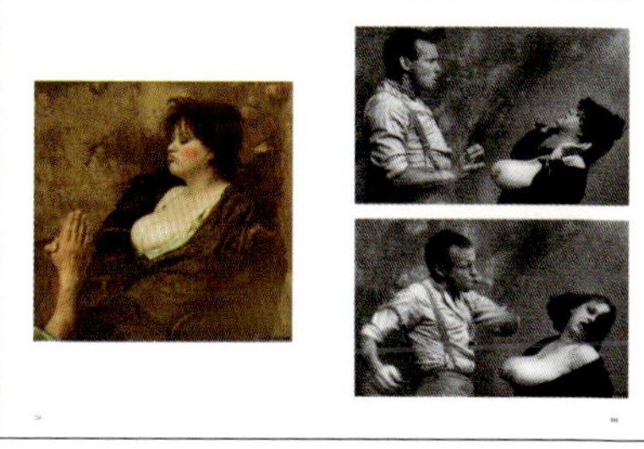

110
Deep Desire, 1985
Tiefes Verlangen
Désir profond

111
Temptation of St. Anthony, 1985
Die Versuchung des heiligen Antonius
La Tentation de saint Antoine

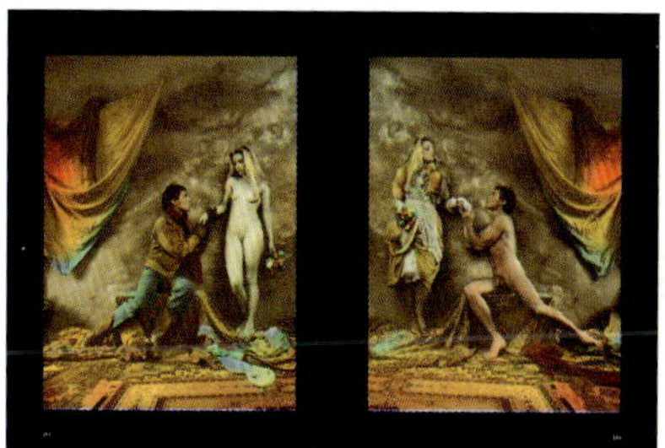

112/113
Wooing, 1988
Liebeswerben
Le Soupirant

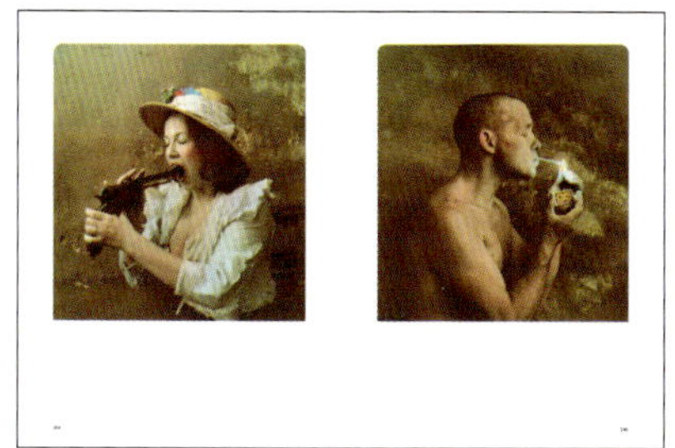

114/115
Portrait of Woman and Man, 1984
Porträt einer Frau und eines Mannes
Portrait d'une Femme et d'un Homme

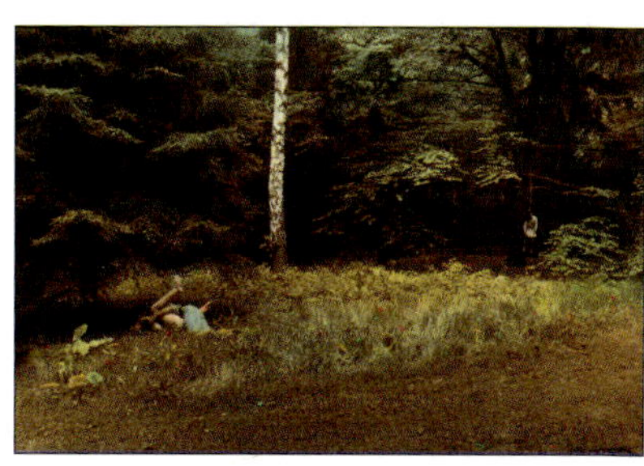

116/117
The Forest of Love and Death, 1990
Der Wald der Liebe und des Todes
Le Bois de l'Amour et de la Mort

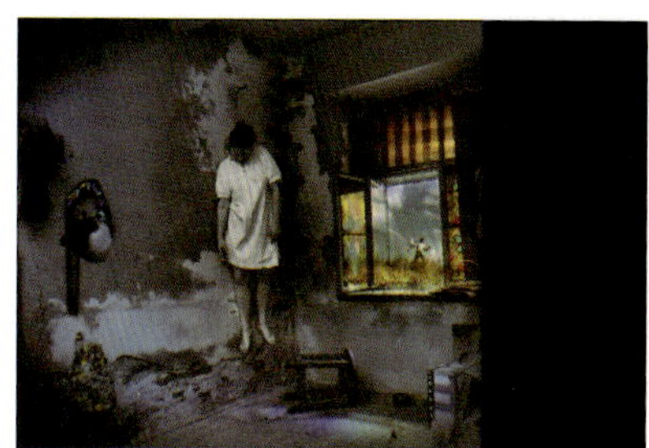

118/119
The Daybreak, 1977
Der Tagesanbruch
Le Lever du jour

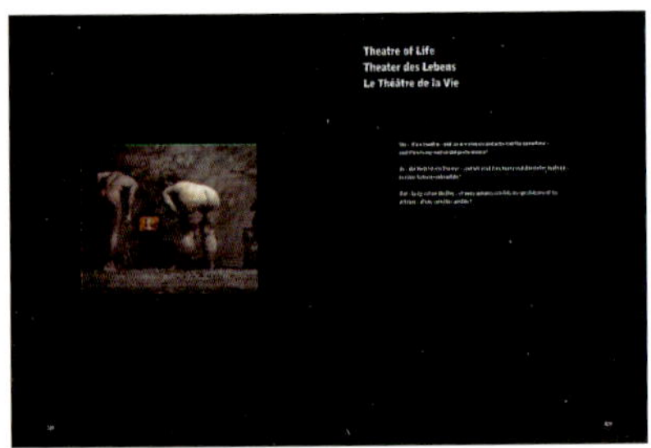

120
T. V. Lovers, 1991
TV-Liebespaar
Les Amoureux de la télé

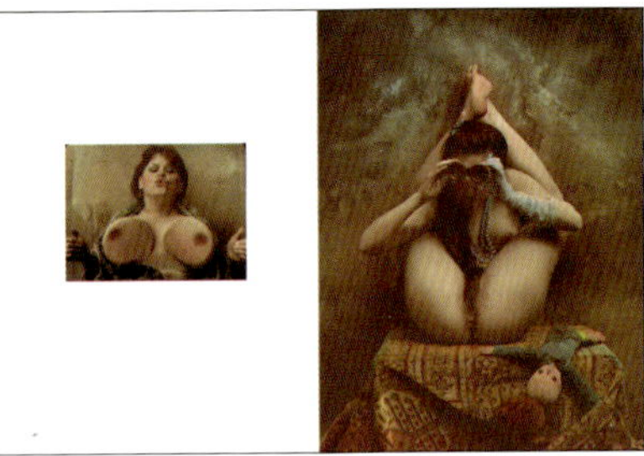

122
Kiss off, 1987
Ein letzter Kuß
Un dernier Baiser

123
Lady in the Theatre Box, 1994
Dame in der Theaterloge
Dame à la loge d'un théâtre

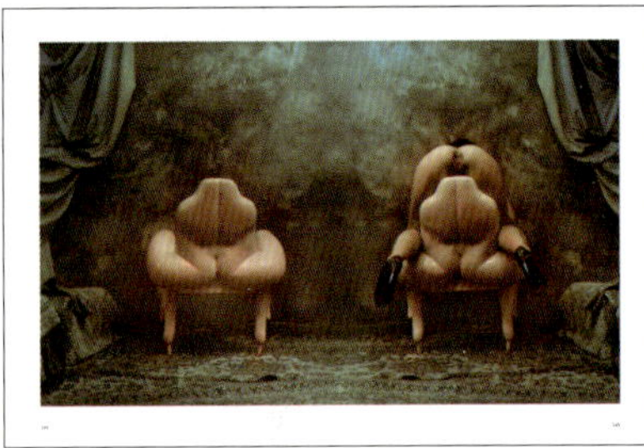

124/125
My New Armchair, 1994
Mein neuer Sessel
Mon nouveau fauteuil

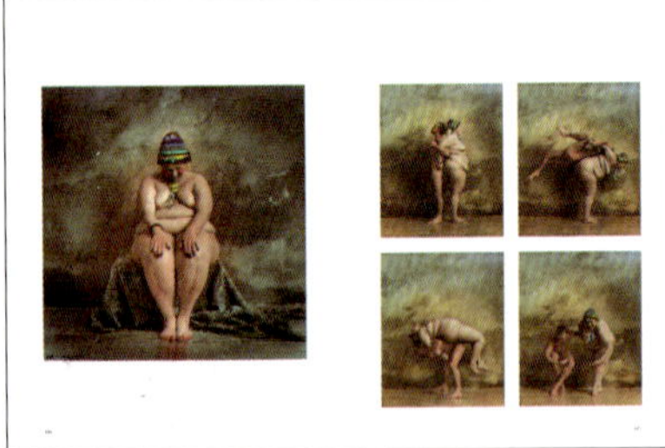

126
Innocence, 1997
Unschuld
Innocence

127
Photographer and His Model – Some Action!, 1997
Der Photograph und sein Modell – Action!
Le Photographe et son Modèle – Action!

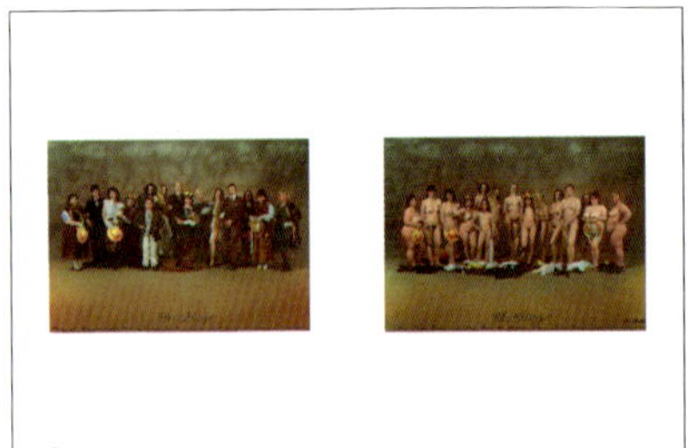

128/129
The Wedding, 1990
Die Hochzeit
Le Mariage

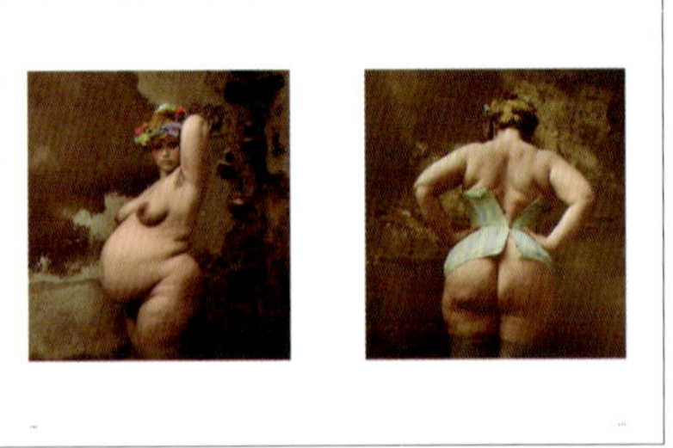

130
The Belly of the Night, 1988
Der Bauch der Nacht
Le Ventre de la Nuit

131
Slavic Beauty, 1988
Slawische Schönheit
Beauté slave

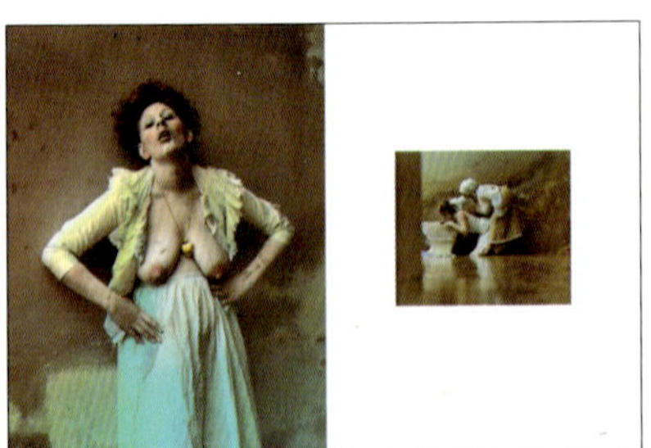

132
Luisa, 1987

133
End of Orgy, 1987
Ende der Orgie
Fin de l'Orgie

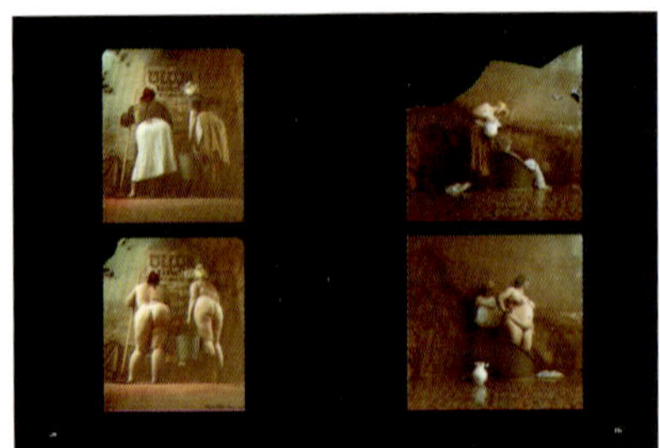

134
Those Ollök Charwomen, 1987
Diese Putzfrauen von Ollök
Ces Femmes de ménage d'Ollök

135
The Bath, 1987
Das Bad
Le Bain

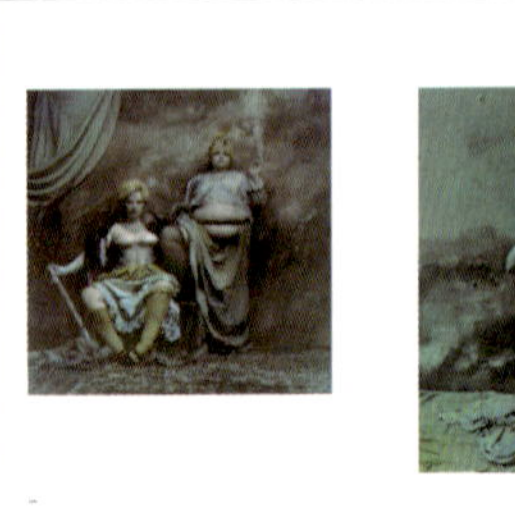

136
Blue Angels, 1993
Blaue Engel
Anges bleus

137
The Burden, 1987
Die Last
Le Fardeau

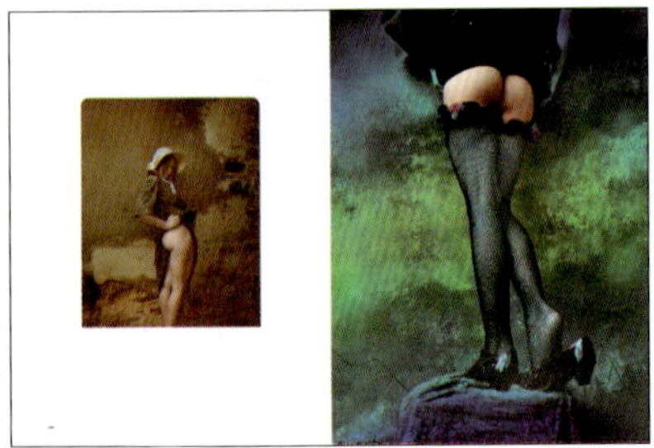

138
Some Legs! 1987
Das sind Beine!
En voilà des jambes!

139
New York, New York, 1985

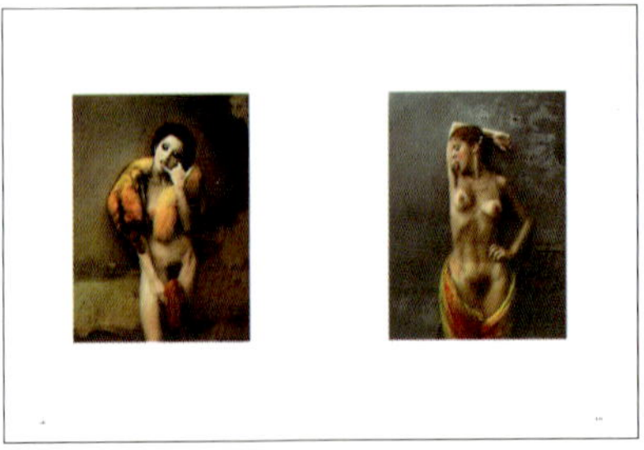

140
Who Cares?, 1987
Wen kümmert's?
Qui s'en préoccupe?

141
Narcissist, 1987
Narzißtin
Narcissique

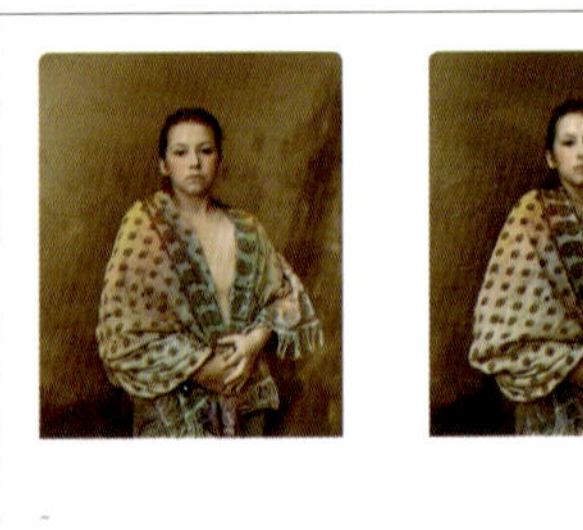

142/143
Quick Change, 1983
Schneller Wechsel
Changement rapide

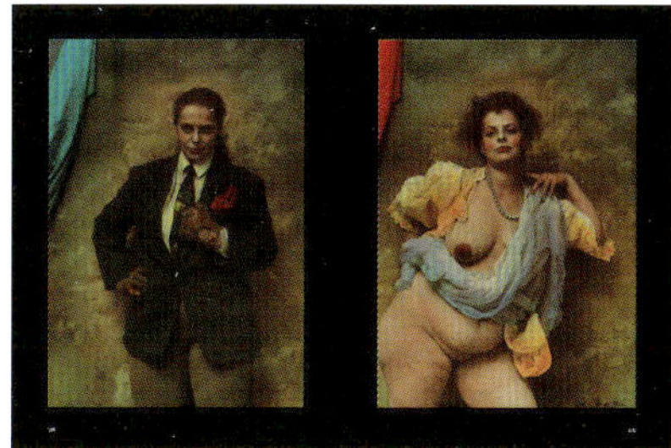

144/145
Boys and Girls (Gabrielle), 1997
Jungen und Mädchen (Gabrielle)
Garçons et Filles (Gabrielle)

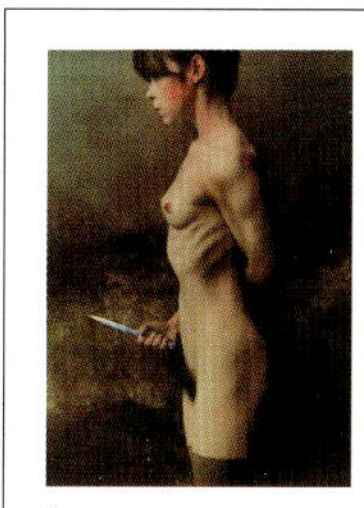

146
The Knife, 1987
Das Messer
Le Couteau

147
Helpless Girl, 1987
Hilfloses Mädchen
Fille sans défense

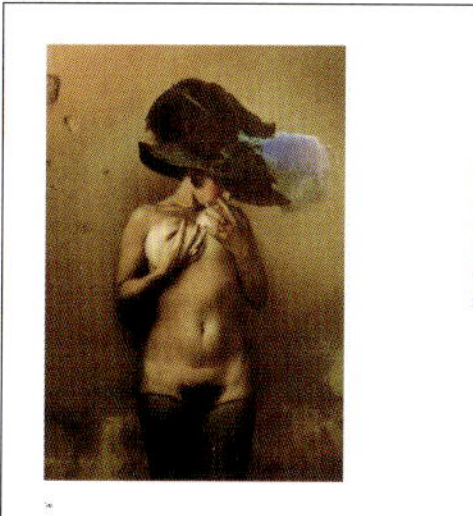

148
Johanna, 1975

149
Saudek Brothers, 1988
Die Brüder Saudek
Les Frères Saudek

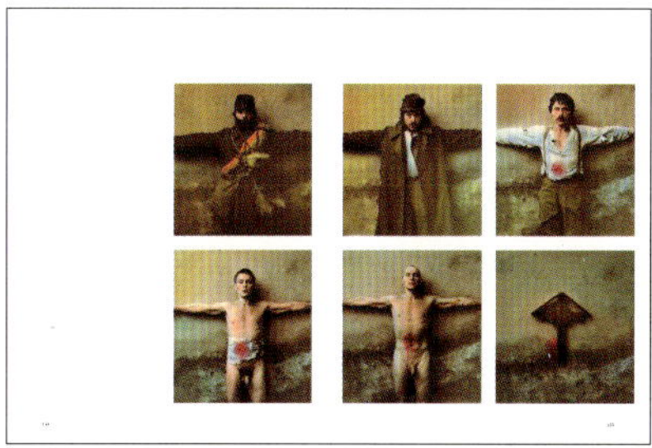

150/151
Target (Death of a Soldier), 1984
Zielscheibe (Tod eines Soldaten)
La Cible (Mort d'un soldat)

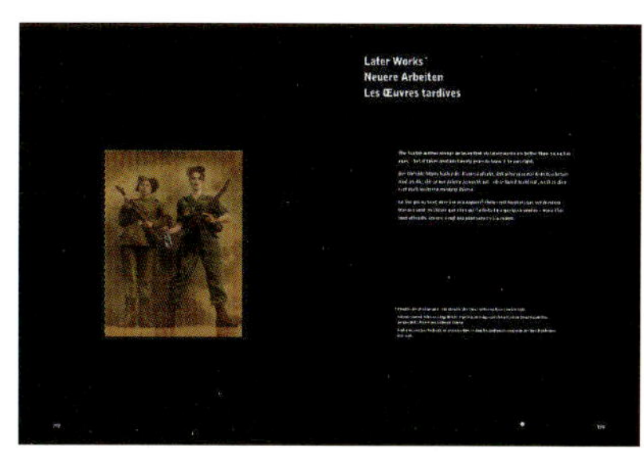

152
Absolut Reunion between East and West, 1998

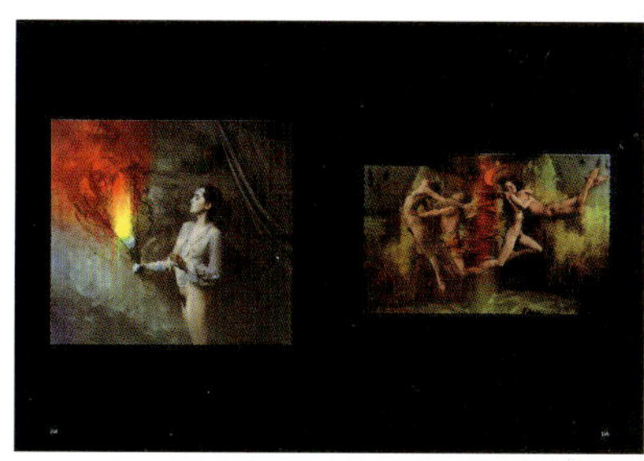

154
The Flame, 1988
Die Flamme
La Flamme

155
Purgatory no. 2, 1987
Fegefeuer Nr. 2
Purgatoire nº 2

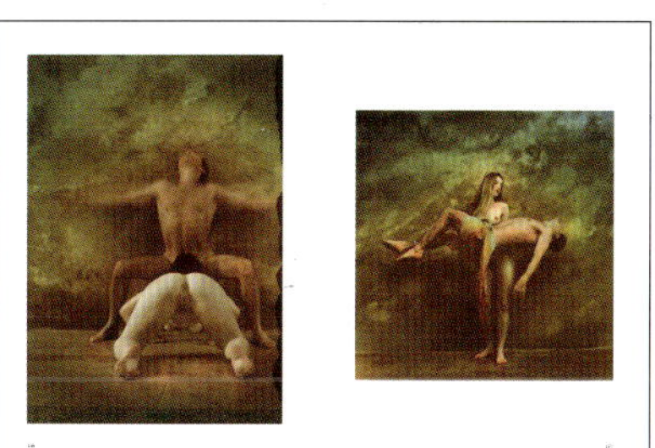

156
The End of the Film, 1997
Das Ende des Films
La Fin du film

157
Pietà, 1990

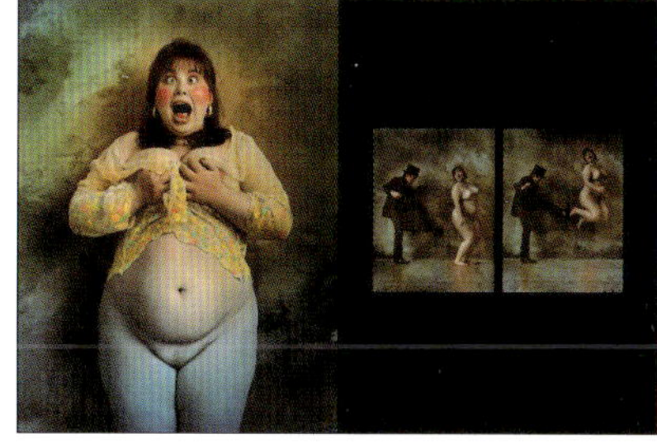

158
Portrait of my Friend Hannelore, 1997
Porträt meiner Freundin Hannelore
Portrait de mon amie Hannelore

159
In the Suburbs, 1997
In der Vorstadt
En Banlieue

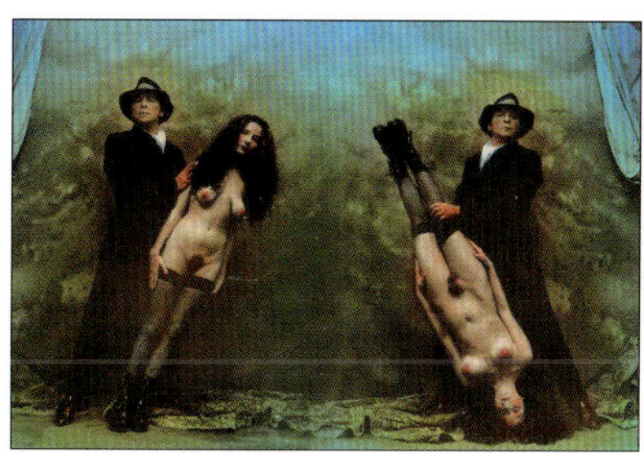

160/161
White Flesh Merchant, 1997
Weißfleischhändler
Marchand de chair blanche

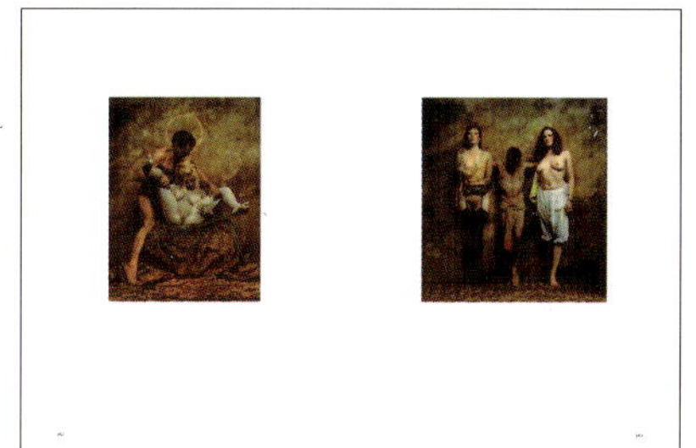

162
The Saint, 1992
Der Heilige
Le Saint

163
Photographer as Jesus, 1991
Der Photograph als Jesus
Le Photographe en Jésus

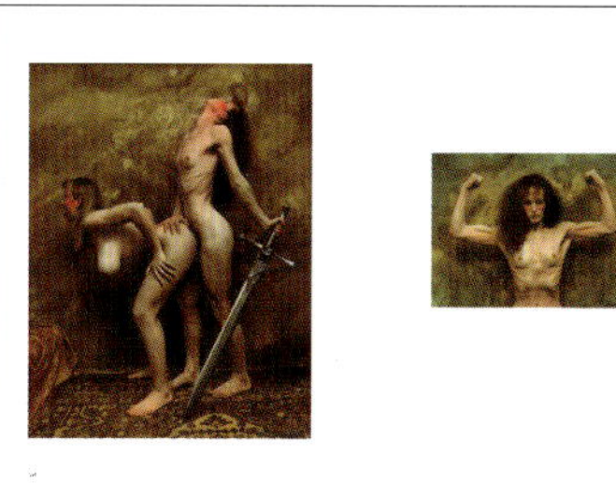

164
Conquest of Paradise, 1995
Die Eroberung des Paradieses
La Conquête du Paradis

165
Sarah goes strong ...!, 1995
Sarah macht auf stark ...!
Sarah joue les dures ... !

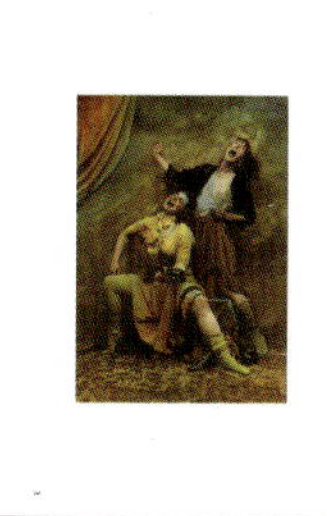

166
Rejoice!, 1993
Frohlocket!
Réjouissons-nous !

167
Czech Girl Singing, 1990
Singendes tschechisches Mädchen
Jeune fille tchèque chantant

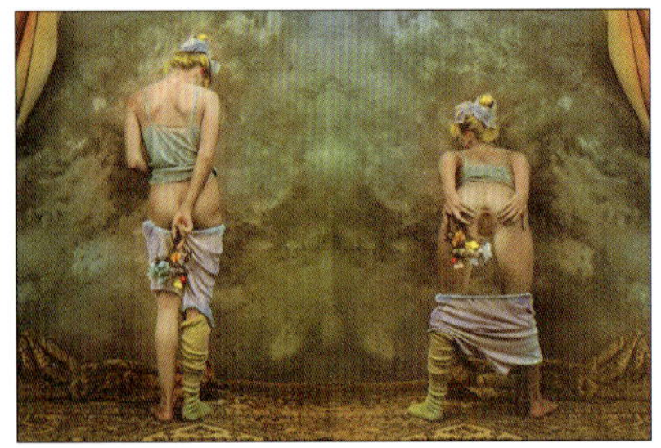

168/169
Just Two Expressions of Sabrina, 1994
Zwei Ansichten von Sabrina
Deux Expressions de Sabrina

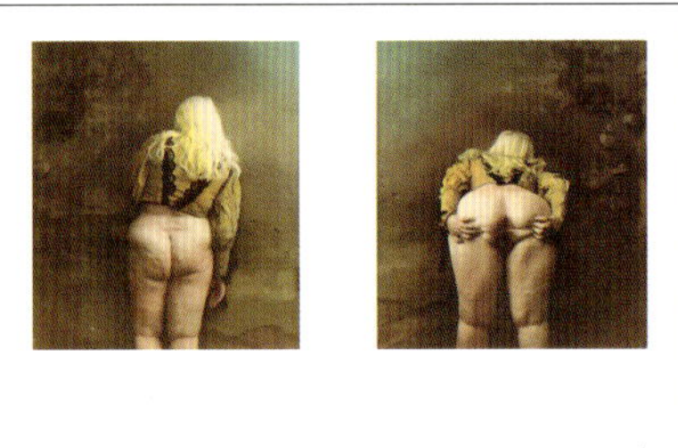

170/171
From the Endless Series: "My Lovers", 1982
Aus der endlosen Folge: »Meine Geliebten«
Extrait de la Série sans fin : « Mes petites amies »

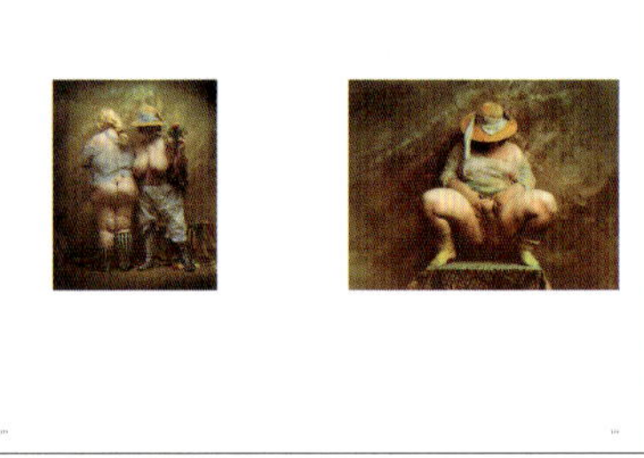

172
Shy Congratulators, 1996
Schüchterne Gratulantinnen
Timides Félicitations

173
Portrait of My Tender Love Marie no. 7, 1992
Porträt meiner zärtlichen Geliebten Marie Nr. 7
Portrait de ma tendre amante Marie nº 7

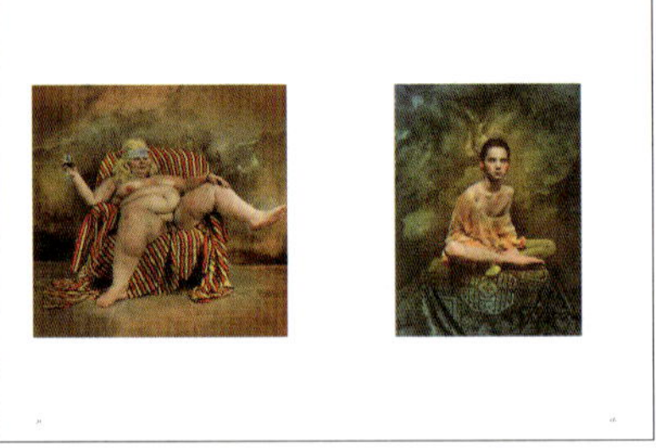

174
Member of the Committee for Public Welfare, 1996
Ein Mitglied des Komitees für öffentliche Wohlfahrt
Membre du Comité de l'Assistance publique

175
Green Eyes of Petra, 1991
Die grünen Augen von Petra
Les Yeux verts de Petra

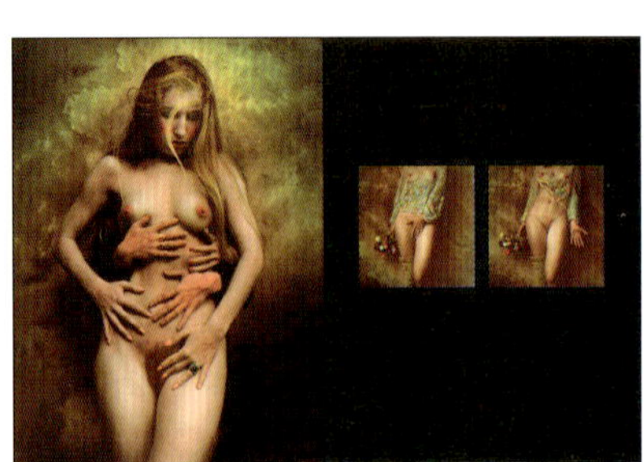

176
Ida, 1990

177
Virgin, 1988
Jungfrau
Pucelle

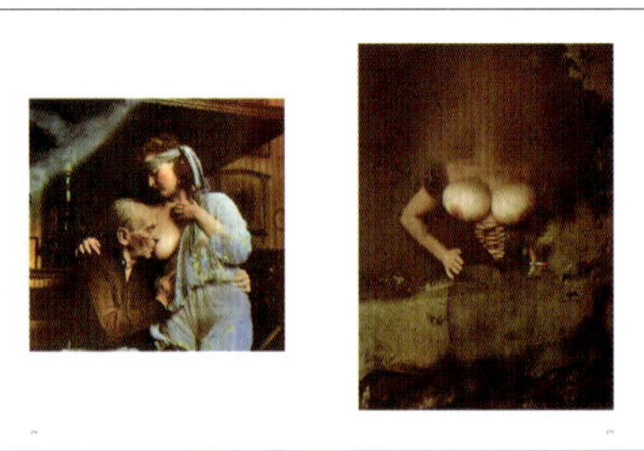

178
Art Nouveau, 1988
Jugendstil
L'Art Nouveau

179
Elusive Dream, 1976
Flüchtiger Traum
Rêve éphémère

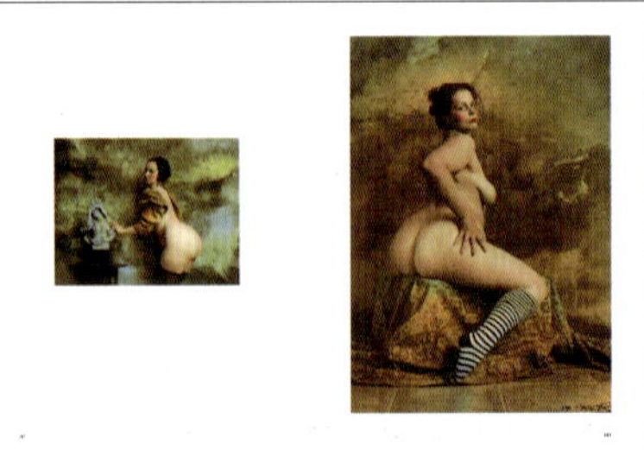

180
Portrait of Lady M., 1984
Porträt der Lady M.
Portrait de Lady M.

181
Portrait of Young Lady G., 1997
Porträt der jungen Lady G.
Portrait de la jeune Lady G.

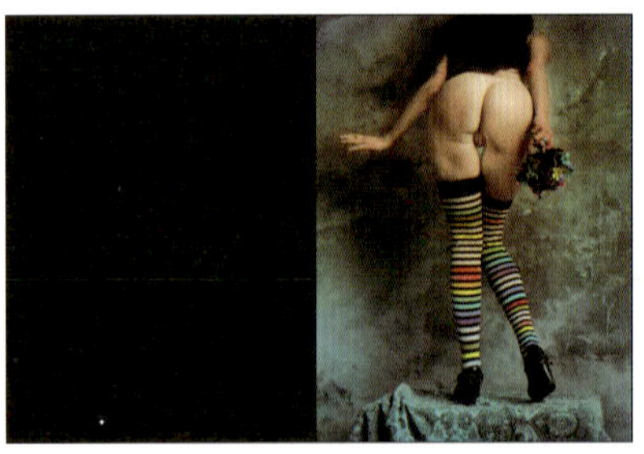

183
I Think it's Gonna Rain, 1997
Es sieht nach Regen aus
On dirait qu'il va pleuvoir

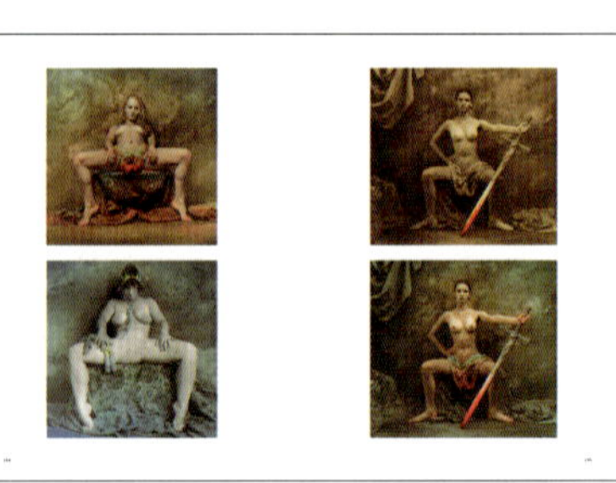

184/1
Portrait of an Innocent Girl, 1997
Porträt eines unschuldigen Mädchens
Portrait d'une Fille innocente

184/2
The Temptation, 1997
Die Versuchung
La Tentation

185/1
Sword, 1996
Schwert
L'Epée

185/2
Petra, 1996

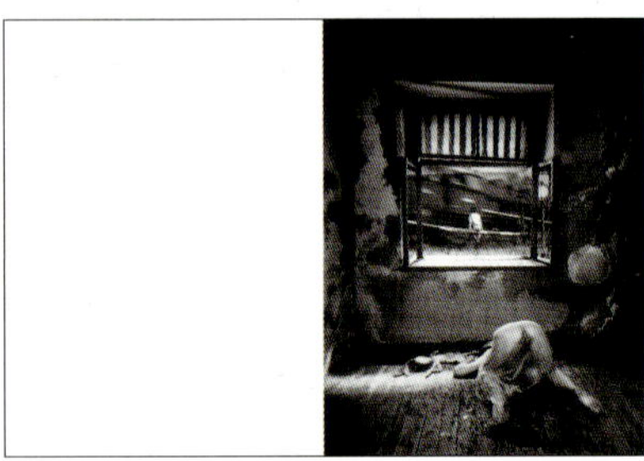

187
End of the Story, 1976
Das Ende der Geschichte
La Fin de l'histoire

Page 6 · Seite 6
Elusive Dreams, 1986
Flüchtige Träume
Rêves éphémères

Page 23 · Seite 23
Where Are You Going, My Little One?, 1968
Wohin des Wegs, mein Kleines?
Où vas-tu, mon petit ?

Page 27 · Seite 27
Home Alone, 1976
Allein zu Haus
Seul à la maison

Biography

1935 Jan Saudek born on the 13 May, the son of a bank clerk in Prague where he grows up and goes to school until the age of 15. His father survives the Theresienstadt concentration camp where his six brothers die.

1950–1983 Works for a printer. Begins to paint and draw. Describes his first camera, a Baby Brownie Kodak: "The only thing you can do with this camera is load the film and press the button to make a picture; that's exactly what I did until 1963."

1953 *My Very First Photograph* – Jan Saudek views this photograph of his brother as his first important artistic work (see p. 30). Works on a farm.

1954–1956 Military service.

1958 Marries Marie with whom he has two children: Samuel and David.

1959 Is given his first 'real' camera, a Flexaret 6 x 6.

1963 First exhibition of his own in Prague.
Decides to become a photographer; inspired by Edward Steichen's exhibition catalogue "The Family of Man" he wants to make a book about the people of his own time.
Only photographs people that he is personally connected with – "You could call it love".

1966 Takes his most famous photograph: *Life* (see p. 44)

1969 Travels to the USA where Hugh Edwards encourages him to continue with photography. First solo exhibition at the University of Indiana, Bloomington.

1970 Separation from Marie.

1972 Discovers the decaying 'cellar wall' which is to become a synonym of his artistic work. Growing international reputation from the mid-seventies onwards. Works together with various artists including Paule Pia (Antwerp and Brussels), Karsten Fricke (Bonn), Marlène and Jean-Pierre Vorlet (Lausanne), Pierre Borhan (Paris), Anita Neugebauer (Basle) and David Travis (Art Institute of Chicago).

1977 Travels to Arles for the exhibition "Rencontres Internationales de la Photographie" and also to Paris.

1976–1984 Collaboration and exhibitions with the Jacques Baruch Gallery, Chicago. In 1983 the first monograph on Saudek, *The World of Jan Saudek*, appears in English, German and French. Starts tinting black and white prints (around 1977).

1984 After years of working in a factory he is given a work permit as a photographer and now, freed from the constraints of earning a weekly wage, he is able to devote himself entirely to photography. He becomes a member of the Unity of Czech Artists, having been ignored for a long time. "With my work I am trying to capture all the things I know and love; and above all I would like to leave behind a sign of the times that have elapsed."

1988–1995 Collaboration and exhibitions with the Galerie Torch in Amsterdam, and from 1990 with the publishers 'Art Unlimited' in Amsterdam.

1989/1991 Fashion pictures for the Japanese firm 'Matsuda'.

1990 Honoured as a 'Chevalier des Arts et Lettres'. The French director, Jerome de Missolz, makes a short film him: "Jan Saudek – Photograph tchèque".

1995 Publishes his first book, *Dopis* (Letters), edited by Sarah Saudek. Since the mid-nineties he has devoted more attention to painting, transferring important motifs from his photographic output to canvas.

1998 Major retrospective of his photographs and paintings in Los Angeles, Bergamot Station Arts Center, BGH Gallery.

Biographie

1935 Jan Saudek wird am 13. Mai als Sohn eines jüdischen Bankangestellten in Prag geboren, wo er bis zum Alter von 15 Jahren die Schule besucht. Saudeks Vater überlebt als einziger von sieben Brüdern das Konzentrationslager Theresienstadt.

1950–1983 Arbeitet in einer Druckerei. Beginnt zu malen und zu zeichnen. Über seine erste Kamera, eine Baby Brownie Kodak, sagt er: »Das einzige, was man mit dieser Kamera tun kann, ist, den Film einzulegen und auf den Knopf zu drücken, um ein Bild zu machen; genau das tat ich bis 1963.«

1953 *My Very First Photograph* – Jan Saudek ist der Meinung, daß diese Aufnahme seines Bruders sein erstes künstlerisch bedeutsames Werk ist. (s. S. 30). Arbeitet auf einem Bauernhof.

1954–1956 Leistet seinen Militärdienst.

1958 Heiratet Marie, mit der er zwei Kinder hat: Samuel und David.

1959 Bekommt seine erste ›richtige‹ Kamera, eine Flexaret 6 x 6.

1963 Erste eigene Ausstellung in Prag. Entschließt sich, Photograph zu werden; inspiriert von Edward Steichens Ausstellungskatalog »The Family of Man« möchte er ein Buch über den Menschen in seiner Zeit machen. Photographiert nur Menschen, zu denen er eine persönliche Beziehung hat – »Man kann es Liebe nennen.«

1966 Entstehung seines berühmtesten Bildes: *Life* (s. S. 44).

1969 Reise in die USA, wo Hugh Edwards ihn ermutigt, mit der Photographie weiterzumachen. Erste Einzelausstellung an der University of Indiana, Bloomington.

1970 Trennung von Marie.

1972 Entdeckung der »Kellerwand«, deren morbide Erscheinung zum Synonym seines künstlerischen Schaffens wird. Seit Mitte der 70er Jahre zunehmende internationale Anerkennung. Zusammenarbeit u. a. mit Paule Pia (Antwerpen und Brüssel), Karsten Fricke (Bonn), Marlène und Jean-Pierre Vorlet (Lausanne), Pierre Borhan (Paris), Anita Neugebauer (Basel) und David Travis (Art Institute of Chicago).

1977 Reise nach Arles anläßlich der Ausstellung »Rencontres Internationales de la Photographie« und nach Paris.

1976–1984 Zusammenarbeit mit der Jacques Baruch Gallery, Chicago. 1983 erscheint seine erste Monographie »Die Welt des Jan Saudek« in englischer, deutscher und französischer Sprache. Beginnt, seine Schwarzweißabzüge zu kolorieren (um 1977).

1984 Bekommt nach jahrelanger Fabrikarbeit seine Arbeitserlaubnis als Photograph und kann sich nun, nach dieser Befreiung von den Zwängen lohnabhängiger Arbeit, ganz der Photographie widmen. Erhält die Mitgliedschaft der Unity of Czech Artists, nachdem er und seine Bilder jahrelang ignoriert wurden. »Ich versuche, mit meiner Arbeit all die Dinge festzuhalten, die ich kenne oder liebe; und vor allem möchte ich ein Zeugnis der verrinnenden Zeit hinterlassen.«

1988–1995 Zusammenarbeit und Ausstellungen zunächst mit der Galerie Torch, Amsterdam, seit 1990 mit dem Verlag »Art Unlimited«, Amsterdam.

1989/1991 Modeaufnahmen für die japanische Firma »Matsuda«.

1990 Auszeichnung als »Chevalier des Arts et Lettres«. Der französische Regisseur Jerome de Missolz dreht einen kurzen Film über ihn: »Jan Saudek – Photograph tchèque«.

1995 Herausgegeben von Sarah Saudek, erscheint sein erstes eigenes Buch: *Dopis* (Briefe). Seit Mitte der neunziger Jahre widmet er sich verstärkt der Malerei, indem er wichtige Motive seines photographischen Werks auf die Leinwand überträgt.

1998 Große Retrospektive in Los Angeles, Bergamot Station Arts Center, BGH Gallery.

Biographie

1935 Fils d'un employé de banque juif, Jan Saudek est né le 13 mai à Prague où il est scolarisé jusqu'à l'âge de 15 ans. De sept frères, le père de Saudek est le seul à avoir survécu au camp de concentration Theresienstadt.

1950–1983 Travaille dans une imprimerie. Commence à peindre et à dessiner. A propos de son premier appareil photo, un Baby Brownie Kodak, il déclare : « La seule chose qu'on peut faire avec cet appareil pour réaliser une photo, c'est mettre la pellicule et appuyer sur le bouton ; c'est exactement ce que j'ai fait jusqu'en 1963 ».

1953 *My Very First Photograph* – Jan Saudek estime que cette photo de son frère est sa première œuvre artistique importante (voir p. 30).
Travaille dans une ferme.

1954–1956 Effectue son service militaire.

1958 Epouse Marie qui lui donnera deux enfants : Samuel et David.

1959 Reçoit son premier « vrai » appareil photo, un Flexaret 6 x 6.

1963 Première exposition à Prague. Décide de devenir photographe ; inspiré par le catalogue d'exposition d'Edward Steichen, « The Family of Man », il désire réaliser un ouvrage sur les gens de son époque.

1966 Réalisation de sa photo la plus célèbre, *Life* (voir p. 44).

1969 Voyage aux Etats-Unis où Hugh Edwards l'encourage à persévérer dans la photographie. Première exposition individuelle à l'University of Indiana, Bloomington.

1970 Se sépare de Marie.

1972 Découvre le « mur de la cave » dont l'aspect morbide devient le synonyme de sa création artistique. Dès le milieu des années soixante-dix, il acquiert une reconnaissance internationale de plus en plus grande. Collabore avec notamment Paule Pia (Anvers et Bruxelles), Karsten Fricke (Bonn), Marlène et Jean-Pierre Vorlet (Lausanne), Pierre Borhan (Paris), Anita Neugebauer (Bâle) et David Travis (Art Institute of Chicago).

1977 Se rend en Arles pour l'exposition « Rencontres Internationales de la Photographie » et à Paris.

1976–1984 Collaboration et expositions avec la Jacques Baruch Gallery de Chicago.
Sa première monographie, « Le Monde de Jan Saudek » paraît en 1983, en anglais, allemand et français.
Commence à colorier ses épreuves en noir et blanc (vers 1977).

1984 Après avoir travaillé de longues années comme ouvrier, il reçoit l'autorisation d'exercer en tant que photographe. Libéré des contraintes d'un emploi salarié, il peut désormais se consacrer entièrement à la photographie. Entre à la Unity of Czech Artists après avoir été ignoré, lui et ses photos, pendant des années. « J'essaie avec mon travail de fixer toutes les choses que je connais ou que j'aime. Et surtout je voudrais laisser un témoignage du temps qui s'écoule. »

1988–1995 Collaboration et expositions avec la galerie Torch d'Amsterdam, puis à partir de 1990 avec les éditions « Art Unlimited » d'Amsterdam.

1989/1991 Photographies de mode pour la firme japonaise « Matsuda ».

1990 Est consacré « Chevalier des Arts et des Lettres ». Le metteur en scène français, Jérôme de Missolz, tourne un petit film sur lui : « Jan Saudek – Photographe tchèque ».

1995 Parution de son premier livre *Dopis* (Lettres) édité par Sarah Saudek. Depuis le milieu des années quatre-vingt-dix, il se consacre de plus en plus à la peinture en reportant sur la toile les motifs importants de son œuvre photographique.

1998 Grande rétrospective de son œuvre photographique et picturale à Los Angeles, Bergamot Station Arts Center, BGH Gallery.

Exhibitions · Ausstellungen · Expositions

1963 Theater am Geländer, Prague
1969 University of Indiana, Bloomington (IN)
1970 Louisville (KY)
1971 Bathouse Gallery, Milwaukee (WI)
Fotochema, Prague
Funke's Cabinet of Photography, Brno, Czech Republic
Gallery of Art and Sculpture, Olomouc, Czech Republic
Haus der Herren von Kunstat, Brno, Czech Republic
1972 Fotochema, Prague
1973 Exchange National Bank, Chicago (IL)
1974 Darkroom Workshop Gallery, Berkeley (CA)
La Photogalerie, Paris
Shado Gallery, Portland (OR)
1975 Peter M. David Gallery, Minneapolis (MN)
Students Hostel, Brno, Czech Republic
1976 Art Institute of Chicago, Chicago (IL)
D. P. M. Gallery, Minneapolis (MN)
Jacques Baruch Gallery, Chicago (IL)
1977 Australian Centre of Photography, Sydney
Church Street Photo Centre, Melbourne
La Photogalerie, Paris
National Gallery of Victoria, Melbourne
Photo Art, Basle, Switzerland
Photo Center, Melbourne
Photogalerie / Bardavil, Paris
Rencontres Internationales de la Photographie (R. I. P.), Arles, France
1978 Cincinnati Art Museum, Cincinnati (OH)
Galeria Il Diaframma, Milan
Galerie im Riek, Essen, Germany
International Museum of Photography at George Eastman House, Rochester (NY)
Kresge Art Center, Michigan City (IN)
Photo Art, Basle, Switzerland
Wroclawska Galerie Fotografie, Wroclaw, Poland
1979 G. Ray Hawkins Gallery, Los Angeles (CA)
Galerie Fiolet, Amsterdam
Galerie Paule Pia, Antwerp, Belgium
Pratt Manhattan Graphic Center, New York
1980 Camden Art Centre, London
Church Street Photo Center, Melbourne
Equivalents Gallery, Seattle (WA)
Fine Art Exposition, Association of International Photography Art Dealers, New York
FNAC-Montparnasse, Paris
Galerie Lichtblick, Dortmund, Germany
Photokina, Cologne
"56/65 ... The Print Club 56th Annual International Competition", Philadelphia
1981 Cincinnati Art Museum, Cincinnati (OH)
Equivalents Gallery, Seattle (WA)
Images Gallery, Sun Valley (ID)
Jacques Baruch Gallery, Chicago (IL)
Kamp Gallery, Saint Louis (MO)
Keystone Gallery, Santa Barbara (CA)
Marcuse Pfeiffer Gallery, New York
Portfolio Gallery, Lausanne, Switzerland
Second Annual Fine Art Photography Exposition, Association of International Photography Art Dealers, New York
1982 Art 1982 Chicago, International Art Exposition, Chicago (IL)
Evanston Art Center, Evanston (IL)
G. H. Dalsheimer Gallery, Baltimore (MD)
Het Pepertje, Depenbeeck, Belgium
The House of Cs. Writers, Prague
Karin Steins Gallery, Frankfurt/M.
1983 University of Iowa Museum of Art, Iowa City (IA)
Wabash College, Crawfordsville (IA)
1984 Bei Liicht, Dudelange, Luxemburg
Jacques Baruch Gallery, Chicago (IL)
Musée national d'art moderne,
Centre Georges Pompidou, Paris
Watari Gallery, Tokyo
1985 Alvar Aalto Museo, Jyvaskylä, Finland
Galerie Le Réverbère, Lyon
Münchner Stadtmuseum, Munich
Suomen Valokü Vataiteen Museum, Helsinki
VALR, Little Rock (AR)
1986 A Gallery of Fine Photography, New Orleans (LA)
Centre National de la Photographie, Paris
Fotografie Forum Frankfurt, Frankfurt/M.
Kicken Gallery, Cologne
Théâtre des Réalités, Caves Ste Croix, Metz, France
Torch Gallery, Amsterdam, Netherlands
1987 Fotografie Forum, Bremen, Germany
Musée d'Art Moderne de la Ville de Paris, Paris
Robert Koch Gallery, San Francisco (CA)
1988 Primavera Fotogràfica, Barcelona
The Second Israeli Photography Biennale, Museum of Art, Ein Harod, Israel
Urbi et Orbi, Paris
1989 Fotografie Forum Frankfurt, Frankfurt/M.
Galerie Nikki Diana Marquardt, Paris
In Extremis, Strasbourg, France
Jan Kesner Gallery, Los Angeles (CA)
1990 Rencontres Internationales de la Photographie (R. I. P.), Arles, France
Robert Koch Gallery, Los Angeles (CA)
Yokohama Gallery, Yokohama, Japan
1991 Ambrosiana, Brno, Czech Republic
Galerie Steltman, Amsterdam, Netherlands
Musée national d'art moderne, Centre Georges Pompidou, Paris
Nicky Akehurst Gallery, London
Portfolio Gallery, London
1992 Galerie Le Réverbère, Lyon
Galerie Municipale du Chateau d'Eau, Toulouse, France
Galerie Thierry Salvador, Paris
Gallery Steltman, Amsterdam, Netherlands
1993 Art Temporis, Klagenfurt, Austria
Galerie David, Bielefeld, Germany
Galerie Faber, Vienna
Galerie Objekte, Munich
Gallery of the City of Bratislava, Bratislava, Slovakia
Vision Gallery, San Francisco (CA)
1994 Galerie Aura, Olomouc, Czech Republic
Gallery for fine Photography, Gdansk, Poland
In Focus, Cologne
Parco Gallery, Tokyo
Prinz, Tokyo
1995 A Gallery for Fine Photography, New Orleans (LA)
Galerie 4, Cheb, Czech Republic
Galerie Objekte, Munich
Krisal Gallery, Geneve
Michalský Dvor Gallery, Bratislava, Slovakia
1996 Krisal Gallery, Geneve
Museum of Art, Olomouc, Czech Republic
1997 Edelman Gallery, Chicago (IL)
Galerie du Chateau d'Eau, Toulouse, France
Kamera- und Fotomuseum, Mölkau, Germany
Ken Damy Museo, Milan
1998 Bergamot Station Arts Center, BGH Gallery, Los Angeles
Centre Interrégional de Conversation du Livre, Arles, France
Galerie für Fotografie, Rotenburg, Germany
Michalský Dvor Gallery, Bratislava, Slovakia
Obecní Dům, Prague, Czech Republic
Vrais Rêves, Lyon, France
1998–99 The Museum of Photography, Tel-Hai, Israel
1999 Stills Gallery, Sydney, Australia

Group Exhibitions

1985 *Das Aktfoto*, Münchener Stadtmuseum, Munich
1990 *Photographie Progressive en Tchécoslovaquie 1920–1990*, Galerie Robert Doisneau, Vanoeuvre-lès-Nancy, France
Tschechoslowakische Fotografie der Gegenwart, Museum Ludwig, Cologne
1993 *Kobe International Fashion Photographies Exhibition*, Kobe City, Japan
1995 *Fotofeis*, Scotland
1996 *Certainty and Searching in Czech Photography of the 1990s*, Prague Castle, Prague
Czech and Slovak Photography from between the Wars to the Present, Fitchburg Art Museum, Fitchburg (MA)
1997 *Fotofeis*, Scotland
Month of Photography, Paris
1998 *Zärtlicher Blick auf schöne Damen*, Museum Ludwig, Cologne

Bibliography · Bibliographie

1969 White, Devon, "Czech photographer tells it the way it is", *Courier-Tribune*, Bloomington, March 23, p. 6

1977 Fárová, Anna, "Jan Saudek", *Fotografie, Zeitschrift Internationaler Fotokunst*, no. 4, Akt & Erotik, Riesweiler, pp. 4–23

"Jan Saudek", *zoom, Magazin für Foto und Film*, no. 48, pp. 68–79

1978 Bennett, Derek, "Jan Saudek: Intuitives statt intellektuelles Schaffen", *Print Letter*, no. 14

Krause, Manfred, "Unschuld und Verruchtheit, Essen-Kettwig: Erstmals fotografische Arbeiten von Jan Saudek", *Westdeutsche Allgemeine Zeitung*, June 13

1979 Flapper, Aad, "Lijfelijke foto's", *Het Parool*, January 16

"Saudek, Jan, Schwarzweiß-Fotografie" (text by Gisèle Freund), *zoom, Magazin für Foto und Film*, no. 4, pp. 50–59

"The World of Jan Saudek Photographs", Jacques Baruch Gallery, Chicago (IL)

1981 *Il teatro de la vita*, (text by Giuliana Scimé), Selezione d'Immagini, Milan

1982 *Contemporary Photographers*, St. James Press, MacMillan Publishers, Great Britain – USA (1982, 1988), p. 660f.

Krzyzanowski, Michel Szulc, "Het fotografisch surrealisme voan Jan Saudek", *Zero*, no. 6, pp. 126–133

Photography Yearbook 1982, Time-Life-Books

"Story from Czechoslovakia, My Country. Photographs and Notes by Jan Saudek", *Aperture*, no. 89, pp. 62–76

"Eine 'verrückte Idee', die Menschheit portraitieren", *Photography 1982/83*, Time-Life-Books

Greeting Cards, Paule Pia Editions, Antwerp

1983 Bennett, Derek, "Berühmte Fotos vorgestellt, Jan Saudek: Ohne Titel, 1978", *Kamera und Schule, Zeitschrift für Foto, Film und AV-Medien*, no. 1, p. 14f.

Gerling, Astrid, "Jan Saudeks erotische Arrangements", *Stern magazin*, no. 51, pp. 130–140

"Jan Saudek. An Interview by Liba Taylor", *creative camera*, no. 225, pp. 1084–1089

Osman, Colin, "The world of Jan Saudek, Reviewed", *creative camera*, no. 228, p. 1206f.

"Portfolio Jan Saudek", *Photographie*, no. 9, pp. 69–78

"Posen für den Poeten mit der Kamera", *Stern magazin*, no. 12, pp. 130–140

The World of Jan Saudek (preface by Anna Fávorá), The Master Collection Book III, RotoVision, Geneve

Postcards, Verlag Dieter Fricke, Frankfurt/M.

1984 Broekman, Wim, "De wered van Jan Saudek", *Foto*, no. 4, pp. 30–35

"Die Welt des Jan Saudek", *visuel*, no 1, pp. 22–24

1985 *Encyclopédie internationale des photographes de 1839 à nos* jours, Camera Obscura, Hermance, Switzerland

1986 *The Male Nude*, ed. by Peter Weiermair, Zurich

Männer sehen Männer, ed. by Peter Weiermair, Schaffhausen, Switzerland

"Poesie aus Prag, Tagebuch von Jan Saudek", *Penthouse*, no. 10, p. 117ff.

"35 Jahre Fotografie – Jan Saudek", Fotografie Forum Frankfurt, Frankfurt/M.

1987 "Jan Saudek. 200 Photographs 1953–1986", Musée d'art moderne de la Ville de Paris, Paris

1988 "The World of Jan Saudek", *Minolta Mirror, An International Magazine of Photography*, 60th Anniversary Issue, pp. 66–81

1990 *Déjà-Vu. A Photography Quarterly* (Japan), no. 2

Tschechoslowakische Fotografie der Gegenwart, Edition Braus, Heidelberg

1991 *Jan Saudek – Life, Love, Death & Other Such Trifles*, Art Unlimited, Amsterdam (Czech edition 1994)

Mrázková, Daniela, *Jan Saudek – Divadlo ivota*, Panorama, Prague (German edition: *Theater des Lebens*)

1992 *The Black & White Art Photographer*, no. 5 (London)

Vis à Vis, no. 10 (Paris)

1993 "Erotik aus dem Keller. Prager Fotokunst kommt nach Düsseldorf", *Express*, August 25

Zollner, Manfred, "Jan Saudek, Moderne Klassiker: 10. Folge", and "Erfolg macht glücklich" (interview) *fotoMagazin*, no. 6, pp. 28–37

Dictionary of international Biography, International Biographical Centre, Cambridge, Great Britain

1994 *Modern Czech Photography (Selective Visions)*, Harn Museum of Art, University of Florida

1995 *Jan Saudek. Jubilations and Obsessions*, Rosbeek Publishers, Amsterdam

Jan Saudek. Dopis (The Letter) edited by Sarah Saudek, Prague

"Jan Saudek im Studio 3000, Polaroid 50x60 Kamera in Prag", *Pròfifoto*, no. 5, pp. 62–69

"Jan Saudek '1895'", (texts and poems by Lionel Chiuch), Krisal Gallery, Geneve

Wall Calendar, BB Art, Prague

1996 *Black and White*, no. 17, pp. 56–61 (Australia)

Photographie des 20. Jahrhunderts. Museum Ludwig Köln, Benedikt Taschen Verlag, Cologne

"Jan Saudek, Ein Interview von Zdenek Primus", *Photonews*, no. 1, p. 4f.

Notecards, Slovart, Prague

1997 "Das Kabinett des Jan Saudek", *Das Magazin, Die Lust zu lesen*, no. 272, Frankfurt/M. pp. 26–36

Freitag, Michael, "Süsse Qual der Jugend", *Frankfurter Allgemeine Magazin*, no. 272, Frankfurt/M. pp. 26–36

The Photography Book, Phaidon Press Ltd., London

Jan Saudek. Photographs 1987–1997, Benedikt Taschen Verlag, Cologne

Jan Saudek, 30 Postcards, Benedikt Taschen Verlag, Cologne, Germany

1998 *Masterpieces of Erotic Photography*, Carlton Books, London

Exhibition Catalogues

1979 *The World of Jan Saudek Photographs*, Jacques Baruch Gallery, Chicago (IL)

1983 *Images from Czechoslovakia*, University of Iowa Museum of Art, Iowa City (IA)

1985 Das Aktfoto, Ästhetik, Geschichte, Ideologie, Ansichten vom Körper im fotografischen Zeitalter, ed. by Michael Köhler and Gisela Barche, Münchener Stadtmuseum, Munich, Luzern

1986 *Jan Saudek*, Alvar Aalto Museo, Jyväskylä, Suomen Valokuvataiteen Museo, Helsinki

Jan Saudek. 35 Jahre Fotografie / 35 Years of Photography, Fotografie Forum Frankfurt, Frankfurt/M., Galerie Rudolf Kicken, Cologne et al., ed. by Manfred Heiting, Frankfurt/M.

1987 *Jan Saudek. 200 Photographies 1953–1986*, Musée d'art moderne de la Ville de Paris, Paris

1988 *Photographische Erinnerungen*, Museum Ludwig, Cologne

The Second Israeli Photography Biennale, Museum of Art, Ein Harod, Israel

1995 *The World of Jan Saudek. Photographs 1959–1995*, Museum of Art, Olomouc, Czech Republic

1997 *The Body in Contemporary Czech Photography*, Macintosh Gallery, Glasgow

1998 *Zärtlicher Blick auf schöne Damen*, Museum Ludwig, Cologne

Special thanks to
Karsten Fricke and Sarah Saudek

Jan Saudek can be contacted at:
Blodkova 6
13000 Prague 3
Czech Republic